'RACE',
CULTURE
AND
DIFFERENCE

'Race', Education and Society

Racism and Education
Structures and Strategies
Edited by Dawn Gill, Barbara Mayor and Maud Blair

'Race', Culture and Difference
Edited by James Donald and Ali Rattansi

Racism and Antiracism
Inequalities, Opportunities and Policies
Edited by Peter Braham, Ali Rattansi and Richard Skellington

These three volumes, all published by SAGE Publications are Readers for the Open University course ED356 *'Race', Education and Society*

(Details of the course are available from the Student Enquiries Office, The Open University, Milton Keynes, MK7 6AG.)

'RACE', CULTURE AND DIFFERENCE

EDITED BY JAMES DONALD AND ALI RATTANSI

SAGE PUBLICATIONS

in association with

The Open University

SAGE Publications Ltd
6 Bonhill Street
London EC2A 4PU

SAGE Publications Inc
2455 Teller Road
Newbury Park, California 91320

SAGE Publications India Pvt Ltd
32, M-Block Market
Greater Kailash – I
New Delhi 110 048

British Library Cataloguing in Publication data

'Race', culture and difference.
  I. Donald, James   II. Rattansi, Ali
  305.8001

  ISBN 0–8039–8579–7
  ISBN 0–8039–8580–0 pbk

Library of Congress catalog card number 91–53240

Typeset by Photoprint, Torquay, Devon
Printed in Great Britain by J. W. Arrowsmith Ltd, Bristol

CONTENTS

PREFACE

This collection of articles, many of them specially commissioned, is one of three volumes that constitute a major component of the Open University course, 'Race', Education and Society. It explores the cultural aspects of 'race', although very much in the light of the critical rethinking of the concept 'culture' to be found in the emerging traditions of poststructuralism and postmodernism. The other two volumes in the series are *Racism and Education: structures and strategies*, edited by Dawn Gill, Barbara Mayor and Maud Blair, and *Racism and Antiracism: inequalities, opportunities and policies*, edited by Peter Braham, Ali Rattansi and Richard Skellington. The former focuses on policies, pratices and experiences of schooling, and their implications in sustaining or challenging racism. The latter is concerned with patterns of differentiation and discrimination across a range of social institutions and practices: the labour market, nationality and migration laws, welfare provision, and so forth. Although the three books have been designed primarily with the needs of Open University students in mind, each can be read independently and will be of interest to a much wider range of readers who wish to study the social and cultural dynamics of 'race' in Britain today.

In order to include as broad a range of materials as possible, some of the previously published articles have been shortened. Editorial cuts are marked by three dots in square brackets: | . . . |. Editorial interpolations are placed in square brackets. In view of the political significance attached to terminology in this field, no attempt has been made to standardize authors' usage of terms such as 'black', 'Black', 'ethnic minority', 'minority ethnic', etc.

The editors would like to thank the following colleagues for their advice during the preparation of this book: Homi Bhabha, Maud Blair, Peter Braham, Phil Cohen, Bob Ferguson, Jagdish Gundara, Stuart Hall, Barbara Mayor and Dick Skellington. They would also like to thank the following for their assistance in the production of the book: Sheila Gilks, June Evison, Gill Marshall, Lesley Passey, John Taylor and Laurily Wilson.

ACKNOWLEDGEMENTS

The authors and publishers wish to thank the following for permission to use copyright material.

Basil Blackwell Ltd for Tariq Madood, 'British Asian Muslims and the Rushdie Affair', *Political Quarterly,* **61**(2), 1990;

Gower Publishing Company for Caroline Knowles and Sharmila Mercer, 'Feminism and Antiracism: an exploration of the political possibilities' from A. Cambridge and S. Feuchtwang (eds), *Anti-racist Strategies,* Avebury (Wildwood), 1990;

HarperCollins Publishers for Frantz Fanon, 'The fact of blackness' from *Black Skins, White Masks,* Paladin, 1970;

Macmillan Publishers Ltd for Paul Gilroy, 'The end of antiracism' from W. Ball and J. Solomos (eds), *Race and Local Politics,* 1990;

The *Oxford Literary Review* for Gauri Viswanathan, 'The beginnings of English literary study in British India', *Oxford Literary Review,* 9, 1987. Copyright © 1987 by *Oxford Literary Review;*

Routledge for Robert Young, 'Colonialism and humanism' from *White Mythologies: Writing History and the West,* 1990;

The University of Chicago Press for Sander L. Gilman, 'Black bodies, white bodies: towards an iconography of female sexuality in late nineteenth century art, medicine and literature' from Henry Louis Gates Jr. (ed.), *Race, Writing, and Difference,* 1987;

Every effort has been made to trace all the copyright holders, but if any have been inadvertently overlooked the publishers will be pleased to make the necessary arrangement at the first opportunity.

INTRODUCTION

A paradox confronts anyone who tries to understand the perplexing and persistent phenomena of 'race' and racism in Europe today. On the one hand, in genetic terms, the physical or biological differences between groups defined as 'races' have been shown to be trivial. No persuasive empirical case has been made for ascribing common psychological, intellectual or moral capacities or characteristics to individuals on the basis of skin colour or physiognomy. Certainly, no good ethical case has been made to justify differential or inequitable treatment on such arbitrary grounds. And yet, on the other hand, it is all too clear that racism still remains a widespread, and possibly intensifying, fact of many people's lives. Reiterating that 'there's no such thing as "race"' offers only the frail reassurance that there *shouldn't* be a problem. It cannot deal with the problems that do exist, because it fails to see them for what they are.

Our pragmatic starting point here is not whether 'race' exists. Instead, we rephrase the question and ask how the category operates in practice. The issue is not how *natural* differences determine and justify group definitions and interactions, but how racial logics and racial frames of reference are articulated and deployed, and with what consequences. 'Race' is conceptualized as 'an unstable and "decentred" complex of social meanings constantly being transformed by political struggle' (Omi and Winant, 1986, p. 68). Getting to grips with the dynamics of 'race', racism and antiracism in Britain today therefore means studying an ever-changing nexus of representation, discourse and power. And that requires a critical return to the concept *culture*.

Why a *critical* rereading of culture? There are two reasons. First, the academic study of the concept has been profoundly transformed in the past twenty years or so. The belated impact of Saussurian semiotics, Althusserian and other neo- and post-marxist theories of ideology, Lacanian psychoanalysis and its account of subjectivity and identity, the tradition of British cultural studies associated with people like Raymond Williams and Stuart Hall, various strands of feminism, Foucault's concern with discourse and power: these are just some of the developments that today make it impossible to think of culture as a finite and self-sufficient body of contents, customs and traditions.

Second, it has been around the definition and significance of culture that some of the sharpest disagreements and disputes in the field of multiculturalism and antiracism have been expressed. One of the most telling strands in the antiracist critique of multiculturalism in the 1970s and 1980s, for example, was that it suffered from an overemphasis on culture. We would give that a slightly different gloss: multiculturalism, certainly as it was translated into educational and political practice, often conflated the question of culture with a particular understanding of *ethnicity*. The positive achievement of this tradition was that it allowed different communities, and their claims over their members, to be acknowledged and valued with a new, official respect.

Its drawback was that a multicultural celebration of *diversity* tended to reproduce the 'saris, samosas and steel-bands syndrome'. That is, by focusing on the superficial manifestations of culture, multiculturalism failed to address the continuing *hierarchies* of power and legitimacy that still existed among these different centres of cultural authority. By exoticizing them, it even colluded in their further disenfranchisement. Despite its apparent relativism, in practice it defined alternative centres of cultural authority primarily in terms of their difference from the norm of English culture, not in their uniqueness and their discontinuities.

'Other cultures', in more technical philosophical terms, were specified in terms of an all-embracing A:not-A opposition, not as a sequence of proliferating A:B, A:C, A:n differences that might call into question the very idea of such a definitive centre of cultural reference and authority. The potential of such different communal traditions and emerging sub-cultures as rivals to the dominant *national* culture in generating and legitimating beliefs, values and behaviour was disavowed. Multicultural-ism thus remained within the political logic of assimilationism. However unwittingly, it endorsed the claims to tolerance and inclusiveness of English national culture and the British state. The limits of this approach were cruelly exposed by intellectual as well as political responses to the *Satanic Verses* affair in the late 1980s. Attempts to accommodate both a sensitivity to difference and a commitment to the universalistic claims of post-Enlightenment liberalism became increasingly convoluted and for-lorn. Under pressure, an aggressive assimilationism began to reassert itself – for instance in Fay Weldon's pamphlet *Sacred Cows* (1989).

Another good reason for antiracist scepticism about culture was the emergence in the 1980s of a 'new racism' based not on ideas of innate biological superiority, but on the supposed incompatibility of cultural traditions (see, for example, Barker, 1981). This presented itself as a worldly acknowledgement that different communities have different values and different ways of life which they have an instinct and a right to defend. There was an increasingly explicit articulation of a 'white ethnic-ity' linking discourses of family and community, national belonging, English patriotism, xenophobia, and popular conservatism. Neo-conserv-ative philosophers asserted that 'the consciousness of nationhood is the highest form of political consciousness' (see Gilroy, 1987, p. 44). The same logic was evident in the self-justification offered by one of the parents who in 1987 withdrew their children from a school in the Yorkshire town of Dewsbury because the majority of pupils were of South Asian origin. This father insisted that all they wanted was for their children to receive a schooling based on English traditions and values. Denying the charge of racism, he protested that: 'It's not a question of race; it's a question of culture.'

In this climate, it is easy to understand why antiracists became impatient with the whole question of culture. It is not individual beliefs and prejudices about 'race' that are the main problem, they argued, nor the contents of different traditions. What matters are the structures of power, the institutions and the social practices that produce racial oppression and discriminatory outcomes. In practice, of course, antiracist intellectuals and activists did not ignore the problematic relationship between the production of racialized meanings and the exercise of power. Rather than pose it as a question of culture, however, they tackled it – often very productively – in terms of *ideology*. This concept has the advantage of stressing that people's perceptions and beliefs are not just the inheritance of a shared ethnic descent, but are rooted in broader economic structures and material interests. It can also provide the rationale for arguing that certain perceptions and beliefs conceal real social contradictions and thus present an inadequate representation of reality.

This made it possible to rethink multiculturalism's psychological interpretation of racism as individual prejudice in more structural and politicized terms. Meanings and beliefs had not become irrelevant, but the coherence and falsity of racist ideas were now ascribed to the function they serve in legitimating social practices that reinforce an unequal distribution of power between groups differentiated in racial and/or ethnic terms (see, for example, Troyna and Carrington, 1990, p. 56).

In such definitions, 'race' is still conceived as a false representation of reality rather than as part of the process of constructing an operative symbolic and social reality: literally, a common sense. By continuing to ask 'is it true?' instead of analysing 'which truth?' and 'whose truth?', antiracists often remain trapped within the paradox we identified at the beginning of this Introduction. While they chastised multiculturalism for identifying racism as the ideas in people's heads when it should be located in institutional structures, they themselves underestimated the resilience, malleability and *power* of 'race' as a discursive category. Their strategies therefore still targeted the *irrationality* of racist beliefs, whereas, as Omi and Winant's definition suggests, the fictional or metaphorical status of the category 'race' in no way undermines its symbolic and social effectuality. 'Race' can produce simplified interpretations of complex social, economic and cultural relations for antiracists as well as racists.

This signals another danger. The term *racism* can be stretched to impose a brittle coherence on multi-faceted phenomena, thus avoiding the need for more diverse and discriminating forms of analysis. It can also impose a constraining and reductionist interpretative grid on the political and cultural life of Afro-Caribbean, Asian and other minority communities in

Britain today. Not only can it homogenize these communities as in-sensitively as assimilationism or multiculturalism. It can also imply that all the experiences and aspirations of their members are exhausted by the fact of racial subordination.

How can the critical reappropriation of the concept of culture proposed here overcome the limitations that we have identified in both multicultur-alism and antiracism? It begins by re-posing the question in terms of cultural authority and individual agency. These cannot be explained simply in terms of shared descent (as they were in some multicultural accounts of ethnicity) or a shared socio-economic location and history (as they are in some antiracist versions of 'the black experience'). Rather, they require a careful analysis of contemporary political struggles over questions of representation, symbolic boundary formation, and identifica-tion. It is in this conflictual dialogue that the meanings of 'race', racism and antiracism are forged, broken and remade.

This suggests a definition of culture that is closer to what many social scientists and cultural theorists would have in mind when they talk about culture than the versions associated with either multiculturalism or antiracism. This is not limited to religious beliefs, communal rituals or shared traditions. On the contrary, it begins with the way that such manifest phenomena are *produced* through systems of meaning, through structures of power, and through the institutions in which these are deployed. In the following summary of current approaches to the analysis of culture, for example, Raymond Williams suggests that it is these interactions which produce the way of life defining a social collectivity:

> ... there is some practical convergence between (i) the anthropological and sociological senses of culture as a distinct 'whole way of life', within which, now, a distinctive 'signifying system' is seen not only as essential but as essentially involved in *all* forms of social activity, and (ii) the more specialized if also more common sense of culture as 'artistic and intellectual activities', though these, because of the emphasis on a general signifying system, are now much more broadly defined, to include not only the traditional arts and forms of intellectual production but also all the 'signifying practices' – from language through the arts and philosophy to journalism, fashion and advertising – which now constitute this complex and necessarily extended field.
> (Williams, 1981, p. 13)

From this point of view, culture is no longer understood as what expresses the identity of a community. Rather, it refers to the processes, categories and knowledges through which communities are defined as such: that is, how they are rendered specific and differentiated.

It is worth observing how devastating this reconceptualization is for the cultural absolutism evident in the National Curriculum introduced into the schools of England and Wales in the wake of the Education Reform Act (1988). Although this had a complex rationale, there is no question that one motive behind it was a desire to reassert a largely factitious national identity – the 'imagined community' of nationhood that is supposed to transcend all inequalities, oppressions and exploitation (Anderson, 1983). In the face of an increasingly miscegenated and polyglot population, the National Curriculum proposed a standard language, a definitive canon of English literature and a single, shared narrative of the nation's history. In classic style, it claimed the legitimacy of anteriority for these. 'Let's get back to the safe, sure way things used to be,' was its implicit message, 'back to the virtues and verities that have served "us" since time immemorial.' The trouble is that the traditions and symbols that embody and transmit these supposedly universal and perennial virtues usually turn out to be modern inventions (Hobsbawm and Ranger, 1983). In that sense, the apparent traditionalism of the National Curriculum was a typical tactic of modern statecraft and modern nation formation.

The rethinking of culture in the light of theoretical advances and political experience over recent years undermines the claims and comforts of community understood in terms of a normative identity and tradition, whether that of nation, religion, ethnicity or 'the black experience'. It emphasizes the contingency of *any* instituted cultural authority. It insists that 'race' and identity are inherently contestable social and political categories: that is why it calls into question multicultural and antiracist paradigms, as well as the logic of assimilation. What new intellectual and political agenda does this reorientation imply? What new possibilities and demands – political, educational, aesthetic – does it create?

Once the apparent coherence and universality of *racism* is questioned, it becomes necessary to grasp the historical and cultural specificity of different racisms. This in turn raises a serious and subversive problem identified by Paul Gilroy: that 'the content of "antiracism" has not always been a direct response to the ideologies and practices of racism' (Gilroy, 1987, p. 114). Both these anti-essentializing moves demand a reconceptualization of community: a shift from the idea of inherited or imposed authority and towards the principles of difference and dialogue. The practical working out of this change can be seen in the syncretism of what Gilroy terms 'black expressive cultures' in contemporary Britain (Gilroy, 1987, ch. 5). It is also particularly striking in the exploration and articulation of hybrid identities – both black and British – of artists, photographers and film-makers like Sonia Boyce, David A. Bailey, Reece Auguitse, Isaac Julien, and Pratibha Parmar.[1] For all its variety, one question that is posed by their work – sometimes explicitly, often implicitly – is this: how might it be possible, in unpropitious times, to create a radically pluralistic culture for a post-colonial society like Britain?

This represents neither the old multicultural celebration of diversity, nor a naïve postmodern embrace of an endless multiplication of cultural identities. The debate about representation and culture is here articulated with a sharper political urgency. Their work raises questions with far-reaching implications for the educational orthodoxies of both multicultur-alism and antiracism. What would be the institutional conditions for a genuine cultural and political democracy, for example? And what would be the role of education and cultural production in the attempt to bring those conditions into being?

A critical rethinking of the relationship between culture, 'race' and politics is the linking thread that runs through the various articles collected together here.

The book is divided into three sections. The first presents a number of critiques of antiracism. Although there are differences between them, each addresses in its own way the range of concerns sketched in this Introduction. In contrast to the 'anti-antiracism' generated by the New Right, all these articles come out of a continuing and committed opposition to the demonstrable inequities and injustices of racism. In exemplary fashion, however, they enact a critical *self*-reflection. What comes under critical scrutiny here are the presuppositions, habits of thought and strategies that, under the banner of Antiracism, dominated political interventions in local authorities, education and the arts from the late seventies to the mid-eighties.

In a wide-ranging challenge to the opposition of multiculturalism to antiracism as an adequate framework for educational debate, Ali Rattansi argues that, in the wake of the Burnage Report, it is necessary to identify new priorities that undermine old certainties. In a similar vein, Paul Gilroy develops his critique of antiracist strategies that remain too firmly embedded within the (municipal) state. He insists that there is more to the emancipation of black people than opposition to racism. The alternative he poses is the creation of a radical, democratic civil society by linking immediate local concerns to globalizing economic and political developments. This entails a new conception of 'micro-political' activity. In reflecting on his own practices as an antiracist teacher, Philip Cohen too argues for more nuanced and localized initiatives to replace what he sees as the overly prescriptive and universalistic policies of the past.

Caroline Knowles and Sharmila Mercer in their article, and Avtar Brah in hers, explore the articulations – actual and potential – between antiracism and feminism. Both articles sustain the case for an anti-essentialist and pragmatic politics, and therefore question the appeal to the category of *experience* in the two movements. Knowles and Mercer reject the idea that there is any general relationship between 'race' and gender as forms of division: rather, both racism and sexism should be 'viewed as a series of effects which do not have a single cause'. They argue that close attention to the processes through which constituencies are constructed and – inevitably temporary – links articulated between them allows for more effective forms of political calculation and intervention. Brah's review of the debate about the inclusiveness and limitations of the category 'black' and of the often fractious engagement between feminism and antiracism shows her to be not unsympathetic to this post-structuralist perspective. Nevertheless, she argues the case for continuing to set the micro-political perspective in the context of a macro-political explanation of social relations.

The second section of the reader outlines some of the diverse phenomena that are often lumped together and explained by the single category of racism. In tracing how the study of English literature took on its claims to be a moralizing influence, Gauri Viswanathan contributes to a history of the subtle stratagems of colonial administration and their contemporary legacy. In doing so, she also shows how a literary education took on this curious status in India *before* the state took any role in popular education in England and before literary studies had been institutionalized as 'English'.

Starting from Manet's two pictures *Olympia* and *Nana*, Sander Gilman unravels their semiotic conditions of existence. His cultural detective work leads him through aesthetic, anthropological and medical discourses about 'race' and sexuality, specifically as they were articulated around the figures of the female Hottentot and the prostitute in the nineteenth century. He uncovers the complex interaction between 'race' and sexuality in the visual representation of the Other, and suggests the sources of the male/white fascination with the mysteries of the female/black. In establishing the relevance for this field of psychoanalytic concepts, Claire Pajaczkowska and Lola Young identify some of the psychological mechanisms involved in the production of individual and social racism. Their article is structured around two case studies in racialized representation: the film *Mona Lisa* and the novel *Beloved*.

In his seminal chapter 'The fact of blackness', from *Black Skins, White Masks*, Frantz Fanon vividly conveys the experience of being Other – 'the desperate struggles of a Negro who is driven to discover the meaning of black identity'. In doing so, he shows how the socially and historically constructed opposition between blackness and whiteness takes on the absolute, unquestionable authority of a natural fact. By exposing the process, Fanon opened the way to the sort of anti-essentialist understanding of racial categories that is the theme of this book.

The third section offers a critical exploration of possible starting points for new strategies, not least by looking anew at some of the difficult and resilient questions about cultural identity and belongingness, about ethnicity and community, that were often glossed over or disavowed in the antiracist movement. Robert Young suggests why the presupposition of a shared humanity cannot provide such a starting point, although it may operate as a horizon of thought, a desirable if always unachievable aspiration. Stuart Hall suggests that certain artistic and aesthetic practices prefigure a new conception of ethnicity, one which would be neither homogeneous nor normative, but always negotiated and in a state of becoming. In his analysis of the *Satanic Verses* affair on British Asian Muslims, Tariq Modood challenges the hegemonic claims of the category 'black' and criticizes the indiscriminate and ill-informed use of the term 'fundamentalism'. As an alternative, he offers a reasoned defence of the demands of community understood in more traditional terms. Drawing in part on her involvement in the organization Women Against Fundamentalism, Nira Yuval-Davis registers some of the potential pitfalls of that approach for women.

James Donald
Ali Rattansi

Note

1 Their work is amongst that explored in a two-part BBC television programme entitled *The Burden of Representation* for the Open University course *'Race', Education and Society*.

References

Anderson, B. (1983) *Imagined Communities: reflections on the origins and spread of nationalism*, London, Verso.

Barker, M. (1981) *The New Racism*, London, Junction Books.

Gilroy, P. (1987) *There Ain't No Black in the Union Jack: the cultural politics of race and nation*, London, Hutchinson.

Hobsbawm, E. J. and Ranger, T. (eds) (1983) *The Invention of Tradition*, Cambridge, Cambridge University Press.

Omi, M. and Winant, H. (1986) *Racial Formation in the United States*, London and New York, Routledge and Kegan Paul.

Troyna, B. and Carrington, B. (1990) *Education, Racism and Reform*, London, Routledge.

Weldon, F. (1989) *Sacred Cows*, London, Chatto.

Williams, R. (1981) *Culture*, London, Fontana.

PART 1

ANTIRACISM
POSSIBILITIES AND LIMITS

1 CHANGING THE SUBJECT?
RACISM, CULTURE AND EDUCATION
ALI RATTANSI

The multiculturalist and antiracist initiatives in education that emerged in the 1980s set themselves extraordinarily difficult tasks. In challenging the structural and cultural marginalization of Britain's black minority communities, they also began to shift the terms around which British national identities had sedimented over the years of colonial domination and imperial grandeur and before.[1] This was an absolutely necessary intervention. This article is written with some knowledge, experience and appreciation of the commitment, the personal costs and the professional risks involved for those engaged in the struggle to reform school curricula, teacher education and other spheres and practices. I do not wish to sell their achievements short. New cultural and political spaces have been opened up, and hegemonic racial identities and structures have been loosened.

Despite these real successes, however, my sense is that now is a time to take stock and to reflect on the theoretical, pedagogic and political foundations of multiculturalism and antiracism. This is a period of transition. Significant changes are under way in the economic, political and cultural formation of black British communities. Older certainties about the nature and direction of black struggles no longer hold. In education, the liberal optimism of the 1985 Swann Report has not only been punctured by the policies of Conservative governments and by the ideological counter-offensive of the New Right. From within the movement, the publication of the Macdonald Report on the tragic events at Burnage High School has been widely interpreted as signalling the failure of the antiracist project in education.

If antiracism is to be effective in education, it is therefore necessary to take a hard and perhaps painful look at the terms under which we have operated so far. We need to understand the extent to which oppositional practices have, wittingly or unwittingly, shared the assumptions of the dominant state-led strategies that have also attempted to respond to the black presence in British education and society. And it is necessary to assess the nature and significance of the polarization between 'multiculturalism' and 'antiracism' in this field, especially given the left's construction of antiracism as representing the more genuinely radical intervention in this field.

The article begins by setting out Swann's terms of reference and contrasts its liberal optimism with the Macdonald Inquiry's condemnation of antiracist policies at Burnage High School. It then sketches in how it was that 'race' came to be constructed as a significant educational issue at all. It interrogates earlier state, academic and other public responses to the black presence in education, and documents their continuing influence and weaknesses in a critique of the debate around the question of black 'underachievement' in education. This is followed by a brief and selective representation of the forms of racism identified within the education system. A sympathetic but rigorous critique of some of the assumptions underlying both multiculturalist and antiracist interventions is then erected, demonstrating some of the unacknowledged weaknesses they share. The article concludes that what is now required is not only a consolidation but also a rethinking of educational interventions if issues of racism, ethnicity and cultural difference are to be adequately addressed in the 1990s and beyond.

From Swann to Burnage

1985 saw the publication of *Education for All*, the 800-page Swann Report on the education of children from ethnic minority groups (DES). Set up in 1979 under the chairmanship of Anthony Rampton, its original brief was primarily concerned with the causes of ethnic minority, and especially 'West Indian', 'underachievement'. Amid a series of controversial resignations and the replacement of Rampton by Lord Swann, the inquiry broadened its scope to consider the creation of an education system appropriate to a multi-ethnic society. (An insider account of the politicking around the Rampton and Swann phases can be found in Parekh, 1989b). Broadly speaking, Swann provided a liberal, semi-official legitimation for tackling issues of racism (or, more accurately, prejudice) and what it coyly referred to as 'cultural pluralism' in *all* schools, including the so-called all-white schools which hitherto had maintained the stance of 'No problem (i.e. blacks) here'. By advocating a non-prejudiced, pluralist 'education for *all*', Swann, however obliquely and weakly, had begun to problematize *whiteness* and the deeply embedded racism of the national culture. It had begun to chip away at the common-sense attribution of 'race' problems simply to a black presence.

Despite the then Education Secretary Keith Joseph's almost instant equivocations, the recommendations of the Report did give some legitimacy and impetus to local education authorities (LEAs) and schools already tentatively and sometimes vigorously pursuing one or another variety of multicultural or antiracist policy. Although it's *naïveté* and many internal contradictions and evasions were easily exposed by its critics (Chivers, 1987), it is arguable that Swann put multiculturalism and at least weak versions of antiracism on the national educational agenda. Multiculturalist and antiracist lobbies could regard this as a partial vindication. The expectation that the Afro-Caribbean and Asian minorities would simply blend into a homogeneous British or even English stew, perhaps adding some harmless spice, was revealed as not only hopelessly unrealistic but symptomatic of a form of racism which regarded 'Britishness' and 'Westernness' as the only touchstones of cultural value. In the aftermath of the urban uprisings of 1980–81 and Scarman's subsequent call for a speedy response from the education system (HMSO, 1981; Scarman, 1982), Swann attempted to construct a liberal consensus in a very troubled area.

Four years later came the Macdonald Report, *Murder in the Playground*, stemming from an inquiry into the murder of 13-year-old Ahmed Iqbal Ullah by a white boy in the playground of Burnage High School in South Manchester. The committee of inquiry, composed of individuals with impressive antiracist credentials – Ian Macdonald, Gus John, Reena Bhavnani, Lily Khan – delivered a strong and, for some, an astonishing condemnation of the antiracist policies apparently vigorously pursued at the school, castigating them as doctrinaire, divisive, ineffectual and counterproductive.

The policies of Dr Gough (the headteacher) and his colleagues were not actually blamed for the fatality. But this is exactly what large sections of the media, especially given Manchester City Council's refusal to publish the full report for fear of litigation, took to be the real meaning of the report. The day after the conclusions had been leaked, *The Daily Telegraph* had no doubts: 'Antiracist policy led to killing', it claimed. Peter Wilby in the *Independent* concluded that antiracist education had been 'a disaster'. In the years between Swann and Burnage the media had in any case had a field day. There had been the row over Ray Honeyford's diatribes against what he regarded as the nightmare of multiculturalism imposed on well-intentioned schools by a combination of the race relations industry and 'volatile', 'half-educated' Asian and Afro-Caribbean parents (Honeyford, 1983, 1984). A group of Dewsbury parents had refused to send their children to a predominantly British Asian school. And moral panics had been orchestrated around 'loony left councils' supposedly banning black dustbin liners, insisting on renaming black coffee 'coffee without milk', and banning 'Ba-ba black sheep' from the classroom – scares which turned out to rest on complete fabrications (Media Research Group, 1987). Meanwhile, in a series of moves capped by the Education Reform Act and the proposals for a national (or, as some were quick to point out, nationa*list*) curriculum, the Conservative government had effectively challenged and undermined the fragile liberal consensus Swann had tried to erect in the mid-1980s.

But how did 'race' come to occupy a place in post-war British education in the first place and what were its terms of entry?

'Race', ethnicity and culture in British educational policy

Recent research has disrupted the conventional narrative which represented the period between the end of the Second World War and the passing of the first Immigration Act in 1962 as an era of *laissez-faire*, with restrictions on black immigration supposedly only being reluctantly considered and implemented in the wake of campaigning by small right-wing elements in parliament and a groundswell of racism in the constituencies, especially in the Midlands. In fact, there was considerable debate in official circles during the time of both the Labour administration of 1945–51 and the subsequent Conservative administration about the consequences of black immigration on the 'racial character' of the British, and several covert and sometimes illegal administrative measures were put into operation to discourage black immigration (Carter, Harris and Joshi, 1987). The inhibitions against introducing full-scale controls against black immigration are likely to have stemmed from their possible impact on Britain's role as head of the Commonwealth and Colonies and concern over the national and international legality of controls based on colour (Solomos, 1989, p. 47). When controls were increasingly applied through successive Immigration Acts, these were always accompanied by official disavowals that black immigrants were the real target. This form of political rhetoric Reeves (1983) has dubbed 'discursive deracialization' (what more appropriately should be called *discursive* deracialization).

By the 1960s the new British Afro-Caribbean and Asian communities had become well aware of the racism embedded in the national culture and institutionalized in the practices of many public and private agencies. They daily encountered 'colour bars' in employment, housing and pubs. Their children had begun to face racial abuse on the streets and in the schools. Documents recently released by Birmingham LEA also reveal the degree of teacher and local authority hostility to the growing black presence in the schools, and the caricatures that had begun to circulate around the lifestyles and 'racial character' of 'Asiatics' and 'West Indians'. Racism, patently, was a problem that required urgent attention. Official policies geared towards the black presence did, indeed, begin to emerge from the DES and some LEAs, often under prompting from agitated schools and headteachers who refused to admit more black pupils (Grosvenor, 1991).

The policies did not develop on the terrain of racism, however, but under the sign of culture. Just as in a previous era an official 'gentling of the masses' by way of induction into a culture of civilization had accompanied the educational and political entry of the working classes into citizenship within the nation, so now assimilation into an imagined British national culture and way of life became the preoccupation of the educational establishment (Open University, 1974; Jones and Kimberley, 1982). The issue of language symbolized and condensed the anxiety provoked by the black presence and became the preferred site for an educational response. Soon after the first Immigration Act, the DES produced its first major intervention, revealingly entitled *English for Immigrants* (1963). Although the primary target for the policy of Anglicization was the Asian communities, schools appeared to be equally concerned with what they regarded as the 'plantation English' of Afro-Caribbean pupils (Grosvenor, 1991). Teaching English, being a metaphor for a policy of enforced cultural assimilation, dovetailed with the view expressed by a large proportion of heads and teachers that 'immigrant' cultures – the desire to hold on to which was seen as evidence of a 'ghetto mentality' – were an educational hindrance requiring vigilant exclusion from the culture of the school (Brittan, 1976). In this spirit, Section 11 of the 1966 Local Government Act offered financial assistance for those authorities finding themselves with substantial proportions of Commonwealth migrant communities 'whose language and customs differ from those of the community'.

The assimilationist thrust was, and still is, through and through essentialist. Like all essentialisms it assumes an obvious, definable, homo-geneous essence (British culture) into which the hapless migrant might be inducted, given a suitable dose of English and an undiluted diet of the official school curriculum. The simultaneous cultural, racial and educa-tional panic and white backlash, moreover, led to a policy of dispersal of black students by bussing, initiated in Southall and gaining DES support and subsequent endorsement by the Labour Education Secretary, Anthony Crosland. Racism and its accompanying cultural essentialism thus received further official backing, although, eventually, protests from black parents, educational critiques, administrative problems and an emergent ideology of cultural pluralism undermined the practice of bussing (Kirp, 1979, p. 69–103).

Something of a shift in official perspectives was signalled by Home Secretary Roy Jenkins's famous demand in 1966 that the ideology of assimilation be replaced by an ethic of 'equal opportunity accompanied by cultural diversity'. Here was an admission that it was not so much an issue of transforming alien black cultures, but a problem of cultures and practices of white racism leading to unequal opportunities. This racializa-tion of the debate was further propelled onto local and national agendas by campaigning black parents and teachers. Afro-Caribbean parents, in particular, had consistently attempted to bring the fate of their children in British schools to public attention. The frustration of Redbridge's black parents, for example, forcing them to initiate an inquiry which was published as *Cause for Concern* (Redbridge Community Relations Council,

1978). Bernard Coard's *How the West Indian Child is made Educationally Sub-Normal in the British School System* (1971) had already given concrete expression to many black parents' justified fears that their children were being systematically mis-classified as educationally sub-normal and relegated to a 'special' education which effectively excluded them from any possibility of acquiring decent qualifications.

By the end of the 1970s, the question of 'underachievement' was firmly on the agenda.

Class, gender and culture in the black 'underachievement' debate

Remember that what became the Swann Inquiry started life under the chairmanship of Anthony Rampton as an investigation into the causes of 'West Indian' 'underachievement' and, in a curious and even paradoxical discourse of exclusion and inclusion, entitled its interim report *West Indian Children in Our Schools* (DES, 1981)! Meanwhile disturbing evidence had begun to accumulate about the relatively poor performance of children of Afro-Caribbean and Asian origin in schools (see Tomlinson, 1983, pp. 27–59 for a useful review). This fragmentary evidence could not, strictly speaking, be regarded as cumulative, being based on a variety of different criteria and deriving from children with varying degrees of residence in Britain, to mention just two complicating factors. (See Troyna, 1984, Open University, 1989a and Rattansi, 1988, for more detailed discussions of the evidence.)

More pertinent here is the curious manner in which categories of class, 'race', gender, ethnicity and culture intersected, or were excluded from, the debates surrounding the performance of pupils of Afro-Caribbean and Asian origin. Cultural and ethnic essentialism, of one variety or another, disfigured much of the debate. In its survey of six LEAs the Rampton Report primarily divided its sample into 'Asian', 'West Indian' and 'Other' school leavers, concluding that while 'Asians' and 'Others' performed equally well at O level and CSE, 'West Indian' school leavers performed significantly worse. On the complex differences of social class, gender and ethnicity, Rampton was conspicuously silent. Actually, the emerging evidence suggested that, once social class differences were taken into account, the performance of 'Asian', 'West Indian' and 'Other' students was more nearly comparable (although not necessarily identical) (Reeves and Chevannes, 1981; Roberts *et al.*, 1983); that it was likely that British Afro-Caribbean girls, for a variety of reasons, were more successful at school level than Afro-Caribbean boys (Driver, 1980; Fuller, 1983); and that pupils of Bangladeshi origin were performing particularly badly (House of Commons, Home Affairs Select Committee, 1986). Even in this last case not enough connections were made between racism and class –

poverty, unemployment, poor housing and racial harassment and violence
– in the lives of the community and its children (CRE, 1979, 1981; Gordon,
1990).

Although it was mindful of such factors as teacher racism and recognized
that 'West Indian' parents expressed considerable interest in their
children's education, the Rampton Report succumbed to other cultural
essentialism which replicated the presuppositions of earlier debates about
working-class families and educational 'underachievement'. It reproduced
American anxieties around cultures of deprivation and the supposed
pathologies of 'the black family', stressing the relatively large proportion
of 'West Indian' mothers who undertook paid employment outside the
home, the incidence of one-parent families, and the supposed ignorance of
'West Indian' parents about the need to help their children academically
at home (DES, 1981, pp. 15ff, 43). Although not to anything like the same
extent as in an earlier period in the United States, quietly and firmly the
British black family was becoming the focus of official anxieties. This was
no doubt reinforced by a growing concern over disaffection and alienation
among black youth, culminating in the 'moral panic' that erupted after
the urban uprisings of 1980–81 (cf. Hall *et al.*, 1978, pp. 16–17 for a
discussion of 'moral panics' and their racialization). Lord Scarman, in
constructing his view of the Brixton disorders expressed anxieties about
the black family in almost identical terms to those of Rampton (Scarman,
1982, pp. 24–5).

By the time the Swann Report came to be written, some progress had
been made in the debate about 'underachievement'. Swann displayed a
much firmer grasp of the significance of socio-economic circumstances in
explaining the fate of students of Afro-Caribbean origin in the education
system and had begun to notice that the achievement of students of
Bangladeshi origin should also give cause for concern. But the terms of
the Report's discussion remained ultimately trapped within the ethnic
and cultural essentialism inherited from Rampton. This emerges clearly
in its tortuous attempt to grapple with what it still regarded as a
fundamental difference between 'Asian' and 'West Indian' patterns of
educational performance. 'West Indian' 'underachievement' was attributed to a combination of poor socio-economic circumstances, which were
exacerbated by racism, and to racism within the education system. Given
the awareness that not all 'Asians' were middle class and/or immune to
racism within the education system, however, how could the apparently
better 'Asian' educational performance be understood?

In the final analysis, the Swann Report not only put aside what it had
already acknowledged about the relatively poor performance of students
of Bangladeshi origin, but ignored evidence that students of Mirpuri
Pakistani origin were also underperforming, while students of East
African Asian origin seemed to be achieving exceptionally well. Social
class and rural–urban contrasts, and different relations with British
colonial states and education systems, are very likely to be involved as

causal influences here, and Swann could well have commissioned research to explore some of the underlying issues. Instead, despite its disavowals and qualifications the Report slid into the trap of singling out 'Asian' culture and especially its main bearer, 'the Asian family', to explain the contrast with 'West Indians'. Asians 'kept their heads down', a strategy supposedly more likely to succeed in a 'hostile' (read: 'racist') environment – a view perhaps based on a selective construction of Jewish history in Britain? – in contrast to the 'West Indian' tendency to engage in protest (against racism). The 'tightly knit' Asian community, symbolized by the 'tightly knit' Asian family was said to be more likely to create a supportive educational environment (DES, 1985, p. 85). The Swann Report thus failed to break with the cultural and ethnic essentialism which had hegemonized debate in this area and which, as we shall see, continues to mark both the 'multiculturalist' and 'antiracist' discourses and programmes of educational reform.

In the period since Swann the collection of official statistics on educational achievements has displayed a slightly greater sensitivity and discrimination. The Inner London Education Authority, before its abolition, had begun to classify its students as being of 'African, African Asian, Arab, Bangladeshi, Caribbean, ESWI (English, Scottish, Welsh and Irish), Greek, Indian, Pakistani, SE Asian, Turkish and Other' origin (ILEA, 1987). Some attempt was made to provide even finer discriminations, Gujerati-speaking pupils being singled out as 'performing better than average', for example (ibid., p. 15). There was even some attention to gender: the ILEA report pointed out that for every ethnic group in its area the mean performance of girls was better than that of boys (ibid., p. 19). But no 'sub-ethnicities' were considered, nor was there any indication of differences in performance on particular subjects. An insight into the way the official terrain is constructed can be gained by noting the exclusion of other categories, which might have yielded different 'problems': 'Muslims', 'Jews', 'Catholics', 'Protestants', etc. Crucially, social class was again a significant absence. If ethnic monitoring recommendations are anything to go by, both in schools and elsewhere, official information on the fate of pupils from the minorities will continue to suffer from this lacuna. Particular cultural and ethnic essentialisms, in other words, look set to structure public debate in the future despite attempts by activists and researchers to press for more sociologically informed discussion. And this will assist the fragmentation around the imagined absoluteness of ethnic differences upon which both the New Right and the 'cultural nationalists' from the ethnic minorities have been premising their demands for cultural separatism in education (cf. Gilroy, 1990).

Discussions around the educational achievements of British Afro-Caribbean and Asian girls are also significant in what they reveal about the contradictions and reductionisms of both public and academic debate in the whole area of racism, culture and education. Take, first, one of the major contradictions.[2] The 'tightly knit' Asian culture and its cultural agent, the 'tightly knit' Asian family, are regarded in the Swann Report and elsewhere as a key influence in producing high educational achievements. But this same culture and family system is held responsible for a widespread pathology supposedly afflicting 'Asian' girls and thus also their education: the malaise of being 'caught between two cultures', an 'identity crisis', a form of individual splitting between two essentialized cultural forms, 'Asian' and 'British/Western'. Avtar Brah and Rehana Minhas (1986), amongst others, have challenged the cultural racism and the insensitivity to the vibrancy of Asian female cultures embedded in this type of representation. Brah's own research has revealed that the larger proportion of Asian girls continue to have strong and supportive relationships with parents and that the degree of inter-generational conflict is not necessarily higher than among white families.

Lest it be thought that the form of cultural essentialism being challenged here appears only in lay public debate, consider this astonishing but revealing passage from Professor John Rex, a leading figure in British 'race relations' research. Contrasting the 'altruistic solidarity' of Asian culture with the Western 'middle-class' culture of 'individualism' and 'competition', Rex concludes: 'Thus, being a good Indian and being a successful middle-class student at the same time are by no means easy goals to attain. There is bound to be breakdown' (Rex, 1982, p. 61). What is meant by class and ethnic reductionism and essentialism is illustrated here by Rex's assumption of deterministic and invariable cultural patterns producing inevitable individual responses. (Cashmore and Troyna, the editors of the volume in which Rex's paper appeared, were widely criticized for their own collapse into a cultural essentialism which accused 'black youth' of being 'arrogant, rumbustious and contemptuous' and having 'a certain fascination for violence' (1982, pp. 18, 33).)

'The Asian woman' is subject to contradictory and ambivalent stereotypification. This figure acts variously as the symbol and chief bearer of the admirably strong, tightly-knit family and culture, as the oppressed subject of traditional Asian patriarchal practices, as a problem because of her failure to learn the language and customs which might allow a smoother integration of her community and children into 'the British way of life', and full of sexual charm and allure produced by a demure seductiveness replete with the promise of a mysterious Oriental eroticism. Afro-Caribbean girls and women, on the other hand, are often represented as crushed under the weight of a triple oppression of class, gender and racism. This common-sense image implies a linear model which sees these burdens as cumulative in operation and effect, although also overlain with images of the strong black woman, the single mother, holding the family together in the face of irresponsible black males, whether they be husbands or disruptive youth.

Most research has thoroughly problematized these conceptions. It is not merely that the incidence of single-parent black families has been exaggerated (Phoenix, 1988), but that class, gender and racism intersect in highly complex and contradictory ways in the lives of black women (Anthias and Yuval-Davis, 1982; Phizacklea, 1983; Ramazanoglu, 1989; Westwood, 1985; Westwood and Bhachu, 1988). The notion of cumulatively disadvantaging oppressions, leading to inevitable failure, is belied by the educational responses of British Afro-Caribbean girls. What research and evidence there is appears to suggest that at school level at least their educational achievements are higher than those of Afro-Caribbean boys, and that they exhibit a greater tenacity in the pursuit of educational qualifications than white girls. Many working-class British Afro-Caribbean girls, it appears, have been adopting a clever and effective strategy which combines resistance and accommodation, instrumentalism and commitment. They work hard at school without giving the appearance of being swots, thus pre-empting derision from their peers. They resist school procedures and rules but not to the point of risking outright confrontation with teachers. And they aspire to interesting and well-paid work but without any illusions about the degree of racial discrimination and sexual segregation in employment. There is, in other words, no simple 'culture of failure' or 'culture of resistance', but rather a complex set of strategies set generally within the context of strong attachments to families and black cultural identities (Fuller, 1982, 1983; Dex, 1983; Riley, 1986; Mac an Ghaill, 1988). Similar complexities need to be acknowledged in the case of British Asian girls (Fuller, 1983; Brah and Minhas, 1986; Mac an Ghaill, 1988).

So far, I have sketched in some of the contours of early educational debates and policy in the field of racism, culture and education and explored the way in which the problem of cultural and ethnic essentialism, in particular, has structured and indeed disfigured public debates and the production of relevant knowledge. This is how the ground was unwittingly prepared for New Right and other interventions based on rigid, absolutist conceptions of cultural and ethnic difference. The issues of social class and racism, as I have argued, have been significant casualties of the discursive formations and apparatuses of knowledge and power which defined the emergence of the black presence as an object of public discussion and policy.[3] It is time to turn more explicitly to the question of racism.

Racism and schooling

One of the fundamental charges levelled by antiracists against the culturalist assumptions underpinning much public and academic debate, especially in the field of education, is that the specificity and significance of racist ideologies and structures have received inadequate attention. Whenever the issue of racism is put on the agenda, they suggest, it is transmuted into questions of prejudice and attitudes, thus leaving a wide range of discriminatory practices and structures unchallenged. This charge is well aimed. As we shall see later in this essay, however, there is a definite, and what at first sight may appear to be surprising, degree of isomorphism between the two perspectives. Before I make that case, it is first necessary to set out, albeit briefly, some of the documented forms of exclusion and violence that are targeted by practices designed to challenge racism in schools.

Racial abuse and violence

The sheer prevalence, intensity and normality of abuse, harassment and violence directed by white students against British Asian and Afro-Caribbean students as part of the informal, popular culture of schools is horrifying. Accounts abound of the distress, trauma and injury involved. The acts range from verbal abuse – continual taunts of 'Paki', 'Nigger', 'Blacky', 'Chocolate face', 'Black bastard' – to vicious physical attacks by both boys and girls in corridors, on playing fields and at bus stops; hospitalization for broken bones, stitches and broken noses is not uncommon. The extent of the problem compelled the Commission for Racial Equality to entitle its survey of racial harassment *Learning in Terror* (1988), giving added weight to other accounts (see, for instance, DES, 1985, pp. 31–5; Kelly and Cohn, 1988; Stronach and Akhtar, 1986). The historical and contemporary experiences of Jewish children attest to the continuing significance of Britain's other racisms and, in the context of another phase of rising anti-semitism, clearly need greater attention (Pilkington, 1990).

In the wake of Burnage the risk of fatality can hardly be denied. To some degree, the racial abuse and violence in schools mirrors that meted out to black minorities in British cities more generally (the anti-semitic parallels must again be recalled). In the absence of adequate police action, this is producing a growing number of self-defence and monitoring groups among black minorities (Gordon, 1990).

The culture of teacher racism

A frequent complaint of black students is that their reports of racial abuse and violence are habitually ignored or their racial elements denied by white teachers. This is only one form of teacher collusion with racialized processes. There are many others, again amply documented. Black students, for example, are not infrequently humiliated with jokes. Common 'witticisms' range from the threat to send a student back to the 'chocolate factory' to be 'remade' to remarks about 'jungle like behaviour', 'Go back to the trees', or 'Stop laughing like monkeys'. (See for instance Wright's chapter in Eggleston *et al.*, 1986, and Macdonald *et al.*, 1989, pp. 140–2.) Many black teachers hardly fare better at the hands of their white colleagues, often finding themselves the butt of racist jokes, hostile remarks and isolation in the staff room. Here is part of an account of the experiences of an extremely well-qualified woman teacher of Afro-Caribbean origin:

> In school she has had to contend with discussions about 'Pakis' in the staff room. One teacher said he would like to send all blacks back on the banana boat, and another told her that he was unable to sit by her because she was black.
> (*The Guardian*, 5 April 1988, reprinted in Open University, 1989a)

The Burnage Report gives a further sense of the routine culture of teacher racism:

> A teacher who showed an interest in Asian culture was asked by a colleague, 'why don't you wear Indian dress?' and was greeted by a mock Indian prayer movement every time she passed this colleague in the corridor.

> A Section 11 teacher who was wearing a hair slide was asked if it was a West Indian hair slide she was wearing. She replied: 'no, it's just a hair slide', and was told 'why don't you take the bone out and wear it through your nose?'

> The wearing of pig badges by a large group of staff, many of whom were members of middle management, after the Deputy Head, Peter Moors, had suggested that pork was less suitable than turkey for the school's Christmas dinner, since it prevented Muslim boys from taking part. Pork scratching packets were pinned to his notice board and he was and still is referred to as 'Porky'.
> (Macdonald *et al.*, 1989, pp. 140–41).

Selection and allocation procedures

Schools are pre-eminently institutional sites for selection and deselection, for the allocation of students to different levels in status hierarchies of subjects in the curriculum and public examinations. The subsequent outcomes are of some significance in determining further educational chances and career opportunities. The various forms of allocative discrimination which operate against black students have been the subject of several investigations. Again, a few instances must suffice to show how the culture of racism, and institutional processes which provide discretionary allocative power to teachers, tend to intermesh and work against many black students. Cecile Wright's research for the Eggleston Report, *Education for Some* (Eggleston *et al.*, 1986), is one of the most compelling documentations of the process at work. It reveals a systematic tendency for able black students to be allocated to sets and streams and entered for examinations below their capacities, and exposes the significance of racist discourses in legitimating these practices (see also Wright, 1987). The obverse of this process is the tendency to channel Afro-Caribbean students, especially, into sports or music on account of supposedly innate physical capacities and 'a natural sense of rhythm' (Carrington, 1983). Careers advice given to both Afro-Caribbean and Asian students is frequently based on conceptions of their supposedly unrealistic and over-ambitious aspirations. Attempts are made to route them into low-level manual work regardless of ability or level of motivation for further education, and discrimination in entry to training schemes acts as a further block to employment and careers (Wrench, 1987, 1990). One symptomatic phenomenon was revealed in my own research in Leicester for an Open University television programme, when I found that many teachers of English were unwilling to come to terms with the interest and creative potential of Asian students in English language, literature and drama. These exclusionary effects of a culture of Englishness embedded in the discourses and practices of English teaching appear rather ironic in view of the significance for the growth of English literary studies of the colonial attempt to 'Anglicize' Indians (Open University, 1989b; Viswanathan, 1987).

School subjects and the production of racialized subjectivities

Caricatured images of 'natives' – African, Asian and Arab – and selective and often fanciful representations of their histories and cultures, reinforced in comics, adventure stories and films, have long been a powerful presence in the official curriculum of British schools (Mackenzie, 1984, 1986; Klein, 1985,; Ahier 1988). They continue to be an important mechanism of exclusion, stereotypification and marginalization, re-inforced as they are by representations in the mass media (Hartmann and Husband, 1974; Hall, 1981; Murdock, 1984).

Institutional procedures

Black minorities have frequently been casualties of rules and procedures which may not have been intended to discriminate against them but which, in effect, do so and there is considerable resistance when the hitherto taken-for-granted procedures are brought into question. Rules about appropriate modes of dress, whether concerning school uniforms or clothing for PE and sports, have been one such arena. Some schools refuse to allow Sikh boys to wear turbans, or girls to cover their legs. These constitute a form of indirect discrimination which in the case of turbans was fought successfully by a Sikh family under the terms of the 1976 Race Relations Act (Dorn, 1985). Other instances include the lack of avail-ability of vegetarian food or halal meat, the failure to communicate school messages to parents in languages other than English, and the absence of policies on racial abuse or equal opportunities. Mention must also be made of the marginalization of many black teaching staff because of their employment in 'community language' teams or as Section 11 teachers. (See the accounts of black teachers at Burnage in Macdonald *et al.*, 1989, pp. 215–44.)

'Multiculturalism' and 'antiracism': a binary opposition?

It is often asserted that the 1980s saw a polarization of two fundamentally opposed educational movements, multiculturalism and antiracism. These were based on different understandings of racism which apparently led to radically divergent programmes of educational reform. In part the debate has been presented as an opposition between a broadly liberal programme – multiculturalism – and an antiracism which claimed for itself the mantle of left radicalism (Dodgson and Stewart, 1981; Mullard, 1984; Troyna, 1987a; Gill and Singh, 1987). It is certainly the case that there have been debates, often acrimonious ones, between self-styled multiculturalists and antiracists.

It is less clear, however, to what extent and in what ways this broad division has actually manifested itself in the classroom and in internal school debates and policies, and in local authority policies. In many institutions complex and varying combinations of the two have been put into practice, and there are in any case many differences and contradictions *within* the two movements (see, for example, Bonnett, 1990). My argument here is that, despite some differences of approach, at a deeper level there are fundamental similarities in conceptualization and prescription between multiculturalism and antiracism which are flawed. Although both movements have made important contributions, my judgement is that their frameworks and policies *share* significant and disabling weaknesses.

I cannot emphasize too strongly that I have not here attempted to provide a detailed exposition or erect a comprehensive critique of multiculturalist and antiracist assumptions and practices. The discussion that follows is necessarily selective, highlighting some key issues, but inevitably neglecting others, for example around the vexed question of cultural relativism and the problems surrounding the marginalization of 'race' policies at the institutional level, which might be treated in a text of quite different length and scope.

Multiculturalism, as expressed in the Swann Report or in the writings of Jeffcoate, James, Lynch and Parekh, is based on the premise that the key issue facing schools is how to create tolerance for black minorities and their cultures in a white nation now characterized by cultural diversity or cultural pluralism. Intolerance is conceptualized basically as a matter of *attitudes*, and is said to be constituted by *prejudice*. The basic educational prescription is the sympathetic teaching of 'other cultures' in order to dispel the ignorance which is seen to be at the root of prejudice and intolerance. The overall social and political project is the creation of a harmonious, democratic cultural pluralism, a healthy cultural diversity. There are internal differences among the multiculturalists, of course, and under relentless criticism from antiracists most multiculturalists have acknowledged the significance of tackling institutionalized racist practices in schools (Lynch, 1986). Nevertheless, these are the key principles held by those who see themselves more as multiculturalists, and continue explicitly to take a critical distance from antiracism (cf. Lynch, 1990, pp. 32–3).

Antiracists have pointed out that in privileging prejudice and attitudes the multiculturalists have neglected racism as embedded in structures and institutions. However, the case against prejudice is even stronger, and more complex.

The case against prejudice

Prejudice, as conceptualized both in the educational literature around multiculturalism and in more specialized psychological discourses, is defined as hostile or negative attitudes based on ignorance and faulty or incomplete knowledge. It is characterized by a tendency to stereotype, that is, a tendency to assign identical characteristics to whole groups regardless of individual variations (Twitchin and Demuth, 1985, p. 170; Aronson, 1980, p. 197). Thus, multicultural handbooks and official reports such as Rampton and Swann warn against the common teacher stereotypes of Afro-Caribbean ('disruptive', 'lazy') and Asian ('industrious', 'passive', 'over-ambitious') students which are also documented in academic research on teachers' attitudes (Brittan, 1976). As we have seen, multi-culturalist accounts emphasize the way in which stereotypes may be affecting classroom encounters (DES, 1985, pp. 46–56, reproduces a piece of research on this by Peter Green); the channelling of Afro-Caribbean students into sports; and the allocation of Afro-Caribbean and Asian students to streams, sets, examinations and career paths which grossly underestimate their abilities and potential.

One major difficulty about these notions of prejudice and stereotype concerns the all too common assumption that individuals hold prejudiced views consistently and express them and act in accordance with them in a systematic and uncontradictory manner. This therefore tends to essentialize 'the prejudiced individual' – the prejudiced teacher or student – who becomes the target for pedagogies that are supposed to cure them of this pathology. There is mounting evidence, however, to suggest a more complex picture. For one thing, many people who might be labelled racially prejudiced on the basis of attitude surveys or expressive behaviour in particular contexts turn out to be more ambivalent and contradictory in their discourses and practices. Thus Billig and Cochrane (1984) report that during their research a white girl, who in discussions with them had expressed strongly racist views, was seen walking out of school arm in arm with an Asian girl. Even more dramatically, Darren Coulbourn, the white boy from Burnage High School who murdered Ahmed Iqbal Ullah and triumphantly proclaimed 'I've killed a Paki', was also known to have collaborated with an Asian boy in burning down the art block and 'used to get into trouble' at school (as the Burnage Report puts it) in the company of an Afro-Caribbean boy. Darren Coulbourn's 'attitudes on race are not clear-cut', the report concludes (Macdonald *et al.*, 1989, p. 8). In Philip Cohen's research (1989b) white working-class youths in south London expressed more or less sympathetic views on blacks depending on the context and topic of conversation. Talking to the researcher about South Africa, they voiced sympathy for the plight of black South Africans. Talking to their mates about British blacks, they tended to complain about becoming second-class citizens in their own country. Although it appears to be the same principle that promotes sympathy for South African blacks in *their* country, this confirms rather than vitiates the point that the form and meaning of racist discourses depends on and varies in context and enables a range of verbal and practical interactions and positions. (Cohen also refers, for instance, to white youth who supported overtly racist immigration policies but dissociated themselves from the National Front; see also the research on white youth reported in Coffield *et al.*, 1986).

Billig's research (1978) on adult National Front members revealed a complexity of attitudes and practices which belies what is, ironically enough, a *social scientific* stereotype of the strongly prejudiced individual who operates with a rigid set or framework of categories. A notable illustration of this complexity even among hard-core racists was the NF official who pointed out that he had been elected by both black and white workmates, despite his well-known NF affiliation, because he fought equally hard for blacks and whites; he claimed a liking for blacks and maintained that he played football and drank with them, although politically he supported repatriation. In the United States, Wellman (1977) has shown how antidiscrimination legislation in the sphere of employment can be supported by people who reject it in the field of housing. This is part of a much wider pattern of contradictions in white attitudes. Investigations in New Zealand have pointed up the complexity and variability of white orientations towards the entitlements of Maoris within the policy (Wetherell and Potter, 1988).

The circulation of contradictory stereotypes is partly responsible for the complexity and ambivalence of discourses surrounding 'race'. This is graphically illustrated by Jenkins's investigations (1985, 1986) of white managers' varying conceptions of the capacities of Asian and Afro-

Caribbean workers. Some regarded Asians as lazy compared with Afro-Caribbeans, while others reversed the comparison. Generally, Asians in Britain have been regarded both as scroungers *and* as so industrious that they are taking over jobs and businesses, as both thrifty *and* flashy. They may be resented or hated, but there is admiration for their supposed 'industriousness', 'ambitiousness', 'enterprise', 'family values', 'respect and care for their elderly', 'respect for authority', and so on. Afro-Caribbeans are seen as both lazy *and* as extraordinarily successful in activities requiring considerable physical exertion and mental discipline such as sport and athletics. Stereotypes, moreover, are subject to historical change and geographical variation and salience. Such ambiguities and variations are particularly evident in New Right discourses but can also be found in popular culture. Afro-Caribbeans may be reviled as 'niggers', but their musical forms and stylistic innovations exercise considerable fascination, attraction and influence in popular culture (Jones, 1988). Some of the most common forms of ambivalence, of course, are expressed in disavowals such as 'Some of my best friends are . . .', or 'You [some] are all right, it's the rest . . .'.

The question of sexuality further complicates racialized encounters, such as racial harassment and violence. These are not simply between 'black' and 'white', but between white and black men (Westwood, 1990), white men and black women, and so on. Both working-class and middle-class masculinities are involved, with defences of the neighbourhood against racialized 'others' which Cohen refers to as the 'nationalism of the neighbourhood' (Cohen, 1988); the proving of masculinity by beating up 'Pakis' (Willis, 1978); the sexual harassment of black women; and an aspect that deserves much greater research, in the middle-class and professional institutional context, the complex intertwining of masculinity, class and racism in the exclusion of blacks from employment or promotion by white male managers.

Racialized discourses are always articulated in context: in an English or history class; in a school corridor, dinner queue or playground; at work or on the streets; in one neighbourhood or another. These different sites can yield complex and shifting alliances and points of tension. (See Nanton and Fitzgerald, 1990, for the complexity of alliances around racial harassment on public housing estates.) The ambivalences generated for many white youth by the attractions of Afro-Caribbean, Afro-American and African musical forms, and their admirations for some aggressive forms of Afro-Caribbean masculinity, have resulted in alliances in particular schools and neighbourhoods between white and Afro-Caribbean youth against Asian youth, while in some schools where black–white conflicts remain submerged the dominant form of racist insult occurs between different ethnic minority groups, for instance Asian and Afro-Caribbean or Cypriot and Vietnamese (Cohen, 1987).

An appreciation of contradiction, ambivalence and context, combined with a sensitivity to the variability of discourses among teachers and their practices also puts into question simplistic models of the process whereby (uncontradictory) teacher stereotypes of black pupils are supposedly translated into discriminatory practices that lead to unequal outcomes. Recent research paints a more complex picture of contradictory teacher attitudes varying within and between schools and provoking a range of responses from black male and female students (Mac an Ghaill, 1989; Foster, 1990). This point is also being registered in relation to sexism in schools (Wolpe, 1989) and has provoked a more general rethinking of educational processes in which poststructuralist theorizing is beginning to exercise a belated, but in my view welcome, influence (Walkerdine, 1991).

The Burnage Report is the first document of its kind to attempt to deal with some of these complexities. It points *inter alia* to the ambivalence of Darren Coulbourn's racism and the significance of the masculine cult of violence that had a strong presence in the all-boys school. It also emphasizes how the generalized context of racism in the school was relevant to their conclusion that the murder of Ahmed Iqbal Ullah was a 'racial' murder.

All this is a far cry from the simplifications of the multicultural discourse of prejudice and the prejudiced subject or individual. But this is not the end of the story. Conceptions of prejudice, and associated forms of multiculturalism in education, are premised on the view that prejudice is primarily caused by ignorance – in this case of black cultures. The educational prescription is therefore a curricular dose of knowledge about those 'other cultures', taught in a variety of sometimes imaginative ways. The problem with this is not merely that there has been very little serious thinking within multiculturalism about how 'cultural understanding' actually occurs, about its forms, mechanisms and limits. What, after all, does it mean to *understand* any culture, including one's own, whatever that might be in ethnic, class, or any other terms? The more subversive possibility is that the discourse of prejudice contains an element that threatens the foundations of multiculturalism from within. That is, there is a contradiction between the *rationalism* of the multiculturalist project, which recommends a reduction of prejudice by teaching a combination of facts and cultural empathy, and the insistence, also within the discourse of prejudice, that prejudice involves a strong element of *irrationalism*.[4]

A further question mark over the practices of multiculturalism concerns the actual effects of teaching about 'other cultures'. Little evidence, sceptics argue, has been adduced to support the claim that such teaching has a significant impact in reducing prejudice. The 'culture contact' hypothesis as investigated by psychologists has produced poor results (Troyna, 1987a). What evidence there is often exists only in the anecdotal form of teacher accounts or in multicultural handbooks (Burgess, 1986; Nixon, 1985). However, the whole question of the effects of teaching around 'race', whether in multiculturalist or other forms, requires recasting in the light of the more complex understanding of racism and racist subjectivities being proposed here. If subjects are contradictorily and ambivalently positioned in discourses and if racist practices are significantly affected by social context, research into the effects of teaching about 'race' cannot operate with the linear and essentialist models used by most conventional psychology and sociology. Far more subtle, long-term ethnographic research has to be undertaken to establish how subjects negotiate such teaching and how subjectivities are recomposed in different contexts. In the absence of such research, Troyna's confident rejection of multiculturalist strategies cannot be sustained, although of course the antiracist argument that teaching about 'other cultures' does not necessarily give an understanding of the racism of one's own remains intact.

Racism and the antiracists

Antiracists have rightly pointed to the limited nature of multicultural-ism's focus on prejudice and attitudes, and its strategy of prejudice reduction by teaching about 'other cultures'. Racism, the antiracists argue, must be challenged head on. That requires a dismantling of institutionalized *practices* of racism, whether in education or in employment, housing, immigration policy, and so on, as well as a direct confrontation with racist ideologies, for example, in the school curriculum. (See, for example, Hatcher and Shallice, 1983; Mullard, 1984; Sivanandan, 1985; Sarup, 1986; Troyna, 1987a; Gill and Singh, 1987.) On closer examination, however, their conception of racism, both at the level of ideology and structures, also suffers from oversimplification, often of a very similar kind.

When racism is addressed as a set of ideologies, for example, none of the antiracist analyses cited above displays an awareness of contradictions, inconsistencies and ambivalences of the kind I have sketched earlier. In this sense, the antiracists' understanding of racist ideologies and racist subjects or individuals is no more sophisticated than that of the multi-culturalists. Also absent is an understanding of the complex intertwining of racism with sexuality (not the same point as the increasingly common reference to the 'triple oppression' of the black woman). It is now quite clear that the complexities of white racism (which is the focus here) cannot be grasped without an exploration of the anxieties and ambivalences generated particularly by white male, but also female, sexual anxieties and desires. From the earliest encounters between Europeans and Others right to the present, these manifest themselves in an endless series of speculations, projections, fantasies and crimes in relation to 'African' and 'Oriental' women and men (Gilman, 1985, 1987; Cohen, 1988; Open University, 1992). This interaction between sexuality and racism is an important source of the irrationalities and resistances encountered by a rational 'facts and empathy' approach, whether of an antiracist of multicultural variety, and poses highly complex problems for any project of deracialization. There are no easy answers here. Even the prescription of a joint approach to issues of sexism and racism (Brah and Deem, 1986) does little more than scratch the surface of a very much deeper problem. Educational and pedagogic strategies developed by feminists more conscious of the need to dig deeper into psychic processes in tackling sexual identities and subjectivities (e.g. Walkerdine, 1991) require more serious attention within antiracism, and have found a sympathetic counterpart in Phillip Cohen's cultural studies approach to antiracism (Cohen, 1987, 1988, 1989a).

In antiracism as much as in multiculturalism, the absence of any serious engagement with issues around sexuality in the 'irrationality' of popular racism is symptomatic of a rationalist understanding of pedagogies and educational processes. In the case of antiracism, this is further under-pinned by an overly rationalist conception of state and dominant class racism. I begin by examining the antiracists' notion of racism as a form of irrationalism.

The mode by which the discourse of *prejudice* consigns racism to a form of irrationalism is, at bottom, a *pathologization* of the individual subject. Racism is interpreted as a form of displacement and objectification deriving from unhealthy neuroses and personality traits. In antiracist analyses the irrationality of popular or working-class racism is concep-tualized primarily as a form of false consciousness. There are several variants of the argument, differing at least in part around the degree of class reductionism and the amount of reflexivity allowed to the working-class racist subject. In the crudest analyses, working-class racism is interpreted as composed of a set of falsehoods perpetrated by one, or a combination, of the following agencies: capital, the ruling class, the mass media, and the state. These are conceptualized as unified, non-contradictory, omniscient 'actors', united by the common objective of dividing the working class along racial lines so as to facilitate the economic exploitation of both sections of the class. The state is viewed as an instrument of capital and state policies such as immigration and race relations legislation are seen as the outcome of deliberate, thus 'rational', manipulation by agents of capital and the capitalist state. The working-class racist, in this construction, is reduced to a 'cultural dope'. That is, he or she is viewed as a passive and helpless victim of ruling class, media and state propaganda. Reformist black activists are also seen as cultural dopes and/or traitors to class and community, bought off by the race relations industry of the Commission for Racial Equality, Community Relations Councils, local authority 'race' posts, community and welfare projects, or multiculturalism. All these have been supposedly cynically instituted by the state–capital complex.

Some of the highly influential writings of Sivanandan, director of the Institute of Race Relations and editor of the journal *Race and Class* fall squarely within this tradition (1974, 1985). These operate within a crude Marxism which became the object of considerable internal criticism within Marxism (see, for example, Gabriel and Ben-Tovim, 1978; Hall, 1980) but which appears to have failed to shift the class reductionism and instrumentalism associated with his project. Other left antiracists, like Madan Sarup, are more aware *in principle* of the pitfalls of such class reductionism, and attempt to disavow it. In practice, however, they often fall back on a similar analysis (Sarup, 1986, pp. 40, 95–8). (It is worth adding that multiculturalists are prone to another essentialism with regard to the state, often seeing it as a neutral and uncontradictory vehicle for educational and other reforms – see Troyna's critique (1987b) of the Swann Report.) Although it is not possible to rehearse here the many deficiencies of the antiracist brand of class reductionism, some of the difficulties are signalled by my description of instrumentalism and the patronizing 'cultural dope' stereotype of the white working-class racist. It is also worth emphasizing the links between a view of racist subjects and ideologies which neglects contradictions and ambivalences and the conception of racism as, simply, a form of false consciousness. Note, too, that nothing is said within such analyses about forms of middle-class racism – the discussion pivots around a simple polarization between a 'ruling' and 'working' class.

Not all antiracists, however, whether in education or elsewhere, appear to subscribe to such a simplified version of the racism-as-false-consciousness argument. Others (e.g. Hatcher and Shallice, 1983) have drawn upon Phizacklea and Miles's North London research which, although in the final analysis conceives of racism as a form of false consciousness, nevertheless gives a more active, reasoning or reflexive role to the working-class racist subject. Phizacklea and Miles (1979, 1980) argue that, in the particular inner-city context that they researched, white racism operated not simply in the form of cultural stereotypes but as part of the process whereby white residents and workers attempted to make sense of public housing shortages, reduction in employment opportunities, and other aspects of urban decline. These features for many whites were primarily associated with the arrival of black settlers, who were thus blamed for the problems. This gave rise to the resentment and hostility which Phizacklea and Miles regard as a characteristic form of modern, inner-city, working-class white racism, although they have been mindful that the findings may only apply to particular sections of the class and in particular areas. Thus racist discourses and practices are seen to emerge in specific forms. More generally, they are seen to flourish in situations of acute competition for scarce resources such as employment and housing and they are exacerbated by the insecurities of rising inflation.

Phizacklea and Miles show some sensitivity to the contradictory nature of working-class consciousness and emphasize that in a number of workers high levels of class consciousness nevertheless coexisted with considerable hostility towards local blacks. They stress the often fragmented and piecemeal character of the racial hostility expressed by some white people in their survey: some of them blamed black settlers for housing shortages but not the loss of employment opportunities, for example. Nevertheless, the forms of racism revealed here are seen as a form of false consciousness based on the

> attempt to understand and explain *immediate daily experience*, while the real reasons for both the socio-economic decline and New Commonwealth immigration are to be found in much more abstract and long-standing social and economic processes which cannot be grasped in terms of daily experience.
> (original emphasis, Phizacklea and Miles, 1979, p. 118)

Note the important educational and pedagogic conclusion Phizacklea and Miles draw from their research: the significance of immediate daily experience in producing and reproducing inner-city working-class racism, in conjunction with the backdrop of a widespread nationalist culture of racism in British society, means that those who express racist hostility 'are very resistant to modification as a result of argument from outsiders' (ibid., p. 120). Phizacklea and Miles warn of the limits of any strategy premised on the assumption (made in the 1970s by the TUC and the Labour Party) that 'the way to eliminate working-class racism was to provide counter-arguments to common racist beliefs', to push out of workers' heads an ideological baggage primarily produced by the dominant class and replace it by 'the truth'.

This research has been expounded at some length here to demonstrate that despite some limitations it is informed by a relatively subtle and complex analysis. Antiracist educators have read it in a simplistic manner, however, much to the detriment of their pedagogic project. Hatcher and Shallice, for instance, having cited Phizacklea and Miles's research, conclude, contrary to the researchers, that in education the key task must be the provision of superior explanations for unemployment, for example, which would also involve discussions of issues of class politics. They stress the significance of a *cognitive* emphasis, and link this to an older labour movement project for the provision of 'really useful knowledge' (Hatcher and Shallice, 1983, pp. 8–10; cf. Troyna, 1987a, p. 316 for a similarly misleading reading of Billig and Cochrane's research). Moreover, while Phizacklea and Miles believe that changes in the material circumstances of the working class can provide only a partial solution to the problem of racist ideologies, the political project of the transformation of capitalism and working-class conditions advocated by Hatcher and Shallice (and other left antiracists in education) squeezes out of consideration the rather important caveat entered by Phizacklea and Miles about the prospects for change in racist ideologies as a result of changes in the material base.

Phizacklea and Miles's own research can be faulted on a variety of grounds. There is little detailed exploration of the contradictions, and none of the ambivalences that might characterize the racism of their subjects (for contrasting discussions see Cohen, 1988, 1991). The analysis is also considerably weakened by the empiricism of their notion of 'direct, immediate experience', which writes out the significance of the complex interpretive *frameworks* through which events, processes and facts are *constructed*. Experience, that is, is *produced*, rather than simply *registered*. The implicit recognition of this in their work is obscured by the distinction they make between 'direct experience' and more 'abstract' 'underlying' causes which cannot be grasped at the level of immediate experience. Moreover, resistances other than those posed by 'immediate experience' are ignored; for instance, possible sexual anxieties provoked by moral panics, common enough in the 1970s and early 1980s, around black 'muggers' and 'rapists'.

Like the multiculturalists, antiracists have often failed to confront the limitations of a rationalist approach to education. The *rationalism* of their educational project is contingent on the supposed *irrationalism* of the racist subject – often conceptualized as a collective, class subject. In the context of schooling one significant issue that is paradoxically neglected is the 'rationality' of the working-class students' resistance to antiracist curricula and classroom discussions in so far as this resistance is bound up with a more generalized opposition to the degrees of surveillance, discipline, authoritarianism and class domination involved in conventional forms of schooling. (The same point can be made against multiculturalist understandings of prejudice.)[5] Like the multiculturalist project of reducing prejudice by teaching about other cultures, the antiracist project of providing superior explanations for unemployment, housing shortages, and so forth, has so far, and for similar reasons, produced only patchy evidence of success. The point is not simply to abandon this type of teaching but to acknowledge and analyse its limitations in the light of a more complex understanding of the nature of racism and to develop forms of educational engagement more likely to open up racist subjectivities and common sense to alternative discourses. More democratic and collaborative pedagogies, as proposed by Troyna and Carrington (1990) and exemplified by some of the projects they have developed, are a step in the right direction. They are still weakened, however, by the absence of a more complex understanding of the contradictions, ambivalences and resistances of the popular cultures of racism amongst white youth.[6] Indeed Troyna and Carrington have themselves expressed doubts about the efficacy of such initiatives (ibid., pp. 114–19).

One index of the theoretical and educational congruences between multiculturalism and antiracism is the underlying similarity between multiculturalist attempts to combat racial prejudice by the provision of 'positive images' and the antiracist injunction to present black histories primarily as narratives of resistance and struggle against racism

(Jeffcoate, 1979; Hatcher and Shallice, 1983, p. 10). The aims are laudable, given the often grotesque caricatures of African, Asian and Arab histories and cultures; the neglect of the destructive, exploitative effects of colonialism and imperialism in school texts and in popular cultural forms such as comics, adventure stories, adult fiction and the cinema; and the absence of any serious treatment of resistance to imperial rule (Mackenzie, 1984, 1986; Klein, 1985). Nevertheless there are difficulties here which must be confronted if both multicultural and antiracist attempts at the development of alternative curricula and popular cultural forms are to avoid oversimplification and naïvety.

There is an unacknowledged disingenuity involved in replacing one lot of selective images with another set of partial representations. Among other things, this opens up the multiculturalists and antiracists to the very charge of propaganda and indoctrination which they level at the textbooks, authors and teachers they are attempting to challenge. It also allows the New Right and sections of the media to connect the purging of 'negative images' from textbooks with other authoritarian or top-down antiracist policies by LEAs and schools and to represent the whole exercise as a Labour left and antiracist 'totalitarian' conspiracy. On this issue, the 'traditionalists', the multiculturalists and antiracists occupy the same epistemological terrain. They all share the misleading assumption that it is possible to produce a singular, uncontestable, objective and accurate representation of the reality external to the literary or photo-graphic or any other text. They thus ignore or obscure a different, more democratic objective: that is, the search for mechanisms for giving voice to a range of representations, and for encouraging a critical dialogue and interrogation of all intellectual and political frameworks. Black artists, photographers, film makers and cultural critics have been in the forefront of demands and attempts to break the bounds of an aesthetic of 'positive images'. They reject the reduction of the diversity of black histories, experiences and cultures to a response to racism, not least because this inhibits the productive exploration of the economic, cultural and sexual differentiations within black communities – for example, 'positive images' tend to privilege middle-class, heterosexual, familial respectability. It also blocks the creativity of black artistic imagination and practices of representation. Look, for example, at the photography of David A. Bailey, the films of Sankofa, the Black Audio Films Collective and Hanif Kureishi, the essays of Paul Gilroy and Kobena Mercer, or the paintings of Sonia Boyce (Areean, 1989; Bailey, 1988; Gilroy, 1987; Mercer, 1988). This work explores questions of racism, ethnicity, nationality and sexual difference in ways which have problematized conventional assumptions and opened up a debate about the diversity and complexity of black British identities and voices. The *educational* implication is not that the contestation of caricatures of black histories and cultures in school texts should cease, but that it should not be premised on the stifling aesthetic of the positive image.

Although, given their underlying premise of cultural pluralism, multi-culturalists tend to be more sympathetic to giving voice to a plurality of positions, their project is vitiated by the tendency to cling to epistemological assumptions more congruent with the discourse of positive images. A decisive break with realist conceptions of the curriculum is long overdue and is a precondition for genuinely pluralist forms of radicalization of the curriculum (Alvarado and Ferguson, 1983; Wexler, 1987). Troyna and Carrington's dissatisfaction with simplistic assumptions about the anti-racist effects of 'culture contact' and white students' 'direct experience' of black realities, as well as their growing awareness of the limits of rationalist pedagogies, points to a need on their part to break with realist assumptions about the curriculum which still underpin their antiracist projects (Troyna and Carrington, 1990).

Both multicultural and antiracist critiques ignore the actual literary and pedagogic devices involved in the construction of subject positions for the child/reader in school texts. They neglect *how* texts construct meanings as opposed to *what* they supposedly mean. As a consequence, the complexity of the processes by which texts which form part of particular school disciplines – history or geography, etc. – have effects on the 'subjects' of schools, the students, is also neglected. Too often, all the protagonists make simplistic assumptions about the ease with which subjectivities are produced by racist or antiracist texts (see, for a contrary analysis, Ahier, 1988).

A last important theme in the antiracists' analysis is their conception of 'institutional racism'. Originating in the Black Power Movement's struggles in the US, the term now generally signifies all the myriad, taken-for-granted ways in which routine institutional procedures, whatever their original purposes, end up discriminating against and disadvantaging black and other ethnic minorities. Examples of some of the forms of institutional racism involved in the education system have been provided earlier in this article. There has been, however, a tendency to use the concept in a reductive manner to imply that racist processes are the only or primary cause of all the unequal outcomes and exclusions which black students experience (Troyna and Williams, 1986; see also Mason, 1982). The significance of the class and gender inequalities which are intertwined with the racism that black students encounter is thus underplayed. This weakens the analysis and suggests inappropriate and possibly divisive policies which ignore discriminations and disadvantages common to white and black students, or which impinge in varying ways upon boys and girls. The hostages to fortune delivered by simplistic uses of institutional racism can be seen in Antony Flew's New Right critique (1984).

An alternative framework

Having criticized the limits of the antiracist account of racism, this is an appropriate point at which to explicate my own conception of racism and to indicate why I think it is more persuasive (cf. Open University, 1992). In my view *racism*, which should be distinguished from *racial discrimination*, should be restricted to discourses which group human populations into 'races' on the basis of some biological signifier – for example, 'stock' – with each 'race' being regarded as having essential characteristics or a certain essential character (as in the phrase 'the British character', or in attributions to 'races' of laziness, rebelliousness, or industriousness) and where inferiorization of some 'races' may or may not be present. Such views may be held alongside others in varying combinations. They may shade off into what might more appropriately be called *ethnocentrism*, where ethnic groups are defined primarily in cultural terms and are regarded as having essential traits. Although overt inferiorization may not be present, there is a tendency to view cultures from within the categories and frameworks of one ethnic group. *Nationalism* may thus be regarded as one form of ethnocentrism, in which cultural groups and their essential characteristics are defined by nationality and the cultural attributes of one or more nations may be regarded as inherently superior or inferior. Nationalism may also contain *racial* elements in so far as particular nations may be regarded as deriving from specific racial stocks; and biologically defined communities may be regarded as the prime source of cultural characteristics.

This type of analytical framework posits a range of views from strong versions of racism to weak versions of ethnocentrism. It has a number of advantages. It recognizes that most discourses, and especially individuals, are likely to express a complex combination of strong and weak racism and ethnocentrism (and nationalism), and that these may change in emphasis in different historical institutional and interpersonal contexts. It has a theoretical structure which allows for the possibility of a variety of 'racisms', depending upon how various elements of 'race', ethnicity and nationality are combined, how they are articulated with gender and class, and how they are related to theories in the natural and social sciences and notions in popular culture and common sense. Also, by restricting itself to the realm of discourse, the definition leaves open the relationship between particular discourses, specific practices of discrimination, and particular unequal or discriminatory outcomes (although bearing in mind that discourses themselves involve acts or practices of expression). *It clearly implies that racism and ethnocentrism are not necessarily confined to white groups.* And it should be added that some degree of ethnocentrism is likely to be endemic because all discourses and individuals necessarily have to use language and categories. All enunciations have to be produced within particular discourses, and these are always liable to contain particular ethnicities and thus likely to position individuals in specific ethnic locations, often in taken-for-granted and deeply unconscious ways.

Moreover, in keeping with my earlier remarks, I would argue that racialized and ethnic discourses and encounters have a tendency to be contradictory and ambivalent in character. These internal complexities are contextually produced and differentially deployed in particular situations and institutional locations. Racialized and ethnic discourses and encounters are also inevitably suffused with elements of sexual and class difference and therefore fractured and criss-crossed around a number of axes and identities.

The contradictoriness and ambivalence of racist discourses and inter-actions are produced by a complex combination of social and psychic structures and forces. For one thing, the sheer range and historical variation of the sites where encounters between 'white' and 'other' have taken place and the immense variety of specialized and popular discourses that have operated in these encounters have by now put into circulation a multitude of selective images. These operate as discursive resources to be drawn upon and articulated in different combinations in particular contexts, thus constantly opening up the possibility of tension, inconsistency and contradiction within and between sites. Sociologically, politically and educationally speaking, difficult but vital questions arise as to how and why particular images, labels, categories, anxieties, forms of rhetoric and practices come to be mobilized around specific sections of a population. How, for example, do various forms of racism, ethnocentrism and nationalism interact with discourses of gender, sexuality, class and generation to produce different stereotypes and practices in official policy programmes and popular culture around 'the Asian woman' or 'black youth'?

In explorations of the texture of racist discourses in recent years, the inner city has been a prime site for investigation. Research into the complexities of urban power relations and conflicts over resources have produced important insights into the operation of complex rhetorics and categories of racialization (Wellman, 1977; Phizacklea and Miles, 1980). But there has been a relative neglect of the general institutional and discursive form of the liberal-democratic, capitalist nation-state and its effects in the production of contradictory discourses around 'race'. That is, racist, ethnocentric and nationalist ideas, which attempt to create strict symbolic and institutional barriers between collectivities, have also to coexist and continually articulate with a variety of discourses and practices around meritocracy, equal opportunities and citizenship rights. This creates a multiplicity of axes for the production of possibly conflicting subject positions and potential practices and interactions.

Nevertheless, it is unlikely that the contradictions and ambivalences of stereotypes in general, and racist discourses in particular, can be fully understood without addressing the operations of the unconscious and the dynamics of psychic reality. This therefore involves a difficult journey through psychoanalytic theories and categories. This is not the place to explain and justify different psychoanalytic accounts of the dynamics of identification, disavowal and ambivalence which characterize racist discourses. One way of viewing the significance of psychoanalytic theories is to conceptualize the unconscious as productive of irrationalities and resistances which simultaneously organize and subvert the operations of conscious subjectivity (Craib, 1989); hence their relevance for transforming the rationalism which underlies the pedagogies of both multiculturalist and antiracist educational practices. But their significance also needs to be grasped with respect to the operations of splitting, desire, fantasy, pleasure and paranoia which are deeply implicated in racist discourses, and which may inherently produce dualities and ambivalences in racialized encounters between selves and others. The psychoanalytic–historical investigations of Gilman (1985, 1987) and Bhabha (1983, 1986) provide contrasting routes into this terrain, while the theoretical, historical and educational work of Philip Cohen, already referred to, constitutes the most significant intervention around antiracist education informed by both psychoanalytic and sociological understanding.

Having set out a critique of multicultural and antiracist conceptions of racism and elements of an alternative theorization, it is time to turn to notions of culture in multiculturalism and antiracism.

The question of culture

Earlier in this article I have argued that the initial debates and policies which emerged in the wake of the growing black presence were characterized by various forms of cultural and ethnic essentialism or reductionism and that this still persists, for example, in the way ethnic monitoring and other official knowledges are produced.

Latter-day multiculturalisms, to turn our attention back to them, have by no means overcome the weaknesses of earlier discourses and policy interventions, despite the greater attention given to cultural pluralism and diversity (cf. Parekh, 1989a). Several key problems can be identified. First, in occupying the terrain of prejudice, there continues – as in so many forms of antiracism – to be a fairly simplistic notion of how racism is culturally reproduced, or transmitted as the preferred term has it. Prejudice acquisition is ascribed to a process of acculturation or socialization from family, peer groups, school curricula, the media, and so on (Lynch, 1987). Contradictory discourses and practices within and between these agencies of socialization are given little serious attention. Secondly, although the diverse bases of cultural differentiation – ethnicity, class, gender, region, etc. – are acknowledged, the primary emphasis in multiculturalist analysis is on ethnicity, such that economic and sexual differentiations within the minority communities, for example, continue to be ignored (cf. Lynch, 1986; Parekh, 1986, 1989a; Verma, 1989).

Thirdly, however, the focus on ethnicity as part of the discourse of cultural pluralism and diversity pays scant attention to the highly complex, contextually variable and economically and politically influenced drawing and redrawing of boundaries that takes place in encounters within the minority communities and in relation to white groups. There is little exploration of the sorts of processes and events reported in research in Manchester (Ward, 1979) and London (Wallman, 1986), for example, which documents the shifting forms of boundary maintenance, division and alliance that emerge in relation to local politics. To put it differently, sociologically speaking there can be no simple additive model of British cultural diversity as composed of a series of ethnic groups, as posited in the discourse of multiculturalism. This implies, in turn, that the foundations of the whole project of teaching about 'other cultures' need to be rethought. The shape and character of ethnic cultural formations is too complex to be reduced to formulas around festivals, religions, world-views and lifestyles. These fail to grapple with the shifting and kaleidoscopic nature of ethnic differentiations and identities and their relation to internal divisions of class and gender. Moreover, as I have remarked earlier, thinking around the question of what it means to understand cultures has hardly begun in multiculturalism, although there is a wealth of material and debate in cultural studies, social anthropology and philosophy upon which to draw (cf. Geertz, 1973, 1983; Clifford and Marcus, 1986). Definitions of culture are either not provided at all or conflate distinct conceptions such as symbolization, ethnicity and lifestyle (see the contributions of Lynch and Verma to Parekh, 1989a).

One consequence of these lacunae in multiculturalist discourse has been a failure to confront issues of cultural *difference*. These are obscured by what I have called the additive model of cultural diversity. The Rushdie scandal has exposed the weaknesses of any benign multiculturalism premised on the assumption of easy harmony and pluralism. The problem of epistemological and cultural relativism, amongst other things, looms large here. Only recently has there been some serious debate within multiculturalism about the issues involved, although with very little guidance on how teachers are to approach and facilitate discussion around the inevitable questions which arise regarding the evaluation of different cultural representations, knowledges and practices. And the debate is apt to collapse into a gross oversimplification of 'other' cultures, for example, with regard to the differing positions and politics of girls and women in Muslim cultures (Troyna and Carrington, 1987).

It might be thought that, given their aversion to the whole terrain of culture, antiracists are generally immune to the kinds of criticisms set out above. This is only partly true. Whereas multiculturalism often collapses analysis and prescription into some form of *ethnic* essentialism, in antiracism cultural essentialism emerges, ironically enough, partly out of the *denial* of ethnicity. Antiracists have tended to reify the notion of community, and, by focusing for understandable reasons on unitary conceptions of 'The black struggle', to marginalize issues of ethnic, class and gender differences in the black communities.[7] Partly influenced by the Black Power Movement in the US, the category 'black' became, for the late 1960s, an important focus, especially among left antiracists, for mobilizing the growing communities of Afro-Caribbean and Asian descent. 'Black', here, denotes not simply an often successful political alliance against racism. It operates as a profoundly cultural category, an attempted representation of particular experiences and a particular construction of unity around those experiences.

The category had a profound influence on antiracist activists and intellectuals of British Afro-Caribbean, African and Asian descent, and it can still serve as a powerful descriptive and political signifier. But the cultural essentialism at its core has begun to disintegrate. In the first place, there has been what one might call an ethnic 'backlash' from British Asian and Afro-Caribbean communities. Some groups within both have protested at the homogenization of different histories, cultures, needs, aspirations and trajectories of migration and settlement, implied in the use of the singular category. Secondly, it has become increasingly clear that the category can marginalize the racialization of other British minorities. Turkish and Greek Cypriots, for example, Jewish people and the Irish have been unable to find a voice within a political and cultural space marked out as 'black'. The category, in other words, functioned both to include and exclude; in so doing it tended not to engage with the *variety* of British racisms. It is true, of course, that the category was never intended to deny the existence of other racisms, nor as an all-encompassing identity that would make ethnicity invisible or irrelevant. Here its hegemony has been challenged by a third cultural and political thrust. A range of 'black' groups have begun to explore, construct and express identities and experiences not exhausted by the experience of and struggle against racism, or the polarization between social democratic and revolutionary strategic positions. In this sense the growing dissolution of the category is also part of the collapse of older certainties and polarities of the British left and the emergence of concerns around *socialist* pluralism (Rustin, 1985; Keane, 1988). We now have in play what Stuart Hall has dubbed 'new ethnicities'. These are evident in the projects of a wide variety of film-makers, artists, novelists, poets and photographers, some of whom I have already referred to. In films such as *My Beautiful Launderette*, *Passion of Remembrance*, and *Sammy and Rosie Get Laid*, or in the paintings of Sonia Boyce and others which formed part of *The Other Story* exhibition at the Hayward Gallery in 1989, complex inter-sections of sexuality, ethnicity and class are imaginatively constructed through representations which break decisively with the framework of positive and negative images.

There is emerging a new cultural politics of difference which overlays the

RACISM, CULTURE AND EDUCATION

older ethnic differences whose divisive effects antiracists have always, rightly, warned against. Neither the multiculturalist nor the antiracist movement in education has yet engaged with these 'new ethnicities'. Nor have they attempted to develop with students their potential for creative explorations of the shifting contours of black and white British cultural and political identities. The issues thrown up by these works are hardly remote from the lives of students. Many of them are engaging in their own complex negotiations and renegotiations around language and music, for example, borrowing elements from 'white', Afro-Caribbean and Asian forms and creating new syncretic versions (Jones, 1988; Hewitt, 1986; Gilroy, 1987).

For these developments to be taken seriously, the multiculturalists will have to abandon their additive models of cultural pluralism and their continuing obsession with the old ethnicities. Antiracists, on the other hand, will have to move beyond their reductive conceptions of culture and their fear of cultural difference as simply a source of division and weakness in the struggle against racism. They need to acknowledge the political significance of questions of national culture and ethnic identity, and to grasp how these intersect with questions of 'race' and racism. They will also have to work through the consequences of other British racisms, especially towards Jewish people and the Irish, and the realignment of older Western–Islamic polarities in the context of the Rushdie scandal.

Political and cultural questions of representation were always implicit in the older conception of 'the black struggle'. Now they have to be re-assessed in a context where older socialist and antiracist certainties no longer hold. We need to move beyond both multiculturalism and antiracism.

Conclusions

I have not provided a manifesto for that next phase in this article. I have merely tried to unravel what I take to be *some* of the main underlying oversimplifications which have informed educational practices in the field of 'race' and education, whether state-led or self-consciously oppositionist. This does not imply, and should not be taken to mean, that everything being practised as multicultural and/or antiracist education in schools is worthless. Much of that work should be defended against its attempted marginalization by the Education Reform Act, the New Right and others. But we do ourselves no service if we neglect to ask fundamental, difficult questions about our understanding of some of the key issues, processes and terms involved; if we ignore contradictions in our underlying discourses; if we fail to grapple with the limitations of our assumptions about pedagogy and how subjects and subjectivities are formed; and if we fail to notice how economic, political and cultural differentiations are undermining older fixities around the ethnic, class and political identities of the minority communities. This was surely the lesson of the Macdonald Inquiry's critique of antiracist education at Burnage High School, and this is what I have tried to indicate through my critical interrogations of the theoretical and pedagogical foundations of multiculturalism and anti-racism – especially in relation to the multifaceted nature of racism and the complexities of its intersection with gender and class (see also Cohen and Rattansi, 1991).

How will it be possible to develop educational practices that will build on existing multicultural and antiracist initiatives, but move beyond them? They will have to take account of contradiction and ambivalence in the operation of racism, avoid cultural and ethnic essentialisms and reductionism, grapple with the limitations of rationalist pedagogies and rationalist assumptions about the translation of formal policies into practices, and engage with the 'new ethnicities' and other differentiations. This is going to be a long and difficult task; difficult, but in my view, absolutely essential.

Notes

I am indebted to Maud Blair, Peter Braham, Phil Cohen and James Donald for their comments on an earlier version of this essay.

1 I have generally used 'black' to signify British communities of Afro-Caribbean, African and Asian descent. Whether the category should be used in this way is a question posed in a later section of this article.

2 'Contradiction' here and elsewhere in the text is not *necessarily* being used in the strict philosophical sense of a *logical* contradiction (cf. Goldberg, 1990a).

3 The general conceptualization here is adapted from Foucault, articulating his earlier work on discourses and discursive formations in *The Archaeology of Knowledge* to his later investigations into the operations of power and knowledge in *Discipline and Punish, Power/Knowledge* and elsewhere. For the influence of Foucault in the fields of 'race', and education see *inter alia*, Goldberg (1990b) and Ball (1990).

4 'Rationality' and 'irrationality' can function within discussions of 'race' in quite different ways (see Goldberg, 1990a). In the present essay 'irrationality' is being used primarily, as in the psychological and educational literature under discussion, to *open up* the area of 'resistances' to discourses which challenge an individual's rhetorics with regard to 'race'. However, as will become apparent later, I give the concept poststructuralist and psychoanalytic inflections by insisting upon the inherently contradictory nature of identities, thus problematizing any easy division between rationality and irrationality either at the level of individuals or discourses. Goldberg (1990a) accomplishes a parallel task, deploying the conceptual apparatus of analytical philosophy. It is likely that future theoretical work will have to break from the problematic of the rational/irrational divide within which the present discussion has been circumscribed by the need to challenge conventional theories of prejudice and racism and by the allusion to a particular understanding and psychoanalysis. The critique of rationalism implied in this essay intersects with the postmodernist reassessment of the Enlightenment project (cf. Boyne and Rattansi, 1990).

5 Such resistances are themselves coded and recorded around 'race', class and gender, with shifting alliances between black and white girls and boys depending upon the nature of the antiracist (or antisexist) initiative and the 'race' and sex of the teacher; cf. Cohen 1987.

6 Troyna's co-author, Carrington, has recently proposed that antiracist work be based on Festinger's conception of the *inability* of individuals to tolerate ambiguity and contradiction (Carrington and Short, 1989). This is very different, almost the opposite of the conception of contradictions and ambivalence proposed in this article. For a critique of Festinger from a perspective much closer to mine see Billig, 1982; see also Wetherell and Potter, 1987; Henriques *et al.*, 1986; and the writings of Wallman, Hall and Bhabha referred to in the text.

7 For a much more sophisticated analysis of ethnicity and community politics see Eade (1989).

References

Ahier, J. (1988) *Industry, Children and the Nation: an analysis of national identity in school textbooks*, Brighton, Falmer.

Alvarado, M. and Ferguson, B. (1983) 'The curriculum, media studies and discursivity', *Screen*, **24**(3).

Anthias, F. and Yuval-Davis, N. (1982) 'Contextualising feminism – gender, ethnic and class divisions', *Feminist Review*, **15**, pp. 62–76.

Areean, R. (1989) *The Other Story: Afro-Asian artists in post-war Britain*, London, Hayward Gallery.

Aronson, E. (1980) *The Social Animal*, 3rd edn, San Francisco, W. H. Freeman.

Bailey, D. A. (1988) 'Re-thinking black representations', *Ten-8*, **31**.

Ball, S. (ed.) (1990) *Foucault and Education: disciplines and knowledge*, London, Routledge.

Bhabha, H. (1983) 'The Other question', *Screen*, **24**.

Bhabha, H. (1986) 'Of mimicry and man: the ambivalence of colonial discourse' in Donald, J. and Hall, S. (eds) *Politics and Ideology*, Milton Keynes, Open University Press.

Billig, M. (1978) *Fascists: a social psychological view of the National Front*, London, Harcourt, Brace, Jovanovich.

Billig, M. (1982) *Ideology and Social Psychology*, Oxford, Basil Blackwell.

Billig, M. and Cochrane, R. (1984) 'I'm not National Front, but . . .' *New Society*, **68**.

Bonnet, K. (1990) 'Anti-racism as a radical educational ideology in London and Tyneside', *Oxford Review of Education*, **16**.

Boyne, R. and Rattansi, A. (eds) (1990) *Postmodernism and Society*, London, Macmillan.

Brah, A. and Deem, R. (1986) 'Towards anti-sexist and anti-racist schooling', *Critical Social Policy*, **6**(1).

Brah, A. and Minhas, R. (1986) 'Structural racism or cultural difference? Schooling for Asian girls' in Weiner, G. (ed.) *Just a Bunch of Girls*, Milton Keynes, Open University Press.

Brittan, E. (1976) 'Multiracial education 2: teacher opinion on aspects of school life', *Educational Research*, **18**(2,3).

Burgess, C. (1986) 'Tackling racism and sexism in the primary classroom' in Gundara, J., Jones, C. and Kimberley, K. (eds) (1986), *Racism, Diversity and Education*, London, Hodder and Stoughton, reprinted in Gill, D., Mayor, B. and Blair, M. (eds) (1992) *Racism and Education: structures and strategies*, London, Sage.

Carrington, B. (1983) 'Sport as a side-track' in Barton, L. and Walker, S. (eds) *Race, Class and Education*, Beckenham, Croom Helm.

Carrington, B. and Short, G. (1989) 'Policy or presentation? The psychology of anti-racist education', *New Community*, **15**.

Carter, B., Harris, C., and Joshi, S. (1987) *The 1951–55 Conservative Government and the Racialisation of Black Immigration*, Warwick, Centre for Research in Ethnic Relations, University of Warwick.

Cashmore, E. and Troyna, B. (1982) 'Black youth in crisis' in Cashmore E. and Troyna, B. (eds) *Black Youth in Crisis*, London, Allen and Unwin.

Chivers, T. (ed.) (1987) *Race and Culture in Education*, Windsor, NFER–Nelson.

Clifford, J. and Marcus, G. (eds) (1986) *Writing Culture: the poetics and politics of ethnography*, Berkeley, University of California Press.

Coard, B. (1971) *How the West Indian Child is made Educationally Sub-Normal in the British School System*, London, New Beacon Books.

Coffield, F., Borrill, C. and Marshall, S. (1986) *Growing Up at the Margins*, Milton Keynes, Open University Press.

Cohen, P. (1987) *Racism and Popular Culture*, London, Centre for Multicultural Education, University of London Institute of Education.

Cohen, P. (1988) 'The perversions of inheritance: studies in the making of multi-racist Britain' in Cohen, P. and Bains, H. (eds) *Multi-Racist Britain*, London, Macmillan.

Cohen, P. (1989a) *The Making of the Indian Cowgirl Warrior*, London, Centre for Multicultural Education, University of London Institute of Education.

Cohen, P. (1989b) *The Cultural Geography of Adolescent Racism*, London, Centre for Multicultural Education, University of London Institute of Education.

Cohen, P. (1991) '"We hate humans": antiracism and antihumanism', London, Centre for Multicultural Education, University of London Institute of Education.

Cohen, P. and Rattansi, A. (1991) *Rethinking Racism and Antiracism*, London, Runnymede Trust.

Commission for Racial Equality (1979) *Brick Lane and Beyond: an inquiry into racial strife and violence in Tower Hamlets*, London, CRE.

Commission for Racial Equality (1981) *Racial Harassment on Local Authority Housing Estates*, London, CRE.

Commission for Racial Equality (1988) *Learning in Terror*, London, CRE.

Craib, I. (1989) *Psychoanalysis and Social Theory*, Hemel Hempstead, Harvester Wheatsheaf.

Department of Education and Science (DES) (1963) *English for Immigrants*, London, DES.

Department of Education and Science (DES) (1981) *West Indian Children in Our Schools*, London, HMSO (The Rampton Report).

Department of Education and Science (DES) (1985) *Education for All*, London, HMSO (The Swann Report).

Dex, S. (1983) 'The second generation: West Indian female school leavers' in Phizacklea, A. (ed.) *One Way Ticket*, London, Routledge.

Dodgson, P. and Stewart, D. (1981) 'Multiculturalism or anti-racist teaching: a question of alternatives', *Multiracial Teaching*, **9**(3).

Dorn, A. (1985) 'Education and the Race Relations Act' in Arnot, M. (ed.) *Race and Gender: equal opportunities policies in education*, Oxford, Pergamon Press.

Driver, G. (1980) *Beyond Underachievement*, London, CRE.

Eade, J. (1989) *The Politics of Community: the Bangladeshi community in East London*, Aldershot, Avebury/Gower.

Eggleston, J., Dunn, D., Anjali, M. and Wright, C. (1986) *Education for Some*, Stoke on Trent, Trentham Books.

Flew, A. (1984) *Education, Race and Revolution*, London, Centre for Policy Studies.

Foster, P. (1990) *Policy and Practice in Multicultural and Anti-Racist Education*, London, Routledge.

Fuller, M. (1982) 'Young, female and black' in Cashmore, E. and Troyna, B. (eds) *Black Youth in Crisis*, London, Allen and Unwin.

Fuller, M. (1983) 'Qualified criticism, critical qualifications' in Barton, L. and Walker, S. (eds) *Race, Class and Education*, Beckenham, Croom Helm.

Gabriel, J. and Ben-Tovim, G. (1978) 'Marxism and the concept of racism', *Economy and Society*, **7**(2).

Geertz, C. (1973) *The Interpretation of Cultures*, New York, Basic Books.

Geertz, C. (1983) *Local Knowledge*, New York, Basic Books.

Gill, D. and Singh, E. (1987) 'Multicultural versus anti-racist science' in Gill, D. and Levidow, L. (eds) *Anti-Racist Science Teaching*, London, Free Association Books.

Gilman, S. (1985) *Difference and Pathology: stereotypes of sexuality, race and madness*, Ithaca, Cornell University Press.

Gilman, S. (1987) 'Black bodies, white bodies: towards an iconography of female sexuality in late 19th art, medicine and literature' reprinted in this volume.

Gilroy, P. (1987) *There Ain't No Black in the Union Jack*, London, Hutchinson.

Gilroy, P. (1990) 'The end of antiracism' reprinted in this volume.

Goldberg, D. (1990a) 'Racism and irrationality: the need for a new critique', *Philosophy of the Social Sciences*, **20**(3).

Goldberg, D. (1990b) 'The social formation of racist discourse' in Goldberg, D. (ed.) (1990) *Anatomy of Racism*, Minneapolis, University of Minnesota Press.

Gordon, P. (1990) *Racial Violence and Harassment*, London, Runnymede Research Report.

Grosvenor, I. (1991) 'Racialisation and the State', unpublished.

Hall, S. (1980) 'Race, articulation and societies structured in dominance' in UNESCO, *Sociological Theories: race and colonialism*, Paris, UNESCO.

Hall, S. (1981) 'The whites of their eyes: racist ideologies and the media' in Bridges, G. and Brunt, R. (eds) *Silver Linings*, London, Lawrence and Wishart.

Hall, S., Critcher, C., Jefferson, T. and Roberts, B. (1978) *Policing the Crisis*, London, Macmillan.

Hartmann, P. and Husband, C. (1974) *Racism and the Mass Media*, London, Davis-Poynter.

Hatcher, R. and Shallice, J. (1983) 'The politics of anti-racist education', *Multiracial Education*, **12**(1).

Henriques, J., Holloway, W., Urwin, C., Venn, C. and Walkerdine, V. (1986) *Changing the Subject*, London, Methuen.

Hewitt, R. (1986) *White Talk – Black Talk: inter-racial friendship and communication amongst adolescents*, Cambridge, Cambridge University Press.

HMSO (1981) *The Brixton Disorders, 10–12 April 1981*, London, HMSO.

Honeyford, R. (1983) 'Multi-ethnic intolerance', *The Salisbury Review*, **4**.

Honeyford, R. (1984) 'Education and race – an alternative view', *The Salisbury Review*, **6**.

House of Commons, Home Affairs Select Committee (1986) *Bangladeshis in Britain*, London, HMSO.

Inner London Education Authority (ILEA) (1987) *Ethnic Background and Examination Results 1985 and 1986*, London, ILEA.

Jeffcoate, R. (1979) *Positive Image*, London, Writers and Readers.

Jenkins, R. (1985) 'Black workers in the labour market' in Roberts, B., Finnegan, R. and Gallie, D. (eds) *New Approaches to Economic Life*, Manchester, Manchester University Press, reprinted in Braham, P., Rattansi, A. and Skellington, R. (eds) (1992) *Racism and Antiracism: inequalities, opportunities and policies*, London, Sage.

Jenkins, R. (1986) *Racism and Recruitment*, Cambridge, Cambridge University Press.

Jones, C. and Kimberley, K. (1982) 'Educational responses to racism' in Tierney, J. (ed.) *Race, Migration and Schooling*, London, Holt, Rinehart and Winston.

Jones, S. (1988) *Black Culture, White Youth*, London, Macmillan.

Keane, J. (1988) *Democracy and Civil Society*, London, Verso.

Kelly, E. and Cohn, T. (1988) *Racism in Schools: new research evidence*, Stoke on Trent, Trentham Books.

Kirp, D. (1979) *Doing Good by Doing Little*, London, University of California Press.

Klein, G. (1985) *Reading Into Racism*, London, Routledge and Kegan Paul.

Lynch, J. (1986) *Multicultural Education*, London, Routledge and Kegan Paul.

Lynch, J. (1987) *Prejudice Reduction and the Schools*, London, Cassell.

Lynch, J. (1990) 'Cultural pluralism, structural pluralism and the United Kingdom' in Parekh, B. (ed.) *Britain: A Plural Society*, London, Commission for Racial Equality.

Mac an Ghaill, M. (1988) *Young, Gifted and Black*, Milton Keynes, Open University Press.

Mac an Ghaill, M. (1989) 'Coming of age in 1980s England: reconceptualising black students' schooling experience', *British Journal of Sociology of Education*, **10**(3), reprinted in Gill, D., Mayor, B. and Blair, M. (eds) (1992) *Racism and Education: structures and strategies*, London, Sage.

Macdonald, I., Bhavnani, R., Khan, L. and John, G. (1989) *Murder in the Playground*, London, Longsight Press.

Mackenzie, J. (1984) *Propaganda and Empire*, Manchester, Manchester University Press.

Mackenzie, J. (ed.) (1986) *Imperialism and Popular Culture*, Manchester, Manchester University Press.

Mason, D. (1982) 'After Scarman: a note on the concept of "Institutional Racism"', *New Community*, **10**(1).

Media Research Group (1987) *Media Coverage of London Councils*, London, Goldsmith's College, University of London.

Mercer, K. (ed.) (1988) *Black Film/British Cinema*, London, Institute of Contemporary Arts.

Mullard, C. (1984) *Antiracist Education: the three O's*, London, National Association for Multiracial Education.

Murdock, G. (1984) 'Reporting the riots' in Benyon, J. (ed.) *Scarman and After*, Oxford, Pergamon Press.

Nanton, P. and Fitzgerald, M. (1990) 'Race policies in local government: boundaries or thresholds?' in Ball, W. and Solomos, J. (eds) *Race and Local Politics*, London, Macmillan.

Nixon, J. (1985) *A Teacher's Guide to Multicultural Education*, Oxford, Basil Blackwell.

Open University, The (1974) E351 *Urban Education*, Block 1, *Education and the Crisis of the Urban School*, Milton Keynes, The Open University.

Open University, The (1989a) E208 *Exploring Educational Issues*, Unit 24, *'Race', Education and Inequality*, Milton Keynes, The Open University.

Open University, The (1989b) E208 *Exploring Educational Issues*, TV13, *Black Girls in Search of Learning*, BBC/Open University.

Open University, The (1992) ED356 *'Race', Education and Society, Course Introduction*, Milton Keynes, The Open University.

Parekh, B. (1986) 'The concept of multicultural education' in Modgil, S., Verma, G., Mallick, K., and Modgil, C. (eds) *Multicultural Education: the interminable debate*, Brighton, Falmer Press.

Parekh, B. (1989a) 'Britain and the social logic of pluralism' in Parekh, B. (ed.) *Britain: a plural society*, London, Commission for Racial Equality.

Parekh, B. (1989b) 'The hermeneutics of the Swann Report' in Verma, G. (ed.) *Education for All: a landmark in pluralism*, Brighton, Falmer Press.

Phizacklea, A. (ed.) (1983) *One Way Ticket: migration and female labour*, London, Routledge and Kegan Paul.

Phizacklea, A. and Miles, R. (1979) 'Working-class racist beliefs in the inner city' in Miles, R. and Phizacklea, A. (eds) *Racism and Political Action in Britain*, London, Routledge and Kegan Paul.

Phizacklea, A. and Miles, R. (1980) *Labour and Racism*, London, Routledge and Kegan Paul.

Phoenix, A. (1988) 'The Afro-Caribbean myth' *New Society*, 4 March.

Pilkington, E. (1990) 'Dilemma of the gauntlet of hate', *Education Guardian*, 18 December.

Ramazanoglu, C. (1989) *Feminism and the Contradictions of Oppression*, London, Routledge.

Rattansi, A. (1988) '"Race", education and British society' in Dale, R. *et al.* (eds) *Frameworks for Teaching*, London, Hodder and Stoughton.

Redbridge Community Relations Council (1978) *Cause for Concern: West Indian pupils in Redbridge*, Redbridge, Redbridge CRC and Black Parents' Progressive Association.

Reeves, F. (1983) *British Racial Discourse*, Cambridge, Cambridge University Press.

Reeves, F. and Chevannes, M. (1981) 'The underachievement of Rampton', *Multiracial Education*, 12(1).

Rex, J. (1982) 'West Indian and Asian youth' in Cashmore, E. and Troyna, B. (eds) *Black Youth in Crisis*, London, Allen and Unwin.

Riley, K. (1986) 'Black girls speak for themselves' in Weiner, G. (eds) *Just a Bunch of Girls*, Milton Keynes, Open University Press.

Roberts, K., Duggan, J., and Noble, M. (1983) 'Young, black and out of work' in Troyna, B. and Smith, D. (eds) *Racism, School and the Labour Market*, Leicester, National Youth Bureau.

Rustin, M. (1985) *For a Pluralist Socialism*, London, Verso.

Sarup, M. (1986) *The Politics of Multiracial Education*, London, Routledge.

Scarman, The Rt. Hon. Lord (1982) *The Scarman Report*, Harmondsworth, Penguin.

Sivanandan, A. (1974) *Race, Class and the State*, London, Institute of Race Relations.

Sivanandan, A. (1985) 'RAT and the degradation of the black struggle', *Race and Class*, 26(4).

Solomos, J. (1989) *Race and Racism in Contemporary Britain*, London, Macmillan.

Stronach, I. and Akhtar, S. (1986) '"They call me blacky": a story of everyday racism in primary schools', *The Times Educational Supplement*, 19 September.

Tomlinson, S. (1983) *Ethnic Minorities in British Schools*, London, Heinemann.

Townsend, H. E. R. and Brittan, E. (1973) *Multiracial Education: need and innovation*, London, Evans/Methuen Educational, Schools Council Working Paper 50.

Troyna, B. (1984) 'Fact or artefact? The "educational underachievement" of black pupils', *British Journal of Sociology of Education*, 5(2), pp. 153–66.

Troyna, B. (1987a) 'Beyond multiculturalism: towards the enactment of anti-racist education in policy, provision and pedagogy', *Oxford Review of Education*, 13(3).

Troyna, B. (1987b) '"Swann's song": the origins, ideology and implications of *Education for All*' in Chivers, T. (ed.) *Race and Culture in Education*, Windsor, NFER-Nelson.

Troyna, B. and Carrington, B. (1987) 'Antisexist/antiracist education – a false dilemma: a reply to Walkling and Brannigan', *Journal of Moral Education*, 16(1).

Troyna, B. and Carrington, B. (1990) *Education, Racism and Reform*, London, Routledge.

Troyna, B. and Williams, J. (1986) *Racism, Education and the State*, Beckenham, Croom Helm.

Twitchin, J. and Demuth, C. (1985) *Multi-Cultural Education: Views from the Classroom*, 2nd edn, London, BBC.

Verma, G. (1989) 'Pluralism: some theoretical and practical considerations', in Parekh, B. (ed.) *Britain: a plural society*, London, Commission for Racial Equality.

Viswanathan, G. (1987) 'The beginnings of English literary study in British India', *Oxford Literary Review*, **9** and in this volume.

Walkerdine, V. (1991) *Schoolgirl Fictions*, London, Verso.

Wallman, S. (1986) 'Ethnicity and the boundary process in context' in Rex, J. and Mason, D. (eds) *Theories of Race and Ethnic Relations*, Cambridge, Cambridge University Press.

Ward, R. (1979) 'Where race didn't divide: some reflections on slum clearance in Moss Side' in Miles, R. and Phizacklea, A. (eds) *Racism and Political Action in Britain*, London, Routledge and Kegan Paul.

Wellman, D. (1977) *Portraits of White Racism*, Cambridge, Cambridge University Press.

Westwood, S. (1985) *All Day, Every Day: factory and family in the making of women's lives*, London, Pluto Press.

Westwood, S. (1990) 'Racism, black masculinity and the politics of space' in Hearn, J. and Morgan, D. (eds) *Men, Masculinities and Social Theory*, London, Unwin Hyman.

Westwood, S. and Bhachu, P. (eds) (1988) *Enterprising Women: ethnicity, economy and gender relations*, London, Routledge.

Wetherell, M. and Potter, J. (1987) *Discourse and Social Psychology*, London, Sage.

Wetherell, M. and Potter, J. (1988) 'Discourse analysis and the identification of interpretative repertoires' in Antaki, C. (ed.) *Analysing Everyday Explanation*, London, Sage.

Wexler, P. (1987) *Social Analysis of Education: after the new sociology*, London, Routledge and Kegan Paul.

Willis, P. (1978) *Learning to Labour*, Farnborough, Saxon House.

Wolpe, A. M. (1989) *Within School Walls: the role of sexuality, discipline and the curriculum*, London, Routledge.

Wrench, J. (1987) 'The unfinished bridge: YTS and black youth', in Troyna, B. (ed.) *Racial Inequality in Education*, London, Allen and Unwin.

Wrench, J. (1990) 'New vocationalism, old racism and the careers service', *New Community*, **16**(3), pp. 425–40, reprinted in Braham, P., Rattansi, A. and Skellington, R. (eds) (1992) *Racism and Antiracism: inequalities, opportunities and policies*, London, Sage.

Wright, C. (1987) 'Black students – white teachers' in Troyna, B. (ed.) *Racial Inequality in Education*, London, Allen and Unwin.

2 THE END OF ANTIRACISM

PAUL GILROY

The task of developing a radical critique of the moralistic excesses practised in the name of 'antiracism' is an urgent task today. The absurdities of antiracist orthodoxy have become a target of critique by the right (Honeyford, 1988; Lewis, 1988), and have formed a backdrop to the bitter debates that have surrounded the publication of *The Satanic Verses*. The dictatorial character of antiracism, particularly in local government, has itself become an important theme within the discourse of popular racism.

These assaults on the fundamental objective of antiracism and the attendant practice of multiculturalism in education, social work and other municipal services have passed largely unanswered and vocal political support for antiracism has been hard to find. This is partly because the cadre of antiracism professionals which was created during the boom years of radicalism on the rates has lost its collective tongue: its political confidence has been drained away. There has been little support from independent black defence organizations and authentic community groups whose actions go far beyond the narrow categories in which antiracism can operate. Meanwhile, many of the ideological gains of Thatcherite conservatism have dovetailed neatly with the shibboleths of black nationalism – self-reliance and economic betterment through thrift, hard work and individual disciplines. The impact of this resolutely conservative and often authoritarian political ideology can be felt right across the field of social and economic policy where an idealized and homogenized vision of 'The Black Community' is the object of a discourse that urges it to take care of its own problems and assume the major burden of managing its own public affairs. This is not a wholly negative development, but in the new atmosphere it creates antiracist initiatives can only appear to be a patronizing and unacceptable form of special pleading. Apart from these important changes, specialized antiracist work within the local state has been increasingly identified as an embarrassment by the Labour Party for whom political commitments to antiracism and multiculturalism are apparently a vote loser.

These developments have created political inertia in what was once an antiracist *movement*. The political forces which once made that movement move are now enveloped in a catastrophe that has two distinct dimensions. Firstly, there is a crisis of organizational forms. In the absence of mass mobilization around antiracist aims, it has been impossible to construct structures that could span the gulf between the elements of the movement which are outside the local state and the residues which are dedicated to remaining within it. This problem is also conveyed in the considerable rift that has opened up between those sections which are ideologically committed to the Labour Party and those which are indifferent if not actively opposed to it. Secondly, and more importantly for what follows, there is a crisis of the political language, images and cultural symbols which this movement needs in order to develop its self-consciousness and its political programme. This problem with the language of antiracism is acutely expressed by the lack of clarity that surrounds the term 'antiracism' itself. It includes the difficulties involved in producing a coherent definition of racism (cf. Miles, 1989) as well as the tension that appears from the need to link an account of the racialization of social and political structures and discourses with an understanding of individual action and institutional behaviour.

For all its antipathy to the new racism of the New Right, the common sense ideology of antiracism has also drifted towards a belief in the absolute nature of ethnic categories and a strong sense of the insurmountable cultural and experiential divisions which, it is argued, are a feature of racial difference. I have argued elsewhere that these ideological failures have been compounded firstly by a reductive conception of culture and secondly by a culturalist conception of race and ethnic identity (Gilroy, 1987). This has led to a position where politically opposed groups are united by their view of race exclusively in terms of culture and identity rather than politics and history. Culture and identity are part of the story of racial sensibility but they do not exhaust that story. At a theoretical level 'race' needs to be viewed much more contingently, as a precarious discursive construction. To note this does not, of course, imply that it is any less real or effective politically.

It is possible, then, that the idea of antiracism has been so discredited that it is no longer useful. It is certain that we have to devise ways to move beyond antiracism as it is presently constituted. I must emphasize that I am thinking not of antiracism as a political objective, or a goal which emerges alongside other issues from the daily struggles of black people, from the practice of community organizations and voluntary groups, even from the war of position which must be waged inside the institutions of the state. I am not talking about the ongoing struggle towards black liberation, for there is much more to the emancipation of blacks than opposition to racism. I am thinking instead of antiracism as a much more limited project defined simply, even simplistically, by the desire to do away with racism.

The antiracism I am criticizing trivializes the struggle against racism and isolates it from other political antagonisms – from the contradiction between capital and labour, from the battle between men and women. It suggests that racism can be eliminated on its own because it is readily extricable from everything else. Yet in Britain, 'race' cannot be understood if it is falsely divorced from other political processes or grasped if it is reduced to the effect of these other relations. Antiracism in this sense is a phenomenon which grew out of the political openings created by the 1981 riots. In the years since then, antiracists have become a discrete and self-contained political formation. Their activism is now able to sustain itself independently of the lives, dreams and aspirations of the majority of blacks from whose experience they derive their authority to speak.

To criticize antiracism necessitates understanding racism and being able to locate the politics of 'race' from which it springs. Analysing what racism does in our society means, first of all, claiming 'race' and racism back from the margins of British politics. Racism is not epiphenomenal. Yet just as racism itself views black settlers as an external, alien visitation, antiracism can itself appear to be tangential to the main business of the political system as a whole.

The apparent marginality of race politics is often an effect of a fundamental tension inherent in antiracist organizing. A tension exists between those strands in antiracism which are primarily antifascist and those which work with a more extensive and complex sense of what racism is in contemporary Britain. This simplistic antifascist emphasis attempts to mobilize the memory of earlier encounters with the fascism of Hitler and Mussolini. The racists are a problem because they are descended from the brown- and black-shirted enemies of earlier days. To oppose them is a patriotic act; their own use of national flags and symbols is nothing more than a sham masking their terroristic inclinations.

The price of over-identifying the struggle against racism with the activities of these extremist groups and grouplets is that however much of a problem they may be in a particular area (and I am not denying the need to combat their organizing) they are exceptional. They exist on the fringes of political culture and for the foreseeable future are destined to have only tenuous and intermittent relationships with respectability. They are a threat but not the only threat. There is more to contemporary racism than the violence they perpetrate. We shall see in a moment that there are problems with the nationalism which goes hand in hand with this outlook.

A more productive starting point is provided by focusing on racism in the mainstream and seeing 'race' and racism not as fringe questions but as a volatile presence at the very centre of British politics, actively shaping and determining the history not simply of blacks, but of this country as a whole at a crucial stage in its development.

The importance of racism in contemporary politics betrays something about the nature of the painful transition this country, and the overdeveloped world as a whole, is undergoing. The almost mystical power of race and nation on the political stage conveys something about the changing nature of class relations, the growth of state authoritarianism, the eclipse of industrial production, the need to maintain popular support for militarism and exterminism and the end of the nation-state as a political form.

The highly charged politics of national identity that have been occasioned by these developments have been transposed into a higher, shriller key by current concern over the appeal of a wide pan-European disposition tailored to the new range of possibilities that flow from tighter political and economic integration of the European Economic Community. This potentially post-national European consciousness has racial referents of its own. It is however felt by elements of both left and right to pose a threat to the sovereignty and cultural integrity of the United Kingdom. Whether it is possible to generate a political discourse capable of articulating the distinctive needs and historical experiences of black Europeans remains to be seen. Though the rich legacy of an extensive black presence on this continent suggests that it may be possible for many commentators, the terms 'black' and 'European' remain categories which mutually exclude each other.

Racism and the ideology of antiracism

The first question I want to ask of contemporary antiracism is whether it does not collude in accepting that the problems of 'race' and racism are somehow peripheral to the substance of political life. My view, which locates racism in the core of politics, contrasts sharply with what can be called the coat-of-paint theory of racism (Gilroy, 1987). This is not, in fact, a single theory but an approach which sees racism on the outside of social and political life – sometimes the unwanted blemish is the neo-fascists, sometimes it is immigration laws, other times it is the absence of equal opportunities – yet racism is always located on the surface of other things. It is an unfortunate excrescence on a democratic policy which is essentially sound and it follows from this that, with the right ideological tools and political elbow grease, racism can be dealt with once and for all, leaving the basic structures and relations of British economy and society essentially unchanged.

Though not always stated openly, the different permutations of this view underpin much of contemporary antiracism. I think there are particular problems posed by the fact that this type of theory is intrinsic to equal opportunities initiatives. The coat-of-paint approach is doubly mistaken because it suggests that fundamental issues of social justice, democracy and political and economic power are not raised by the struggle against racial subordination.

Seeing racism as determining rather than determinate, at the centre rather than in the margins, also means accepting that Britain's crisis is centrally and emphatically concerned with notions of race and national identity. It has been held together, punctuated and periodized by racial politics – immigration, the myriad problems of the riotous 'inner city' and by the loony left. These terms are carefully coded and they are significant because they enable people to speak about race without mentioning the word. The frequent absence of any overt reference to 'race' or hierarchy is an important characteristic of the new types of racism with which we have to deal. This kind of coded language has created further strategic problems for antiracism. It is easy to call Mr Honeyford, the Bradford headteacher, a racist and to organize against him on that basis but less easy to show precisely how and why this is the case.

We must be prepared to focus unsentimentally on antiracism's inability to respond to other distinctive aspects of these new forms of racism. Apart from the way that racial meanings are inferred rather than stated openly, these new forms are distinguished by the extent to which they identify race with the terms 'culture' and 'identity', terms which have their own resonance in antiracist orthodoxy. The new racism has a third important feature which enables it to slip through the rationalist approach of those who, with the best will in the world, reduce the problem of racism to the sum of power and prejudice. This is the closeness it suggests between the idea of race and the ideas of nation, nationality and national belonging.

We increasingly face a racism which avoids being recognized as such because it is able to link 'race' with nationhood, patriotism and nationalism, a racism which has taken a necessary distance from crude ideas of biological inferiority and superiority and now seeks to present an imaginary definition of the nation as a unified *cultural* community. It constructs and defends an image of national culture – homogeneous in its whiteness yet precarious and perpetually vulnerable to attack from enemies within and without. The analogy of war and invasion is increasingly used to make sense of events.

This is racism that answers the social and political turbulence of crisis and crisis management by the recovery of national greatness *in the imagination*. Its dreamlike construction of our sceptred isle as an ethnically purified one provides a special comfort against the ravages of decline. It has been a key component in the ideological and political processes which have put the 'Great' back in Britain. The symbolic restoration of greatness has been achieved in part through the actual expulsion of blacks and the fragmentation of their households, which is never far from page three in the tabloids.

The shock of decline has induced Britons to ask themselves a question first posed by Enoch Powell: What kind of people are we? The emphasis on culture and the attendant imagery of the nation composed of symmetrical family units contributes to a metaphysics of Britishness which has acquired racial referents. I can illustrate this by referring to a poem which was part of a racist leaflet circulated in Haringey during the 1987 election. It was illustrated by a picture of Bernie Grant, the black Labour candidate, with the hairy body of a gorilla. It read:

Swing along with Bernie, it's the very natural thing
He's been doing it for centuries and now he thinks he's king
He's got a little empire and he doesn't give a jot
But then the British are a bloody tolerant lot
They'll let him swing and holler hetero-homo-gay
And then just up and shoot him in the good old British way.

These lines signify a powerful appropriation of the rights and liberties of the freeborn Briton so beloved of the new left. The rhyme's historical references demonstrate how completely blackness and Britishness have been made into mutually exclusive categories, incompatible identities. The problems which Bernie represents are most clearly visible against the patterned backdrop of the Union Jack. The picture of him as a gorilla was necessary on the leaflet because the words make no overt mention of his race. The crime which justifies lynching him is a form of treason, not racial inferiority.

This culturalist variety of racism and the cultural theory of 'race' difference linked to it hold that the family supplies the units, the building blocks from which the national community is constructed. This puts black women directly in the firing line: firstly, because they are seen as playing a key role in reproducing the alien culture, and, secondly, because their fertility is identified as excessive and therefore threatening.

It has become commonplace to observe that the precious yet precarious Churchillian, stiff-upper-lip culture which only materializes in the midst of national adversity – underneath the arches, down in the air-raid shelters where Britannia enjoyed her finest hours – is something from which blacks are excluded. The means of their exclusion is identified in the colourful deviancy which is produced by their pathological family forms. Pathology and deviancy are the qualities which define distinct and insubordinate black cultures. This applies in different yet parallel ways to both Afro-Caribbean and Asian populations, whose criminality violates the law – the supreme achievement of British civilization.

Deviancy, so the argument runs, has its roots in generational conflict which appears along cultural lines. The antisocial activities of the 'Holy Smokes' in west London's Asian gangland are, in a sense, parallel to the barbarous misdemeanours of the Afro-Caribbean Yardies on London's proliferating frontlines. The 'racial' criminal subcultures of each group are seen to wantonly violate the laws and customs which express the civilization of the national community and in so doing provide powerful symbols which express black difference as a whole. To be a street criminal is therefore to fulfil cultural destiny.

For a long while, the crime question provided the principal means to underscore the *cultural* concerns of this new nationalist racism. Its dominance helped us to understand where the new racism began in Powell's bloody nightmare of the aged white woman pursued through the streets by black children. However, crime has been displaced recently at the centre of race politics by another issue which points equally effectively to the incompatibility of different cultures supposedly sealed off from one another forever along ethnic lines. This too uses images of the black child to make its point – the cultural sins of the fathers will be visited on their children. Where once it was the main streets of the decaying inner city which hosted the most fearsome encounter between Britons and their most improbable and intimidating other – black youth – now it is the classrooms and staffrooms of the inner-city school which frame the same conflict and provide the most potent terms with which to make sense of racial difference.

The publication of *Antiracism: an assault on education and value*, the book of essays edited by Frank Palmer (1987), confirmed the fact that the school has become the principal element in the ideology with which the new right have sought to attack antiracism. While it is important not to be mesmerized by the gains and strengths of the new right – as many radicals are – it is essential to understand *why* their burgeoning anti-antiracism has focused upon education. From their perspective, schools are repositories of the authentic national culture which they transmit between generations. They mediate the relation of the national community to its youthful subjects – future citizens.

Decaying school buildings provide a ready image for the nation in microcosm. The hard fought changes which antiracists and multiculturalists have wrought on the curriculum mirror the bastardization of genuine British culture. Antiracism initiatives that literally denigrate educational standards are identified as an assault on the traditional virtues of British education. This cultural conflict is a means through which power is transposed and whites become a voiceless ethnic minority oppressed by totalitarian local authority antiracism. The racists are redefined as the black racists and Mr Honeyford, dogged defender of freedom, is invited to Number 10 Downing Street for consultation. In *The Independent* of 23 July 1987 Baroness Cox argues that black parents are motivated to demand their own separate schools not by dissatisfaction or frustration with the way that racism is institutionalized in state education, but because they want 'a good old-fashioned British education' for their children.

I think we have to recognize that the effect of these images and the conflicts from which they spring in Brent or Bradford has been to call into question any antiracist or multicultural project in education and indeed the idea of antiracism in general. The new racism's stress on cultural difference and its absolutist conception of ethnicity have other significant effects. It is now not only a feature of the relationship between blacks and whites. It enters directly into the political relations between the different groups which, in negotiating with each other, promise to construct a unified black community from their diversity.

The potentially unifying effects of their different but complementary experiences of racism are dismissed, while the inclusive and openly politicized definitions of 'race' which were a notable feature of the late seventies have been fragmented into their ethnic components, first into Afro-Caribbean and Asian and then into Pakistani, Bangladeshi, Bajan, Jamaican and Guyanese in a spiral. This boiling down of groups into their respective ethnic essences is clearly congruent with the nationalist concerns of the right, but it is also sanctioned by the antiracist orthodoxy of the left and by many voices from within the black communities themselves which have needed no prompting to develop their own fascination with ethnic differences and thus reduce political definitions of 'race' to a narcissistic celebration of culture and identity.

I have argued that antiracism has been unable to deal with the new forms in which racism has developed. In particular, it has been incapable of showing how British cultural nationalism becomes a language of race. The power of this patriotic political language is there for all to behold. It puts the vital populist force into those processes for which 'Thatcherism' serves as a reasonable shorthand term. However, it does not appear to be the exclusive property of the right. Its magical populist appeal will tempt political pragmatists of all hues. I am afraid there are segments of the left who are especially envious of its capacity to animate the groups which were once regarded as their traditional supporters. Unfortunately, Labour's blustering 'patriotism of freedom and fairness', like its recent attempts to 'take crime seriously', is no less saturated with racial connotations than the Conservative versions of these arguments. This is not to say that the right and left are necessarily the same, but rather that they converge at key points and share an understanding of what is involved in the politics of 'race'.

The Bernie poem seamlessly knitted together images invoking empire, sovereignity and sexuality, with a concluding exhortation to violence. There is nothing about this combination of themes which marks it out as the exclusive preserve of the right. It is another example of how the racism which ties national culture to ethnic essences, which sees custom, law and constitution, schools and courts of justice beset by corrosive alien forces, has moved beyond the grasp of the old left/right distinction.

This populist character of the new racism works across class lines as well as within them. It can link together disparate and formally opposed groups, leading them to discover the morbid pleasures of seeing themselves as 'one nation'. It transmits the idea of the British people as the *white people*. While Labour seeks to simply snatch the language of one nation from the Tories, the danger here can only grow and it is compounded because it is by no means clear how far a reconstituted and emphatically 'un-loony' socialism may go in negotiating its own language of toughness on immigration and nationality, even perhaps on humane socialist repatriation. [. . .]

Racial justice and civil society

I think it is important to concede that what we can loosely call the anti-antiracist position associated with sections of the new right and with populist politics has fed on crucial ambiguities in antiracist and multicultural initiatives.

The definition of racism as the sum of prejudice and power can be used to illustrate these problems. Power is a relation between social groups not a possession to be worn like a garment or flaunted like an antiracist badge. Prejudice suggests conscious action if not actual choice. Is this an appropriate formula? The most elementary lessons involved in studying ideas and consciousness seem to have been forgotten. Racism, like capitalism as a whole, rests on the mystification of social relations – the necessary illusions that secure the order of public authority.

There are other aspects of what has become a multiculturalist or antiracist orthodoxy which can be shown to replicate in many ways the *volkish* new right sense of the relationship between race, nation and culture – kin blood and ethnic identity. I have already mentioned how the left and right distinction has begun to evaporate as formally opposed groups have come to share a sense of what race is. These problems are even more severe when elements of the black community have themselves endorsed this understanding. Here I am thinking of the definition of race exclusively in terms of culture and identity which ties certain strands in antiracism to the position of some of the new right ideologues.

By emphasizing this convergence I am not saying that culture and identity are unimportant, but challenging the routine reduction of race to them alone which obscures the inherently political character of the term. The way in which culture is itself understood provides the key to grasping the extraordinary convergence between left and right, antiracist and avowedly racist over precisely what race and racism add up to.

At the end of the day, an absolute commitment to cultural insiderism is as bad as an absolute commitment to biological insiderism. I think we need to be theoretically and politically clear that no single culture is hermetically sealed off from others. There can be no neat and tidy pluralistic separation of racial groups in this country. It is time to dispute with those positions which, when taken to their conclusions, say 'there is no possibility of shared history and no human empathy'. We must beware of the use of ethnicity to wrap a spurious cloak of legitimacy around the speaker who invokes it. Culture, even the culture which defines the groups we know as races, is never fixed, finished or final. It is fluid, it is actively and continually made and re-made. In our multicultural schools the sound of the steel pan may evoke Caribbean ethnicity, tradition and authenticity, yet they originate in the oil drums of the Standard Oil Company rather than the mysterious knowledge of ancient African griots.

These theoretical problems are most visible and at their most intractable in the area of fostering and adoption policy. Here, the inflated rhetoric and culturalist orthodoxies of antiracism have borne some peculiar fruit. The critique of the pathological views of black family life that were so prevalent in Social Services during the late seventies and early eighties has led directly to an extraordinary idealization of black family forms. Antiracist orthodoxy now sees them as the only effective repositories of authentic black culture and as a guaranteed means to transmit all the essential skills that black children will need if they are to 'survive' in a racist society without psychological damage. 'Same-race' adoption and fostering for 'minority ethnics' is presented as an unchallenged and seemingly unchallengeable benefit for all concerned. It is hotly defended with the same fervour that denounces white demands for 'same race' schooling as a repellent manifestation of racism. What is most alarming about this is not its inappropriate survivalist tone, the crudity with which racial identity is conceived nor even the sad inability to see beyond the conservation of racial identities to possibility of their transcendence. It is the extraordinary manner in which the pathological imagery has simply been inverted so that it forms the basis of a pastoral view which asserts the strength and durability of black family life and, in present circumstances, retreats from confronting the difficult issues which result in black children arriving in care in the first place. The contents of the racist pathology and the material circumstances to which it can be made to correspond are thus left untouched. The tentacles of racism are everywhere, except in the safe haven which a nurturing black family provides for delicate, fledgling racial identities.

The forces of antiracism

I want to turn now to the forces which have grouped around the antiracist project and to the question of class. There is a problem here in that much of the certainty and confidence with which the term has been used have collapsed along with the secure life-time employment which characterized industrial capitalism. Today, for example, I think it means next to nothing to simply state that blacks are working class when we are likely to be unemployed and may not recognize our experience and history in those areas of political life where an appeal to class is most prominent. Class politics do not, in any case, enjoy a monopoly of political radicalism. Obviously people still belong to classes, but belief in the decisive universal agency of the dwindling proletariat is something which must be dismissed as an idealist fantasy. Class is an indispensable instrument in analysing capitalism, but it contains no ready-made plan for its overcoming. We must learn to live without a theological faith in the working class as either a revolutionary or an antiracist agent.

There is a major issue here, but I want to note it and move on to consider a different aspect of how race and class intersect. A more significant task for class analysis is comprehending the emergence of a proto-middle class grouping narrowly constituted around the toeholds which some blacks have been able to acquire in the professions, mostly those related directly to the welfare state itself – social work, teaching, and now antiracist bureaucracies. A Marxist writer would probably identify this group as the first stirrings of a black petit bourgeoisie. I do not think this grouping or grouplet is yet a class either in itself or for itself and it may never become one. For one thing it is too small; for another it is too directly dependent on the state institutions which pay its wages. But it is with this group that antiracism can be most readily identified and we need to examine it on its own terms and in its relationship to other more easily identifiable class groupings. It is obviously in an uncomfortably contradictory position – squeezed between the expectations of the bureaucracies on which it relies and its political affiliation to the struggles of the mass of blacks which it is called upon to mediate, translate and sometimes police. It is caught between the demands of bureaucratic professionalism and the emotive pull of ethnic identification.

This not-yet-class plays a key role in organizing the political forces of antiracism centred on local authorities. It involves three opposed tendencies which have evolved an uneasy symbiosis. They are not wholly discrete. The campaign for autonomous Black Sections in the Labour Party, for example, involves elements of each of them. First, there is the equal opportunities strand, which has its roots in the social democratic 'race' interventions of the 1960s. It has also borrowed heavily from the experience of Afro-America's shift into electoral politics – the black mayors' movement and so on. This tendency is proud and secure in its bureaucratic status and it identifies equality (antiracism) with efficiency and good management practice. Policy questions dominate political ones and antiracism emerges from the production of general blueprints which can be universally applied. Of course, equal opportunities afford an important interface between struggles around race and gender and they can be a locus of possible alliances. However, in the context of local authorities these initiatives can also host a competition between different political forces over which of them is going to take immediate priority. We should therefore be wary of collapsing antiracism let alone black emancipation into equal opportunities.

The second tendency is what used to be called Black nationalism but is now fragmented into multiple varieties, each with its own claim to ethnic particularity. It is now emphatically culturalist rather than political, each ethnic or national group arguing for cultural relativism in the strongest form. Very often, these mutually unintelligible and exclusive ethnic cultures just happen to be the same as the groups which common sense tells us are 'races'. Perversely and ironically, this tendency has happily co-existed with old-style Labourism for which ethnic absolutism and cultural relativism have provided an obvious means to rationalize and balance its funding practices.

The third tendency is the most complex. It unendingly reiterates the idea that class is race, race is class and is both black and white. Its spokespeople have sought refuge from inter-ethnic conflict in some of the more anachronistic formulae of socialist class politics. For them class is the thing which will unify the diverse and end the polyphonic ethno-babble in the new municipal Tower of Babel. Class remains synonymous with organized labour, regardless of the fact that in the context of local authorities organized labour is not always very radical. This tendency overlooks the role which the bureaucratic hierarchy plays in coercing the actually existing working class into antirace line. So far its class-based line has been almost exclusively animated by a critique of race awareness training – a practical strategy which has been thrown up in the grating between the first two tendencies. This is an important issue, but it is nonetheless the most gestural and superficial aspect of deeper problems, namely culturalism and ethnic absolutism. This tendency has mistaken the particular for the general – racism awareness training is a symptom, not a cause in its own right.

Apart from their conceit, these diverse yet inter-dependent groupings share a statist conception of antiracism. In making the local state the main vehicle for advancing antiracist politics they have actively confused and confounded the black community's capacity for autonomous self-organization. Here, we must make an assessment of the politics of funding community organizations and the dependency which that creates.

There is every likelihood that the versions of antiracism I have criticized will wither away as the local state structures on which they have relied are destroyed by the conflict with central government. But antiracist activities encapsulate one final problem which may outlive them. This is the disastrous way in which they have trivialized the rich complexity of black life by reducing it to nothing more than a response to racism. More than any other issue this operation reveals the extent of the antiracists' conceptual trading with the racists and the results of embracing their culturalist assumptions. Seeing in black life nothing more than an answer to racism means moving on to the ideological circuit which makes us visible in two complementary roles – the problem and the victim.

Antiracism seems very comfortable with this idea of blacks as victims. I remember one simplistic piece of Greater London Council propaganda which said 'We are all either the victims or the perpetrators of racism'. Why should this be so? Suffering confers no virtue on the victim; yesterday's victims are tomorrow's executioners. I propose that we reject the central image of ourselves as victims and install instead an alternative conception which sees us as an active force working in many different ways for our freedom from racial subordination. The plural is important here for there can be no single or homogeneous strategy against racism because racism itself is never homogeneous. It varies, it changes and it is *always* uneven. The recent history of our struggles has shown how people can shrink the world to the size of their communities and act politically on that basis, expressing their dissent in the symbolism of disorderly protest while demanding control over their immediate conditions. However you feel about the useless violence of these eruptions, it was the riotous protests of 1981 which created the space in which political antiracism became an option.

We must accept that for the years immediately ahead these struggles will be essentially defensive and probably unable to make the transition to more stable, totalizing forms of politics. But the challenge we face is the task of linking these immediate local concerns together across the international division of labour, transcending national boundaries, turning our back on the state and using all the means at our disposal to build a radical, democratic movement of civil society. This kind of activity could be called the micro-politics of race, though in practice, as where we align ourselves with the struggles of our brothers and sisters in South Africa, it is more likely to prove the micro-politics of race's overcoming.

References

Gilroy, P. (1987) *There Ain't No Black in the Union Jack*, London, Hutchinson.

Honeyford, R. (1988) *Integration or Disintegration*, London, Claridge Press.

Lewis, R. (1988) *Anti-Racism: a mania exposed*, London, Quartet.

Miles, R. (1989) *Racism*, London, Routledge & Kegan Paul.

Palmer, F. (1987) *Antiracism: an assault on education and value*, London, Sherwood Press.

Source: Ball, W. and Solomos, J. (1990) *Race and Local Politics*, London, Macmillan.

3 'IT'S RACISM WHAT DUNNIT'
HIDDEN NARRATIVES IN THEORIES OF RACISM

PHILIP COHEN

In their articles in this volume Ali Rattansi and Paul Gilroy have argued the case for new strategies in antiracist education that avoid what the Burnage Report criticized as its 'moral, symbolic and doctrinaire' forms. This article is also a contribution to that process of critical revision, and therefore inevitably involves an element of self-reflection, focusing on some of the ideas and approaches which I have used in my own antiracist work over the years.[1]

The story begins with two examples taken from work in the early 1980s. The first is a transcript taken from some ethnographic research which I carried out into the culture of racism amongst young white men living on a large council estate in South London. This was part of a wider project to develop forms of youth work to counter the appeal of the National Front amongst this group. The second is the text of an unofficial lampoon that was being circulated among junior officers in the Metropolitan Police in 1982, in the wake of the Scarman Report. I was given it at the end of a stormy course on race relations given to staff at Hendon Police College. Shortly afterwards the lecturer who was responsible for arranging the course was sacked for leaking essays that revealed the extent of racism amongst the cadets, and a programme of 'human awareness training' was introduced instead.

The two texts provide vivid evidence of the continuing reality of racist cultures in Britain. I do not provide a detailed analysis of them here, but use them as a reference point for raising a number of issues about different approaches to understanding and tackling the kind of racism which they represent. I have in fact used these texts many times for study purposes in a variety of settings: with teachers, community activists, academics and 'race professionals'. It is the experience of listening to the responses or readings which have been triggered by them which has led me to question the nature of the arguments usually put forward by antiracists to explain racism.

It is often said that one of the problems with antiracism is that it knows what it is against, but not what it is for. But do we really know enough about the whys and wherefores of racism? If not, then perhaps the models of racism which are implicitly or explicitly present in antiracist policies and practices may be inhibiting the development of more positive and effective strategies? What alternative models are possible?

Before we even begin to consider how such questions could be productively posed, let alone answered, it is perhaps worth asking what it means to have a model of something at all. There are a number of different senses in which the word has come to be used, both in the social sciences and in everyday parlance. It may refer to a scaled down version of reality such as a model car, or to a form of symbolic representation such as a map. In both cases the model is a device which reduces the complexity of what is represented, by selectively reproducing only those details which are deemed significant or useful for the purpose at hand. A model car doesn't have to contain all the elements of an internal combustion engine in order to work as a toy! A map does not have to indicate all the features of the terrain in order to help people find their way about it. There is, however, another meaning which can be given to the term: the model as an ideal, an exemplary type or paradigm, as in model pupil, worker or wife. These constructions also involve a process of selective reproduction in which certain features are privileged and others ignored. For example, the 'model' pupil is one who is always eager to follow the teacher's line of instruction and is never bolshy or bored!

One of the things I want to argue is that in order to construct certain exemplary models of antiracist policy and practice it has been necessary to operate in terms of a reductive representation of racism, one which not only scales down its reality, but ignores its more complex features. It is this 'reductionism', this disavowal of complexity for the sake of pursuing moral certainties or political ideals, which has lead to the present crisis of antiracist education. In taking this line of thought for a walk I have had to develop a model of antiracism itself, and this in the more properly social scientific sense of the word – the model as a typology of instances. I have tried to identify the pattern of presuppositions which underlay common-sense arguments about the meaning of my two study texts; I look both at their theoretical adequacy as explanatory models of racism, and at their rhetorical power as a means of winning consent for certain 'exemplary' or 'ideologically correct' formulations of how antiracist work should be done.

Although I do not develop this aspect of the analysis here, I also suggest that the images or metaphors which are applied to define racism by analogy hold the key to understanding people's emotional investment in antiracist positions. It is just as necessary to be aware of the role which desire, displacement and fantasy play in our own practices, as it is in relation to the perverse ideo-logic of racism itself. In the light of this discussion I offer some indications as to how a strategy of reading might be applied to the study of racist discourses, and invite readers to try out this approach on the two study texts, not in order to produce 'the right answer' but to compare what is gained and what lost in detail and depth of understanding by applying this kind of model compared to the others. At times this may seem a difficult and roundabout journey. But it will prove to be a necessary and worthwhile one if it leads us in the direction of a less doctrinaire and therefore more properly educational form of antiracism.

From the wrong side of the tracks

Fighting talk

You got into a fight the other night. What happened?

Well, there was a **fair** fight between one of my brothers and this coloured kid, right? They started one on to one. And my brother won, right? And half of the blacks said 'Right, let's leave it at that.' But the other lot come down the next night, and the night after that, and the night after that, all week they come down, about 40, 50 of them, from all over . . . Shepherd's Bush, Notting Hill, White City . . .
. . . black city (*laughter*) . . .
. . . and there's just our lot from the estate.

What started the first fight?

I dunno, you never know, do you, it just happens . . .

Did all the black people come from outside the area?

All from outside, weren't they (*general assent*) . . . Well **one** lived here, the rest came from outside.

Would you go outside the area to fight blacks?

No, not really. You see, if we went outside our area we'd get nicked . . . remember that time the police come down and they said 'if you're on your own territory we'll nick the others, but if you're outside, we'll nick *you*.' So we let the blacks come down to *us*, we didn't go looking for them. And on the Friday night we was fetching bottles and sticks and everything and we hid them ready. And the Old Bill came down and found them and nicked us, even after what they'd said. And we got done for conspiracy to cause GBH. Nine of us got done. But the blacks they just let them go. They just put them in the meat wagon and dropped them up town.

Why do you think the police let them go?

Race relations . . . Race Relations Act. If the coons get nicked they start complaining, saying the police are nicking them unfairly . . .

Do you think the police in this area are biased against young white people?

No, they're not biased against white people they're biased against **us**! They know quite a few of us, don't they, and if they see you, they nick you. But if they see a bunch of black kids hanging around they won't nick them.

. . . Blacks reckon the opposite; they reckon the police are picking on them.

. . . Nearly every day round our area you used to get searched. The Law come over if you were in a group. If you hang about after 10pm they come over and say 'If you lot ain't out of here in five minutes, you're nicked, the lot of you.'

. . . Yes, there used to be a bigger lot you know, like 18, 19. Now they're off and married, so **we** hang about and get the trouble.

What are the girls doing in all this?

Well, it depends. Sometimes they egg you on, you know. Most times they just hang about and watch if there's a fight. If there's real trouble with the blacks most of them don't want to know. But a few of them they're worse than us, ain't they?

Yeah but some of them are really scared of the coons, ain't they? Like there was this girl, she worked in the paper shop down the road, and there was this black kid who kept pestering her all the time, so we had to go down and sort him out. He left her alone after that.

What did your parents have to say about all this?

Well, they saw there was more of them [the blacks] than us. And they saw the Old Bill nicking us and letting the coons go. And they was right behind us.

. . . Yes, cos they seen the trouble from the balconies, you know.

. . . Everyone was looking over the balcony. There was a big audience. **Everyone** was out. Some of the older blokes, they come out, and they started fighting as well! (*laughter*) One bloke come down from the flats with just a pair of trousers and a vest on and **he** started having a go!

. . . Yes, when they see all the white kids getting nicked, all the parents was going mad about it.

. . . and we got a petition!

. . . Yes, we just went round the houses and we said to the people, you know, why we was getting nicked, and they just signed their names. We got 100 names in three days!

Are most of the people on this estate white?

It used to be didn't it? (*general assent*) But not no more, since they started bringing coloured families in. Now it's about half and half.

When they first come over here it was probably all right. But then more and more come and they all started acting flash, like they owned the place and that's when all the trouble started.

I went down the Kentucky in the High Street the other day, I had just come out, I was just standing there, when these black kids come up and start jostling me and then they nicks my chicken and chips. Just like that, in front of my nose. I mean I might think of doing something like that, but I'd never actually dare to do it . . .

What other changes have there been?

Well, they just keep building flats don't they? They're opening a new lot now at the top of the road there. It just keeps on getting bigger and bigger . . .

. . . and how many flats have gone to blacks in just the last few years? That's where my first house was, where they are now.

It was good when we were smaller; it was much better wasn't it? (*general agreement*)

. . . Where our flats are, all it is now is green and trees and everything. There used to be rubbish dumps and mud and all that and we used to have a laugh there, you know what I mean?

. . . There used to be a lot of older houses and we used to all go in them. But they've been knocking everything down. I mean we can't even have a bonfire round our way now, can we, without them phoning the police.

The last laugh?

The following instructions are to be brought to the attention of all officers.

Dress: No 2 trousers (pressed) boots (shone) reinforced helmets. Truncheons and whistles must be carried. Non-authorised clothing: crash helmets, steel capped boots, jogging shoes and squad ties will not be worn.

Inspectors in charge of serials will search their officers to ensure that no officers have concealed six foot scaffold poles or pick axe handles in their pockets.

Protective clothing: the only protective item allowed is a Police 'Long Service and Good Conduct Medal' which should be worn in a prominent position so as to allow the Local Youth to identify old policemen who they do not like, from young policemen whom they like even less.

The following practices have been noted and should cease forthwith: Missiles thrown at the police should not be picked up and thrown back as once the missile has hit the ground it is deemed 'out of play'. However missiles in mid flight may be headed back although, prior to this, helmets should be removed to prevent damage to the helmet plate.

The practice, especially among members of shield serials, of 'whooping like cowboys and indians' and beating of truncheons on riot shields must cease as this tends to frighten and intimidate rioters.

The practice of 'blacking up' faces is definitely not appropriate in present conflict.

Officers who are unfortunately set alight by petrol bombs should not run down the road screaming, but should lay down with dignity and await their turn to be put out.

Before leaving for Brixton, Inspectors should brief their men on local customs and traditions.

It has been statistically proved that the young of the area are six times more helpful than youngsters in the rest of the country at carrying ladies bags. This action leads to about sixty misunderstandings a week.

Brixton, like the rest of the country has its take away shops, only here the service includes jewellers, Burtons, Woolworths, and camera shops; in fact most shops can be regarded as 'in the scheme'.

The youngsters of the area hold celebrations similar to our Guy Fawkes Night, when pubs, shops, homes and policemen are set alight.

Finally should any elderly residents approach officers complaining of being assaulted or mugged, they should be closely questioned to ascertain if they are trying to provoke a riot.

Reading ideologies

Simply to denounce the sort of racism which is evident in these texts does not in itself enable us to understand why this culture comes into being, and how it is perpetuated. These questions should properly be the subject of extensive research and debate, since on the answers hang decisive issues of antiracist strategy. We should not have to anguish over what needs to be done to stop the physical and mental havoc which such racists wreak on black people. This can be limited and even stopped by resolute political action. But it is not so easy to legislate out of existence the cultures which produce these practices. The stick-and-carrot approach to 'race relations' has done little to shift the moral economy of the street gang, or that of the rank-and-file police. For at this level we are dealing with underlying causes, rather than immediate effects.

How those causes are identified will affect political priorities and is also partly influenced by them. If you believe that racism is essentially a product of economic or political structures, then you will concentrate all your efforts on trying to change these. Better opportunities for ethnic minorities in the housing and labour markets, plus more houses and jobs, equals less racism. If you grant racist ideologies their own relatively autonomous conditions of existence, however, you might be inclined to give a higher priority to educational or cultural issues, whilst at the same time taking care, not to bracket out their links to other dimensions of racism. You might, for example, be concerned that more and better jobs or housing for black people might produce a white backlash and result in more, not less, racism, unless it was accompanied by educational initiatives.

These different standpoints also have implications for the way racist discourses themselves are understood. In the first case, they are held to reflect or express social realities external to them and to need no further analysis than that. In the second case, how the discourses are constructed is seen as an integral part of the power which they exercise in and through material practices of discrimination. Here discourse analysis becomes a central aspect of antiracist education.

Let us focus then on some of the contexts in which discussion about racism takes place. When I have used these texts in workshops, we have usually started by reading them through silently, before breaking into small groups to discuss them in detail. Initial 'gut' reactions have varied from righteous indignation to cynical amusement, from vocal anger to silent embarrassment. One surprising aspect of these responses was the way they were almost always followed or overlaid by a sense of satisfaction, even pleasure, at having documentary evidence to support particular explanations of racism, and particular ideological standpoints related to them.

At one level this is hardly surprising. Presented with such explicitly racist material and asked to make intellectual sense of it, most people's reactions are likely to be anchored to positions in which they have an emotional and material stake. If you are black you find yourself being addressed directly as an object – and potential subject – of verbal and physical attack. They're talking about you and no one else! As a result you may be motivated to read the texts as confirming the existence of a persistent and all-pervasive racism inherent in white society. In contrast, if you are white, and unless you actually subscribe to racist arguments, you will want to find ways of dissociating yourself from the views expressed here. You may try to do this by defining or explaining racism in terms which are specific to these two instances, but which also count you out. If you happen to be a policeman, however, or a friend of one of the 'lads', but do not happen to share their attitudes towards black people, you are in an even more awkward and complicated position; how can you avoid being spoken for by those who 'represent' you in the text? Only by finding evidence to 'prove' that these particular 'spokesmen' are in fact 'unrepresentative' and speak neither for you, nor for anyone but themselves.

This implies a certain kind of model of racism and its mode of representation, one which stresses the element of negotiation or contradiction in the way people are positioned in and by racist discourses. I am not saying that people who are directly subjected to racism are inevitably attracted to one-dimensional argument or that those who are not necessarily take a more sophisticated view. But it clearly is much more difficult and heroic for any group of people who are on the front line of discrimination to adopt a nuanced reading of racism's multiple forms than for those who are or want to be distanced from its processes and effects.

As a rule, how particular groups are located *vis-à-vis* racist discourse intimately affects the reading strategies their members adopt towards specific instances, and this in turn underwrites the explanatory procedures used to interpret and make common sense of them. In most of our workshops the study texts would be used as a kind of mirror writing whose 'decoding' simply confirmed what was always and already known or felt to be inscribed in them. The problem was not so much the offensive content of the material, since there was no one who was not familiar with it. Rather it was the terms of that very familiarity which pre-empted any new reading.

For those who claimed to have seen or heard it all before, racism was always the same old story. But this also held the depressing implication that nothing much had changed since 1981, and that the antiracist movement had largely failed to shift either popular attitudes or state policies. It was very rare that this conclusion was actually reached however. Such ineffectiveness, it was usually argued, had nothing to do with any deficiency in antiracist strategy or method. On the contrary, it only proved how deep rooted racism was and how successful the New Right had been in discrediting these initiatives. But from another point of view, the chronic repetitions of racist discourse were here being used as a defence against recognizing unpalatable truths.

There was, however, a minority of readers who detected something rather old fashioned in both 'fighting talk' and the police communiqué. They argued that a new racism based on arguments about cultural difference had largely taken over the arenas of public debate.[2] This opened up an interesting line of enquiry. How far had popular or institutional racism been transformed during the 'Thatcher decade', and by what? Has the next generation of unemployed white youth followed in the footsteps of their elder brothers or taken a new route? Have police attitudes hardened or changed as a result of public pressure?

We will come back to these substantive questions later on. For the moment what concerns me is the sources of these two positions. Clearly they are symptomatic of investments in different kinds of discourse. Those who had been formed by the politics of black nationalism, or roots radicalism, or by the various schools of classical Marxism all in different ways stressed the continuities with the past. They were much more likely to stick to the 'maginot line' of municipal antiracism and therefore, paradoxically, to experience any shift away from that defensive position as a retreat. Those who did not inhabit this universe of discourse had less difficulty in accepting possible discontinuities between different movements or forms of racism. Equally, though, they tended to fetishize the 'new' at the expense of a more properly conjunctural analysis.

How do these different ways of understanding contemporary racism relate to the ideologies of reading which were applied to the study texts? Is it just that people selectively applied to the task in hand some of the ideas they had come across in reading various books? Or was the way they engaged with these theoretical explanations of racism governed by the same conditions as applied to their reading of the 'primary' material? That question raises a further and even more interesting one about the status of different kinds of accounts. Are theories just another kind of story, or do they constitute a radically distinct form of discourse?

Teleological tales

Theories which aim to explain social phenomena do so through methods of investigation and interpretation which strive for internal consistency, comprehensiveness, and conceptual clarity. Sometimes it is argued that this requires a form of discourse which breaks with principles of narrative continuity and follows a purely analytic order of exposition, albeit one which remains open ended and exploratory. From this position nothing would be assumed a priori about the meaning of our study texts (how far they qualified as racist, for example) until their actual conditions of existence had been exhaustively examined.

Social theories do not, of course, operate in an ideological vacuum, nor do they create one around themselves as a result of some special 'scientific' procedure. The same theory may take on quite different political, moral and even existential meanings according to particular circumstances of context and conjuncture. As a result theoretical discourses are traversed by narrative structures which form a hidden thread running through the argument.[3] Whereas in many cases this is only one dimension, albeit an important one, in the case of what we might call *theoretical ideology* it constitutes the main organizing principle.[4] For here a particular epistemology is subsumed within a rhetoric of special pleading for a chosen reference group (the black community, the proletariat, the intelligentsia, women, the professions). Such groups are constructed as the bearers of privileged knowledge or agency, by virtue of their social location. As such they are invested with a unique role as makers of history, or as critics of society. This is above all a narrative role, a role within a storyline which is unfolded as a teleology, that is a narrative moving towards a preordained conclusion, which structures the logic of preceding events.[5] Within this framework, in other words, societies or individuals are made to develop according to certain 'laws of motion' which are inscribed in their very mode of being. It is because certain groups are held to exemplify the working of these laws that their structural positions or social attributes are held to possess a special explanatory power, or to equip them with a special 'totalizing' consciousness.

Teleologies produce stable narratives in which the meaning of any conjuncture can be read off from the 'stage' it is supposed to represent in the dynamic unfolding of some ultimate and pre-defined goal. This is the *diachronic*, or *historicist* version. Alternatively the nature of any institution is read off from its underlying role in reproducing the social structure of which it is a part. This is the *functionalist* or *synchronic* version. Either form of explanation acts as an insurance policy taken out against the contingency of actions and events. Their outcome is guaranteed always and already to be inscribed in the process of their unfolding, according to certain overarching principles of causality.[6]

How does this work in the case of theories of racism? Perhaps the dominant account still belongs to the Whig interpretation of history. This is a story of continuing progress, from the barbarity of slavery to the enlightenment of the contemporary race relations industry. The onward march of reason and tolerance is led by their 'natural' standard bearers, the European intelligentsia, and its various allies, who wage an unremitting battle against the irrational prejudices of both masses and traditional elites. The emancipation of the poor and oppressed is thus made part of a civilizing process, which is often seen to be conditional on assimilating their demands to the discourses of humanism and rationalism.[7]

This is a fairy story version of race relations and it may reflect the hubris or wishful thinking of an intelligentsia which sets up its own preferred cultural practices as a referential model for everyone else. Increasingly it has been challenged by a rival account which might be called a 'teleology of the oppressed'. Here things do not get better and better, they go from bad to worse. The onward march of racism is traced through historical time and institutional space, from some presumed point of origination which defines its essential character, to a present conjuncture which is the summation of its effects. This narrative is often linked to another in which the victims of racism trace their own onward march, as an epic journey of emancipation from bondage, in which they alone carry the banner of human progress. These narratives can be read as two sides of the same story. The identity of Jews, blacks and others is made to depend on its inscription within an unfolding logic of racial oppression, which in turn is specified in terms of its formative effects upon their experience.[8]

At one level, then, racism tends to be read as a kind of horrific soap opera in which the surface incidents are ever changing, but the underlying plot remains constant, generating one episode of discrimination after another, punctuated by atrocities which have no end even though paradoxically the final, cataclysmic outcome is never in doubt: for it will be the fire next time, the Armageddon which puts an end to chronic injustice, once and for all. Past and present struggles are transformed into 'epiphanies', special moments in which the conditions of oppression are transcended and which prefigure the ultimate goal of Liberation.

Such triumphalist narratives can be empowering in the symbolic sense that they invest ethnic minorities with special powers of knowledge and action. They break the signifying chains which have so often bound the project of emancipation to a strategy of cultural assimilation. Yet this radical autonomy of means and ends is itself dependent upon a circumscribed and self-confirming discourse of origins and destinies. It is like turning to the end of the story before you begin reading it, to find out if the baddies got their just deserts, or the good guys won. Or, as one of my students once put it to me, ironically, when I was still preaching this gospel, 'I know, Sir, it was racism what dunnit.'

Why are 'teleological tales' so central to the common sense of antiracism? I suspect that part at least of the explanation lies in the pressures which structures of racism exert on the forms of resistance to it. I am thinking here of two distinct but linked operations which constitute racism as a discursive practice. The first is a totalizing strategy which dissolves every distinction into the all-inclusive distinction of race: for example you are always and already defined as Jewish irrespective of age, class, gender, culture, or any other feature which might place you in a category with non-Jews. The other is a strategy of discrimination which magnifies and exploits every kind of social distinction (of wealth, culture status, etc.) to be found within a designated subject population and gives it a racist connotation as signifying certain 'exclusive traits'.

Used together these two strategies comprise that peculiar language game known as a double bind.[9] Thus if you are Jewish and working class, your Jewishness is used to disqualify you from membership of labour organizations; but equally if you are Jewish and poor, your poverty is made to signify the essentially parasitic nature of your 'race' on the host community. How has the power of this system of classification been dealt with by those who have been victims of its perverse games of inclusion and exclusion?

Perhaps the main defence has been to construct an imagined community of resistance which cuts across all internal divisions by emphasizing the levelling effects of racist oppression. In this way diaspora communities are able to subsume all their disparate histories within a single meta-narrative which irons out all the 'wrinkles'. This may take the form of a genealogy which enables the present generation to see its own experience prefigured in the struggles of its ancestors, or to trace an unbroken line of descent to certain common codes and practices which define its 'roots'. Alternatively, it may provide a means of translating atrocity stories from simple acts of individual testimony into public iconographies, monuments in the living museum of collective memory. In either case, another chapter is added to a 'founding text', a text which both authorizes its own dissemination, and gives everything which is recounted in it the imprimatur of a special truth: this is the word of a chosen people.

Here we can see the influence of religious ideologies in furnishing common sense explanations of racial intolerance and persecution.[10] What often begins with a vision of racism as a global force of evil often becomes focused down into a conspiracy directed against a chosen people in a way which invests their suffering and sacrifices with a special redemptive meaning. The principle of salvation may be theological, as in the case of religious fundamentalism; or it may be purely secular, as with ethnic nationalism; or it may involve some combination of the two. But in every case the populist element is reinforced by a particular practice of reading and writing the founding text which stresses the prescriptive or predictive value of an elective destiny. This religious dimension is conserved as a subtext in many political ideologies, where it furnishes particular articles of faith in the self-emancipation of ethnic minorities, or in their special role as makers of their own history. In this context Marxism furnishes its own distinctive teleology of the oppressed, which can easily be transposed from class to nation or 'race'. Here the myth of the founding text is most clearly articulated to that of the founding fathers, whose word lays down the laws of a history in which women and children do not count.[11]

These narratives do not work only to unite across space and time. They play a vital role in glossing over discontinuities in the here and now. Where a minority within an ethnic minority successfully pursues a strategy of contest mobility, and rises to positions of relative power and affluence, the teleologies of roots radicalism can reassert the organic links binding those who are moving onwards and upwards to those still in the ghetto. The racial success story turns those who have made it into narrative role models for the next generation, who are pledged to follow in their footsteps 'one day'. The elision between the onward march of the struggle against racism and the upward mobility of those who lead it, with its easy equation between individual success and collective emancipation has proved one of the more effective seductions offered by western democracies. It enables those who enter the professional middle class to avoid the worst traps of assimilation while disavowing the material advantages which now separate them from their erstwhile peers.

In such ways teleological tales of race and racism reinforce the imagined community of resistance at those points where divisions of class, gender or ethnicity threaten to break through. They ease the pain of lived contradictions, furnishing missing links between origins and destinies, stitching together scattered histories into a singular totalizing consciousness of what it means to be black or Muslim, Palestinian or Jew. The story lines which are woven together in this way are often spellbinding. Their telling and retelling relay important principles of hope rooted in political and moral certainties about the outcome of struggle. But do they really cauterize the wounds of historical separation and loss? Or do they merely invite us to count and compare our scars? Do these theoretical ideologies provide a strategic grasp of racism, or do they raise expectations which they cannot fulfil?

Language games

In this section I shall try to uncover some of the theoretical assumptions and rhetorical devices at work in 'common-sense' responses to the 'Fighting talk' and 'Last laugh' texts. The following examples are typical of the sort of comments which were made. All the speakers, some white, some black, were active in antiracist campaigns.

Statement A: Racism as institutionalized false consciousness

Britain is an intrinsically racist society . . . it's institutionalized . . . it runs right through everything like letters in a stick of rock. You've only got to look at history . . . slavery which led into colonialism which developed into full-blown imperialism, right on up to the present-day immigration policies. And now Mrs Thatcher comes along and tells us we've got to *return* to Victorian values. As if they've ever been left behind as regards the treatment of black people! Obviously a lot of this racism has seeped down from the top; for example the police are part of a racist legal system so you've got to expect them to hold those views. It's the only way they can go around harassing and criminalizing black kids and think they're doing a good job. They're complaining because blacks are fighting back – that's all. As for the white kids on the estate, they experience the immediate effects – unemployment, bad housing, but they're in no position to understand or tackle the actual underlying causes. Society tells them they're rubbish, because they can't find jobs, but it also tells them that they are better than the blacks. So it's not surprising they draw the racist conclusions – the blacks are getting jobs, housing etc. at their expense; and so they become fodder for the National Front.

Statement B: Racism as irrational prejudice

Racism poisons a lot of children's minds – they grow up in an environment with all these images around them, in comics, newspapers, TV, films, plus everything they hear from the family or friends – they just cannot help taking it in. So they grow up just assuming that whites are the goodies and blacks are the baddies and pass the same stereotypes onto their children. It's not their fault, they just don't know any better. As a teacher I try to do what I can, but in a lot of cases you come up against a brick wall with a lot of racist graffitti on it! The boys are the worst, especially if they're in gangs like the ones here. They seem to think that they've got to prove how manly they are. As for the police, they seem to think and behave in much the same way. I should imagine that the police force attracts people who have got particular hang-ups about race. They're hardly likely to have the most tolerant or liberal attitudes are they! We've got to hope that something will happen to make these people change their minds, but do leopards ever change their spots?

Statement C: Racism as white power

From a black perspective you're up against a white power structure and it doesn't really matter whether you're being beaten up or abused by the police or by a group of kids on the street, it all comes down to the same thing – racism. If you go for a job, or a place to live and they send you away, it's racism. Discrimination can be institutionalized and done procedurally as a matter of course behind the scenes or it can be out in the open with insults to your face, but the result is the same. It's so many stabs in the back . . . It's the whole system which is fucking us up. That's why it's only black people who will put an end to racism; our whole experience tells us that.

Statement D: Racism as class rule

Racism just boils down to ruling-class propaganda; you've only got to look at the popular Tory press, churning it out day after day, all owned and controlled by capitalists who've got a direct interest in setting white workers against black and undermining the unity of the working class. The same papers are read by those kids and by the coppers who nick them, and basically they've both swallowed the same lies.

Statement E: Racism as rational self interest

I think that's absolute nonsense. They're not as stupid as you make out. They're much more likely to be acting out of self interest. If you know that employers are using immigrants as cheap labour, and that they're being used to undercut your rates of pay, you're going to be against that. If you think that you're more likely to keep the price of your house high by keeping blacks out, then you'd be likely to go for that. And if you're a policeman on the beat, with an eye on promotion, what easier way to keep your arrest rate up than to go out and pull in some black kids off the street. Put it the other way round, what incentives have the police or the white working class got *not* to be racist?

These views do not, of course, exhaust the range of possible antiracist positions. They all bear on actual realities, and contain elements of genuine insight. They may be deployed in a variety of circumstances to greater or lesser effect. For example, the argument about institutionalized racism in Statement A can be used to counter denials about the existence and effects of racial inequalities. The denunciation of white racism in C is often used to make white people feel guilty about their structural or historical implication in the oppression of black people and to force them to concede the legitimacy of black demands. In contrast the explanations of racism in terms of prejudice (B) or self interest (E) offer 'get out clauses' for whites and pinpoint specific types of motive or intent which may yield tactical priorities in antiracist work. The identification of racism as a capitalist ploy (D) draws on a particular kind of political rhetoric which under some conditions may mobilize sections of the left or the labour movement in defence of the black community.

When they are cited in the context of discussion or debate, arguments about irrationality and its cultural transmission (B) are frequently used as a strategy of professional empowerment on the part of teachers, who define racism in such a way to privilege their own role, as guardians of reason and enlightenment, in combating it. Equally the enunciation of statements C and D may enable certain individuals to dominate the group in the name of an 'imagined community' of race or class which they either claim or are made by others to represent.

The pragmatics of all these statements – the ways they are used to produce certain effects on the people to whom they are addressed – are thus tied to their propaganda value for particular campaigns or positions, or to their instrumental value in furthering the personal or political objectives of particular individuals or groups. But however effective these arguments may be in political debate, that does not make them necessarily adequate as theoretical explanations of racism.

I would argue that the persuasive force of these statements owes a great deal to their teleological format. In Statement A the history of racism is rigidly determined by specific laws of development. Each phase is the outcome of the one before, whilst bearing the chronic imprint of an interior design. Equally, when the argument goes synchronic it locates racism in the structure of society, as key to the way the whole functions. Statement C starts from the same premise, but is an even more explicit version of a teleology of the oppressed. Every instance of racism is explicable as the effect of a white power structure whose overthrow is the historical mission of black people. Rhetorically its strategy of reiteration attempts to unify different groups into one political bloc by appealing to a single source of oppression which they all share. Statements D and E offer alternative views of racism as goal-directed behaviour on the part of groups who are held to have an intrinsic interest in pursuing these ends. Statement B seems to admit the greatest amount of contingency into the determination of outcomes, but nevertheless still falls back on a tendential law to explain how racism is reproduced.

The problem with all these formulations is that they are *reductionist*: that is, they claim that complex and multi-faceted phenomena can be explained by a single, simple cause. These explanations are therefore limited. They tell only part of the story, and leave out any elements which do not fit into their chosen line of argument. I would identify two main types of reduction in these examples. Statements A and C operate according to the procedures of *radical holism*.[12] They explain the actions or attitudes of particular individuals or groups, and the meaning of particular events, as the expression of an over-determining social totality – 'capitalist society', 'patriarchy', or 'the white power structure' – which supervenes in every case to determine the form of all social eventualities. The method consists in extrapolating from concrete relations those properties which can be directly subsumed under these higher order abstractions. Other features of the phenomena which cannot be treated in this way are ignored or denied any narrative or causal significance. Thus, for example, an account of some episode of social conflict is constructed in which the discrete personalities of the protagonists are regarded as irrelevant to the outcome, and they are treated simply as the bearers or supports of certain political ideologies or economic forces. In practice the effect is to dissolve the psychic into the social, and reify the social, turning it into an inert structural process. This tendency is present in most theories of 'institutionalized racism'.[13]

The reductionism at work in the other three statements moves in exactly the opposite direction. This mode of explanation has been called *methodological individualism*,[14] for it seeks to disaggregate all larger institutional and historical entities into the practices and relations of the individuals or groups who compose or inhabit them. Structural processes are rendered down into social or psychological properties, which are then erected into totalizing principles of explanation. All macro-level features which cannot be made intelligible in this way are regarded as being of secondary importance to the outcome of the story. For example statements B, D and E all assume that the outcomes of 'race relations' are explicable at a micro-level, in terms of the intrinsic propensities of particular individuals or groups: working-class children or parents (B), capitalists (D) or white residents or policemen (E). From this standpoint racism appears to be a matter of individual prejudice which, even when institutionalized, is ultimately sustained by the attitudes and actions of racists. Propositions generated by this type of reduction do not necessarily agree about the conditions under which racist positions or practices are adopted, as witness the dispute between D and E.

The two types of explanation appear to have rather different political implications. Holistic theories suggest that racism cannot be eliminated without the radical transformation of state, economy and civil society – whether this entails the dismantling of key institutions or the overthrow of the power structure as a whole. Whether or not methodological individualists subscribe to such views, for them, the important point is that the levers of power are to be found in the hands of strategically placed individuals or groups. This does not make their account any less deterministic. Attitudes are still read off from attributes. What differs is that holists derive attributes from structural location, and individualists from relational properties. In one case what counts is the 'objective positions' which 'white people' as such occupy within the 'racist power structure'; in the second it is their socialization, or cultural traditions which racializes their relationships to blacks.

In practice, then, these explanatory models can be either antagonistic or complementary. Elements from both can be combined at the level of common-sense argument. For example, in the heat of debate it is not unusual to hear radically holistic denunciations of 'capitalism', or 'the racist power structure', which imply the need for their wholesale destruction, followed in the next breath by appeals to specific individuals or groups to 'change the system' by virtue of their special predisposition to do so. There is a good example of this in Statement C's juxtaposition of 'the whole system' with the specific appeal to black people to put an end to racism.

Such switches between the two forms of reductionism have several payoffs. They get the argument out of a tight corner, and make for a less fatalistic scenario. This particular example (C) may conceivably make it easier for community activists to occupy positions of influence within existing power structures without being accused of 'selling out'. Above all, however, it makes it possible to yoke together a generic model of racism as a global ideological form with a highly differentiated notion of its relational properties, in a way which makes its enactment or sufferance the monopoly of specific individuals or groups. Everything in a given society is made to explain its racism, and this racism, in turn, is made to explain everything about a particular ethnic minority within it.[15]

This practice of stitching together the two kinds of reduction into a single statement, which combines sweeping generalization with particularistic reference, is central to the discursive strategies which the Burnage Report criticized as 'moral, symbolic and doctrinaire' antiracism. The double reduction formula is explicitly stated in the equation *racism =*

power + *prejudice* which was widely adopted within the movement during the 1980s.[16]

It would be unfair to make too many demands of the statements I have quoted. They are examples of people thinking on their feet, trying to rationalize their responses to texts which 'hit below the belt'. The aim was often to convince fellow students (and me) of the force of their own political perspective. My point is not to criticize the theoretical deficiencies of these statements. On the contrary, I would argue that the embedded narratives I have identified here can also be found in more elaborated academic discourses.

Problematics

There are forceful defences to be made of both holism and individualism as theoretical models within the social sciences. The problem here is their application as practical models for understanding and tackling racism. When they are deployed in arguments like the ones we have just looked at, they tend to be strong on moral denunciation but weak in their inclusiveness and weight of explanation. This inevitably reduces their strategic purchase on racist practices.

The holistic statements in terms of institutional racism (A) and white power (C) articulate what has been called the dominant ideology thesis in the social sciences.[17] This perspective has been associated with the function of ideology in creating the perceptions and beliefs in individuals deemed necessary to reproduce the political and economic structures of class and/or ethnic hegemony. These conditions are institutionalized through forms of discourse and power which establish a pervasive framework of values, beliefs, ideals and aspirations. As a result, the ideology of the dominant class – or 'race' – comes to be accepted as self evident 'common sense' by large sections of society, including groups who would seem to have little to gain from them. Existing patterns of inequality can thus be experienced as both necessary and legitimate, while the very possibility of alternative social arrangements becomes unthinkable or marginalized.

This is a complex formulation which in practice can be given various emphases. In every case, however, there is the assumption that forms of subjectivity can be read off from objective conditions of domination/ subordination. In invoking slavery, colonialism, imperialism and contemporary immigration legislation, for example, Statement A stresses the weight of history and the continuity of practices in achieving this effect. The idea of the pervasiveness and invisibility of racism in Statement C underlines the inertia of institutions and the sticking power of 'ideological cement'. There is agreement about the role of ideology in legitimating racial inequality, but in one case (A) this is related to the existence of a dominant (though unidentified) class, while in (C) it is a question of a dominant 'race'. Where this model comes up against its own limitations is in explaining 'popular' or working-class racism.[18] In so far as these subordinated forms of racism are granted some relative autonomy, and are not treated as simply an echo of the dominant ideology, the argument usually reverts to the classical tenets of a 'necessary false consciousness'. This is what happens in Statement A.

The main problem with the concept of necessary false consciousness is the conjunction of these three terms.[19] Are the phenomena which it discloses really necessary, in the sense of being an inevitable concomitant of social structures? (There are plenty of white working-class boys and even a few policemen who do not hold pronounced racist views.) Are they false in the sense of being definable in opposition to some 'true' or 'correct' consciousness? Are they solely to do with consciousness (in so far as they relate to ontological stakes or emotional investments in racist ideology which may be pre- or even un-conscious)?

The arguments advanced by methodological individualists do not necessarily escape these problems. The propositions advanced by the teacher in Statement B are a good case in point. An apparently holistic analysis of racist images and their ideological effect is followed in the second sentence by a switch into an argument about the way racism is reproduced through processes of transmission in micro-contexts like the family or peer group. The crucial question here is what makes individuals receptive or resistant to racist ideas. The answer seems to be that it depends on their immediate environment, how they are socialized, their level of education or 'culture'. The assumption is that children from 'deprived backgrounds' are more likely to adopt racist attitudes and arguments because their cultural milieu is unable to equip them with a more enlightened understanding of the causes of their problems.[20]

This model of working-class culture as pathological or deficient is often given a holistic twist and linked to notions of 'necessary false consciousness'. To treat racism as a matter of irrational prejudice is really a micro-reductive variant on this theme. In the case of Statement B racism is entailed in a set of inherited predispositions passed on from one generation to another. The initial supposition of environmental determinism makes space for the role of education in interrupting or reversing the trend, but this possibility gets weaker as the argument proceeds and its reductionism gathers strength. The final reference to 'leopards not changing their spots' shows just how far this explanation has moved onto the terrain of 'race' thinking itself. Racism is 'naturalized' to the point where it ceases to be a cultural norm (and as such contestable) and becomes instead a quasi-biological trait, a symptom of inherent individual pathology.

The pathological model reaches its apotheosis in attempts to explain the origin and distribution of racist beliefs in terms of the personal characteristics of those who espouse them.[21] This finds academic expression in psychological theories of prejudice. In Statement B this story line is applied to the police force to suggest that the young white working-class men who enter the force are to a large extent preselected, and irrespective of recruitment and training policies are likely to be authoritarian personality types who flourish in a para-military environment and 'have a hang-up about race'.

The difficulty with this argument is that whatever factor of psycho-social pathology is associated with racism or racists can be shown to exist just as widely in other institutions, or groups. There is also a problem in principle with the inferences that can be made from such evidence, especially the assumption that the nature of a regime can be deduced from the unconscious motives or conscious intentions of the people who run it. It does not follow that, because the legal system systematically discriminates against black people, such discrimination is its *raison d'être*, or even that it is the outcome of the undoubted prejudices of the police or judiciary. The argument could far more plausibly be turned on its head: the 'latent function' of the operation of unofficial suspect categories may be to make the administration of (in)justice more efficient and 'rational', which in turn institutionalizes these practices and gives them the status of 'due legal process'.

There is, however, another version of methodological individualism which proceeds from the opposite, and apparently more promising starting point – namely that racism is a rational or calculating strategy on the part of specific individuals or groups seeking to maximize their political or economic interests. One example might be the 'divide and rule' thesis presented in Statement D. It is in the interests of employers to use immigrants as a source of cheap labour and this also usefully weakens the workforce politically by creating internal divisions. As capitalists own and control the popular press they are able to spread disinformation about ethnic minorities and fan the flames of popular prejudice against them. The rationality attributed to racism thus coincides with a presumed calculation of class interest: racism is a means to maximize profit, which is the individual aim of every capitalist enterprise.[22]

This is a double reduction, inferring psychological motive or intention from economic or political effect. It is the 'profit motive' which conditions the attitudes and actions of individual employers (as exemplified in their recruitment and training policies) and creates the general conditions of racial discrimination, which the 'press barons' in turn deliberately exploit to sell more newspapers. But how to explain the collective, and indeed international dimensions of capitalism and racism, which can and do operate independently of any local patterns of linkage? To answer this it becomes necessary to invent a global conspiracy theory in which the 'objective interests' of capitalism and racism always and already coincide, and are actively co-ordinated by the many agents of the ruling class. This, then is a micro-reductive version of the dominant ideology thesis. The other side of the divide-and-rule thesis is that working-class racists are seen as the dupes of 'bourgeois propaganda'. The idea of racism as a product of ignorance or superstition is conserved for 'the uneducated masses' while it remains a 'rational choice' for the elite.

The notion of 'rational choice' introduces us to another, more sophisticated conception of the rationality of racism, and one which does not require this kind of double standard.[23] Starting from the premise that actions and attitudes are motivated by the maximization of self interest, the focus is on the micro-social conditions under which the ideology of individualism may be transcended, and collective aims given priority. Thus, as Statement E argues, under certain conditions white workers or residents may get together to freeze out black immigrants because their presence is felt to depress wages or house prices, or to threaten allocation policies which have hitherto made certain jobs or housing the preserve of the indigenous population. This racist behaviour is rational, because such strategies of social closure are logically consistent with the aims of protecting white privilege, and this can best be done through organized forms of discrimination, rather than at the level of individual expressions of prejudice. This seems an apt description of the defensive strategies associated with a racism of relative affluence caught at a particular moment of its crystallization. How far, though, is that an appropriate model to apply to the more aggressive racism of relative deprivation exampled in the 'fighting talk' transcript? And are there not more general problems with such a 'rationalistic' theory of racism.

If the rationality of an action is judged solely by its realism then clearly reason must always be a characteristic of those who have the power to put their policies into practice, never of those who oppose them. Even if we admit that an element of calculation usually enters into racist practices, rather than blind hatred, it is clear that this model ignores the deeper reaches of the racist *imagination*, the structures of feeling and phantasy which are embedded in even the most rationalized forms of racist argument and action. Also, in giving racist explanations the status of realist accounts, without in any way questioning their ideological construction, common sense is taken at its face value. It is only because they assume that the entry of black families into their neighbourhood makes it 'undesirable', for example, that white residents 'act rationally' to keep them out and protect the value of their properties. The assumption is both racist and ignores the importance of macro-economic factors in determining levels of demand in the housing market. The model takes such actions for granted because its reduction of macro to micro has bracketed out the conditions under which it might be put in question.

Imagining racism: phantasy, metaphor and the ideal type

Rational choice models, like class conspiracy theories, can be considered as micro-reductive variations on the dominant ideology thesis, just as, I suggested earlier, the concept of racism as necessary false consciousness could be regarded as a macro-reductive correlate of 'irrational prejudice' arguments. These principles of correspondence articulate two fundamentally different ways of conceptualizing racism. In the first case (dominant ideology/rational choice) racism is regarded as *functional* to the society or the individual, in the sense of maintaining the power of specific groups. In the second case (necessary false consciousness/irrational prejudice) racism is seen as *dysfunctional* because it distorts the perception of reality and generates division amongst those who should be on the same side.

This distinction also bears on the pragmatics of these models as they are applied in the context of political debates and campaigns. The 'functional' argument provides a discursive strategy which is useful for implicating all sorts of groups and individuals in racism who would otherwise have cast-iron alibis. For the same reason it is also an effective device for constructing a 'common enemy' or 'system' for people to unite against. The 'dysfunctional' argument can be a useful ploy against those who officially represent the unity of particular institutions of state or civil society. If they do not want to be held responsible for 'increasing racial tension' on the street, or the shop floor, they had better do x, y, or z. Of course such arguments may well backfire. You are not likely to shake the beliefs of ex-colonials by arguing that racism was and still is 'functional' to their way of life! And you may find that instead of making antiracism the rational choice for trade union officials and other bureaucrats, you are encouraging them to see immigration as dysfunctional, rather than racism! But there never is any guarantee about the outcome of this or any other pragmatics.

It is not in any case possible to pin a particular explanatory model to a specific political strategy or standpoint. For example, it is often assumed that multiculturalism is methodologically individualist, and reduces racism to an individual pathology of prejudice, whilst antiracism is radically holist and insists on the primacy of structural processes. Our discussion suggests that this is not always the case. Rational choice theories are often popular amongst left antiracists inspired by a particular reading of Marx.[24] Equally, some radical versions of multiculturalism make use of holistic arguments about power and ideology to legitimate ethnic minority cultures as an educational resource.[25] Where multiculturalists and antiracists share common ground is in their general reliance on problematics which make the detailed reading and analysis of racist discourses seem irrelevant. This, I have argued, is evident both at the level of theoretical explanations and in the common-sense models of understanding which are deployed in the five statements I have quoted.

What all these approaches have in common is their *essentialism*. By this I mean their tendency to explain racism in terms of an 'ideal type' or model, which makes certain a priori assumptions about its origins, causes, meaning and effect. These assumptions correspond to particular forms or experiences of racism, which are translated into universal criteria defining its 'essence'. Types of racism which do not conform to this model are either ignored, marginalized, or 'redescribed' in ways which deny their independent significance. Racism becomes defined in terms of features which are specific to the black (or Afro-Caribbean) experience, for example, or to the peculiarities of English history, so that anti-semitism, or the specific articulations of racism which have developed in, say, the Irish or Scottish contexts, or in other European countries, are treated as 'special cases', because their inclusion would 'deconstruct' the ideal type. At the same time, at a micro level an assumption is made about who is racist and who is not in terms of a set of essential defining properties or predispositions.[26]

This is not to suggest that each of the sample antiracist statements does not have something pertinent to say about the particular instance of racism which it privileges as paradigmatic. But putting these accounts together does not unfortunately add up to a multi-dimensional model which could provide the basis for a general theory; it only amplifies their essentialism. Indeed it is when these statements strive to go beyond themselves to grasp the complexities of the phenomena to which they refer that they are most likely to resort to rhetorical devices. These often take the form of images and metaphors which are used to define racism by analogy.[27] For example in Statement A, the persistence of racism is compared to a stick of lettered rock. What does this image signify in this context? A principle of continuity which is 'inscribed' in such a way that it can only be established by breaking into it, but which nothing can interrupt or change! This is an example of an attempt to grapple with the issue of discontinuity from within a problematic which allows it no space. The resultant image, far from putting reductionism in question, turns racism into a perpetual seduction of the senses.

Just how difficult it is to move beyond this kind of thinking can be seen from Statement B. Here the principle of continuity is rooted directly in the process of generational transmission. Racism is likened to a poison which children take in, if not from their mother's breast, then at least from its mechanical substitutes. It is a dangerous substance which, once internalized, enters 'into the system' and attacks its defences. In many statements of this sort racism is likened to a contagious disease, which people catch off each other, or a cancer in the body politic, something which can only be stopped by either eliminating its carriers, or protecting others, especially children, from contact with its 'breeding grounds'. Short of such drastic screening processes the 'germs of racism' will go on spreading.

In Statement C a rather different metaphor is at work. Racism operates everywhere, working now openly, now secretly to stab black people in the back. This idea of a white conspiracy, between police, unemployed youth, employers, and the mass media relies on the assumption that equivalent effects in disparate contexts must be produced by the same omnipresent agency or cause. Such constructions are 'paralogical' in the sense that the conclusions do not strictly follow from the premises. In this case the image seems to be informed by a phantasy of some omnipotent power of destruction which 'penetrates everywhere', and is bent on 'fucking people up'. A rather similar phantasy informs the divide-and-rule thesis except that here it is the ruling class whose power is both all-pervasive, and works to sow the seeds of rivalry amongst those 'brothers and sisters' subjected to its tyrannical will.

The force of such metaphors is all the greater because of the unconscious effect which racist discourse itself exerts. For this is above all a discourse which ties a congenital link between origins and destinies, and which draws on images of birth and blood, the functions of the body and sexual reproduction, kinship and filiation, to do so.[28] It is not surprising that such symbolism should unconsciously echo or evoke those infantile structures of representation through which identities and differences are first negotiated and invested with a sense of mastery, or that these models should be reproduced in the way racism is itself conceptualized.[29] Of course these constructions are never just phantasies. The conspiracy theory of racism makes sense of a particular social reality: it is because the police force, which is supposed to uphold justice and protect ethnic minorities from racist attacks, is itself responsible for so much of the violence and injustice suffered by black communities that it is experienced as being part of the same oppressive system as the gang of white unemployed youth who are beating up people on the street. It is this kind of objective correspondence which makes it possible for the experience of racism to become connected to paranoid structures of feeling and phantasy which originate at a quite different and more unconscious level of representation.

In general, the more persecutory and overpowering the reality principles of racism, the more likely it is that they will be 'totalized' in this way. Logically such constructions should make ethnic minorities feel even more powerless than they actually are. But paradoxically, or rather, paralogically, they have the opposite effect. This is because they are embedded in what I have called a teleology of the oppressed. These metaphors are important rhetoric devices in narratives of empowerment and emancipation, where they are used to 'naturalize' particular victimologies, and even, sometimes, to justify the enterprise of revenge.

The issue is whether making the protean forms of racism seem more omnipotent, cohesive and enduring than they are does after all serve to strengthen and unify the antiracist movement, or whether it reinforces the more sectarian elements within it. On the positive side, I would argue that these devices may make it easier to withstand setbacks, to hold on to a belief in ultimate victory when times are hard, because they all underline the continuities of racial oppression. Indirectly this may also help legitimate an autonomous space of representation for ethnic minorities who have been otherwise silenced or marginalized, a place where they can find their own political voice, in their own mother tongue. But, on the other hand, this perspective produces global strategies which have little purchase on concrete instances, and tend to assume instead the burden of a messianic project in which the enemy is supposedly being smashed, crushed, or stamped out for ever. Pushed to the limit it leads to splitting the world into a racialized opposition between goodies and baddies. And once this kind of polarization is set in motion, it becomes a self-fulfilling prophecy in which everyone who is not with us is against us. If you're white, you're not part of the solution you're part of the problem . . .

It must be a matter of personal judgement, as well as political debate, as to whether the gains outweigh the losses when it comes to sustaining such a manichean, 'black and white' view of the world. In my view, in the longer term, and in the context of the more complicated state of contemporary race relations in Britain, the 'fix' or 'hold' or 'take' which this standpoint offers seems likely to prove disappointing. Even if the catechisms of 'correct thought' are updated and find new roots, and old up-beat endings are set to more popular and contemporary tunes, they will not be able to generate the more intricate models or maps which are required to confront successfully the types of racism which are evidenced by our two transcripts. But what kind of resources or strategies could be committed, both theoretically and practically to this task?

Notes in the margin

In what follows I am going to use a general procedure for reading texts to examine specific features of racist discourse to be found in 'Fighting talk' and 'The last laugh' and to suggest a series of questions which they raise as an agenda for further research and debate. To begin with we need to be aware of the extra-discursive realities which environ these statements. These reality principles may be alluded to, or they may be disavowed in various ways, but in either event they set limits and conditions to what is articulated about racism. First and foremost we have to consider the immediate social contexts in which the statements are made: in one case an intervention in a youth project on a council estate dominated by the particular group of boys being interviewed; in the second case a course run for police officers who had special responsibility for training cadets in the art of 'good community relations'. In both cases people who were directly or indirectly implicated in racial harassment were asked to reflect on their actions and attitudes by an outsider who did not share their views; moreover, as a researcher I was concerned to elicit evidence about racist assumptions or practices which as an educator I was also concerned to challenge. How did this relationship and the context in which it occurred 'overdetermine' these texts? How did it affect the way the story about the fight is told, for example, or the uses to which the unofficial communiqué was put?

We also need to look at the wider political conjuncture. The backdrop to 'Fighting talk' was the growing appeal of the National Front to sections of the white working class in inner city areas where youth unemployment was high. My actual intervention was linked to wider attempts to combat these influences by developing a new cultural politics of antiracism based around 'two tone music'.[30] In the second instance public criticism of the policing of the urban disorders and riots of 1981/82, coupled with mounting evidence of systematic discrimination against the black community, created a situation in which the practices of the 'copper on the beat' came under close scrutiny both from within the force itself and from various watchdog bodies.[31] Clearly these sets of circumstances influence the pragmatics of these statements, in ways that we have to unravel by close analysis.

Finally there are some deeper structural factors which constitute the hidden or unconscious premises of these types of racist discourse. Here, perhaps we need to frame 'Fighting talk' within a historical perspective, to consider the particular versions of ethnicity and body politics which developed within working-class cultures, as well as their complex articulation to dominant ideologies of race, nation and Empire. Similarly, to understand where the police are coming from we should look at the changing role which the institutions and practice of law have played in racializing the place occupied by immigrant populations within the urban social structure, as well as the internal contradictions of the apparatus of enforcement itself.[32]

To say that these factors of context, conjuncture and wider conditionality are 'extra-discursive' does not mean that discourses do not enter into their determination, only that they involve processes which cannot be reduced to this effect. By the same argument, the way such factors are constructed discursively does not always correspond to the role which they play in other, non-discursive, forms of racial discrimination. Sometimes the relationship may be direct but the reference deleted. The fact that several of the boys were active members of the National Front, for example, had an all too direct bearing on how they positioned themselves as narrators of the fight, even though they were anxious to characterize their role as merely voicing public opinion on the estate. Equally, the unofficial communiqué was undoubtedly part of a rank-and-file protest against pressures for reform generated by the Scarman Report, even if no mention is made of it!

Often the relation is more oblique. The eliciting context of 'Fighting talk' was one in which the boys may have been quite strongly motivated to impress the researcher by exaggerating the extremity of their views on race. Nevertheless they are constrained from deploying the usual wind-up techniques by their overriding concern to justify their actions and attitudes to someone who disapproved of them but whom they perceived to be in a position to influence their situation for better or worse. So we have a rehearsal of grievances centring on the injustices they feel they have suffered as a result of black immigration into the area. The element of playing to the gallery is conserved in the way they portray the fight as a piece of street theatre, with the adults cheering them on from the balconies, while the girls offer silent support, as the boys defend the honour of the white community against the 'black invasion'. In this way they achieve the desired effect of both showing off their street fighting skills and justifying their moral commitment to racism, while positioning me, alongside their parents and girl friends as admiring spectators of their 'protection racket'. Of course while they may be imagining that they are bending my ear and creating a good impression, they are also providing me with the kind of evidence I am looking for about the gendered and generational aspects of this kind of racism. But would the story have been told in quite the same way if I had been black, or a woman, or nearer their own age and social background? Indeed would it have been told at all?

Such questions point up the importance of recognizing how the reality principles of power are reworked 'intra-discursively'. Consider the boys' version of the 'numbers game' at the beginning of 'Fighting talk': 'and the other lot come down the next night, and the night after that and the night after that, all week, about 40, 50, from all over . . .' The use of reiteration coupled with vocal register (increased pitch and speed of delivery) served to convey a dramatic atmosphere of mounting racial conflict in which excitement is tinged with anxiety (defused here by the joke about 'black city'). This structure of feeling is produced by a particular rhetorical device, providing an image which resonates with an unstated discourse about 'waves of black immigration swamping the British way of life' – a theme which Thatcherism was in the process of popularizing at the time. Note how blacks are invested with vastly exaggerated powers of social combination whilst the ethnic majority are reduced to minority status – 'just our lot from the estate'. In this way the real principles of powerlessness which govern these boys' lives are both doubled over and displaced by the sense of being overpowered or outnumbered by a group which in political and demographic terms are in an even weaker position than they are.

A rather different reworking is to be found in 'The last laugh'. Its rhetorical effectiveness comes from the way the language of official communiqués issued by the command structure to other ranks is deliberately parodied. The impersonality of this discourse of power is here used to signify an unfeeling bureaucracy out of touch with the realities of policing a riot – 'Officers who are unfortunately set alight should lie down patiently and wait their turn to be put out.' This regulatory code is put to even greater effect when it is used to turn an exchange of missiles between rioters and police into a surreal game of football in which the rules have been deliberately bent to give the 'opposing team' an unfair advantage!

All texts contain elements of metacommunication – devices which refer the recipient to a preferred reading of the relational contexts in which the statements are being made. 'Fighting talk' stakes its claim to credibility through the narrative conventions of autobiographical realism; the continual citation of 'first hand' experience conveys an implicit message that it is their encounter with black people which has led these boys to adopt racist arguments and not any external ideological influence. In fact the function of such eye- and ear-witness accounts as the 'Kentucky fried chips' incident is to authorize and authenticate the racialization of experience by making it seem like an entirely spontaneous and natural process, and one for which blacks themselves must be held responsible.

In 'The last laugh' a quite different strategy of citation is adopted, one which consciously aims to draw the reader's attention to the problematic status of the text. For all its underground samizdat quality, this document is designed to be discovered in order to draw the attention of the police authorities to the strength of rank-and-file feeling. So here the use of quasi-official language to make a series of provocatively racist statements serves to undermine the credibility of the authorized version of 'community relations' by contrasting its unrealistic viewpoint with the putative realities of 'the job'. As an example of this consider the use made of multiculturalism ('briefing about local customs and traditions') and quasi-sociological jargon ('it is statistically proven . . .') to comment ironically about the kind of theories they have encountered during their training in community relations. Citation is here an act of revenge against what is seen as a liberal apologetics for black crime.[33]

Other sources of quotation may be more disguised or unconscious. For example there are echoes of colonial discourse in the way the boys make a distinction between the 'good blacks' (who accept the verdict of the first, lost fight) and the 'bad blacks' who cry foul and fight back, trying to reverse the verdict of a society which has made them permanent losers. And it is there in the way the police communiqué constructs its surreal anthropology of Brixton and the 'alien black presence'. Yet the picture that all this conjures up of a thin red, white and blue line defending civilization and the British sense of 'fair play' against serried ranks of black barbarians is suddenly counterpointed by an even more arresting image – that of the police themselves who are frightening the local inhabitants of Brixton by whooping like red indians, and beating on their shields like Zulu warriors. Why do the police characterize themselves as 'behaving like savages' in this way? Is it a consciously ironic reversal of the negative stereotype of blacks? Or a distanced comment on the fact that this is how a lot of people actually see them? Does it even speak from some recognition, however disavowed, that police practices transgress the 'rules of civilized conduct' which they are supposed to be upholding, and nowhere more obviously than in their treatment of black people? In this context what is the significance of the ironic statement prohibiting 'blacking up' given its double connotation as a practice of camouflage used in night-time military manœuvres, and as a means for white entertainers to impersonate blacks?

Between the lines

To stop our enquiry at this point would be to bracket out those elements which I suggested earlier constitute the deep structures of these texts. To understand the cultures of racism from which these texts are produced we need to moved from a formal or semiotic level of analysis to a consideration of more substantive issues. I start from an apparent paradox. Here we have a gang of unemployed white boys who imagine themselves to be some kind of local ruling class, and who feel outraged that this omnipotent position is being usurped by groups of black youth who are even more disadvantaged than they are. And there is a group of policemen, empowered by the State with all the prerogatives of coercion, who imagine themselves to be a beleaguered and oppressed minority victimized by an all-powerful conspiracy between the white liberal establishment and the black community. The racist imagination turns the world upside down, but it does so through a conservative appropriation of existing structures and discourses of power. The white boys impute an imaginary position of advantage to blacks, which allows them not only to deny the actual conditions of black oppression, but to claim them as their own, in order to justify exclusionary practices which keep blacks 'one down' and themselves 'one up'. The police, who routinely bend the rules in black areas, portray the youth of Brixton as doing the same, acting as if they were 'above the law' because of special measures designed to protect them from the consequences of their illegal actions – a fairly apt description of the police's own position until very recently.

This kind of 'trading places' certainly has played its part in fuelling the dynamics of racial envy. The white boys admire the cheek of the black lad who nicks their Kentucky'n'chips, as well as wanting to beat him up for it, just as many of them secretly envy and try to emulate the black street style which at another level they experience as so invasive. Similarly, police outrage at 'blacks getting away with murder' is often tinged with grudging respect for the way they flout authority. But envy is an ambivalent structure of feeling; it involves the desire to possess certain idealized attributes of the Other *and* the desire to destroy them because they signify what is felt to be lacking. The racism of relative deprivation, with its constant refrain 'the blacks are taking *our* jobs, houses, women and now *our* exams' plays upon this sense of 'getting our own back'.

The central paradox of this kind of 'trading places' is that through the very symmetry of its inversions it postulates imaginary correspondences between black and white positions even as it seeks to naturalize difference and domination. Is this because the construction of racialized identities depends on the existence of the Other, while at the same time it is this 'alien presence' which is seen to be such a threat to identity that its total annihilation is required? Are racial double standards (viz., good/bad natives) and double binds (damned if you are different and damned if you are like the master race) a function of this contradictory or dual relation to the Other? Or do we have to look to more concrete and historically specific forms of mediation to explain the racialization of envy and desire?

In this context, it is perhaps worth noting that the body politic oscillates between two contradictory modes of address towards the civil population. There are those who are hailed as the backbone of 'the nation', and who are often idealized as the defenders of 'ancient liberties and laws' associated with the 'free-born Englishman'; and there are those who are denigrated as a 'race' apart, the 'enemy within', the 'Other England'. This device has served to draw a moral dividing line between the 'respectable' and 'rough' elements of the working class, as well as between indigenous and immigrant populations. Moreover, it has been reworked within the cultural forms and practices of a whole variety of subaltern groups.[34]

Both indigenous and immigrant working classes have at various times staked claims to be considered the true backbone of 'the nation' (as against a decadent aristocracy or unpatriotic bourgeoisie for example) through various institutions of public propriety (churches, labour organizations, community associations) which at the same time defend the integrity of their own traditions against negative influences in the wider society. By definition this is largely an enterprise of elders and women who are charged with transmitting these traditions to a new generation. But there are also groups within these communities which have taken the other route, and adopted the position of a 'race apart', investing it with a positive image as a means of asserting the distinctiveness of their own culture and its powers of resistance to the dominant society. This has been largely an enterprise of male youth, asserting their own 'body politics' of the street through rules and rituals of territoriality. In these contrasting ways imagined communities of ethnicity and neighbourhood have been sustained, giving these groups a sense of pride in both their historical origins and their present place. But this has also ensured that when these structures become racialized, elders and women become mobilized around the defence of public proprieties while male youth become locked in struggles for territorial dominance. Indigenous working-class cultures of racism have thus been internally fragmented by strong sexual and generational divisions, as well as being externally mirrored in the forms of resistance mobilized by immigrant communities against them.

The police have played a key role in the development of this configuration. The maintenance of legal definitions of public order, based on a principle of 'free circulation', inevitably brings them up against the annexation of the street by male youth culture. In practice it proved logistically impossible to observe the strict letter of the law or to completely suppress these cultures. Instead, in many localities informal norms of public order were negotiated which recognized popular sovereignties of place, in return for co-operation from 'responsible' internal agencies of social control. There is an example of this in 'Fighting talk' where the police are recorded as using the white boys' own rules of territoriality as a device to keep them apart from blacks ('if you're on your own territory we'll nick the others, but if you're outside, we'll nick you'). The boys are furious when the police break their own rules by arresting them for public order offences while they are fighting on their home ground. This puts the Law literally and metaphorically on the side of the blacks, who are also deemed 'out of order' for having broken the rules of a fair fight. And this in turn mobilizes the forces of public propriety in the shape of community elders who want to 'clean up the estate' and who willingly sign the petition to keep it as white as possible.

The irony in the situation is that the real double standard involved in policing the area is not applied to white youth, but to their black counterparts. For until very recently the police made no concession to black street culture, but instead rigidly interpreted and ruthlessly enforced statutory norms of public order, first through the notorious 'Sus' law (abolished after a long campaign by black and civil liberties groups) and then through routine powers of search and arrest. Moreover, it is through such means that the discretionary powers and prerogatives of the copper on the beat come to be exercised. The practices associated with harassment are so jealously guarded, not just because they articulate a culture of institutionalized racism within the force, but because they form part of a system 'workers' control' against the encroachment of line management. The fact that the police are positioned as at once the backbone of the State and a pariah within civil society in a way that is similar, though not identical, to that of the working class adds a further twist to the tale.

The racialization of place, the construction of a political geography in which certain areas like Brixton and White City are coded in terms which mark them out as 'front lines' of racial confrontation (inner city/urban jungle/ghetto) is thus the outcome of complex antagonisms within and between the police force and working-class communities, and is reinforced from both sides. It is complimented by a racialization of time, the construction of a 'golden age' before the blacks/Jews/Irish came. In 'Fighting talk' the two are tied together in the nostalgic account of an idyllic childhood landscape, all large back gardens and open public spaces, where you could mooch about for as long as you wanted. This daydream of a space and time of unbounded freedom is rudely interrupted by the advent of the forces of the State (in the form of the municipal bulldozer) and the Asian shopocracy (as property owners). This unholy alliance is not only supposed to have destroyed the traditional amenities of working-class community life, but to have robbed these boys of their childhood patrimony as well!

It is hard to see anything like the controlling hand of a single dominant ideology in all this, given the complex shifts of power and positioning which are in play in these constructions. If there is a common underlying theme or thread it would seem to be the unstated assumption that 'anyone can make it if they try, and if they conform to the rules'; those who fail must suffer from some congenital lack of capacities, or be of an alien disposition. This would seem to invite an invidious comparison between white youth who are unemployed and their more successful black peers. But this is avoided through the assertion that blacks are being given an unfair advantage by the hidden helping hand of the race relations industry. Thus black achievement has nothing to do with their struggles and the white boys' failure is dissociated from any implication of personal inadequacy. For their own very different purposes the police adopt elements of this working-class position in their battle against their superiors. In both cases we seem to be dealing with a *subordinated racism* which becomes 'common sense' as a result of its articulation through a *dominant but non-racist ideology* of competitive individualism – a situation which is the exact opposite of what is normally argued!

The question of individualism raises the issue of whether we are dealing with a 'new racism' or merely an updated version of the old 'race and empire' story. There certainly are continuities in the way black people are characterized. I have tried to indicate some of them, and no doubt other readers of these texts will find others. I believe that the major discontinuity lies in the discursive forms through which positions of racial superiority are constructed. Instead of self-confident assertions whose utterance actually enacts the superiority that is claimed, and which make it possible to identify with 'the master race', as being and having everything that the subject races lack, we have discourses which resort to all manner of rhetorical devices to construct a narrative of special pleading marked by highly ambiguous and ironic self-reference and a litany of real or imagined grievance. This is a racist discourse profoundly marked by the fractures of identity which produced it, and consequently one whose internal contradictions are both more explicitly articulated and more strongly disavowed. For example, it has become more difficult than ever to reconcile the proprietary brand of 'backbone of the nation' style racism, with the aggressive body politics of the 'territorial armies' who march under the banner of Millwall or Manchester United. The last-night-of-the-prommers may wave the same flag as England's World Cup supporters but they do not, at the end of the day, dance to the same tunes.

This seems to me to be a real cause for celebration. The popular culture of racism is neither so unified, nor the positions within it so fixed as is sometimes supposed. Not every aspect of 'Fighting talk' is racialized. There is the comment which allows a black perspective to momentarily emerge ('Blacks reckon the opposite; they reckon the police are picking on them'). Some members of the group were avid supporters of reggae – they loved the music even while they hated the people who made it. And there were elements of their life history which remained open to non-racist articulation. These are all points of possible engagement for antiracist work. Even police culture is not monolithic. The officer who handed us the unofficial communiqué was risking his neck by taking a public stance against racism amongst his colleagues. 'Grassing up your mates' and co-operating with the 'enemy within' (antiracists, liberals, etc.) are both capital crimes in this rank-and-file code, yet he had enough moral courage and support to bring this material out into the open for discussion.

This finally leads us into a series of other more practical questions. Should the youth workers have tried to integrate these boys into 'the community', or to isolate them from it? Would it have been a good tactic to try and exploit adult hostility towards this group on account of their delinquent activities, rather than highlight their racist involvements which clearly did have a measure of adult support? Would such a move have made it easier or more difficult to confront the local police about their failure to protect the black community from racial attack? In the longer term, is there a risk that in focusing attention on such 'hard core' racist groups there is a danger of making them seem glamorous? Is it more productive to concentrate on doing antiracist work with parents and younger children, to try to minimize the influences exerted by such gangs as role models for the next generation? Or is this a counsel of despair which makes the culture of racism seem more entrenched and unchangeable than it really is?

As regards the police, should the publication of racist statements like the unofficial communiqué be made a disciplinary offence, or would this merely strengthen rank-and-file resistance to the implementation of antiracist policies within the force? Would it be more useful to devise training regimes in which such attitudes could be systematically confronted? What kind of changes in police structure and ideology would be necessary before such regimes could influence actual police behaviour towards black people on the street?

Even if there never will be any easy answers to such questions, and certainly not ones which could be read off from some kind of 'correct analysis', it is still the case that the better informed we are about the complexities which underlie them the quicker we will be able to learn from our mistakes.[35]

Relative autonomy rules

I have outlined one possible approach to reading discourses, whether racist or antiracist, which suggests that what is going on in and between them may be more complex and contradictory than is often allowed. To regard them as an example of a clear-cut binary opposition between good and evil, or rationality and irrationality fails to engage with the kinds of investments which they actually entail. I have examined these 'other scenes' of theoretical and political ideology in detail elsewhere.[35] Here I just want to concentrate on what may be required if we are to shift to a different mode of argumentation. What needs to be changed in the 'etiquettes' of antiracism to create the conditions for a more productive debate?

There are a number of unwritten rules or axioms which perhaps need to be questioned. The first and most restrictive of these might be called the 'totalization' rule. According to this any theoretical statement, or political initiative, is supposed to tackle racism as a whole, all at once, and once and for all. If it fails to do so it is condemned as being 'reformist', or 'liberal' or even 'racist'. I suggest that we substitute for this what might be called a 'relative autonomy' rule. Just as different sites or forms of racism have their own conditions of existence and articulation, so they require specific modes of analysis and intervention, each of which has its own criteria of efficacy. This rule may help to keep clear the distinction between those interventions which seek to challenge the structural conditions under which racist discourses are directly or indirectly reproduced, and those strategies which aim to interrupt their circulation in specific micro-contexts, and/or introduce alternative story lines. Both are necessary but they require radically different forms of organization and styles of action. Success at the level of macro-institutional policies does not automatically produce a knock-on effect at the level of everyday social interaction, and local 'grass roots' initiatives do not necessarily yield models which are applicable to strategies of structural transformation. This is no reason to rubbish what is achievable by these different means. Ironically, one reason why so many antiracist initiatives have failed is because they have assumed some kind of transitive relation between policy and practice. But as anyone who has sat on an equal opportunities working party will tell you, it is one thing to formulate policies and quite another to implement them. And partly this is because the closer you get to concrete 'race relations' the less likely they are to conform to the models which have informed policy making.[36]

A second problem is the way ethnic credentialism has been used to canonize certain texts, or underwrite certain schools of thought as possessing the authentic or correct perspective on racism. The unwritten rule of this knowledge/power game is that one set of rather benign standards are applied to texts produced by 'ethnic' writers (black, Jewish, Irish etc.) and other far more critical ones to work produced by those who lack such 'authorizations'. The exploitation of ethnicity may perhaps work as a form of primitive accumulation of cultural capital, but it does nothing to enlarge the audience or scope of such work, which is why most artists and writers of any stature have rejected this appellation, even if they have benefited indirectly from it. The attempt to insist that a particular intellectual tradition or body of work possesses a monopoly of the truth about racism because it 'objectively corresponds' to the experience of those subjected to it, is part of the same game.[37]

Against all this I would propose a rule of limited self-reference. Any work or practice should first of all be judged on its own merits independently of the ethnic origins, affiliations or status of its author. Such judgements should be based on criteria which are directly and internally related to the form as well as the content of the text. It is quite appropriate to apply political criteria to a political statement such as a manifesto, or policy document. It is not appropriate to judge a novel or film, a work of art or philosophy in political terms if the work in question does not take that form (i.e., does not organize itself in terms of political discourse). Applying purely literary, cinematic, aesthetic or philosophical criteria to such work does not mean that it cannot be located in terms to which value judgements may be attached. It is certainly possible to identify the features of a racist aesthetic or an antiracist philosophical practice, for example, and to assess the contribution which a particular work makes to their development.[38]

A corollary of this· rule, and a condition of its operation, is the establishment of a proper intellectual division of labour, one which is no longer based on the rival claims of totalizing theories or disciplines. For example, historical materialism may have a lot to tell us about the political economy of immigrant labour and the unequal exchange between metropolitan capitalism and the third world, but it has proved quite incapable of grasping the micro-foundations of racist ideologies. Equally, psychoanalysis is proving an indispensable method for investigating the deeper reaches of the racist imagination, but produces the most absurdly reductionist theories when it tries to apply its concepts to explaining the rise of fascism or the nation-state.[39] Respect for the relative autonomy of these levels, and of the different modes of enquiry appropriate to them is a *sine qua non* of developing anti-reductive perspectives.

A further difficulty has arisen concerning the priority which has been given to judicial or quasi-judicial measures in the attempt to suppress racist discourses. Although it is certainly necessary to protect ethnic minorities from verbal attack, and to signal society's disapproval of all forms of racial abuse, it does not follow that criminalization is always the best method of doing this. Not only does it risk making heroes and martyrs out of the perpetrators, but in practice it has led to a damaging split between reactive strategies, which are aimed at highly specific target groups, and proactive· approaches which rely on nebulous generalities, viz., 'creating the right ethos'. More seriously, forms of discipline and surveillance may be developed to police – and hopefully deter – discriminatory behaviour in public settings, whilst the informal cultures of racism which actually sustain these practices are relegated to an untouchable realm of 'private attitude'. When attempts are then made to intervene at this latter level, they often use the same procedures as are applied to the public realm. This is what occurred with racism awareness training (RAT). RAT may have succeeded in driving the culture of racism underground, but enforced privatization did not always silence; in many cases it resulted in more secretly coded forms of expression, which actually strengthened popular resistance to antiracism.[40]

The excessive reliance on punitive powers and sanctions to interdict racist ideologies in this external way is a characteristic of the harsh 'super egoism' associated with doctrinaire antiracism. Instead I would suggest a rule of proportional response. If people are using racist language to actively intimidate members of ethnic minorities it is appropriate to use whatever sanctions may be necessary to stop them from doing so. When racist jokes, stories and images are used as a device of social closure, to culturally exclude ethnic minorities, then they should be tackled by specific educational means coupled with measures to counter their exclusionary effect.[41]

The ground rules I have proposed for antiracist work are not enforceable. They are not even prescriptive. They explicitly rule out any attempt to impose a single correct line or approach. By definition they can only work if they are voluntarily agreed upon within a framework of democratic discussion. They address the need to develop an antiracism without the comforts of immutable definitions and impermeable boundaries, or the moral certitudes which go with them. But in advocating a new pluralism of effort I am not suggesting we adopt an aimless relativism where 'anything goes'. On the contrary, the demands which are now made on intellectual and political commitment are if anything more stringent. It requires us to recognize, for example, that the issue of race is not only a minefield of vested interests, but a site where powerful structures of feeling – anger, hatred, pain and envy – are inevitably in play, and subject to strategies of sublimation or disavowal. We have to continually interrogate our theories and practices in the light of that 'hidden agenda'. Yet if we know how to read between the lines, if we become as sensitive to the silences and ambiguities of discourse as we already are to its more vociferous and oppressive forms then perhaps we may be better placed to exploit contradictions of racism. That, it seems to me is not a counsel of despair, but a principle of hope.

Notes

1 A shortened version of this article was presented to a British Sociological Association seminar on 'New Perspectives on Racism' in June 1991. I am grateful to John Solomos, Stuart Hall and other members of the seminar for their useful comments and criticisms. The text underwent intensive treatment at the James Donald Clinic for Psychosemantic Disorders. If the cure has not been complete, this should be attributed solely to the resistance of the author. Many of the ideas developed here were first discussed with Ali Rattansi, for whose encouragement and support I am especially grateful. The first transcript was produced in collaboration with Dave Robins as part of a project funded by the Leverhulme Trust. The second text was produced in the context of a course run with Tuku Mukherjee. None of the above should be held responsible for any of the views expressed here.

2 The notion of a 'new racism' based on a discourse of cultural difference (or ethnicism) rather than on biological characteristics was first argued by Barker (1981). Reeves (1983) considers the shift to a more secretly coded idiom to be a feature of 'new racism'. There is some historical research to suggest that neither the use of cultural signifiers nor of indirect expressions is new, but occurs in particular discursive conjunctures. The influence of Thatcherism and the New Right is discussed in Gordon and Klug (1990) and the contribution to Deakin *et al.* (1986). The question of whether we are entering a period in which distinctively 'post modern' forms of racist discourse prevail is discussed briefly later in this article and at greater length in Cohen (1991).

3 For a recent survey of theories and debates around the concept of ideology see Eagleton (1991). An interesting attempt to distinguish between different ideology types can be found in Therborn (1987). A good summary of these debates in relation to race can be found in Miles (1990). On the theory of ideological articulation see Laclau (1977).

4 The notion of theoretical ideology, as distinct from socio-practical ideology, was first proposed by Althusser (1971). The particular usage of the term proposed here owes something to the formulations in Lyotard (1986), in focusing on the knowledge/power games played by intelligentsias.

5 For a general introduction to the debate about teleological explanations see Wright (1976). For a discussion of the philosophical doctrines associated with this idea see Nagel (1979). On the application of this model within the human sciences, and especially psychology, see Bodem (1978). On the link between teleological and utopian thought see Mannheim (1991).

6 The terms *synchronic* and *diachronic* derive from linguistics; the first is used to denote the system of binary oppositions which characterize a linguistic structure and the second refers to the rules governing the succession of its instances in an utterance. The same distinction has been applied to the analysis of cultural forms. For example, a cuisine could be identified in terms of its synchronic order of tastes (sweet/savoury; bland/spiced) and the sequential order in which these tastes are presented in the course of a meal. Theories can similarly be identified in terms of which order they privilege in explaining social phenomena. Functionalist theories, which assign meaning and purpose to any element in terms of the role which it is held to play in maintaining the system of which it is a part, necessarily privilege the synchronic. Historicism, which ascribes meaning and purpose to an element by virtue of the logic of its development focuses on the diachronic.

7 For an elegant exposition of the Whig interpretation of race relations history see Mason (1962). For a critique of humanistic perspectives on racism see Balibar and Wallerstein (1989) and Cohen (1991). A trenchant critique of rationalistic approaches is made by Goldberg (1990); some of the implications of this critique for antiracist education are explored in Cohen (1991). For a more general analysis of the Enlightenment tradition see Porter and Rousseau (1990) and Hulme and Jordanova (1990).

8 On teleological narratives of black oppression see Taylor (1989) and Davis and Gates (1985). On Jewish examples see Eisen (1983) and Neusner (1984).

9 The concept of double bind was originally produced by Bateson (1972) in the context of his research into schizophrenic patterns of family communication. It was further elaborated as part of a more general theory of the pragmatics of human communication by Watzlawick, Beavan and Jackson (1967). Rosolato (1978) has reworked the concept within a psychoanalytic framework heavily influenced by the work of Klein and Lacan. The relevance of the double bind concept for post-modernist accounts of identity is suggested by the work of Billig (1982 and 1991).

10 The role of religious ideologies and especially Christianity in giving a special redemptive value to experiences of political oppression or economic exploitation was of course strongly emphasized – and condemned – by Marx. The more positive role which these ideologies play in sustaining utopias of liberation is explored by Bloch (1986). For a more

sociological discussion of this phenomenon see Berger (1979). On its specific application to popular theories of racism see Neusner (1984).

11 On patriarchal ideologies of the text and their relation to forms of political power see Hampton (1990). For a general introduction to discourse analysis see Fairclough (1989).

12 For a general discussion of different models of reductive explanation, which has influenced much of what follows, see the article by Levine *et al.* (1987).

13 For an account of institutionalized racism from a radical holist position see Troyna and Williams (1986).

14 For a critique of methodological individualism see Levine *et al.* (1987). For a defence of this position see Elster (1985).

15 For a critique of 'global particularism' and its role in promoting ethnocentric perspectives on racism see Rodinson (1983).

16 The formula 'power plus prejudice equals racism' was used as a kind of catechism in the early days of antiracism, and was for example enshrined in ILEA's famous policy statement in the early 1980s.

17 For a critical discussion of the dominant ideology thesis, albeit one which rather throws the baby out with the bathwater, see Abercrombie *et al.* (1980).

18 On working-class racism in post-war Britain see Miles (1979) and Phizacklea (1980). For a wider historical perspective see 'The perversion of inheritance' in Bains and Cohen (1988).

19 The concept of necessary false consciousness was originally formulated in Lukács (1971). An attempt to develop and apply this concept to an understanding of racism can be found in Gabel (1975). Gabel's work dissolves Lukács' structural analysis of the phenomenology of class relations into a humanistic psychology of alienation.

20 Deficit or pathological models of working-class culture developed around the problematic of multiple deprivation in the early 1960s. The effect was to attribute lack of social mobility on the part of the unskilled working class to their lifestyle, rather than to the structural factors which had produced it. Deficit models were associated with various attempts at compensatory education aimed at integrating this stratum within a framework of petit bourgeois aspiration. Although by the late 1960s this model had become largely discredited as far as the white working class were concerned, it gained a new lease of life in the field of race relations. For a good critique of these developments see Gilman (1985) and Centre for Contemporary Cultural Studies (1982).

21 For the social psychology of prejudice see the classic study by Bagley and Verma (1979) and for a more recent overview of this perspective see Bethlehem (1988).

22 For a classic statement of a left antiracist position based on the divide-and-rule thesis see Edgar (1977). His position is today mainly associated with the propaganda recruitment campaigns of far left groups who seek to increase their influence amongst ethnic minority and immigrant communities.

23 For a general statement of the rational choice theory of racism see Hechter, 'Rational choice theory' in Rex and Mason (1986).

24 On rational choice theories within Marxism see Roemer (1982), Elster (1985) and Levine *et al.* (1987).

25 For a discussion of holistic approaches to multiculturalism see Foster (1990).

26 Rodinson's critique of Zionist and Muslim fundamentalism (1983) demonstrates the exclusionary tendencies supported by essentialized readings of history.

27 On the use of metaphorical and analogical thinking in ideological constructions of the Other see Zizek (1989).

28 Sibony (1978) has pioneered a micro-foundational theory of racist ideology in terms of its specific structures of unconscious representation. Unlike other psychoanalytic theories which reduce racist ideology to mechanisms of the individual psyche, Sibony has isolated an elementary structure of phantasy, ritual and myth which operates at the level of collective representations. Elsewhere I have tried to develop this approach in analysing the popular culture of racism (Bains and Cohen, 1988; Cohen, 1991).

29 For a general discussion of the role which the unconscious plays in the formation of ideology see the work of Zizek (1989).

30 On this conjuncture see Gilroy and Lawrence in Bains and Cohen (1988).

31 On the 'Swamp 81' operation in Brixton see Scarman (1981). Criticism of the policing of black communities came from many quarters and perspectives. See for example Bishton (1978), Benyon (1986) and Institute of Race Relations (1987).

32 The historical analysis of popular cultures of racism is only just beginning. For the mid to late Victorian period see Samuel (1981), Lorimer (1978), Humphries (1981) and the contributions to Duane and MacKenzie (1986). On the history of policing see Steedman (1984) and Cohen, 'Policing the working-class city' in Young (1981).

33 For a study of police culture see Young (1991) and for a more general analysis of policy strategy see Keith and Murji (1989).

34 For a more detailed presentation of this argument see Bains and Cohen (1988).

35 Some recent attempts to construct anti-reductive theories of racist ideology which foreground its multiple dimensions of articulation include Gilroy in Bains and Cohen (1988), Fields (1990), Balibar and Wallerstein (1989) and Goldberg (1990).

36 It is perhaps indicative of the lack of grounded social research in this field that the two most important studies of concrete situations should have been the product of judicial or quasi-judicial enquiries. Both the Scarman Report (1981) and the findings of the Burnage Inquiry (1989), despite their very different orientations and purposes, expose complexities which have been glossed over in most antiracist analyses.

37 On the uses of ethnicity see the contributions to Sollors (1989) and Anthias and Yuval-Davis (1992). On the construction of new ethnicities in Britain see the article by Hall in this book (1992). On its wider European dimension see the contributions to Liebkind (1989).

38 Recent essays in reconstructing a diaspora aesthetic which are not beholden to the kind of fundamentalist positions on race criticized here can be found in work of writers such as Toni Morrison, *Beloved* (1987) and Charles Johnson, *Middle Passage* (1991) on the black experience of slavery; Salman Rushdie's *Satanic Verses* (1988) and *Imaginary Homelands* (1991) and Hanif Kureishi's *My Beautiful Laundrette* (1986) on the post-colonial condition. The work of Primo Levi has performed a similar service for the Jewish community in deconstructing moralistic accounts of the Holocaust, for example in *If This is a Man* (1987) and *The Drowned and the Saved* (1988).

39 There have been many attempts to use psychoanalytic concepts to explore the subjective conditions or effect of structures of power and exploitation analysed in Marxist political economy; for example Wilhelm Reich on German fascism (1975), Frantz Fanon on French colonialism (1986) and Joel Kovel on racism in the USA (1987). None of this work has been entirely successful in so far as it seeks to establish principles of correspondence between the two sets of concepts (or the realities they denote) without introducing any mediating devices. The result is often to combine two complementary forms of reductionism in a single analysis. I would argue that the problem of mediations has not been so much solved by Foucault and the poststructuralists, as is often claimed, but put in abeyance.

40 For a good critique of racism awareness training see Sivanandan (1985).

41 On racism and sexism in playground cultures see MacDonald *et al.* (1989), Kelly and Cohn (1988) and Cohen and Haddock (1992).

References

Abercrombie, N. *et al. The Dominant Ideology Thesis*, London, Allen and Unwin.

Althusser, L. (1971) *Lenin and Philosophy*, London, Verso.

Anthias, F. and Yuval-Davis, N. (1992) *Racialized Boundaries*, London, Routledge.

Bagley, C. and Verma, V. (1979) *Racial Prejudice*, London, Routledge.

Bains, H. and Cohen, P. (1988) *Multiracist Britain*, Basingstoke, Macmillan.

Balibar, E. and Wallerstein, E. (1989) *Race, Nation, Classe*, Paris, Grasset.

Barker, M. (1981) *The New Racism*, Manchester, Manchester University Press.

Bateson, G. (1972) *Steps to an Ecology of Mind*, London, Paladin.

Benyon, J. (1986) *A Tale of Failure: race and policing*, Coventry, Centre for Ethnic Relations.

Berger, P. (1979) *Facing Up to Modernity*, Harmondsworth, Penguin.

Bethlehem, C. (1988) *A Social Psychology of Prejudice*, London, Croom Helm.

Billig, M. (1982) *Ideology and Social Psychology*, Oxford, Blackwell.

Billig, M. (1991) *Ideological Opinion: studies in rhetorical psychology*, London, Sage.

Bishton, D. (1978) *Talking Blues*, Birmingham, AFFOR

Bloch, E. (1986) *The Principle of Hope*, Oxford, Blackwell.

Bodem, M. (1978) *Purposive Explanation in Psychology*, Hassocks, Harvester.

Centre for Contemporary Cultural Studies (1982) *The Empire Strikes Back*, London, Hutchinson.

Cohen, P. (1991) *Monstrous Images, Perverse Reasons*, University of London Institute of Education, Centre for Multicultural Education.

Cohen, P. and Haddock, L. (1992) *The Schooling of Little Englanders*, London, Routledge.

Davis, C. T. and Gates H. L. (1985) *The Slave's Narrative*, Oxford, Oxford University Press.

Deakin, N. *et al.* (1986) *The New Right: image and reality*, London, Runnymede.

Duane, P. and Mackenzie, J. (eds) (1986) *Imperialism and Popular Culture*, Manchester, Manchester University Press.

Eagleton, T. (1991) *Ideology*, London, Verso.

Edgar, D. (1977) 'Racism, fascism, and the National Front', *Race and Class*, **19**(2).

Eisen, A. (1983) *The Chosen People in America*, Bloomington, Indiana University Press.

Elster, D. (1985) *Making Sense of Marx*, Cambridge, Cambridge University Press.

Fairclough, N. (1989) *Language and Power*, Harlow, Longman.

Fanon, F. (1986) *Black Skins, White Masks*, London, Pluto.

Fields, B. (1990) 'Racism in America', *New Left Review*, **181**.

Foster, P. (1990) *Policy and Practice in Multicultural and Antiracist Education*, London, Routledge.

Gabel, F. (1975) *False Consciousness*, Oxford, Blackwell.

Gilman, S. (1985) *Difference and Pathology*, Ithaca, Cornell University Press.

Goldberg, D. (1990) 'Racism and irrationality', *Philosophy of Science*, 20(3).

Gordon, P. and Klug, F. (1990) *New Right, New Racism*, London, Searchlight.

Gorz, A. (1982) *Farewell to the Working Class*, London, Pluto.

Gramsci, A. (1971) *The Prison Notebooks*, London, Merlin.

Hall, S. (1992) 'New ethnicities' in this volume.

Hall, S. and Jacques, M. (eds) (1991) *New Times*, London, Verso.

Hampton, C. (1990) *Ideology of the Text*, Milton Keynes, Open University Press.

Hebdige, D. (1987) *Cut n Mix*, London, Comedia.

Hewitt, R. (1988) *White Talk, Black Talk*, Cambridge, Cambridge University Press.

Hulme, P. and Jordanova, L. (1990) *The Enlightenment and its Shadow*, London, Routledge.

Humphries, S. (1981) *Hooligans or Rebels*, Oxford, Oxford University Press.

Institute of Race Relations, (1987) *Policing against Black People*, London, IRR.

Johnson, C. (1991) *Middle Passage*, London, Picador.

Jones, S. (1987) *Black Culture, White Youth*, Basingstoke, Macmillan.

Keith, M. and Murji, K. (1989) *Reifying Crime, Legitimating Racism*, Basingstoke, Macmillan.

Kelly, E. and Cohn, T. (1988) *Racism in Schools*, Stoke on Trent, Trentham Books.

Kovel, J. (1987) *White Racism: a psychohistory*, London, Free Association Books.

Kureishi, H. (1986) *My Beautiful Laundrette*, London, Faber.

Laclau (1977) *Politics and Ideology in Marxist Theory*, London, Verso.

Levi, P. (1987) *If This is a Man*, London, Abacus.

Levi, P. (1988) *The Drowned and the Saved*, London, Abacus.

Levine, A., Sober, E. and Wright, E. (1987) 'Marxism and methodological individualism', *New Left Review*, **162**.

Liebkind, K. (1989) *New Identities in Europe: immigrant ancestry and the ethnic identity*, Aldershot, Gower.

Lorimer, D. (1978) *Class, Colour and the Victorians*, Leicester, Leicester University Press.

Lukács, G. (1971) *History and Class Consciousness*, London, Merlin.

Lyotard, J.-F. (1986) *The Post Modern Condition*, Manchester, Manchester University Press.

Mac an Ghaill, M. (1988) *Young, Gifted and Black*, Milton Keynes, Open University Press.

MacDonald, I. *et al.* (1989) *Murder in the Playground*, London, Longsight Press.

Mannheim, K. (1991) *Ideology and Utopia*, London, Routledge.

Mason, P. (1962) *Prospero's Magic*, Oxford, Oxford University Press.

Miles, R. (ed.) (1979) *Racism and Political Action*, London, Routledge.

Miles, R. (1990) *Racism*, London, Routledge.

Morrison, T. (1989) *Beloved*, London, Chatto and Windus.

Murray, R. (1989) *Life after Ford*, Cambridge, Polity.

Nagel, E. (1979) *Teleology Revisited*, New York, Columbia University Press.

Neusner, J. (1984) *Messiah in Context*, Philadelphia, Fortress Press.

Phizacklea, A. (1980) *Labour and Racism*, London, Routledge.

Porter, R. and Rousseau, G. (1990) *Enlightenment and Exoticism*, Manchester, Manchester University Press.

Reeves, F. (1983) *British Racial Discourse*, Cambridge, Cambridge University Press.

Reich, W. (1975) *The Mass Psychology of Fascism*, Harmondsworth, Penguin.

Rex, J. and Mason, D. (1986) *Theories in Race and Ethnic Relations*, Cambridge, Cambridge University Press.

Rodinson, M. (1983) *Cult, Ghetto, State*, London, Al Saqui Press.

Roemer, J. (1982) *A general theory of class and exploitation*, Cambridge, Mass., Harvard University Press.

Rosolato, G. (1978) *La Relation d'Inconnu*, Paris, Gallimard.

Rushdie, S. (1988) *Satanic Verses*, Harmondsworth, Penguin Viking.

Rushdie, S. (1991) *Imaginary Homelands*, London, Penguin/Granta.

Samuel, R. (1981) *East End Underworld*, London, Routledge.

Scarman (1981) *The Brixton Disorders*, London, HMSO.

Sibony, D. (1978) 'L'affet ratial', in *La Haine et le Désir*, Paris, Grasset.

Sivanandan, A. (1985) 'RAT and the degradation of Black struggle', *Race and Class*, **26**(4).

Sollors, W. (1989) *The Invention of Ethnicity*, Oxford, Oxford University Press.

Steedman, C. (1984) *The Policing of the Victorian City*, London, Routledge.

Taylor, P. (1989) *Narrative of Liberation*, London and Ithaca, Cornell University Press.

Therborn, G. (1987) *Power and Ideology*, London, Verso.

Troyna, B. and Williams, J. (1986) *Race, Education and the State*, London, Croom Helm.

Watzlawick *et al.* (1967) *The Pragmatics of Human Communication*, New York, Columbia University Press.

Wright, L. (1976) *Teleological Explanation*, London and Berkeley, California University Press.

Wulff, H. (1988) *Twenty Girls*, Stockholm, University of Stockholm Press.

Young, J. (1981) *Capitalism and the Rule of Law*, London, Hutchinson.

Young, M. (1991) *An Inside Job: policing and police culture*, Oxford, Clarendon Press.

Zizek, S. (1989) *The Sublime Object of Ideology*, London, Verso.

4 FEMINISM AND ANTIRACISM
AN EXPLORATION OF THE
POLITICAL POSSIBILITIES

CAROLINE KNOWLES
AND SHARMILA MERCER

Despite lengthy consideration in feminist publications the relationship between feminist and antiracist politics remains obscure and contentious.[1] We intend to contribute to these debates. But first let us make our position clear. Our interest is not purely academic. We are feminists interested in political intervention. Our theoretical orientation and standards of judgment derive from this position. Of the accounts we explore we ask the question: what is the mode of politics sustained by this position? Whom is it likely to mobilize in support? What sorts of issues is it capable of addressing? Is it likely to be successful in opposing racism and sexism? We are interested in political action and results. But of course these concerns have theoretical implications which need to be explored. We shall argue that there is no general relationship between race and gender. There are only temporary and specific relationships which emerge in particular instances and are, therefore, accessible only through case studies and examples.

We shall also demonstrate that there are no inevitable or permanent relationships between groups of people organized in political discourse (constituencies) and political interests and positions. Women are not inevitably oppressed by men or capitalism. Oppression is not inevitable. It is a set of detailed practices which can be challenged by feminist politics. We will argue that the category 'woman' is a social construct, construed in specific instances by agencies in the public domain with which women come into contact. Interests articulated on behalf of women are claims locating women in terms of stated political objectives. Relationships between categories of the population and political objectives are therefore construed in political discourse. There is nothing inevitable or necessary about them. The category 'woman' divided into black and white by many black feminists is offered for further deconstruction in order to identify specific constructions of womanhood and to calculate the political interests implicated. This deconstruction occurs by demarcating constituencies who share a set of political interests (a position) in relation to a particular issue. In this way we establish a politics organized around issues as opposed to qualification for membership of a struggle. Our approach means that the conventional categories of political discourse (women, black women, black people and so on) based on physical qualification are reorganized into temporary configurations based on interests calculated in relation to particular issues and political struggles.

Black women in Britain and America have been rightly angered by claims advanced within white feminist politics to represent women which blatantly ignore or misrepresent their concerns. Many feel that the main analytical categories used to demarcate women's oppression, the family, patriarchy and reproduction, do not give an adequate account of the lives of black women. [. . .]

There is, as many black feminists have suggested, little to indicate any major theoretical support for issues concerning predominantly poor and black women. Struggles around immigration, deportation and social security have attracted the support of individual white women, but have not figured predominantly in white feminist analyses. They are not part of the representative images of contemporary British feminism. Perhaps there is reticence about issues which implicate men as allies. Where white feminists have taken up issues relevant also to men, such as nuclear defence, they have done so in a manner which excludes men as political allies. But part of this is a reluctance to identify or engage with racism, for feminist theory is still puzzling over the relationship between race and gender as forms of social division (Barrett and McIntosh, 1985). [. . .]

Feminism

Despite the political and theoretical diversity of feminism, feminists have in common a recognition of themselves as a social category separating them from and placing them in opposition to others. We also have a collective identity in public imagery. Although we are suggesting that the content of feminist politics is a site of struggle, it is possible to identify a general direction and set of objectives, the content of which needs to be spelled out in each case. In this context a feminist perspective is one which prioritizes the identification of, and opposition to, actions, practices or procedures which have the effect of excluding women or disadvantaging them relative to men. Sexism in this context is a series of effects, not intentions (though it might also be this) which can be identified, monitored and challenged. Sexism need not be considered the prerogative of men, capitalism or the state. It need not have a cause, only a multiplicity of effects resulting from the actions and practices of diverse agencies. Sexism is evident in the construction of womanhood by, for example, a diversity of agencies promoting particular health and educative norms in the conduct of family life with which women come into contact.

The dissection of the feminist constituency by race has, in debates in *Feminist Review*, *Spare Rib*, *Race and Class* and the work of Hazel Carby (1982) and Pritibha Parmar (1982), occurred along three dimensions which establish the specificity of black women. The black female constituency as an object of political analysis is demarcated by the experience of race and gender oppression, a common history of revolt and its analytical distinctiveness in feminist discourse organized around the family, patriarchy and reproduction. We propose to examine each of these in turn and see what is at stake in their use.

The family, patriarchy and reproduction are the main general terms around which an understanding of female oppression is organized in white feminist discourse. It is precisely around this kind of an issue that an understanding of the *unitary* nature of female oppression, so rightly offensive to black feminists, has been built. The response of feminists such as Carby (1982), Parmar (1982) and Bhavnani and Coulson (1986) has been to establish the specificity of black women and their relationship to the family, patriarchy and reproduction. Therein lies a paradox. 'Black women' is a term which is used by black feminists to incorporate a diversity of lifestyles and yet it is also retained as an undifferentiated category for analysis on the grounds that black women are united by the forces of racism.

Family

Debates about the status of the family for black and white women focus on the extent to which it operates as a force for exploitation and oppression. What black feminists have rightly designated 'white feminism' (because of the narrowness of its focus) maintains that the family is one of the key sites of female oppression.[2] Black feminists, on the other hand, maintain that the black family is a qualitatively different proposition from the family structures in which white women are involved.[3] Black women, argues Carby, are less dependent on men and are not oppressed by the family. Indeed, black feminist analysis of the family is that it is part of the resistance (to racist oppression) rather than collusion in it. White feminists have responded to this by acknowledging that black women in Britain live within different kinds of family arrangements. Barrett and McIntosh (1985), for example, regard this admission as an attempt to deal with what they consider the rather narrow ethnocentrism of the women's movement. They nevertheless maintain that the family is still a site for the perpetuation of gender inequalities which many black women may wish to escape. To support this they quote the views of some Indian women reported in *Manushi* magazine.[4] This leads them to comment that opposition to immigration laws and procedures which split up families may be problematic for feminists because it involves enforcing nuclear family, heterosexist norms. This is clearly an area where feminist and antiracist objectives come into conflict. Immigration procedures operate in a racist manner in singling out black families for harassment, and feminists may justly be accused of racism in supporting, for whatever reasons, actions which, in challenging the family, specifically disadvantage black families.

It seems to us that the term 'family' lends itself to infinite variation, that it contains within it choice and flexibility for negotiation between its members over the conditions in which they inhabit a common living space. We are here using the term 'family' to indicate any living arrangement which is referred to as a family. The position of black women in their families, once we reject the stereotypes of the Afro-Caribbean one-parent family and the Asian woman without rights of disposal over her body and labour power, is infinitely varied. We therefore support the black feminist challenge to the unitary nature of the family as a site of female oppression, but argue that the family cannot just be divided into black and white. Nor does this distinction − between black and white families − correspond to distinctions made between families by agencies in the public domain. The black family, like the white family, does not take a particular form. The term 'black family' is in fact a political construct. It designates a constituency to be mobilized in political struggle − against racism − part of which must be reclaimed by black women from the clutches of another set of political claims − white feminism.

Reproduction

Black women have also sought to establish their analytical distinctiveness from white women over the issue of reproduction. They point out that, while white women have prioritized struggles to defend limited abortion rights, black women are fending off the willingness of medical agencies to curtail their fertility. The use on black women of Depo Provera, a contraceptive drug injected into the muscle which has been known to cause sterility, is often cited to support a different attitude by medical agencies to black and white mothers (Carby, 1982). Both struggles, in fact, are about the rights of women over their own reproductive capacities. It is also entirely possible that the manner in which medical agencies, who control access to abortion, sterilization and fertilization (with *in vitro* fertilization techniques), deal with women's requests is informed by their conception of adequacy in mothering. Such delicate assessments are capable of being made in ways which disadvantage black women.

Reproduction is doubtless an arena in which racial differences between women are a focus for unequal treatment. Further research would identify the practices through which such inequalities are produced. This approach side-steps concerns over the use of Depo Provera until we are able to establish on whom it is used in Britain. (We suspect, from discussions with community nurses, that it is used on women not trusted by medical agencies to control their own fertility. Some of these women may be black, but others will be white and judged deficient as mothers because of handicap or presumed low intelligence.) We do not know how Depo Provera is used in Britain, yet it always features in arguments about race and reproduction. As such, it is a fairly shaky basis on which to demarcate a unitary black female constituency. We do know that it is used on black women in third-world countries, as are other drugs which do not meet the necessary safety standards in Britain, but this needs to be taken up and challenged with the agencies reponsible for their use and distribution in the third world. Learning about the use of a drug like Depo Provera in a third-world country will indicate how black women are perceived and treated in that particular social context, but it is difficult to see what this might tell us about the position of black women in Britain.

Patriarchy

Patriarchy is the final analytical construct we wish to discuss over which black feminists have distanced themselves from the women's movement. Since the 1970s the use of the term 'patriarchy' in the context of women's politics and academic debate has become increasingly elaborate. The impetus for this has been provided by the critiques of black feminists who, like Carby, suggest that because of racism black men do not benefit from patriarchal social structures in the same way as white men and that benefit from patriarchy does not distinguish black men from black women. 'Black women have been dominated "patriarchally" in different ways by men of different "colours"' (Carby, 1982). This has encouraged white feminists to be more cautious of their use of this term as indicative of the female condition and a commonality among women. Yet few white feminist writers are prepared to jettison patriarchy as a central analytical concept. This is because, in their view, it ultimately unites all women in a common sisterhood as undifferentially oppressed subjects, all of whom have in common a disadvantaged relation to men, and it is precisely this unity which provides the force for resistance. This is certainly true of Barrett and McIntosh in their replies to criticism by black feminists in *Feminist Review*. They see the concept of patriarchy as 'one with a valuable but specific purchase' (Barrett and McIntosh, 1985, p. 37). They reject it as a noun but retain it as an adjective, descriptive of certain types of social relations 'characterized by the personal, often physical, exploitation of a servility whose causes are usually economic and always strictly regulated through a hierarchical order' (Barrett and McIntosh, 1985, p. 37). Patriarchy is retained as an analytical concept and with it a privileging of gender over other social divisions. It is this which black feminists find most offensive: the privileging of gender over race in a permanent hierarchy of social divisions. Having established the primacy of gender, it remains only to establish how this is dissected by race. This is the task which Barrett and McIntosh, as well as many other white feminists, prioritize. Thus racial divisions are relegated to a secondary importance.

The establishing of a primacy of one form of social division over another in effect is establishing which form of oppression, gender or racial oppression, has primacy as a political issue. We shall argue later that this is not an issue which can be decided once and for all. Rival primacies involve difficult negotiations between the politics of gender equality and the politics of racial equality, or which constituency has priority, black people or women. These priorities can only be established in relation to specific issues and the political configurations in which they occur.

Oppression

A black female constituency is further demarcated in many black feminist accounts by the experience of oppression.[5] It is this which, it is suggested, unites black women and places them in opposition to white women. The experience of which black women speak arises from being both black and female in a white society which, it is argued, is by definition racist. Oppression is organized around race and gender divisions, with race divisions being accorded a permanent primacy in the establishment of political priorities. This is the opposite of the white feminist position which asserts the primacy of gender. Racial oppression is presented as the result of forms of interaction between black women (and black men) and British society and a range of British social institutions in particular. Racial oppression – it is supposed – is obviously something which black women share with black men [. . .] And this poses difficulties in the construction of a feminist politics which, in general, seeks not only to exclude men but place them in an antagonistic relationship to women.

Racial oppression, for us, is a vague formulation which needs to be deconstructed and 'operationalized' in terms of its detailed practices. We think of racial disadvantage, racism or racial inequality in terms of practices, procedures and actions which have the effect of excluding, providing unequal access for or in some way disadvantaging black people. This is similar to the conception of gender inequality we outlined earlier. The practices and procedures which constitute racism and sexism are likely to be different and there is no particular relationship between the two. Our notion of race and gender oppression is also significantly different from that of authors such as Carby (1982) and Bourne (1983) in that it does not attempt to identify a single cause or source of disadvantage.

Accounts such as Carby's and Bourne's identify a general set of processes in which disadvantage is inevitably and permanently inscribed. Capitalism, colonialism and patriarchal social systems are frequently identified as producing inherent race and gender inequalities which, in various ways, serve the needs of the systems they perpetuate. The grim inevitability of sexism and racism is the message of these accounts which deal with 'state racism' and 'institutionalized sexism'. Opposition to these general 'isms' is necessarily all-embracing, reaching beyond the manifestations of the problem to the structures of the system itself. Thus, ultimately, all forms of struggle are focused on capitalism and its political organization, the 'state'. But when, as we are suggesting, racism and sexism are viewed as a series of effects which do not have a single cause, a different kind of politics is established. There is no need to accept these inequalities as inevitable or to develop strategies which strike at the very root of capitalist and patriarchal relations. We need only to identify the practices and procedures throughout a range of social institutions (some of which may belong to what is referred to as the 'state' and others of which may not) which have the effect of producing racial and gender disadvantage. These can then be monitored and challenged by feminists and antiracists. The advantage of our approach over the ones we criticize is that it allows small-scale direct political challenges to the concrete practices which produce race and gender inequalities. We argue strongly for a deconstructionist approach to any notion of oppression which is used to account for the position of women and black people. We do not wish to participate simply in the elaboration of accounts of our own oppression. Neither do we wish to celebrate that oppression with meetings and rallies. We prefer a mode of politics which engages with the details of the oppression and which is capable of ending it.

A prominent feature of many accounts of race and gender is the presentation of oppression as an 'experience'.[6] Such accounts often convey the impression that experience occurs in an unmediated encounter between particular categories of the population and their social and political environment. White women will, the argument goes, experience sexism, just as black women will experience sexism and racism. But what is experience? Can the constituency exposed to it support the claims made upon it to engage in political struggle? Experience is being used to demarcate qualification for membership of particular political struggles. Black people are therefore expected to experience racism. Those who deny its existence are accused of false consciousness.

We argue, on the contrary, that experience has no such immediacy. Experience is organized by our understanding of the manner in which our social environment is organized. 'Racism' and 'sexism' are political constructs. They are ways of interpreting behaviour and events and require political education. The use of experience as a condition of political involvement has also to face up to the argument that experience can be as different as different people claim it to be. There may, therefore, be no end to the divisions and distinctions claimed by an apparently unitary constituency. Women will experience their femininity in different ways depending partly on the combination of circumstances in which their lives are enmeshed. It is therefore unlikely that all black women, or even all black women in Britain, will experience racism and sexism in a uniform manner. This makes the task of spokespeople very difficult. Those who speak on behalf of black women need to be aware that their accounts of oppression, grounded in experience, are open to counterclaim by other black women. We are made particularly aware of this when Parmar and Carby claim to speak on behalf of 'black women' irrespective of country of residence and differing socio-political circumstances.

Afro-American and black British women need to recognize that African women may not share their conception of femininity nor their notion of oppression. This point is illustrated by the example of a Nigerian feminist group started in 1982, 'Women in Nigeria'.[7] In developing a notion of black women's oppression in Nigeria, this group obviously did not attach the same importance to racism as black British or black American women who live in a hostile environment. Neither did they challenge marriage or the family as legitimate forms of social organization. They did not see the family as oppressive to women and it was not considered acceptable to live outside family structures. Their concerns focused on the need for land reforms, rural development and the need to examine relations between women (co-wives) in polygamous marriages. Interestingly, they also made no attempt to differentiate their position or interests from the minority of white American and European women who also operated in this group, because they were setting the political agenda on behalf of all the group.

Political organizations frequently guard against the expression of a diversity of experience by their members through establishing a set of discursive constraints within which they operate. These organize their agenda-setting exercises and the manner in which they are able to prioritize and deal with issues. 'Experience' for group members then becomes organized in terms of these discursive priorities which are, to some extent, a guarantee against the diversity offered by the politics of experience.

Can experience serve as the basis for political organization? We have already indicated that experience is used as a political device to demarcate a constituency; to establish who may legitimately be involved in a particular struggle. Qualification for membership is an important part of feminist and antiracist political organization in Britain and elsewhere. We will later argue that political struggles could more effectively be built around issues, and not biogenetic categories of the population, but we maintain that black people have better access than anyone else to understanding the various effects we refer to as racism, just as women have better access to understanding the effects of sexism. With the aid of a political education, they are more likely than others to feel its effects and are therefore in a better position to direct political initiatives against it. We completely agree, therefore, that black people must have a privileged position in any antiracist struggle, but insist that within the category 'black' there will be those who have a particular grasp on specific issues (for example, women who have been subject to deportation) and because of this are more likely than others to understand what is involved in opposing particular practices, and their expertise should be recognized in any strategies adopted to counter this particular form of racism. We return to this point in our discussion of political constituency and representation, but it is worth emphasizing here that our prioritization of issues, as the basis for political constituencies and opening up struggles to all who wish to participate, does not challenge the importance within them of those who feel the effects of particular discriminatory practices.

Resistance

A historically constructed capacity for revolt further organizes the claims of black feminists to a distinctiveness from white women. Carby and Parmar, particularly, have claimed that the capacity for revolt against oppression, whether organized in opposition to slavery, colonialism or modern-day racism, both sets black women apart and places them in opposition to white women.

Description of resistance to slavery and colonialism involves an appeal to history. We now propose to examine the status and purpose of history in some black feminist accounts. All histories are organized around political projects. They are reconstructions of the past directed by specific intentions and priorities. The claim that most conventional accounts of history are presented in a manner which organizes disparate events around the achievements of white men indicates that such accounts are directed by the political project of adding validity to the existing social order in which women and black men are rendered invisible. In this context the accounts of history which focus on the conditions of working-class people and the oppression and achievements of women and black people are a welcome departure. Many black feminist accounts of history, however, go further than the excavation of dead heroines and the filling of gaps and absences left by histories directed by less progressive purposes. The central purpose of Carby's and Parmar's accounts of history, for example, is to establish the unity of a black (male and female) constituency through its capacity for revolt against oppression in whatever form it occurs. Their purpose is to show that, historically, black women have not been passive, but active in their opposition to colonialism and to racism in Britain. The political project here is the reconstruction of past oppressions which serve to unify a black constituency because it must be united in order to oppose racism.

We have two problems with this. We welcome a reconstruction of black women's history so as to mobilize black people in opposition to racism. But we do not think that accounts such as Carby's and Parmar's allow this, because they do not indicate either a target or a strategy except in the vaguest terms. We need a historical account which specifies what, precisely, is to be opposed, and, secondly, how this might be achieved. A black history which does not meet these criteria cannot sustain a contemporary onslaught against racism, for it has no strategy and no specific set of actions to oppose. An amorphous concept of oppression which collapses colonial domination, slavery and contemporary racism makes a nonsense of identifying practices and actions disadvantaging black people which need to be opposed. These accounts of history are limited by their inability to identify specific targets for antiracist politics. Instead they construct two groups of oppositional subjects, one black, the other white. The racism to be challenged becomes personified in the bodies of white people. It is they who are to be opposed, for they embody the racism from which black people suffer. We do not deny that some white people are responsible for certain sorts of racial exclusions, but argue that in developing antiracist strategies it is helpful to know exactly how they are racist, so that their actions can be challenged.

We are critical of Carby's and Parmar's accounts of history because they are inadequate in developing struggles against racism. It is fair to ask of them: having constructed your constituency for the struggle against racism, how do you propose to mobilize it? And whom or what will you mobilize it against? For state racism and white power make far too vague an enemy. In the end this kind of account lays itself open to the criticism that it is far more interested in establishing the capacity of its constituency for resistance than in mobilizing it in a struggle against racism. If black history cannot address the political possibilities of antiracism, then perhaps it needs to be rewritten so that it can.

We have argued that the capacity for resistance is a key component of many black feminists' constructions of a black female constituency. What is created in the process of resisting oppression in the case of black people is a 'culture of resistance and rebellion' (Livingstone and Murphy, 1985). Carby and Parmar, for example, present their arguments in the context of a Centre for Contemporary Cultural Studies (CCCS) publication (1982), which prioritizes the study of forms of resistance. Resisting populations may be youth, black youth, black women or black people. Their vanguard position in any struggle is derived from the conditions in which higher forms of political consciousness are likely to develop. For example Bourne, writing in the journal *Race and Class* (1983), implies that revolutionary consciousness is predominantly a capacity of those less directly incorporated into capitalist relations of production. Estranged from production, the argument goes, woman is drawn closer to the community and, in an almost Rousseauesque sense, has, therefore, a better grasp of its need for liberation. In this manner an opposition is set up between community and state and all forms of resistance are supported, irrespective of their political intentions, because they all ultimately constitute a challenge to state power, and hence to the capitalist system.

This account contains no guide for action. Can all projects and struggles be equally politically valid? And what happens when contradictions arise between struggles? In this kind of analysis contradiction is impossible. All struggles ultimately aim to overthrow the capitalist state. The insistence on the idea of the uniformity of capitalist oppression creates a uniform category of oppressed which can then be divided on any basis – gender, colour, age, class – as long as such divisions can be sustained and demonstrated in political argument.

Racism and the women's movement

Just as a black female constituency is organized around its analytical distinctiveness in the accounts we have examined (the experience of oppression and a history of revolt) so white women are said to be united both by their oppositional and oppressive relationship to black women and by a failure to recognize black women's distinctiveness in developing accounts of female oppression in feminist writing. The accusation that the women's movement is racist is partly informed by its exclusion of black women's political concerns and by a misrecognition of their lives and social arrangements when black women are included. The women's movement also stands accused of racism on a second count; its members have historically and currently acted as agents of oppression of black women. A common theme in the writings of many black feminists is an insistence that 'white women stand in a power relationship as oppressors to black women' (Carby, 1982, p. 214). This relationship of power and oppression between black and white women is described as being constituted both contemporaneously, because white women benefit from the exploitation of black people, and historically, because they have benefited from colonialism and eugenicism. Racism, historically consti-tuted in this manner, has a special status in explaining the current relationship between black and white women.

The white women's movement has responded uneasily to these accu-sations. Some white feminist accounts have been prefaced with apologies for not reflecting the concerns and experiences of black women. Some went so far as to admit that this was both remiss and Eurocentric on their part, but denied charges of racism (Barrett and McIntosh, 1985). On the other hand, many have accepted in discomfited silence the criticism of being oppressive inheritors of colonial gain. It is a silence induced by an uneasy feeling that in Britain the women's movement, as part of white society, lacks a history of racial guilt. It is this that white feminists are being reminded of when they are asked to acknowledge their own inherent racism. What is strongly evident is black feminist anger and white feminist *angst* around the whole issue of feminism and antiracism. Missing are any systematic discussions of what might be the initiatives that could incorporate and develop feminist antiracist strategies.

As feminists who are committed to developing antiracist political initiatives, we are interested in precisely how the women's movement is racist, as we should like to challenge any racist practices (and we are sure there are many) which occur in developing the cause of feminism. To this end we should like to further investigate the claim that the women's movement is racist in order to see how racism is constituted in these claims. Does, for example, the exclusion of black women's lives and concerns from white feminist writing constitute racism, or, as Barrett and McIntosh (1985) claim, merely indicate a Eurocentrism on the part of the British women's movement? To Barrett's and McIntosh's attempts to broaden their analysis of family forms so as to include an understanding of ethnic difference, Bhavnani and Coulson (1986) have replied that the lives of black women are 'tacked on' rather than central to an analysis which fails to jettison patriarchy and hence gender as the primary form of social division. Barrett and McIntosh are arguing for both the specificity of women and their ultimate reduction to a universal analytical category, according them a unity as oppressed subjects; and Bhavnani and Coulson are quite right to object to their concerns being overridden in this manner.

But is this racism, however? Racism by our account constitutes a set of practices which exclude or in some way disadvantage black people. We argue that accounts such as Barrett's and McIntosh's are clearly unhelpful in developing antiracist strategies, given that ultimately they do not even recognize the analytical distinctiveness of black women, believing divisions between women to be disabling of political struggle. But we do not think that they, or their theoretical approach, are responsible for contributing to material black female disadvantage. Accounts which do not recognize the lives, struggles and social position of black women are narrow and Eurocentric. They are ill-informed and disabling of antiracist struggles but they are not in themselves racist because they do not materially disadvantage black women.

Let us examine the argument that white women are and have been beneficiaries of black oppression. Ramazanoglu (1986) reiterated Hazel Carby's challenge to the women's movement when she said 'There is a power relation between black and white women in Britain since these relationships are historically structured by racism'. This statement has not drawn much of a response from white feminists. Ramazanoglu's and Carby's history is one which constructs a present-day reality: '. . . white women cannot avoid the legacy of racism within feminism . . . the dominance of eugenicism (in birth control movements) . . . the eager acceptance by the majority of the suffragettes of imperialistic nationalism, and at best, the failure of anti-rape campaigns to challenge racist stereotypes of the sexuality of black men' (Bhavnani and Coulson, 1986).

We will look at this historical legacy of racism before considering the present-day racism of feminist politics and how one may have a bearing upon the other. It is quite widely argued that white women benefited from the oppression of black people through eugenicist assumptions and colonial systems. It is quite clear that black men and women were oppressed through eugenicist assumptions and colonial systems. We use the plural 'systems', for they were clearly diverse and cannot be regarded as producing a uniform oppression. It is also clear that some white people benefited from these indefensible systems of exploiting black labour. What is not clear, and has not in our view been made clear, is how white women as a uniform category cutting across class and other boundaries, benefited from black exploitation. Following the work of Poulantzas (1975) and Wright (1985) on class, which has demonstrated the benefits of deconstructing social categories, it seems to us lacking in analytical sophistication to insist that white women are united by the fact that black people were and are exploited from a multiplicity of sources. Some white women benefited from colonialism. Others (for example, poor and working-class women) did not. So can this form a basis for claiming a political unity between white women? This is not to deny that black people were and are exploited, but what oppresses one group does not necessarily benefit those to whom they are counterposed in the exercises of constituency building.[8]

It is also unclear from this kind of argument precisely how colonial oppression underwrites and informs the present-day nature of black oppression in Britain. It is assumed that there is a historic link through different forms of oppression from the eighteenth and nineteenth centuries to the present day. Obviously, the forms of oppression and disadvantage which black people suffer in Britain today are distinct from those which persisted in British colonies hundreds of years ago. If disadvantage is socially construed, then clearly it takes specific forms. If this is so, then the manner in which colonial oppression informs our understanding of present-day black disadvantage needs to be stipulated. It is likely that the colonial connection is a device for ensuring the building of an antiracist political constituency. Our criticism of this is only that it is by no means clear to us how developing a constituency organized around its opposition to colonialism can be mobilized in a struggle against racism in Britain today.

We are interested in understanding how feminist politics today develops and construes forms of racial disadvantage. Feminist politics are quite capable, in our view, of generating racial inequalities. We argue that it is politically more relevant and useful to try to identify when and how this takes place, so that such practices can be challenged.

How does feminism generate black disadvantage?

In what ways can feminism as a mode of political engagement promote or generate black disadvantage? Before dealing with this we should first like to reiterate the point made by many black feminists, that white feminist politics has neglected an engagement with some of the key dimensions of black women's oppression. Its failure to activate campaigns around issues relevant to black women means that it has failed to challenge the forms of disadvantage from which black women suffer. We have already argued that this failure amounts to Eurocentrism, ignorance and unsisterly behaviour, but not racism. Nevertheless, we think it is high time that feminist politics took up issues relevant to black and to poor women. Its failure to do so indicates a reluctance to deal with racism and a setting of political priorities which places a low premium on black feminist struggles. But a failure to challenge racism is not the same as its active promotion. We are looking for examples of how feminist politics has promoted black disadvantage. An example might be the use of immigration controls and procedures by a women's refuge to deport a black violent husband whose right to remain in Britain is contingent upon his marriage to a British national.

Let us look at actual examples which disadvantage black women. In some areas of inner London white feminists have taken initiatives over the lack of nursery provision to set up parent-run community nurseries. These frequently use parents as workers and are organized around certain assumptions about parenting which include feminist ideas about sharing between men and women, the provision of non-sexist toys and books and often of particular diets. The effect of these arrangements in some areas, for example the London Borough of Hackney, has been the exclusion of black children and parents. This is not the intention, but an effect of the manner in which such groups are constituted. These nurseries are often anxious to attract black families, not realizing that the conception of parenthood held by those involved, while guided by feminist intentions, in effect privileges not only white but middle-class parents. Their requirement of parental involvement excludes single parents who need to work, many of whom in this area are black and working class. This example illustrates our conception of racism as practices which have the effect of disadvantaging black people and shows how a feminist initiative can have the effect of excluding black people from resources which are in very short supply. It is possible to cite many other instances where, in local allocation processes in certain inner-city areas, white feminists capture resources and exclude other women, many of whom are black.

Feminism, like socialism, is a political construct which provides many opportunities for generating racial disadvantage and exclusion. We argue that this sort of approach of citing instances of racism is more helpful than some of the general formulations of racism within feminism which we have examined. Our approach at least proffers the opportunity to counter and resist racism. It provides a guide to action, since once we identify feminist practices which have exclusionary effects they can be challenged.

In the example we have cited, an antagonistic relationship has developed between race and gender disadvantage, and the strategies which may be deployed to address them. This is not in any sense inevitable. Another example reveals a shift in this relationship. Take the example of the closure of a local authority nursery used by black and white families who are allocated places on the basis of 'need'. In an area like the London Borough of Hackney, for example, 'need' is construed by the social services in terms of family stress likely to lead to their intervention. In this case, both black and white mothers form a single constituency in political struggle over this issue. For although black and white mother-hood are likely to be differently constructed by agencies in the public domain and this will affect allocation processes, in the case of the withdrawal of facilities already in use black and white mothers hold a common position in trying to retain their nursery. [`. . .]

Deconstructing the antiracist and feminist constituency

[. . .] The deconstruction of constituencies is not an arbitrary process, neither is it guided by an understanding of cultural difference (Asian, Afro-Caribbean, and so on). Because constituencies are organized around issues their boundaries are constantly changing. We will later comment on the implications of this for the relationship between constituency and political struggle.

Let us take as an example the constituencies organized by the issues raised in the 1986 DHSS consultative paper covering research on embryos, surrogacy and *in vitro* fertilization. We take this because it was a response to the Warnock Report which has implications for the control of female fertility, for many years seen as a key site of struggle for feminists, and because the DHSS were soliciting submissions on these issues which might influence policy making and future legislation on an important issue on which feminist voices ought to be heard. Feminist responses were slow in coming, we think, because, in the context of specific policy making, it is quite difficult to say what a feminist position might be. A feminist position, at a most general level, is one which enhances or defends the interests of women. Those who defend patriarchy as a theoretical explanation of the position of women are stuck with the idea that all women share a common set of interests at some general level. Let us apply this to the issue of surrogacy and see if it is sustained.

Evidently, commissioning and donating mothers will have not only different but conflicting interests in cases where the biological mother has difficulty in giving the child up to the commissioning mother.[9] What do we, as feminists, recommend in the way of drafting legislation to protect women? We would have to ask the question: which set of female interests should we support? Once we consider the construction of femininity in relation to specific issues, a fragmentation of the constituency 'women' has to take place in order for us to make any decisions about support and strategy. It becomes clear that not all women share a set of interests and that accounts of patriarchy do not help us make sense of a complex issue such as surrogacy.

Once we admit division in the female constituency, there are difficult dilemmas which have to be negotiated as far as political allegiances are concerned. Women are not a uniformly disadvantaged set of subjects; female disadvantage is very uneven. But even to express it in this way somehow assumes that woman is a disadvantaged category created elsewhere and maintained and reproduced by the effects of legislation and documents such as the DHSS consultative document. We instead suggest that female disadvantage is created by a multiplicity of mechanisms, including the proposed legislation we refer to. In it women are constructed in terms of their child-bearing capacities, or lack of them. This for us is not the reflection of a set of distinctions made elsewhere; this is one of the mechanisms in which the social category 'woman' is created and maintained, mostly as a disadvantaged subject, but sometimes not.

The division of the female constituency into two on this issue is a division especially significant in this example and we offer it in support of our claim that constituencies are organized in response to particular issues. They are not permanent divisions. A different issue – take the demand for *in vitro* fertilization services – would divide women in an entirely different manner. It divides women around who can afford to pay, as these services are also available privately, and who is judged suitable for motherhood by the consultant in charge.

Another example can be used to indicate how it is necessary in developing antiracist struggles to accept divisions in the black constituency. If racism is an effect of practices which exclude or disadvantage black people, then it does not necessarily follow that they have a single cause. Indeed, as we have argued, racism may be the effect of practices developed by a multiplicity of agencies, all of which are not covered necessarily under the rubric of the 'state'. An example drawn from social services involvement in black families will here be useful in making a number of points about gender and racism.

There are studies on the relationship between black families and social service departments which indicate that one-parent families are much more likely than two-parent families to have their children removed.[10] In some areas of London, families of Afro-Caribbean origin are over-represented in the population of one-parent families. Family assessments by social workers which are negative about one-parent families have the consequence of disproportionately removing the parental rights of black women (who are more likely than men to be heads of single-parent families) over their children. This is an example of a racist effect. But it is also an example of a racist effect which is gender specific. Men and women are judged as parents by social work agencies by different standards. A study of parental assessments in cases of suspected child abuse reveals that women are not only construed as responsible for child care, as they are in different ways by health and education agencies, but that they are also held responsible for the neglect and abuse of children in a way which fathers are not.[11] In cases where these assessments are being made of black families, any account of racial disadvantage suffered needs to take account of the fact that black men and black women suffer different kinds of racism.

Here is an example of a specific relationship between gender and race. Social work assessments of black mothers organize what may be crude stereotypical conceptions of race around a particular reading of the relationship between femininity and motherhood. This is likely to be different for black (including Asian) mothers and white mothers and will be cross-cut by a multiplicity of other factors. Black men in this example are racially disadvantaged in an entirely different way from black women. They are more likely to have to deal with the less liberal aspects of what is referred to as the 'state', the police and courts. Men in general, and black men in particular, are disadvantaged in discourses and practices relating to criminality. In other words, there is no general way in which race and class and gender are related even over an issue as specific as this. Yet all three concepts are likely to inform a social worker's reading of the family situation.

If we continue this example of the relationship which might exist between social services departments and black families, further divisions in the black family become apparent. Even a cursory examination of issues such as child abuse indicate that black (and white) parents and children have differently constituted interests. Children have a clear interest in avoiding serious physical and emotional damage at the hands of their parents. In some cases this may entail their physical removal from the parental home. It should not be assumed that an antiracist position on social work intervention in black homes may be equated with non-intervention. This can have disastrous consequences for black children, as some of the more severe cases of child abuse, which have led to death because social workers have failed to make an adequate assessment of black families, testify.[12] What benefits black mothers, in this case, may constitute disadvantage for their children. Defending the rights of black mothers against what might be prescriptive and racist assessments by social workers may disadvantage another part of the black constituency, children. Again, these are difficult dilemmas which have to be negotiated in developing antiracist strategies.

It should by now be clear that developing antiracist struggles is not as simple a matter as it is often presented. Social work practices may produce racial disadvantage in ways which are age specific as well as gender specific. The development of antiracism needs to take account of the same specificities.

Concluding comments

All of this lays us open to the charge that in suggesting divisions in the black constituency in this way we are weakening any struggle against racism. We have already argued that the construction of a black constituency around the experience of oppression and a capacity for revolt is a political construct. (Black people are constructed as a single constituency, united by their oppression and a predisposition for revolt, so as to operate as a force against racism.) The demarcation of black and white women as analytically distinct oppressed groups is, of course, part of this process. Black women have to be reclaimed back into the constituency from feminism. Our deconstruction of the black constituency is seen, therefore, as a threat to its mobilization as an antiracist force. But this is only so because of an assumed relationship between political constituencies and objects of political struggle in the conventions of progressive or revolutionary political discourse.

A political constituency is usually derived from the notion of a 'community' as it is organized in the conventions of political philosophy[13] and pluralist sociology[14]. It is in fact a curious fusion of these discourses in that it refers to a group of subjects who are identifiable in two senses: as a recognizable and physically distinguishable category of any given population (women, black people, travellers, and so on), and, what is read off from that, a specifiable if rather general set of interests (the ending of capitalism, patriarchy or whatever). These two dimensions are inextricable; the one sustains and gives force to the other. In this kind of formulation, groups of subjects exist in tandem to what are in fact claims to articulate a set of interests or political demands on their behalf. As we see it, there is no necessary relationship between a group of subjects and a set of political objectives. These are constructed.

Our use of the term 'political constituency' is similar to this in some respects. But instead of a parallel existence of subjects and claimed interests, we see constituencies as organized by specific issues as they arise on the political agenda. In other words groups of subjects (constituencies) are created in terms of a commonality of interests around the specifics of policies. Hence a recognized category like black women is unlikely to be constructed by an issue such as the deportation of widows whose British citizenship is gained through marriage. Not all black women are affected by this issue. The primary constituency of this kind of struggle is likely to be a small group of more recently arrived Asian women. They will have a special interest in and knowledge of the issues involved in mounting any campaign against this kind of deportation. There is no need in our view to construct a broader constituency for the purposes of mounting a campaign. We do not need to insist that this is an issue affecting all black women. The conventions of progressive struggles have tended, in this way, to be inclusive of anyone who can be shown to have the slightest stake in an issue. The greater the diversity of people included in a struggle, the more tenuous the links between them and the more general the struggle has to be – in effect against all forms of oppression. Once we get down to the details of that oppression so that it can be opposed, any unity constructed evaporates.

All of this incorporation follows from the conventions which stipulate that no one will join in a political struggle unless their interests are served in so doing. We suggest in place of this formulation that in any political struggle we identify precisely the practices which have to be challenged. Having done this we can identify the primary constituency which will have a special place in any campaign. But having identified the issues it is then open to all people sympathetic to that cause to identify themselves as part of the struggle. Political struggle then involves a choice of political allegiances rather than qualification for membership. This kind of approach has a potential mobilizing capacity far greater than struggles built around qualification for membership.

What emerges from all of this, theoretically and politically, is a reconstruction of conventional modes of political engagement. A constituency, used in the context of what we describe as a direct or 'primary' constituency, is a temporary association of people united by a common position or set of interests in relation to a given issue. This cross-cuts race and gender divisions in any number of ways. 'Interest' and 'position' are not in this context used as they are in discourses on political economy to indicate an essential social nature with a permanent set of attributes. Neither are they deployed in the sense in which they are used in discourses between categories of the population and a generalized set of political demands. They are used here to indicate a temporary association between individuals and a potential set of political demands which may counter or reinforce the manner in which individuals are located in positions by the agencies with which they deal.

Our approach displaces political alignments built around qualification for membership of antiracist and antisexist struggles. It deconstructs commonly accepted political constituencies and the generalized political objectives with which they are associated. It offers in its place a mode of engagement with specific incidents, practices and actions which have the effect of generating various forms of race and gender disadvantage. It is a politics which allows action to challenge racism and sexism in any arena, promoted by a range of agencies.

We have demonstrated that there is no general relationship between race and gender as forms of social division. These are constructs which have only temporary relationships construed by the issues through which they are articulated. Because there are conflicts, in some cases, between feminist and antiracist objectives, because feminism is capable of racism (just as antiracism is capable of sexism) feminists and antiracists sometimes have to make difficult choices about where their allegiances lie. Accusations of racism made by black feminists have been a productive influence on issues of race and gender. They have raised questions which cannot be addressed by feminist theory. The manner in which constituencies are demarcated in black feminist accounts has led us to question the basis for constructing constituencies in political struggle. If we are to go beyond the reaffirmation of our oppression as white women and as black women, if we are to make advances in human equality and challenge that oppression, then we need a different mode of political engagement as feminists and as antiracists. The approach we suggest allows just that. It allows political intervention around issues and instances of inequalities. But it has certain theoretical implications which we have explored concerning the construction of constituencies and the centrality of issues. It postulates temporary links between groups of subjects with interests and positions. It involves the construction and reconstruction of political constituencies in struggle and some difficult dilemmas for feminists and antiracists.

Notes

1 See Carby (1982), Parmar (1982), various articles in *Feminist Review*, No. 17 (1984), Bourne (1983), Barrett and McIntosh (1985), Bhavnani and Coulson (1986), Livingstone and Murphy (1985), a number of articles in *Spare Rib* (debates with 'Women of colour') and Anthias and Yuval-Davis (1983).

2 See for example Barrett (1980).

3 See for example Carby (1982).

4 *Manushi* is a feminist magazine published in Delhi and relates to women's struggles in India.

5 See for example Carby (1982) and Parmar (1982).

6 See various articles in *Feminist Review* (1984).

7 This is a group started by Nigerian feminist academics (mostly but not exclusively women) who first met at the University of Zaria in 1982.

8 Constituency building refers to the arguments supporting the unity of a group of subjects in political discourse.

9 A commissioning mother is a woman who 'rents' the womb of another for the purposes of acquiring a child by her husband or partner. A donating mother is the woman who gives birth to a child for a commissioning mother.

10 Greater London Council (1983); Commission for Racial Equality (1983).

11 This refers to a piece of research carried out in the London Borough of Brent (Knowles, unpublished, 1985).

12 An example of this is offered by the killing of a child of Afro-Caribbean origin, Jasmine Beckford, by her stepfather in Brent (1985). See London Borough of Brent, *A Child in Trust* (1986).

13 See for example the work of Rousseau (1979).

14 See for example the work of Kuper and Smith (1971) and Kuper (1973).

Bibliography

Alexander, S. and Taylor, B. (1980) 'In defence of patriarchy', *New Statesman*, 1 February.

Amos, V. and Parmar, P. (1984) 'Challenging imperial feminism', *Feminist Review*, **17**.

Anthias, F. and Yuval-Davis, N. (1983) 'Contextualising feminism – gender, ethnic and class divisions', *Feminist Review*, **15**.

Barrett, M. (1980) *Women's Oppression Today*, London, Verso.

Barrett, M. and Coward, E. (1982) 'Letter', *M/F*, **17**.

Barrett, M. and McIntosh, M. (1982) *The Antisocial Family*, London, Verso.

Barrett, M. and McIntosh, M. (1985) 'Ethnocentrism and socialist feminist theory', *Feminist Review*, **20**.

Bhavnani, K. K. and Coulson, M. (1986) 'Transforming socialist feminism: the challenge of racism', *Feminist Review*, **23**.

Bourne, J. (1983), 'Towards an antiracist feminism', *Race and Class*, **15**.

Carby, H. (1982) 'White woman listen. Black feminism and the boundaries of sisterhood' in Centre for Contemporary Cultural Studies, *The Empire Strikes Back*, London, Hutchinson.

Centre for Contemporary Cultural Studies (1982) *The Empire Strikes Back*, London, Hutchinson.

Commission for Racial Equality (1983) *Children in Care*, London, CRE.

Coward, R. (1980) 'Socialism, feminism and socialist feminism', *Gay Left*, **10**.

Coward, R. (1983) *Patriarchal Precedents*, London, Routledge & Kegan Paul.

Davis, A. (1981) *Women, Race and Class*, London, Women's Press.

DHSS (1986) 'Legislation on human infertility services and embryo research', Cmnd 46, London, HMSO.

Feminist Review (1984) 'Many voices one chant', Feminist Review, **17**.

Feuchtwang, S. (1980) 'Socialist feminist and antiracist struggles', *M/F*.

Feuchtwang, S. (1982) 'Occupational ghettoes', *Economy and Society*.

GLC (5 October 1983) *Ethnic Minorities Committee Report*, London, GLC.

Knowles, C. (1985) *Child Abuse in the London Borough of Brent* (unpublished).

Kuper, L. (1973) *Race, Class and Power*, London, Duckworth.

Kuper, L. and Smith, M. G. (1971) *Pluralism in Africa*, Los Angeles, African Studies Centre.

Livingstone, J. and Murphy, I. (1985) 'Racism and the limits of radical feminism', *Race and Class*, **26**.

Parmar, P. (1982) 'Gender, race and class: Asian women in resistance' in CCCS, *The Empire Strikes Back*, London, Hutchinson.

Poulantzas, N. (1975) *Classes in Contemporary Capitalism*, London, NLB.

Ramazanoglu, C. (1986) 'Ethnocentrism and socialist feminist theory', *Feminist Review*, **22**.

Rousseau, J.-J. (1979) *The Social Contract* and *Discourses*, London, Dent.

Rowbotham, S. (28 December 1979) 'The trouble with patriarchy', *New Statesman*.

Spare Rib (1984) Articles around debates with 'Women of colour'.

Wilson, A. (1978) *Finding a Voice*, London, Virago.

Women in Nigeria Group (1985) *Women in Nigeria Today*, London, Zed.

Wright, E. O. (1985) *Classes*, London, Verso.

Source: Cambridge, A. and Feuchtwang, S. (eds) (1990) *Antiracist Strategies*, Aldershot, Avebury Press.

5 DIFFERENCE, DIVERSITY AND DIFFERENTIATION

AVTAR BRAH

Difference, diversity, pluralism, hybridity – these are some of the most debated and contested terms of our time. Questions of difference are at the heart of many discussions within contemporary feminisms. In the field of education in Britain, questions of identity and community continue to dominate debates surrounding 'multiculturalism' and 'antiracism'. In this article, I consider how these themes might help us to understand the racialization of gender. No matter how often the concept is exposed as vacuous, 'race' still acts as an apparently ineradicable marker of social difference. What makes it possible for the category to act in this way? What is the nature of social and cultural differences and what gives them their force? How does 'racial' difference then connect to difference and antagonism organized around other markers, like 'gender' or 'class'? Such questions are important because they can help to explain people's tenacious investment in notions of identity, community and tradition.

One recurrent problem in this area is *essentialism*: that is, a notion of ultimate essence that transcends historical and cultural boundaries. Here I argue against an essentialist concept of difference while simultaneously problematizing the issue of 'essentialism'. At what point, and in what ways, for example, does the *specificity* of a particular social experience become an expression of essentialism? In reviewing feminist debates, I suggest that black and white feminism should not be seen as essentially fixed oppositional categories but rather as historically contingent fields of contestation within discursive and material practices in a post-colonial society. In similar vein, I shall be arguing that analysis of the interconnections between racism, class, gender and sexuality must take account of the positionality of different racisms with respect to one another. Overall, I underline the importance of a macro-analysis that studies the interrelationships between various forms of social differentiation empirically and historically, but without necessarily deriving them all from a single determining instance. In other words, I shall also be trying to avoid the danger of 'reductionism'.

The article is divided into three parts. In the first, I address the various notions of 'difference' that have emerged in recent discussions of how extensively the term 'black' can be used to define the experience of African-Caribbean and South Asian groups in post-war Britain. The second section is concerned with the ways in which issues of 'difference' have been framed with respect to racism within feminist theory and practice. My primary focus here is on the ongoing debate in Britain. I conclude with a brief examination of some conceptual categories used in the theorization of 'difference' and suggest that greater clarity in how we conceptualize 'difference' may aid in developing sharper political strategies for social justice.

What's in a name? What's in a colour?

Over the past few years the usage of the term 'black' to refer to people of African-Caribbean and South Asian descent in Britain has been the subject of considerable controversy. It is relevant to address some of these arguments as they often centre around notions of difference.

The African-Caribbean and South Asian people who migrated to Britain in the post-war period found themselves occupying a broadly similar structural position within British society as workers performing predominantly unskilled or semi-skilled jobs on the lowest rungs of the economy. Although the ideologies which racialized them were not identical in content there were similarities in their encounters with racism in arenas such as the workplace, the education system, the housing market, and the health services. Their 'non-whiteness' was a common referent within the racism confronting them. These groups were then commonly described in popular, political, and academic discourses as 'coloured people'. This was not a simple descriptive term. It had been the colonial code for a relationship of domination and subordination between the colonizer and colonized. Now the code was re-worked and re-constituted in and through a variety of political, cultural and economic processes in post-war Britain.

The term 'black' was adopted by the emerging coalitions amongst African-Caribbean and South Asian organizations and activists in the late 1960s and 1970s. They were influenced by the way that the Black Power movement in the USA, which had turned the concept of Black on its head, divested it of its pejorative connotations in racialized discourses, and transformed it into a confident expression of an assertive group identity. The Black Power movement urged black Americans to construe the black community not as a matter of geography but rather in terms of the global African diaspora. Eschewing 'chromatism' – the basis of differentiation amongst blacks according to lighter or darker tone of skin – 'black' became a political colour to be worn with pride against colour-based racisms. The African-Caribbean and South Asian activists in Britain borrowed the term from the Black Power movement to foster a rejection of chromatism amongst those defined as 'coloured people' in Britain.

The politics of solidarity between African-Caribbean and South Asian activists of the period were also influenced by the history of anti-colonial struggles in Africa, Asia and the Caribbean. The fusion of these two influences in the formation of a project concerned to address the social condition of post-colonial subjects in the heart of the British metropolis meant that the concept of black has been associated with rather distinctive and somewhat different meanings in Britain as compared with the USA.

Recently British usage of the term 'black' has been criticized by commentators like Hazareesingh (1986) and Modood (1988). They argue that the 'black' in Black Power ideology referred specifically to the historical experience of people of sub-Saharan African descent, and was designed to create a positive political and cultural identity amongst black Americans. When used in relation to South Asians the concept is *de facto* emptied of those specific cultural meanings associated with phrases such as 'black music'. The concept can incorporate South Asians in a political sense only, and they therefore conclude that it denies Asian cultural identity. Clearly there is some force in this argument. It is certainly the case, as we have already noted, that the Black Power movement's mobilization of the term 'black' was an attempt at reclaiming an African heritage that had been denied to black Americans by racism. But, as a historically specific political project located in the socio-political and economic dynamics in the USA, the Black Power ideology did not simply reclaim a pre-given ancestral past. In that very process, it also *constructed* a particular version of this heritage.

Given that cultural processes are dynamic, and the process of claiming is itself mediated, the term 'black' does not have to be construed in essentialist terms. It can have different political and cultural meanings in different contexts. Its specific meaning in post-war Britain cannot be taken to have denied cultural differences between African, Caribbean and South Asian people when cultural difference was not the organizing principle within this discourse or political practice. The concrete political struggles in which the new meaning was grounded acknowledged cultural differences but sought to accomplish political unity against racism. In any case, the issue of cultural difference cannot be posed purely in terms of differences between South Asian and African-Caribbean cultures. There are, for example, many differences between African and Caribbean cultures (which also include cultures of people of South Asian descent). Cultures in the diasporas always have their own specificity. In other words, even when the use of the 'black' is restricted to sub-Saharan Africa and its diasporas, it can be said, within the parameters of the terms set by the critics, to deny the cultural specificities of these diverse groups.

A second criticism of the ways in which 'black' has been employed in Britain has been that the concept is meaningless since many South Asians do not define themselves as black, and many African-Caribbeans do not recognize them as such. This assertion hinges partly on the criterion of numbers, but without providing supporting numerical evidence. In my own research I have found that South Asians will frequently describe themselves as 'kale' (black) when discussing issues of racism. But since the whole social being of South Asian and African-Caribbean peoples is not constituted only by the experience of racism, they have many other identifications based on, for example, religion, language and political affiliation. Moreover, as many demonstrations and campaigns show, the concept of black was mobilized as part of a set of constitutive ideas and principles to promote collective action. As a social movement, black activism has aimed to generate solidarity; it has not necessarily assumed that all members of the diverse black communities inevitably identify with the concept in its British usage.

Another area of contention has centred on the distribution of resources by the state to different categories of consumers. It is argued that the term 'black' serves to conceal the cultural needs of groups other than those of African-Caribbean origin. This particular critique is often steeped in 'ethnicism'. Ethnicism, I would suggest, defines the experience of racialized groups primarily in 'culturalist' terms: that is, it posits 'ethnic difference' as the primary modality around which social life is constituted and experienced. Cultural needs are defined largely as independent of other social experiences centred around class, gender, racism or sexuality. This means that a group identified as culturally different is assumed to be internally homogeneous, when this is patently not the case. The 'housing needs' of a working-class Asian living in overcrowded conditions on a housing estate, for instance, cannot be the same as those of a middle-class Asian living in a semi-detached house in suburbia. In other words, ethnicist discourses seek to impose stereotypic notions of 'common cultural need' upon heterogeneous groups with diverse social aspirations and interests. They often fail to address the relationship between 'difference' and the social relations of power in which it may be inscribed. It is clearly important that the state should be sensitive to the plurality of needs amongst its citizens. But we need to be attentive to the ways in which 'needs' are socially constructed and represented in various discourses.

There is another aspect to the ethnicist critique of the use of the term 'black' by the local state. Ethnicism does not seem to differentiate between 'black' as a term adopted by subordinate groups to symbolize resistance against oppression *and* the appropriation of the same term by some local authorities as a basis for formulating policies for the allocation of resources (Sivanandan, 1985; Gilroy, 1987; Cain and Yuval-Davis, 1990). The term has different meanings in the two contexts and signifies potentially different social and political outcomes, but ethnicism seems to conflate these different meanings. Furthermore, certain politicians may deploy the discourse of 'ethnic difference' as a means to create their own power base rather than to empower those whose 'needs' are supposed to be better met by jettisoning the term 'black'. It is unlikely that replacing 'black' by some other politically neutral descriptions will secure more equitable distribution of resources.

What kind of a terminology has been proposed to replace 'black'? Writing from somewhat different political perspectives Hazareesingh (1986) and Modood (1988) come to rather similar conclusions. Hazareesingh suggests that the use of black should be confined to people of African descent and that people from the South Asian subcontinent should all be subsumed under the concept of 'Indian' on the grounds of a shared 'culture in a historical sense'. But there is an immense diversity of cultures in the subcontinent which have emerged and been transformed under varying material and political circumstances. Furthermore, these cultures are underpinned by class, caste, religious, regional and linguistic differences and divisions. So in what sense can one speak of a common Indian culture? Hazareesingh's construction of this commonality in terms of a shared experience of imperialism and racism is vulnerable to the same criticism he directs against those who support 'black' as a political colour. He too privileges historical and contemporary processes of domination, and the role of the state in mediating these, as centrally important in structuring people's experiences. His view of a common Indian culture could also be seen by many South Asians as 'an attempt to straitjacket their experience'. Given the position of the modern state of India *vis-à-vis* other countries of the Asian subcontinent, Hazareesingh's concept of 'Indian' might be construed by some as reinforcing a hegemonic project in that region. How will Pakistanis or Bangladeshis recognize themselves in this definition, given the recent history of partition?

Unlike Hazareesingh, Modood employs the term 'Asian' as against 'black' which he claims 'sells short the majority of the people it identifies as black', and against 'South Asian' which he dismisses as an academic term. Leaving aside the fact that Asia covers a much larger part of the globe than the subcontinent of South Asia, it is his definition of 'Asian' which is particularly problematic: 'what I mean by an "Asian" identity', he states, 'is some share in the heritage of the civilisations of old Hindustan prior to British conquest' (Modood, 1988, p. 397). First, the term Hindustan as used by the Mughals referred largely to the northern states of latter-day India. More importantly, Modood seems to attribute a unified identity to pre-colonial India which, by implication, was destroyed by the British Raj. Historical evidence shows, however, that pre-colonial India was a heterogeneous entity, and that people were much more likely to define themselves in terms of their regional, linguistic or religious identity than as Hindustanis. Indeed, it may be possible to argue that 'Indian identity' as a set of identifications with a nation-state was the outcome of resistance and struggle against colonialism rather than something that existed prior to this period.

The main point I wish to stress through this foray into the debate surrounding the use of 'black' in Britain is how difference is constructed within these competing discourses. That is, the usage of 'black', 'Indian' or

'Asian' is determined not so much by the nature of its referent as by its semiotic function within different discourses. These various meanings signal differing political strategies and outcomes. They mobilize different sets of cultural or political identities, and set limits to where the boundaries of a 'community' are established. This debate has to an extent been echoed within feminism. And it is against this general background that I turn to issues of 'difference' within feminism.

Is sisterhood global?

In 1985 I attended the International Women's Conference in Nairobi. There, over 10,000 women from over 150 countries gathered to address questions of our universal subordination as a 'second sex', yet the most striking aspect of this conference was the heterogeneity of our social condition. The issues raised by the different groups of women present at the conference, especially those from the Third World, served to underline the fact that issues affecting women cannot be analysed in isolation from the national and international context of inequality (Brah, 1988; Mohanty, 1988).

Our gender is constituted and represented differently according to our differential location within the global relations of power. Our insertion into these global relations of power is realized through a myriad of economic, political and ideological processes. Within these structures of social relations we do not exist simply as women but as differentiated categories such as *working-class* women, *peasant* women, *migrant* women. Each description references a specificity of social condition. And real lives are forged out of a complex articulation of these dimensions. As is currently being increasingly recognized in feminist theory and practice, *woman* is not a unitary category. Yet, this does not mean that the noun 'woman' is meaningless. It too has its own specificity constituted within and through historically specific configurations of gender relations. But in different womanhoods the noun is only meaningful – indeed only exists – with reference to a fusion of adjectives which symbolize particular historical trajectories, material circumstances and cultural experiences. Difference in this sense is a *difference of social condition*. At this level of analysis the focus is on the social construction of different categories of women within the broader structural and ideological processes within societies. No claims are made that an individual category is internally homogeneous. Working-class women, for instance, comprise very diverse groups of people both within and between societies. Class position signals certain commonalities of location within the social structure but class articulates with other axes of differentiation such as racism, heterosexism or caste in delineating the precise social position of specific categories of women.

The primary objective of feminism has been to change the social relations of power embedded within gender. Since gender inequalities pervade all spheres of life, feminist strategies have involved a challenge to women's subordinated position within both state institutions and civil society. The driving force behind feminist theory and practice in the post-war period has been its commitment to eradicate inequalities arising from a notion of sexual difference inherent in biologically deterministic theories, which explain women's position in society as a result of innate differences. Despite evidence that sex differences in cognitive behaviour among infants are slight and the psychological similarity between men and women is very high, research to establish innate differences continues unabated (Segal, 1990; Rose *et al.*, 1984). Feminists do not, of course, ignore women's biology but they challenge ideologies which construct and represent women's subordination as resulting from their biological capacities.

The ways in which questions of biology are addressed varies within different feminisms. Radical feminist accounts, for example, tend to identify women's biologically based subordination as the fundamental basis of gender inequality. The relations of power between men and women are seen as the primary dynamic of women's oppression almost to the exclusion of other determinants such as class and racism. Radical feminist perspectives often represent women's procreative abilities as an indicator of certain psychological qualities which are uniquely and universally female. These qualities are assumed to have been undermined through patriarchal domination and thus have to be rediscovered and reclaimed. Sexual difference in the form of presumed unique female attributes and qualities may be celebrated. It has been argued that whilst repudiating biological determinism embedded within patriarchal discourses, some versions of radical feminism in turn construct a trans-historical notion of essential femaleness in need of rescuing and recapturing beyond patriarchal relations (Weedon, 1987; Segal, 1987; Spelman, 1988).

Socialist feminism, on the other hand, has been based on the assumption that human nature is not essential but is socially produced. The meaning of what it is to be a woman – biologically, socially, culturally and psychically – is considered to be historically variable. Socialist feminism has mounted a powerful critique of those materialist perspectives which prioritize class, neglect the social consequences of the sexual division of labour, privilege heterosexualities and pay scant attention to the social mechanisms which prevent women from attaining economic, political and social equality. This strand of feminism distances itself from the radical feminist emphasis on power relations between the sexes as the almost exclusive determinant of women's subordination.

On the whole, and especially until very recently, western feminist perspectives of whatever kind have paid little attention to the processes of racialization of gender, class or sexuality. Processes of racialization are, of course, historically specific, and different groups have been racialized differently under varying circumstances, and on the basis of different signifiers of 'difference'. Each racism has a particular history. It arose from a particular set of economic, political and cultural circumstances, has been reproduced through specific mechanisms, and has found different expression in different societies. Anti-black racism, anti-Irish racism, anti-Jewish racism, anti-Arab racism, different varieties of Orientalisms: all have distinctive features.

The specific histories of these various racisms place them in particular relationship to each other. For example, there are several similarities in the social experience of the Irish and black groups in Britain. Both sets of people have a history of being colonized by Britain, their migration patterns to Britain share common features, both groups occupy predominantly working-class positions within the British class structure, and they both have been subjected to racism. But anti-black and anti-Irish racism situates these groups differently within British society. As white Europeans, the great majority of Irish people are placed in a dominant position *vis-à-vis* black people in and through the discourses of anti-black racism, even when the two groups may share a similar class location. In other words, we assume different subject positions within various racisms. Analysis of the interconnections between racism, class, gender and sexuality must take account of the *positionality* of different racisms with respect to one another.

A second example may illustrate the above point further. African-Caribbean and South Asian communities have developed different responses to racism because their experiences of racism, though similar in many ways, have not been identical (Brah and Deem, 1986). State policies have impacted differently on these communities. African-Caribbean communities have mobilized far more around their collective experience of the criminal justice system, particularly the police and the courts, whereas Asian groups have been much more actively involved in defending communities against violent racial attacks, racial harassment on housing estates, and in organizing campaigns against deportations and other issues arising from the effects of immigration laws. The stereotypic representations of African-Caribbean and South Asian communities have also been substantially different. The gendered discourses of the 'nigger' and the 'Paki' in post-war Britain represent distinctive ideologies, yet they are two strands of a common racism structured around colour/phenotype/culture as signifiers of superiority and inferiority in post-colonial Britain. This means that African-Caribbean, South Asian and white groups are relationally positioned within these structures of representation. By their behaviour and actions they may reinforce these structures or alternatively they may assume a political practice which challenges these different strands of anti-black racism.

There is a tendency in Britain to see racism as 'something to do with the presence of Black people'. But it is important to stress that both black and white people experience their gender, class and sexuality through 'race'. Racialization of white subjectivity is often not manifestly apparent to white groups because 'white' is a signifier of dominance, but this renders the racialization process no less significant. We need to analyse the processes which construct us as 'white female', 'black female', 'white male', 'black male' etc. We need to examine how and why the meaning of these words changes from plain descriptions to hierarchically organized categories under given economic, political and social circumstances.

Black feminism, white feminism

During the 1970s there was a lack of much serious and sustained mainstream academic engagement with issues of gendered exploitation of post-colonial labour in the British metropolis, racism within state policies and cultural practices, the racialization of black and white subjectivity in the specific context of a period following the loss of Empire, and the particularities of black women's oppression within feminist theory and practice. This played an important part in the formation of black feminist organizations as distinct from the 'white' Women's Liberation Movement. These organizations emerged against the background of a deepening economic and political crisis and an increasing entrenchment of racism. The 1970s was a period when the Powellism of the 1960s came to suffuse the social fabric, and was gradually consolidated and transmuted into Thatcherism in the 1980s. The black communities were involved in a wide variety of political activity throughout the decade. There were major industrial strikes, several led by women. The Black Trade Union Solidarity Movement was formed to deal with racism in employment and trade unions. There were massive campaigns against immigration control, fascist violence, racist attacks on person and property, modes of policing that resulted in the harassment of black people, and against the criminalization of black communities. There were many self-help projects concerned with educational, welfare and cultural activities. Black women were involved in all these activities but the formation of autonomous black women's groups in the late 1970s injected a new dimension into the political scene.

The specific priorities of local black women's organizations, a number of which combined to form a national body – the Organization of Women of Asian and African Descent (OWAAD) – varied to an extent according to the exigencies of the local context. But the overall aim was to challenge the specific forms of oppression faced by the different categories of black women. The commitment to forging unity between African, Caribbean and Asian women demanded sustained attempts to analyse, understand and work with commonalities as well as heterogeneity of experience. It called for an interrogation of the role of colonialism and imperialism and that of contemporary economic, political and ideological processes in sustaining particular social divisions within these groups. It required black women to be sensitive to one another's cultural specificities while constructing common political strategies to confront sexism, racism and class inequality. This was no easy task and it is a testimony to the political commitment and vision of the women involved that this project thrived for many years, and some of the local groups have survived the divisive impact of ethnicism and remain active today (Bryan *et al.*, 1985; Brixton Black Women's Group, 1984).

The demise of OWAAD as a national organization in the early 1980s was precipitated by a number of factors. Many of these divisive tendencies have been paralleled in the women's movement as a whole. The organizations affiliated to OWAAD shared its broad aims but there were political differences amongst women on various issues. There was general agreement that racism was crucial in structuring our oppression in Britain but we differed in our analysis of racism and its links with class and other modes of inequality. For some women racism was an autonomous structure of oppression and had to be tackled as such; for others it was inextricably connected with class and other axes of social division. There were also differences in perspectives between feminists and non-feminists in OWAAD. For the latter, an emphasis on sexism was a diversion from the struggle against racism. The devaluation of black cultures by the onslaughts of racism meant that for some women the priority was to 'reclaim' these cultural sites and to situate themselves 'as women' within them. Whilst this was an important project there was, at times, more than a hint of idealizing a lost past. Other women argued that, whilst the empowering aspects of culture did need to be affirmed and validated, it was equally important to examine how culture is also a terrain on which women's oppression is produced and reproduced. The problem of male violence against women and children, the unequal sexual division of labour in the household, questions of dowry and forced marriages, clitorodectomy, heterosexism and the suppression of lesbian sexualities: all these were issues demanding immediate attention. Although most women in OWAAD recognized the importance of these issues, there were nonetheless major differences about priorities and political strategies to deal with them.

Alongside these tendencies there was an emerging emphasis within the women's movement as a whole on identity politics. Instead of embarking on the complex but necessary task of sifting out the specificities of particular oppressions, identifying their similarities or connections with other oppressions, and building a politics of solidarity, some women were beginning to differentiate these specificities into hierarchies of oppression. The mere act of naming oneself as a member of an oppressed group was assumed to vest one with moral authority. Multiple oppressions came to be regarded not in terms of their patterns of articulation/interconnections but rather as separate elements that could be added in a linear fashion, so that the more oppressions a woman could list the greater her claims to occupy a higher moral ground. Assertions about authenticity of personal experience could be presented as if they were an unproblematic guide to an understanding of processes of subordination and domination. Declarations concerning self-righteous political correctness sometimes came to substitute for careful political analysis (Adams, 1989; Ardill and O'Sullivan, 1986).

Despite the fragmentation of the women's movement, black women in Britain have continued to raise critical questions about feminist theory and practice. As a result of our location within diasporas formed by the history of slavery, colonialism and imperialism, black feminists have consistently argued against parochialism and stressed the need for a feminism sensitive to the international social relations of power (Carby, 1982; Parmar, 1982; *Feminist Review*, 1984; Brah and Minhas, 1985; Brah, 1987; Phoenix, 1987; Grewal *et al.*, 1988; Mama, 1989; Lewis, 1990). Hazel Carby's article, 'White women listen', for instance, presents a critique of such key feminist concepts as 'patriarchy', 'the family' and 'reproduction'. She criticizes feminist perspectives which use notions of 'feudal residues' and 'traditionalism' to create sliding scales of 'civilized liberties', with the 'Third World' seen at one end of the scale and the supposedly progressive 'First World' at the other. She provides several illustrations of how a certain type of western feminism can serve to reproduce rather than challenge the categories through which 'the West' constructs and represents itself as superior to its 'others'.

These critiques have generated some critical self-reflection on the part of white feminist writers. Barrett and McIntosh (1985), for example, have attempted to re-assess their earlier work. They acknowledge the limitations of the concept of patriarchy as unambiguous and invariable male dominance undifferentiated by class or racism, but wish to retain the notion of 'patriarchal' as signifying how 'particular social relations combine a public dimension of power, exploitation or status with a dimension of personal servility' (p. 39). Having made this point, they fail to explore in any systematic way how and why the concept of the 'patriarchal' helps us to engage with the interconnections between gender, class and racism. The mere substitution of the concept of patriarchy by patriarchal relations will not by itself deal with the charges of ahistoricism, universalism or essentialism that have been levelled at the former, although, as Walby (1990) argues, it is possible to provide historicized accounts of patriarchy. As a response to recent reconceptualizations of patriarchy, Joan Acker suggests that it might be more appropriate to shift 'the theoretical object from patriarchy to gender, which we can define briefly as structural, relational, and symbolic differentiations between women and men' (Acker, 1989, p. 238). She remains cautious about this shift, however, as 'gender', according to her, lacks the critical political sharpness of 'patriarchy' and could much more easily be co-opted and neutralized within 'mainstream' theory.

Patriarchal relations are a specific form of gender relations in which women inhabit a subordinated position. In theory, at least, it should be possible to envisage a social context in which gender relations are not associated with inequality between the sexes *qua* women and men. I would argue in favour of retaining the concept of 'patriarchal' without necessarily subscribing to the concept of 'patriarchy' – whether historicized or not – because I hold serious reservation about the analytic or political utility of maintaining system boundaries between 'patriarchy' and the particular socio-economic and political formation (for example, capitalism or state socialism) with which it articulates. The issue is not whether patriarchal relations pre-date capitalism or state socialism, for they patently do, but how they are manifested within these systems in the context of a history of colonialism and imperialism in different parts of the globe. Structures of class, racism, gender and sexuality cannot be treated as 'independent variables' because the oppression of each is inscribed within the other – is constituted by and is constitutive of the other.

Acknowledging the black feminist critique, Barrett and McIntosh stress the need to analyse the ideological construction of white femininity through racism. This in my view is essential since there is still a tendency to address questions of inequality through a focus on the victims of inequality. Discussions about feminism and racism often centre around the oppression of black women rather than exploring how both black and white women's gender is constructed through class and racism. This means that white women's 'privileged position' within racialized discourses (even when they may share a class position with black women) fails to be adequately theorized and processes of domination remain invisible. The representation of white women as 'the moral guardians of a superior race', for instance, serves to homogenize white women's sexuality at the same time as it fractures it across class in that the white working-class woman, although also presented as 'carrier of the race', is simultaneously constructed as prone to 'degeneracy' because of her class background. Here we see how class contradictions may be worked through and 'resolved' ideologically within the racialized structuration of gender.

Barrett and McIntosh's article generated considerable debate (Ramazanoglu, Kazi, Lees and Safia-Mirza in *Feminist Review*, 1986; Bhavnani and Coulson, 1986). Whilst acknowledging the importance of the reassessment of a part of their work by two prominent white feminists, the critics argued that their methods of re-examination failed to provide the possibility of radical transformation of previous analysis, thus leaving the ways in which 'race' features within social reproduction largely untheorized. Although Barrett and McIntosh note that socialists are divided as to whether the social divisions associated with ethnicity and racism should be seen as absolutely autonomous of social class, as reducible to social class, or as having historical origins but articulating now with the divisions of class in capitalist society (1985, p. 38), they do not signal their own analytical preference on these issues. This is a surprising silence in an article whose aim is to advance our understanding of conceptual and theoretical concerns in the field.

I would argue that racism is neither reducible to social class or gender nor wholly autonomous. Racisms have variable historical origins but they articulate with patriarchal class structures in specific ways under given historical conditions. Racisms may have independent effectivity, but to suggest this is not the same as saying, as Caroline Ramazanoglu (1989) does, that racism is an 'independent form of domination'. The search for grand theories specifying the interconnections between racism, gender and class has been less than productive. They are best construed as historically contingent and context-specific relationships. Hence, we can focus on a given context and differentiate between the demarcation of a category as an object of social discourse, as an analytical category, and as a subject of political mobilization without making assumptions about their permanence or stability across time and space. This means that 'white' feminism or 'black' feminism in Britain are not essentialist categories but rather they are fields of contestation inscribed within discursive and material processes and practices in a post-colonial terrain. They represent struggles over political frameworks for analysis; the meanings of theoretical concepts; the relationship between theory, practice and subjective experiences; and over political priorities and modes of mobilizations. But they should not, in my view, be understood as locating 'white' and 'black' women as 'essentially' fixed oppositional categories.

More recent contributions to the debate make the point that, irrespective of the intentions of the authors, antiracist feminist discourses of the late 1970s and 1980s did not always facilitate political mobilization. Knowles and Mercer (this volume), for example, take the position that Carby's and Bourne's emphasis on the inscription of racism and gender inequality within processes of capitalism, colonialism, and patriarchal social systems produced functionalist arguments – that sexism and racism were inherent within these systems and served the needs of these systems to perpetuate themselves. They believe that this approach demanded nothing short of an all-embracing struggle against these 'isms' that thereby undermined more localized, small-scale political responses. Their own method of dealing with this is to suggest that racism and sexism be 'viewed as a series of effects which do not have a single cause' (p. 110). I would accept the arguments that the level of abstraction at which categories such as 'capitalism' or 'patriarchal relations' are delineated does not provide straightforward guidelines for concrete strategy and action, and also that racism and sexism are not monocausal phenomena. Nonetheless, I am not sure how treating racism and sexism as a 'series of effects' provides any clearer guidelines for political response. The same 'effect' may be interpreted from a variety of political positions, and lead to quite different strategies for action. Taking up a specific political position means that one is making certain assumptions about the nature of the various processes that underline a social phenomenon of which a particular event may be an effect. A focus only on 'effects' may render invisible the workings of such ideological and material processes, thereby hindering our understanding of the complex basis of inequalities. Although crucial in mobilizing specific constituencies, the single-issue struggles *as ends in themselves* may delimit wider-ranging challenges to social inequalities. The language of 'effects' in any case assumes the existence of some causes. The main issue is not whether we should jettison macro-level analysis of gender or racism in relation to capitalism, colonialism or state socialism in favour of empirically grounded analysis of the concrete manifestations of racism in a given local situation, but how each is overdetermined by, and also helps to determine, the others.

I share Knowles and Mercer's reservations about analytical and political perspectives in which social inequality comes to be personified in the bodies of the dominant social groups – white people, men, or heterosexual individuals in relation to racism, sexism or heterosexism – but we cannot ignore the social relations of power that inscribe such differentiations. Members of dominant groups do occupy privileged positions within political and material practices that attend these social divisions, although the precise interplay of this power in specific institutions or in interpersonal relations cannot be stipulated in advance, may be contradictory, and can be challenged.

A somewhat different critique of black feminist writing challenges the validity of black feminism as representing anything more than the interests of black women (Tang Nain, 1990). By implication black feminism is cast as sectarian in comparison with radical or socialist feminism. This comparison is problematic since it constructs black feminism as outside radical or socialist feminism. In practice, the category 'black feminism' in Britain is only meaningful *vis-à-vis* the category 'white feminism'. If, as I have argued earlier, these two categories are contingent rather than essentialist, then one cannot ask the question as Tang Nain does whether 'black feminism' is open to all women without simultaneously asking the same question of 'white feminism'. Tang Nain's characterization of radical or socialist feminism as 'open to all women' flies in the face of massive evidence which shows that in Britain and the USA at least, these feminisms have failed to take adequate account of racism and the experience of racialized groups of women. The ideology of 'open to all' can in fact legitimize all kinds of *de facto* exclusion. Socialist feminism, for example, cannot really include women who are subjected to racism unless it is a non-racist socialist feminism, or lesbian women unless it is simultaneously non-heterosexist, or lower-caste women unless it is also non-casteist. But these issues cannot be realized in the abstract, nor can they be settled once and for all, but through ongoing political struggles.

For similar reasons, Floya Anthias and Nira Yuval-Davis' critique of the category 'black' on the grounds that it failed to address diversity of ethnic exclusions and subordinations seems misplaced (1982). The boundaries of

a political constituency formed around specific concerns is dependent upon
the nature of the concerns and their salience and significance in the lives
of the people so affected. Black feminism constructed a constituency in
terms of the gendered experience of anti-black racism. White ethnic
groups who were not subjected to this particular form of racism could not,
therefore, be part of this constituency. This does not mean that their
experiences of, say, anti-semitism are any the less important. Rather,
anti-black racism and anti-semitism cannot be subsumed under each
other. This becomes patently clear if we compare the experience of a white
Jewish woman and black Jewish woman. The black woman is simultaneously positioned within two racialized discourses. Anthias and Yuval-
Davis make some incisive points about ethnicity as a category of social
differentiation, but their contention that 'black feminism can be too wide
or too narrow a category for specific feminist struggles' (p. 63) remains
problematic since the emergence of the black women's movement as a
historically specific response is a testament that organization around the
category 'black women' is possible. This need not preclude coalitions
across other boundaries, and black women have worked with white
women on several issues of common concern. Any alternatives to the
political category 'black', such as 'women of colour' or some term as yet not
in currency, may emerge through organic involvement in new struggles
set against a changed economic and political climate. But they cannot be
willed in the abstract or decided in advance.

My proposition that 'black' and 'white' feminisms be addressed as non-
essentialist, historically contingent discursive practices implies that black
and white women can work together towards the creation of non-racist
feminist theory and practice. The key issue then is not about 'difference'
per se, but concerns the question of who defines difference, how different
categories of women are represented within the discourses of 'difference',
and whether 'difference' differentiates laterally or hierarchically. We need
greater conceptual clarity in analysing difference.

Difference, what difference?

It is evident that the concept of difference is associated with different
meanings in different discourses. But how are we to understand
'difference'? A detailed discussion of this topic is beyond the scope of this
article but I would like to suggest four ways in which difference may be
conceptualized and addressed: difference as experience, difference as
social relations, difference as subjectivity and difference as identity.

Difference as experience

Experience has been a key concept within feminism. Women's movements
have aimed to give a collective voice to women's personal experiences of

social and psychic forces that constitute the 'female' into the 'woman'. The everyday of the social relations of gender – ranging from housework and childcare, low-paid employment and economic dependency to sexual violence and women's exclusion from key centres of political and cultural power – have all been given a new significance through feminism as they have been brought out of the realm of the 'taken for granted' to be interrogated and challenged. The personal, with its profoundly concrete yet elusive qualities, and its manifold contradiction, acquired new meanings in the slogan 'the personal is political' as consciousness-raising groups provided the forums for exploring individual experiences, personal feelings, and women's own understandings of their daily lives.

The limitations of the consciousness-raising method (empowering though it was for some women) as a strategy for systematically challenging the structures of gender inequality have been widely acknowledged. Nonetheless there was at least an implicit recognition in this mode of working that experience did not transparently reflect reality, but instead it was a constellation of mediated relationships, a site of contradictions to be addressed collectively. This insight is quite often missing from current discussions about differences between women where difference and experience are used primarily as a 'commonsensical term' (Barrett, 1987). Hence, the need to re-emphasize a notion of experience not as an unmediated guide to 'truth' but as a practice of making sense, both symbolically and narratively; as struggle over material conditions and over meaning.

Difference as social relations

The emphasis here is on social relations at the level of the social structure. A group usually mobilizes the concept of difference in this sense of a social relation when addressing the structural, political, and historical basis of the commonality of its experience. Experience is understood here primarily in terms of collective histories.

In practice, the *everyday of lived experience* and *experience as a social relation* do not exist in mutually exclusive spaces. For example, if we speak of 'North African women in France', we are, on the one hand, referring to the *social relations* of gendered post-coloniality in France. On the other hand, we are also making a statement about the *everyday experience* of this post-coloniality on the part of such women, although we cannot specify, in advance, the particularity of individual women's lives or how they interpret and define this experience. In both instances, the question of how difference is defined remains paramount. Are perceptions of difference in a given context a basis of affirming diversity or a mechanism for exclusionary and discriminatory practices? Do discourses of difference legitimize progressive or oppressive state policies and practices? How are different categories of women represented within such discourses? How do the women themselves construct, or represent the specificity of their experience? Under what circumstances does 'difference' become the basis of asserting a collective identity?

Difference as subjectivity

Issues of difference have been central to theoretical debates around subjectivity. A key question facing us is: how are racialized subjects formed? But the question of racialization of subjectivity has not yet received much attention within feminist theory which has been preoccupied with the status of 'sexual difference' in the formation of subjectivity. Feminists have turned to psychoanalysis (notably its post-structuralist and object-relations variants) and to forms of deconstructionist thought to understand the processes of identity formation.

With the growing awareness that women's innermost emotions, feelings, desires and fantasies, with their multiple contradictions, could not be understood purely in terms of the imperatives of the social institutions and the forces of male domination, feminists have approached psycho-analysis for a more complex account of the trials and tribulations of psychic life. Dissatisfied with the social conditioning approaches to women's psychology, some feminists have looked to Lacan's re-reading of Freud for a non-reductive understanding of subjectivity. Post-structuralist accounts have proved attractive to feminism for they seek to problematize 'sexual difference': sexual difference is something to be explained rather than assumed. Subjectivity is seen as neither unified nor fixed – rather it is something that is constantly in progress. Compelling arguments have been made in favour of the importance of psychoanalysis for feminism against those critics who assume that the notion of a fragmented sexual identity constantly in process is at odds with the feminist project of constructing oppositional consciousness through collective action (see Rose, 1986; Penley, 1989; Minsky, 1990).

These arguments are convincing, but certain issues still need to be addressed. The enormous contribution of individuals such as Fanon notwithstanding, much work is yet to be undertaken on the subject of how the racialized 'other' is constituted in the psychic domain. How is post-colonial gendered and racialized subjectivity to be analysed? Does the privileging of 'sexual difference' and early childhood in psychoanalysis limit its explanatory value in helping us to understand psychic dimensions of social phenomena such as racism? How do the 'symbolic order' and the social order articulate in the formation of the subject? In other words, how is the link between social and psychic reality to be theorized? There is also the issue of how certain psychoanalytical discourses are themselves implicated in the inscription of racism (Dalal, 1988).

Difference as identity

Our struggles over meaning are also our struggles over different modes of being: different identities (Minh-ha, 1989). Identity is never a fixed core.

On the other hand, changing identities do assume specific, concrete patterns, as in a kaleidoscope, against particular sets of historical and social circumstances. Our cultural identities are simultaneously our cultures in process, but they acquire specific meanings in a given context. Social phenomena such as racism seek to fix and naturalize 'difference' and create impervious boundaries between groups. The modalities of difference inscribed within the particularities of our personal and collective historical, cultural and political experience – our ethnicities – can interrogate and challenge the strangulating imagination of racism but the task is a complex one, for ethnicities are liable to be appropriated by racism as signifiers of permanent boundaries. Hence, the 'Englishness' of a particular class can come to represent itself via racism as 'Britishness' against those ethnicities that it subordinates – such as those of the Irish, Scottish, Welsh, black British, or the ethnicities of the formerly colonized world. But, as I noted earlier, white/European ethnicities are subordinated differently from non-white, non-European ethnicities.

It should be possible through political practice to retrieve ethnicity from racialized nationalist discourses so that it can be manifested as a non-essentialist horizontality rather than hierarchically organized difference. As Stuart Hall says:

> The fact that this grounding of ethnicity in difference was deployed, in the discourse of racism, as a means of disavowing the realities of racism and repression does not mean that we can permit the term to be permanently colonized. That appropriation will have to be contested, the term disarticulated from its position in the discourse of 'multi-culturalism' and transcoded, just as we previously had to recuperate the term 'black', from its place in a system of negative equivalences. (Hall, this volume, p. 257)

But the project is always beset with difficulties. Since ethnicities are always gendered they construct sexual difference in specific ways. The appropriation of a particular ethnicity cannot be assumed to necessarily involve challenging gender inequalities unless this is undertaken as a conscious objective. Indeed, the reverse may be the case. Similarly, depending upon the context, ethnicities may legitimize class or caste divisions by proclaiming and stressing only the unity of an otherwise heterogeneous group.

So how can we claim ethnicities that do not reinforce inequalities? The project is complex but broadly will entail a variety of concrete practices at the economic, political and cultural level designed to undermine the relations of power that underlie these inequalities. There will be the need to remain vigilant of the circumstances under which affirmation of a particular collective experience becomes an essentialist assertion of difference. This problem may arise not only in relation to dominant ethnicities but also dominated ethnicities. In their struggle against the hegemonic, universalizing imperatives of the former, the latter may also take recourse to constructing essentialist differences. This can be especially problematic for women if the cultural values that the groups in question excavate, recast, and reconstruct are those that underscore women's subordination.

Although I have argued against essentialism, it is not easy to deal with this problem. In their need to create new political identities, dominated groups will often appeal to bonds of common cultural experience in order to mobilize their constituency. In so doing they may assert a seemingly essentialist difference. Spivak (1987) and Fuss (1989) have argued in favour of such a 'strategic essentialism'. They believe that the 'risk' of essentialism may be worth taking if framed from the vantage point of a dominated subject position. This will remain problematic if a challenge to one form of oppression leads to the reinforcement of another. It may be over-ambitious, but it is imperative that we do not compartmentalize oppressions, but instead formulate strategies for challenging all oppressions on the basis of an understanding of how they interconnect and articulate.

References

Acker, J. (1989) 'The problem with patriarchy', *Sociology*, **23**(2).

Adams, M. L. (1989) 'Identity politics', *Feminist Review*, **31**.

Anthias, F. and Yuval-Davis, N. (1982) 'Contextualising feminism', *Feminist Review*, **15**.

Ardill, S. and O'Sullivan, S. (1986) 'Upsetting an applecart: difference, desire and lesbian sadomasochism', *Feminist Review*, **23**.

Barrett, M. (1987) 'The concept of difference', *Feminist Review*, **26**.

Barrett, M. and McIntosh, M. (1985) 'Ethnocentrism and socialist-feminist theory', *Feminist Review*, **20**.

Bhavnani, K. K. and Coulson, M. (1986) 'Transforming socialist feminism: the challenge of racism', *Feminist Review*, **23**.

Bourne, J. (1983) 'Towards an anti-racist feminism', *Race and Class*, **25**(1).

Brah, A. (1987) 'Women of South Asian origin in Britain: issues and concerns', *South Asia Research*, **7**(1).

Brah, A. (1988) 'A Journey to Nairobi' in Grewal *et al.* (eds) *Charting the Journey*, London, Sheba.

Brah, A. and Deem, R. (1986) 'Towards anti-sexist and anti-racist schooling', *Critical Social Policy*, Issue 16.

Brah, A. and Minhas, R. (1985) 'Structural racism or cultural difference: schooling for Asian girls' in Weiner, G. (ed.) *Just a Bunch of Girls*, Milton Keynes, Open University Press.

Brixton Black Women's Group (1984) 'Black women organising autonomously', *Feminist Review*, **17**.

Bryan, B., Dadzie, S. and Scafe, S. (1985) *Heart of the Race*, London, Virago Press.

Cain, H. and Yuval-Davis, N. (1990) 'The "Equal Opportunity Community" and the anti-racist struggle', *Critical Social Policy*, Issue 29, **10**(2).

Carby, H. (1982) 'White women listen! Black feminism and boundaries of sisterhood' in CCCS, *The Empire Strikes Back*, London, Hutchinson.

Dalal, F. (1988) 'The racism of Jung', *Race and Class*, **24**(3).

Feminist Review (1984) 'Many voices, one chant: black feminist perspectives', *Feminist Review*, **17**.

Feminist Review (1986) 'Feedback: feminism and racism', *Feminist Review*, **22**.

Fuss, D. (1989) *Essentially Speaking*, London, Routledge.

Gilroy, P. (1987) *There Ain't No Black in the Union Jack*, London, Hutchinson.

Grewal, S., Kay, J., Landor, L., Lewis, G., Parmar, P. (1988) *Charting the Journey*, London, Sheba.

Hazareesingh, S. (1986) 'Racism and cultural identity: an Indian perspective', *Dragons' Teeth*, **24**.

Knowles, C. and Mercer, S. (1990) 'Feminism and anti-racism' in Cambridge, A. and Feuchtwang, S. (eds) *Anti-racist Strategies*, Aldershot, Avebury (Wildwood).

Lewis, G. (1990) 'Audre Lorde: vignettes and mental conversations', *Feminist Review*, **34**.

Mama, A. (1989) 'Violence against black women: gender, race, and state responses', *Feminist Review*, **32**.

Minh-ha, T. (1989) *Women, Native, Other: writing post coloniality and feminism*, Indianapolis, Indiana University Press.

Minsky, R. (1990) '"The trouble is it's ahistorical": the problem of the unconscious in modern feminist theory', *Feminist Review*, **36**.

Modood, T. (1988) '"Black" racial equality and Asian identity', *New Community*, **14**(3).

Mohanty, C. T. (1988) 'Under Western eyes: feminist scholarships and colonial discourses', *Feminist Review*, **30**.

Parmar, (1982) 'Gender, race and class: Asian women in resistance' in Centre for Contemporary Cultural Studies *The Empire Strikes Back*, London, Hutchinson.

Penley, C. (1989) *The Future of an Illusion: film, feminism and psychoanalysis*, London, Routledge.

Phoenix, A. (1987) 'Theories of gender and black families' in Weiner, G. and Arnot, M. (eds) *Gender under Scrutiny*, Milton Keynes, Open University Press.

Ramazanoglu, C. (1989) *Feminism and the Contradictions of Oppression*, London, Routledge.

Rose, J. (1986) *Sexuality in the Field of Vision*, London, Verso.

Rose, S., Kamin, J. and Lewontin, R. C. (1984) *Not in Our Genes*, Harmondsworth, Pelican Books.

Segal, L. (1987) *Is The Future Female?*, London, Virago Press.

Segal, L. (1990) *Slow Motion: changing masculinities, changing men*, London, Virago Press.

Sivanandan, A. (1985) 'Race and the degradation of black struggle', *Race and Class*, **26**(4).

Spelman, E. V. (1988) *Inessential Woman: problems of exclusion in feminist thought*, London, Women's Press.

Spivak, G. (1987) *In Other Worlds: essays in cultural politics*, London, Methuen.

Tang Nain, G. (1990) 'Black women, sexism and racism: black or anti-racist?', *Feminist Review*, **37**.

Walby, S. (1990) *Theorizing Patriarchy*, Oxford, Basil Blackwell.

Weedon, C. (1987) *Feminist Practice and Poststructuralist Theory*, Oxford, Basil Blackwell.

PART 2

'US' AND 'THEM'

6 THE BEGINNINGS OF ENGLISH LITERARY STUDY IN BRITISH INDIA

GAURI VISWANATHAN

This paper is part of a larger inquiry into the construction of English literary education as a cultural ideal in British India. British parliamentary documents have provided compelling evidence for the central thesis of the investigation: that humanistic functions traditionally associated with the study of literature – for example, the shaping of character or the development of the aesthetic sense or the disciplines of ethical thinking – are also essential to the process of sociopolitical control. My argument is that literary study gained enormous cultural strength through its development in a period of territorial expansion and conquest, and that the subsequent institutionalization of the discipline in England itself took on a shape and an ideological content developed in the colonial context. [. . .]

1

English literature made its inroads in India, albeit gradually and imperceptibly, with a crucial event in Indian educational history: the passing of the Charter Act of 1813. This act, which renewed the East India Company's charter for commercial operations in India, produced two major changes in Britain's role with respect to its Indian subjects: one was the assumption of a new responsibility towards native education, and the other was a relaxation of controls over missionary work in India.

Without minimizing the historical importance of the renewal of the Company's charter, it would be safe to say that the more far-reaching significance of the Charter Act lay in the commitment enjoined upon England to undertake the education of the native subjects, a responsibility which it did not officially bear even towards its own people. Hitherto, measures to educate the natives were entirely at the discretion of the Governor-General at Calcutta and the Company was in no way obligated to attend to their instruction. Indeed, reluctant as it was to spend any more money on the natives than necessary, the East India Company was all too willing to abide by the practice in England where education was not a state responsibility. The Charter Act, however, radically altered the prevailing state of *laissez-faire* in Indian educational matters. The 13th Resolution categorically stated that England was obligated to promote the 'interests and happiness' of the natives and that measures ought to be adopted 'as may tend to the introduction among them of useful knowledge, and of religious and moral improvement'.[1]

The pressure to assume a more direct responsibility for the welfare of the natives came from several sources. The earlier and perhaps more significant one, decisively affecting the future course of British adminis-trative rule in India, was the Westminster Parliament. Significantly, the goal of civilizing the natives was far from being the central motivation in these first official efforts at educational activity. Parliamentary involve-ment with Indian education had a rather uncommon origin in that it began with the excesses of their own countrymen in India. The extra-vagant life-styles of the East India Company servants, combined with their ruthless exploitation of native material resources, had begun to raise serious and alarming questions in England about the morality of the British presence in India. It was an issue that was too embarrassing for Parliament to ignore without appearing to endorse Company excesses. But unable to check the activities of these highly placed 'Nabobs', or wealthy Europeans whose huge fortunes were amassed in India, it sought instead to remedy the wrongs committed against the natives by attending to their welfare and improvement.

Yet however much parliamentary discussions of the British presence in India may have been couched in moral terms, there was no obscuring the real issue, which remained political not moral. The English Parliament's conflict with the East India Company was a long-standing one, going back to the early years of trading activity in the East Indies when rival companies clashed repeatedly in a bid to gain exclusive rights to trade in the region. The East India Company, formed from two rival companies, eventually became the only group of English merchants entitled to carry on English trade. But the clamour for a broadening of commercial privileges in India never died down, and Parliament found itself besieged by Free Trade groups lobbying to break the Company monopoly. In 1813 it had no choice but to concede them greater trading privileges.

Moreover, the English Parliament itself was becoming alarmed by the danger of having a commercial company constituting an independent political power in India. By 1757 the East India Company had already become virtual master of Bengal, and its territorial influence was growing steadily despite numerous financial problems besetting it. But in the absence of any cause for interference in the activities of the Company, the British Crown could conceivably do little to reorganize the Company's system of administration and win control of its affairs. Pitt's India Bill of

1784 had earlier rejected an outright subordination of the political conduct of the Company to the Crown, and the government remained ambiguously placed in relation to the Company. Not until the last quarter of the eighteenth century, when reports of immorality and depravity among Company servants started pouring in, did Parliament find an excuse to intervene, at which point, in the name of undertaking responsibility for the improvement of the natives, it began to take a serious and active interest in Indian political affairs. It was a move that was to result in a gradual erosion of the unchallenged supremacy of the Company in India.

One cannot fail to be struck by the peculiar irony of a history in which England's initial involvement with the education of the natives derived not from a conviction of native immorality as the later discourse might lead one to believe, but from the depravity of their own administrators and merchants. In Edmund Burke's words, steps had to be taken to 'form a strong and solid security for the natives against the wrongs and oppressions of British subjects resident in Bengal'.[2] While the protective-ness contained in this remark may seem dangerously close to an attitude of paternalism, its immediate effect was beneficial, as it led to a strength-ening of existing native institutions and traditions to act as a bulwark against the forces of violent change unleashed by the British presence.

This mission to revitalize Indian culture and learning and protect it from the oblivion to which foreign rule might doom it merged with the then current literary vogue of 'Orientalism' and formed the mainstay of that phase of British rule in India known as the 'Orientalist' phase. Orientalism was adopted as an official policy partly out of expediency and caution and partly out of an emergent political sense that an efficient Indian administration rested on an understanding of Indian culture. It grew out of the concern of Warren Hastings, governor-general from 1774 to 1785, that British administrators and merchants in India were not sufficiently responsive to Indian languages and Indian traditions. The distance between ruler and ruled was perceived to be so vast as to evoke the sentiment that 'we rule over them and traffic with them, but they do not understand our character, and we do not penetrate theirs. The consequence is that we have no hold on their sympathies, no seat in their affections'.[3] Hastings' own administration was distinguished by a toler-ance for the native customs and by a cultural empathy unusual for its time. Underlying Orientalism was a tacit policy of what one may call reverse acculturation, whose goal was to train British administrators and civil servants to fit into the culture of the ruled and to assimilate them thoroughly into the native way of life. The great scholars produced by eighteenth-century Orientalism – William Jones, Henry T. Colebrooke, Jonathan Halhed, Charles Wilkins – entirely owed their reputations to a happy coincidence of pioneering achievement and official patronage. Their exhaustive research had ambitious goals, ranging from the initiation of the West to the vast literary treasures of the East to the reintroduction of the natives to their own cultural heritage, represented by the Orientalists as being buried under the debris of foreign conquest and depredations.

Yet no matter how benign and productive its general influence might appear [. . .] there is no denying that behind Orientalism's exhaustive inquiries, its immense scholarly achievements and discoveries, lay interests that were far from scholarly. Whether later Orientalists were willing to acknowledge it or not, Warren Hastings clearly understood the driving force of Orientalism to be the doctrine that 'every accumulation of knowledge, and especially such as is obtained by social communication with people over whom we exercise a dominion founded on the right of conquest, is useful to the state: it is the gain of humanity'[4] [. . .] Aside from his obviously questionable assumptions about the 'right of conquest', what is most striking about this statement is the intellectual leap it makes from knowledge which is useful to the state to knowledge which becomes the gain of humanity. The relationship of power existing between England and India is certainly one condition allowing for such a leap, but more to the point is the role of the state in mediating between the worlds of scholarship and politics. For Hastings, it was not merely that the state had a vital interest in the production of knowledge about those whom it rules; more importantly, it also had a role in actively processing and then selectively delivering that knowledge up to mankind in the guise of 'objective knowledge'.

A peculiar logic runs through the argument and it has to be monitored closely if one is to appreciate Hastings' keen understanding of the powerful reinforcing effect of Orientalist scholarship upon state authority. The acquisition of knowledge about those whom it governs is clearly perceived to be of vital importance to the state for purposes of domination and control. But the fact that this knowledge eventually passes into the realm of 'humanistic' scholarship (again through the agency of the state) confers a certain legitimacy upon the quest and, by extension, upon the state which promotes it. In other words, even though 'social communication' may have its roots in the impulse to enforce domination over the natives, as Hastings has no hesitation in acknowledging, its political motivation is nullified by virtue of the fixed body of knowledge it produces and makes available to the rest of mankind. The disinterestedness and objectivity which this now shared and therefore 'true' knowledge purports to represent help to confirm the state's 'right of conquest', which duly acquires the status of the *sine qua non* of knowledge-production. What therefore appears on the surface as a rhetorical leap is in fact the carefully controlled effect of a self-fortifying dialectic.

As a candid acknowledgement of the implicit political goals of Orientalism, Hastings' argument belies some of the arbitrary distinctions that are at times made between Orientalism and Anglicism, the countermovement that gained ascendancy in the 1830s. Briefly, Anglicism grew as an expression of discontent with the policy of promoting the Oriental languages and literatures in native education. In its vigorous advocacy of

Western instead of Eastern learning, it came into sharp conflict with the proponents of Orientalism, who vehemently insisted that such a move would have disastrous consequences, the most serious being the alienation of the natives from British rule. However, while it is true that the two movements appear to represent diametrically opposed positions, what is not adequately stressed in the educational literature is the degree to which Anglicism was dependent upon Orientalism for its ideological programme. Through its government-supported researches and scholarly investigations, Orientalism had produced a vast body of knowledge about the native subjects which the Anglicists subsequently drew upon to mount their attack on the culture as a whole. In short, Orientalist scholarship undertaken in the name of 'gains for humanity' gave the Anglicists precisely the material evidence they needed for drawing up a system of comparative evaluations in which one culture could be set off and measured against the other. [...] It would be more accurate to describe Orientalism and Anglicism not as polar opposites but as points along a continuum of attitudes towards the manner and form of native governance, the necessity and justification for which remained by and large an issue of remarkably little disagreement.

To understand the forces enabling the shift along a sliding scale from Orientalism to Anglicism, it is necessary first to distinguish the various political and commercial groups entering the Indian scene. Warren Hastings was succeeded in the governor-generalship by Lord Cornwallis (1786–93), who found himself at the helm of a government seriously compromised by financial scandals and deteriorating standards. For this state of affairs the new governor-general squarely laid the blame on the earlier policy of accommodation to the native culture. In his view the official indulgence towards Oriental forms of social organization, especially government, was directly responsible for the lax morals of the Company servants. If the Company had sorely abused its power, what better explanation was there than the fact that the model of Oriental despotism was constantly before its eyes? To Cornwallis, the abuse of power was the most serious of evils afflicting the East India Company, not only jeopardizing the British hold over India but, worse still, dividing the English nation on the legitimacy of the colonial enterprise.

The most pressing task therefore was to ensure that no further abuse would occur. In the process of working towards this end, Cornwallis evolved a political philosophy that he believed would be consistent with British commercial aims. His theoretical position was that a good government was held together not by men but by political principles and laws, and in these alone rested absolute power. The Oriental system lacking a strong political tradition (and in this belief Cornwallis was doing no more than echoing a view that was common currency); he turned to English principles of government and jurisprudence for setting the norms of public behaviour and responsibility by which administrators were to function. Determined to run a government that would remain free of corrupting influences from the native society, Cornwallis concentrated his entire energies on the improvement of European morals on English lines. The natives engaged his attention only minimally; for the most part, he appeared wholly content to leave them in their 'base' state in the belief that their reform was well beyond his purview.

Clearly, the first steps towards anglicization were aimed at tackling the problem of corruption within the ranks. To this extent [. . .] Anglicism began as a defensive movement. But even in this form it was not without elements of aggression towards the native culture, as is apparent in certain measures that Cornwallis adopted to streamline the government. Convinced that contact with natives was the root cause of declining European morals, he resolved to exclude all natives from appointment to responsible posts, hoping by this means to restore the Englishman to his pristine self and rid him once and for all of decadent influences.

Predictably, the exclusion of Indians from public office had serious repercussions on Anglo-Indian relations. The personal contact that Englishmen and Indians had enjoyed during Hastings' administration vanished with Cornwallis, and the result was that a more rigidified master–subject relationship set in. One historian, Percival Spear, has gone so far as to suggest that this event marks the point at which there developed 'that contempt for things and persons Indian . . . and which produced the views of a Mill or a Macaulay'.[5] Denied all opportunities for expression as a result of the harsh measure, public ability declined steadily. But curiously when this occurred, it was taken to mean that civic responsibility had never existed in India, thus giving rise to one of the most durable legends of British rule: that the Indian mind was best suited to minor pursuits of trade but not to government or administration.

With Cornwallis charting an apparently serious course for administrative rule on English principles, one would expect Anglicism as a cultural movement to have triumphed much earlier than it actually did (i.e., the 1830s). Its momentum was badly shattered, however, by the cultural policy of his immediate successors, a group of skilled and politically astute administrators who had all at one time served under Lord Wellesley, a governor-general (1798–1805) noted for his caution and reserve, and later under the Marquess of Hastings under whose governor-generalship (1812–23) British rule was more firmly consolidated. Conservative in their outlook and fiercely romantic in their disposition, these accomplished officers – John Malcolm, Thomas Munro, Charles Metcalf, and Mountstuart Elphinstone – had no use for the impersonal, bureaucratic system of government carved out for India by Cornwallis. It is helpful to recall that these men came to power at a time when England's wars both abroad and within India had come to an end and the task of consolidating the empire lay before them. Under such altered circumstances the earlier Company policy of expediency and caution was clearly outmoded.

But for reasons pertaining to their aristocratic backgrounds, feudal beliefs and romantic temperament, this new generation of administrators was fiercely resistant to replacing the rule of men with the rule of law. It is true that in certain respects the form of government they favoured was no different from their predecessor's, particularly in its commitment to the liberal doctrine of protection of property rights. But the kind of relationship they envisaged between ruler and ruled was an outright rejection of the abstract and impersonal one of the Cornwallis system in which the mechanistic operations of law had ultimate authority. Distrusting the power of law to effect changes either in individuals or in society, they belonged to an older tradition which, as Eric Stokes points out, 'saw the division of society into ruler and ruled as a natural ordering, and which envisaged submission to authority as necessary to the anarchic nature of man'.[6] With its strong feudal overtones, the form of government they wanted for India was a frankly paternalistic one, firm yet bene-volent, and open to the native traditions of law, government, and religion.

While Cornwallis had no particular interest in either promoting or discouraging Oriental learning, as long as Englishmen were not com-pelled to go through its studies, his successors by no means shared his indifference. Indeed, they were shrewd enough to see that it was entirely in their interest to support Orientalism if it meant the preservation of the feudal character of British rule. Their espousal of Orientalism might lead one to suspect a return to the earlier Company policy of Warren Hastings. But to do so is to ignore the changed political circumstances under which the Orientalist policy now received patronage. Hastings' wholehearted enthusiasm for Orientalism was in large part a response to the volatile and uncertain political position of Britain in India. A touch of adhocism was unmistakable in his approach, as is evident in an educational policy that failed to show any signs of being informed by a clear conception of government or a distinct political philosophy. To gain the affection of the people was his primary goal. If that meant British patronage of the native traditions and systems of learning, he could conceive of no better tactic than to allow the immediate situation to guide and shape policy.

But Wellesley's officers were too conscious of England's by then strengthened position in India to resort to the promotion of native culture as a purely defensive measure. Rather, Orientalism represented for them the logical corollary of a precise and meticulously defined scheme of administration. In that scheme, as was noted earlier, the British government was to function as a paternal protectorate governing India not by direct rule (that is, through the force of British law) but through various local functionaries. In other words, the Cornwallis system of centralized administration was spurned in favour of one which was more diffuse, and operated through a network of hierarchical relationships between British officers at one level and between the British and the Indians on another. Now in order to draw the Indians into this hegemonic structure, it was imperative for the British administration to maintain an alliance with those who formed the traditional ruling class. This was essential partly to reconcile the indigenous elite to their displaced status but partly also to secure a buffer zone for absorbing the effects of foreign rule, which, if experienced directly by the masses, might have a disastrous impact.

This scheme of administration, at once more personal and more rigidly stratified in its conception, was further bolstered by the philosophy that no political tradition could be created anew or superimposed on another without a violent rejection of it by the pre-existing society. For a new political society to emerge, it was argued that the native tradition and culture had to provide the soil for its growth. The imagery of grafting that permeated the discourse around this time pointed to an emerging theory of organicism that conceived of political formation as a part of a process of cultural synthesis.[7]

These theoretical and practical considerations made Orientalism a highly appealing cultural programme to Wellesley's subordinates. In it may be seen the first seeds of what came to be known as the Filtration Theory, which was predicated on the notion that cultural values percolate downwards from a position of power and by enlisting the co-operation of intermediate classes representing the native elite. The Filtration Theory is conventionally associated with Macaulay's Anglicism, and it is in his famous 1835 Minute that it is advanced most forcefully as a theory of culture. But its unacknowledged forebear was the Orientalism of Wellesley's administration. The differences between an intermediate class of native elite educated in the vernaculars and one educated in English are by no means inconsequential, nor is it the intention here to minimize them. But despite the conflict over language, the Orientalist and Anglicist programmes assumed a common method of governance: in both, an influential native class was to be co-opted as the conduit of Western thought and ideas.

This phase of British rule, roughly spanning the first twenty years of the nineteenth century, acquires a special significance in this narrative for marking the historical moment when political philosophy and cultural policy converged to work towards clearly discernible common ends. The promotion of Orientalism no less than Anglicism became irrevocably tied from this point onwards to questions of administrative structure and governance: for example, how were Indian subjects to be imbued with a sense of public responsibility and honour, and by what means could the concept of a Western-style government be impressed on their minds to facilitate the business of state?

Such questions also implied that, with the reversal of the Cornwallis policy of isolationism from Indian society and the hierarchical re-ordering of the Indian subjects for administrative purposes, the problem of reform was no longer confined to the British side but extended more actively to the Indian side as well. The more specialized functions devolving upon a government now settling down to prospective long-term rule brought the Indians as a body of subjects more directly into the conceptual management of the country than was the case in either Hastings' or

Cornwallis' time. As a result, the 'Indian character' suddenly became a subject of immense importance, as was the question of how it could best be moulded to suit British administrative needs.

But curiously it was on this last point that Orientalism began to lose ground to Anglicism. For even though it appeared to be the most favourable cultural policy for a feudal-type administration, its theoretical premises were seriously undermined by the gathering tide of reform that accompanied the restructuring of government. This was a government that had grown acutely aware of both its capacity for generating change (thus far internally) and its own vested authority over the natives. The Orientalist position was that a Western political tradition could be successfully grafted upon the native without having to direct itself towards the transformation of that society along Western lines. But as a theory it found itself at odds with the direction of internal consolidation along which British rule was moving. The strengthening of England's position in India, as exemplified by a recently co-ordinated and efficient administrative structure, put the rulers under less compulsion to direct change inward than to carry over the reformist impulse to those over whom they had dominion.

That tendency was reinforced by two outside developments. One was the opening of India to free trade in 1813, which resulted in the Private Trade and City interests steadily exerting stronger influence on the Crown at the expense of the Indian interest. The 'Private Traders' had no tradition of familiarity with India behind them and, according to the historian C. H. Philips, 'could hardly expect to retain the good opinion of either the Board of Control or of their governments in India'.[8] Removed from direct knowledge of the country they were ruling, these new political groups were more prone to taking decisions that reflected their own biases and assumptions about what was good for their subjects than what the existing situation itself demanded.

A second and more important influence in the thrust towards reform was exerted by a group of missionaries called the Clapham Evangelicals, who played a key role in the drama of consolidation of British interest in India. Among them were Zachary Macaulay, William Wilberforce, Samuel Thornton, and Charles Grant, and to these men must be given credit for supplying British expansionism with an ethics of concern for reform and conversion. Insisting that British domination was robbed of all justification if no efforts were made to reform native morals, the missionaries repeatedly petitioned Parliament to permit them to engage in the urgent business of enlightening the heathen. Unsuccessful with the earlier Act of 1793 that renewed the Company's charter for a twenty-year period, the missionaries were more triumphant by the time of the 1813 resolution, which brought about the other major event associated with the Charter Act: the opening of India to missionary activity.

Although chaplains had hitherto been appointed by the East India Company to serve the needs of the European population residing in India,

Parliament had consistently refused to modify the Company charter to allow missionary work in India. The main reason for government resistance was an apprehension that the Indians would feel threatened and eventually cause trouble for England's commercial ventures. The insurrection at Vellore, near Madras, in 1806 was blamed on proselytizing activity in the area. The fear of further acts of hostility on religious grounds grew so great that it prompted a temporary suspension of the Christianizing mission. Despite assurances by influential parliamentary figures like Lord Castlereagh that the natives would be as little alarmed by the appearance of Christian ministers as 'by an intercourse with the professors of Mahometanism, or of the various sects into which the country was divided',[9] the British government remained unconvinced [. . .] The Bible was proscribed and scriptural teaching forbidden.

The opening of India to missionaries, along with the commitment of the British to native improvement, might suggest a victory for the missionaries, encouraging them perhaps to anticipate official support for their Evangelizing mission. But if they had such hopes, they were to be dismayed by the continuing checks on their activities, which grew impossibly stringent. Publicly, Parliament demanded a guarantee that large-scale proselytizing would not be carried out in India. Privately, though, it needed little persuasion about the distinct advantages that would flow from missionary contact with the natives and their 'many immoral and disgusting habits'.

Though representing a convergence of interests, these two events – of British involvement in Indian education and the entry of missionaries – were far from being complementary or mutually supportive. On the contrary, they were entirely opposed to each other both in principle and in fact. The inherent constraints operating on British educational policy are apparent in the central contradiction of a government committed to the improvement of the people while being restrained from imparting any direct instruction in the religious principles of the English nation. The encouragement of Oriental learning, seen initially as a way of fulfilling the ruler's obligations to the subjects, seemed to accentuate rather than diminish the contradiction. For as the British swiftly learned to their dismay, it was impossible to promote Orientalism without exposing the Hindus and Muslims to the religious and moral tenets of their respective faiths – a situation that was clearly not tenable with the stated goal of 'moral and intellectual improvement'.

2

This tension between increasing involvement in Indian education and enforced noninterference in religion was productively resolved through the introduction of English literature. Significantly, the direction to this solution was present in the Charter Act itself, whose 43rd section empowered the Governor-General-in-Council to direct that 'a sum of not less than one lac of rupees shall be annually applied to the revival and improvement of literature, and the encouragement of the learned natives of India'.[10] As subsequent debate made only too obvious, there is deliberate ambiguity in this clause regarding which literature was to be promoted, leaving it wide open for misinterpretations and conflicts to arise on the issue. While the use of the word 'revival' may weight the interpretations on the side of Oriental literature, the almost deliberate imprecision suggests a more fluid government position in conflict with the official espousal of Orientalism. Over twenty years later Macaulay was to seize on this very ambiguity to argue that the phrase clearly meant Western literature, and denounce in no uncertain terms attempts to interpret the clause as a reference to Oriental literature:

> It is argued, or rather taken for granted, that by literature, the Parliament can have meant only Arabic and Sanskrit literature, that they never would have given the honourable appellation of a learned native to a native who was familiar with the poetry of Milton, the Metaphysics of Locke, the Physics of Newton; but that they meant to designate by that name only such persons as might have studied in the sacred books of the Hindoos all the uses of cusa-grass, and all the mysteries of absorption into the Deity.[11]

This plea on behalf of English literature had a major influence on the passing of the English Education Act in 1835, which officially required the natives of India to submit to its study. But English was not an unknown entity in India at that time, for some natives had already begun receiving rudimentary instruction in the language more than two decades earlier. Initially, English did not supersede Oriental studies but was taught alongside it. Yet it was clear that it enjoyed a different status, for there was a scrupulous attempt to establish separate colleges for its study. Even when it was taught within the same college, the English course of studies was kept separate from the course of Oriental study, and was attended by a different set of students. The rationale was that if the English department drew students who were attached only to its department and to no other (that is, the Persian or the Arabic or the Sanskrit), the language might then be taught 'classically' in much the same way that Latin and Greek were taught in England.

It is important to emphasize that the early British Indian curriculum in English, though based on literary material, was primarily devoted to language studies. However, by the 1820s the atmosphere of secularism in which these studies were conducted became a major cause for concern to the missionaries who were permitted to enter India after 1813. Within England itself, there was a strong feeling that texts read as a form of secular knowledge were 'a sea in which the voyager has to expect shipwreck'[12] and that they could not be relied on to exert a beneficial effect upon the moral condition of society in general. This sentiment was complemented by an equally strong one that for English works to be studied even for language purposes a high degree of mental and moral cultivation was first required which the mass of people simply did not have. To a man in a state of ignorance of moral law, literature would appear indifferent to virtue. Far from cultivating moral feelings, a wide reading was more likely to cause him to question moral law more closely and perhaps even encourage him to deviate from its dictates.

Ironically, much the same argument was made even by staunch Orientalists like Horace Wilson, who criticized prevailing pedagogical practices on the grounds that 'the mere language cannot work any material change'. Only when 'we initiate them into our literature, particularly at an early age, and get them to adopt feelings and sentiments from our standard writers, [can] we make an impression upon them, and effect any considerable alteration in their feelings and notions'.[13]

One missionary in India, the Rev. W. Keane, argued that while European education had done much to destroy 'heathen' superstition, it had not substituted any moral principle in its place. The exclusion of the Bible had a demoralizing effect, he claimed, for it tended to produce evils in the country and to give the native mind

> unity of opinion, which before it never had . . . and political thoughts, which they get out of our European books, but which it is impossible to reconcile with our position in that country, political thoughts of liberty and power, which would be good if they were only the result of a noble ambition of the natural mind for something superior; but which when they arise without religious principles, produce an effect which, to my mind, is one of unmixed evil.[14]

The missionaries got further support from an unexpected quarter. The military officers who testified in the parliamentary sessions on Indian education joined hands with them in arguing that a secular education in English would increase the natives' capacity for evil because it would elevate their intellects without providing the moral principles to keep them in check. Argued a major in the British Army, 'I have seen native students who had obtained an insight into European literature and history, in whose minds there seemed to be engendered a spirit of disaffection towards the British Government'.[15]

The uneasiness generated by a strictly secular policy in teaching English served to resurrect Charles Grant in the British consciousness. An officer of the East India Company, Grant was one of the first Englishmen to urge the promotion of both Western literature and Christianity in India. In 1792 he had written a tract entitled *Observations on the State of Society among the Asiatic Subjects of Great Britain*, which was a scathing denunciation of Indian religion and society. What interested the British in the years following the actual introduction of English in India was Grant's shrewd observation that by emphasizing the moral aspect, it would be possible to talk about introducing Western education without having to throw open the doors of English liberal thought to natives; to aim at moral improvement of the subjects without having to worry about the possible danger of inculcating radical ideas that would upset the British presence in India. Moral good and happiness, Grant had argued, 'views politics through the safe medium of morals, and subjects them to the laws of universal rectitude'.[16] The most appealing part of his argument, from the point of view of a government now sensing the truth of the missionaries' criticism of secularism, was that historically Christianity had never been associated with bringing down governments, for its concern was with the internal rather than the external condition of man.

Underlying all the various appeals to the dogmas of rationality and morality was a growing awareness that the value of English literature was interlocked with other social institutions committed to the communication of 'enlarged notions of duty and the social relations on which it is founded'. Among the most important of these was the institution of religion. In English social history the function of providing authority for individual action and belief and of dispensing moral laws for the formation of character had traditionally been carried out through the medium of church-controlled educational institutions. Until the beginning of the nineteenth century, education in England was fully integrated with the church and shared many common features – curricula, goals, practices. Even when, by mid-nineteenth century, the ideological supremacy of the established churches was eroded and its integration with education replaced by new institutional relationships, the churches continued to function as interest groups influencing educational development.

The aristocracy maintained a monopoly over access to church-dominated education and instituted a classical course of studies that it shared with the clergy, but from which the middle and working classes were systematically excluded. The classical curriculum under church patronage became identified as a prerequisite for social leadership and, more subtly, as the means by which social privilege was protected. This alliance between church and culture consecrated the concept of station in life and directly supported the existing system of social stratification: while the classical curriculum served to confirm the upper orders in their superior social status, religious instruction was given to the lower orders to fit them for the various duties of life and to secure them in their appropriate station. The alliance between church and culture was thus equally an alliance between ideas of formative education and of social control.

Two educational movements in eighteenth-century England illustrate the powerful influence of the church in institutionalizing certain kinds of texts and excluding others. Both the Charity School movement and the Sunday School movement grew out of concern over the alarming rise of urban squalor and crime and out of a conviction that unless the poor were brought back into the Christian orbit, the relatively harmonious order that had been carefully laid would be shattered. Only instruction in sound

Christian principles, it was averred, would prevent such a catastrophe, and 'such little portions of Holy Scripture as recommend industry, gratitude, submission and the like vertues' were duly prescribed. Hannah More summed up the educational philosophy of social control adopted by these institutions when she declared, 'Principles, not opinions, are what I labour to give them'.[17]

Apart from the Bible, required reading in these institutions consisted of religious tracts, textbooks, parables, sermons, homilies, and prayers, many of which were specially written for inclusion in the curriculum. [...] Interestingly, these works were part of what was labelled the 'literary curriculum'. The religious bias of a course of studies restricted to the Bible and catechism meant that secular writing of any kind, by which was generally meant works of the imagination, was kept out of the institutional mainstream. As late as the 1860s, the 'literary curriculum' in British educational establishments remained polarized around classical studies for the upper classes and religious studies for the lower. As for what is now known as the subject of English literature, the British educational system had no firm place for it until the last quarter of the nineteenth century, when the challenge posed by the middle classes to the existing structure resulted in the creation of alternative institutions devoted to 'modern' studies.

It is quite conceivable that educational development in British India may have run the same course as it did in England, were it not for one crucial difference: the strict controls on Christianizing activities. Clearly, the texts that were standard fare for the lower classes in England could not legitimately be incorporated into the Indian curriculum without inviting violent reactions from the native population, particularly the learned classes. And yet the fear lingered in the British mind that without submission of the individual to moral law or the authority of God, the control they were able to secure over the lower classes in their own country would elude them in India. Comparisons were on occasion made between the situation at home and in India, between the 'rescue' of the lower clases in England, 'those living in the dark recesses of our great cities at home, from the state of degradation consequent on their vicious and depraved habits, the offspring of ignorance and sensual indulgence', and the elevation of the Hindus and Muslims whose 'ignorance and degradation' required a remedy not adequately supplied by their respective faiths.[18] Such comparisons served to intensify the search for other social institutions to take over from religious instruction the function of communicating the laws of the social order.

3

It was at this point that British colonial administrators, provoked by missionaries on the one hand and fears of native insubordination on the other, discovered an ally in English literature to support them in maintaining control of the natives under the guise of a liberal education. With both secularism and religion appearing as political liabilities, literature appeared to represent a perfect synthesis of these two opposing positions. The idea evolved in alternating stages of affirmation and disavowal of literature's derivation from and affiliation with Christianity as a social institution. [Thus] the minutes of evidence given before the British Parliament's Select Committee, and recorded in the 1852–53 volume of the *Parliamentary Papers*, [. . .] reveal not only an open assertion of British material interests but also a mapping out of strategies for promoting those interests through representations of Western literary knowledge as objective, universal, and rational.

The first stage in the process was an assertion of structural congruence between Christianity and English literature. Missionaries had long argued on behalf of the shared history of religion and literature, of a tradition of belief and doctrine creating a common culture of values, attitudes, and norms. They had ably cleared the way for the realization that as the 'grand repository of the book of God' England had produced a literature that was immediately marked off from all non-European literatures, being 'animated, vivified, hallowed, and baptized' by a religion to which Western man owed his material and moral progress. The difference was poetically rendered as a contrast between

> the literature of a world embalmed with the Spirit of Him who died
> to redeem it, and that which is the growth of ages that have
> gloomily rolled on in the rejection of that Spirit, as between the
> sweet bloom of creation in the open light of heaven, and the rough,
> dark recesses of submarine forests of sponges.[19]

This other literature was likened to Plato's cave, whose darkened inhabitants were 'chained men . . . counting the shadows of subterranean fires'.

The missionary description was appropriated in its entirety by government officers. But while the missionaries made such claims in order to force the government to sponsor teaching of the Bible, the administrators used the same argument to prove that English literature made such direct instruction redundant. They initiated several steps to incorporate selected English literary texts into the Indian curriculum on the claim that these works were supported in their morality by a body of evidence that also upheld the Christian faith. In their official capacity as members of the Council on Education, Macaulay and his brother-in-law Charles Trevelyan were among those engaged in a minute analysis of English texts to prove the 'diffusive benevolence of Christianity' in them. The process of curricular selection was marked by weighty pronouncements of the 'sound Protestant Bible principles' in Shakespeare, the 'strain of serious piety' in Addison's *Spectator* papers, the 'scriptural morality' of Bacon and Locke, the 'devout sentiment' of Abercrombie, the 'noble Christian sentiments' in

Adam Smith's *Moral Sentiments* (hailed as the 'best authority for the true science of morals which English literature could supply').[20] The cataloguing of shared features had the effect of convincing detractors that the government could effectively cause voluntary reading of the Bible and at the same time disclaim any intentions of proselytizing.

But while these identifications were occurring at one level, at another level the asserted unity of religion and literature was simultaneously disavowed, as evidenced in a series of contradictory statements. The most directly conflicting of these maintained, on the one hand, that English literature is 'imbued with the spirit of Christianity' and 'interwoven with the words of the Bible to a great degree' so that 'without ever looking into the Bible one of those Natives must come to a considerable knowledge of it merely from reading English litereature'.[21] But in the same breath a counterclaim was made that English literature 'is not interwoven to the same extent with the Christian religion as the Hindoo religion is with the Sanskrit language and literature'.[22] Charles Cameron, who succeeded Macaulay as President of the Council on Education, attempted to provide an illustration for the latter position by arguing that though Milton assumed the truth of Christianity, his works did not bear the same relation to the doctrines of Christianity as did Oriental literature to the tenets of the native religious systems. But when pressed by his examiners to explain the point further, he refused to elaborate, admitting only 'a difference in degree'.[23]

It is certainly possible to interpret the contradiction as an unimportant and inconsequential instance of British ambivalence or inconsistency of policy. But to do so is to ignore the operation of a more subtle ideological activity, where a body of texts came to be removed from their social formation and then assigned functions that obscured the historical forces which produced them. The difference that Cameron hesitated to specify had long before been named by missionaries when they termed Western literature a from of intellectual production, in contrast to Oriental literature which, they claimed, set itself up as a source of divine authority. The Serampore Baptist William Carey best expressed the missionary viewpoint when, comparing the Indian epic the *Mahabharata* to Homer, he lamented that '[were] it, like his Iliad, only considered as a great effort of human genius, I should think it is one of the first productions in the world, but alas! it is the ground of Faith to Millions of men; and as such must be held in the utmost abhorrence'.[24]

The distinction served to emphasize the arbitrariness of the Oriental conception of truth, which derived its claims from the power of the explicator (that is, the class learned in Arabic and Sanskrit) to mediate between the popular mind and sacred knowledge. For various reasons colonial administrators found it a useful distinction and appropriated it for their own purposes. The most important of these was the undermining of the powerful hold of the learned classes over the native population, a position strengthened enormously by their function as sole explicators of texts construed as divine knowledge. The government reasoning went along these lines: if by blurring the lines between literature and religion, the native ruling classes had arrogated all power to decipher texts unto themselves, would not an erosion of that power base ensue if the authority vested in the explicator were relocated elsewhere – that is, if authority were reinvested in a body of texts presented as objective, scientific, rational, empirically verifiable truth, the product not of an exclusive social or political class but of a consciousness that spoke in a universal voice and for the universal good?

The relocation of authority in the body of knowledge represented by English literary texts was greatly facilitated by the fact that an historical model existed for it in the Protestant Reformation and the beginnings of an empiricist tradition of thought. Members of the Council on Indian Education seized on the analogy between the British presence in India and the Reformation in Europe to make two related arguments. [. . .] *One*, the characterization of English literature as intellectual production suggested a different process of reading, requiring the exercise of reason rather than unquestioning faith. A major implication of this difference for a native Indian population completely under the control of their learned classes was the fortification of the individual mind against coercive interpretations imposed by those classes. The history of the 'despotic Orient' was adequate proof that a literature claiming to provide divine revelation diluted the capacity of the individual mind to resist the manipulative exertions of a priestly caste. Not only did Oriental literature lull the individual into a passive acceptance of the most fabulous incidents as actual occurrences; more alarming, the acceptance of mythological events as factual description stymied the mind's capacity to extrapolate a range of meanings for analysis and verification in the real world.

Reason as conceived here is made synonymous with the moral imagination, and the moral imagination in turn with the ability to make discriminations and choose judiciously from a wide spectrum of possible meanings. The logic of associating reason with an approach to literary texts as types of human activity was a simple one: the products of human consciousness must submit to interpretation because their creating subject is man not God, man in all his imperfection and fallibility. Because interpretation by definition entails a multiplicity of response, the receiving mind is pressured to weigh the truth-value of each of the various possibilities. The effect of such plurality is the activation of rational processes of discrimination and judgement – intellectual skills entirely alien to a literature conceived as divine agency.

Two, as an example of human invention drawing its material from an empirically perceived world, English literature disciplined the mind to think and reason from the force of evidence, an activity deemed to be wholly foreign to Oriental religions and literatures. The elevation of individual and closely observed experience over received tradition gave the literature of England a scientific character that served to objectify the knowledge it contained. In the British view the element of doubt attending upon the evidence of the senses curiously made it a more reliable tool than articles of faith in the establishment of truth. For the empirical sense set the mind in a state of intellectual restlessness where it had to do battle continually with error until a full knowledge of the truth was reached. Thus, an individually realized truth, being neither *a priori* nor predetermined, defied the arbitrary definitions laid down by class or caste. Having proceeded through the stages of empirical investigation – of observation, analysis, verification, and application – it consequently had greater claims to universal, objective knowledge than a truth laid down by received tradition.

Given the elaborate manner in which English literature was set up as the highest example of empirical reasoning, its transformation into scientific, rational, and objective truth was all but a *fait accompli*. The Scottish missionary Alexander Duff, for example, had no difficulty in defining the literature of England as a group of texts that supplied a complete course of knowledge free of error in every branch of inquiry, literary, scientific, and theological. By contrast, the literature of India, he claimed, could not produce 'a single volume on any one subject that is not studded with error, far less a series of volumes that would furnish anything bearing the most distant resemblance to a complete range of information in any conceivable department of useful knowledge'.[25] The force of his argument lay in offering a definition of literature that linked it with the production of scientific knowledge and the material improvement of the material conditions of mankind. By the same token, the definition dismissed the notion of literature as the transmission and perpetuation of cultural tradition, the argument by which the learned classes had retained their hold over the native population.

But having said this, Duff raised by implication a perplexing, more complicated set of questions: to what extent would the earlier identification of English literature with Christianity cause problems for the promotion of identification with science? Was it possible to have a sustained unity of the moral and the intellectual imperatives given the constraints placed upon evolving a coherent educational policy for British India? Or were the claims of religion and science – the former urging devotion to the articles of faith laid down by the established church and the latter to a secular, nonpartisan conception of knowledge – so irreconcilable that only the temporary suspension of the one would permit the practical realization of the other?

Charles Cameron's reticence may take on more meaning in the context of this imperative, for his unspoken assumption was that the distinctiveness of English literature lay in its double stance towards reason and faith, utility and tradition, empiricism and revelation – a stance obscuring its affiliations with institutional religion (and the entire system of social and political formation of which it was a part) through its appeal to an objective, empirical reality. In other words, the political significance of

English literature rested on its inclining one's thoughts towards religion while maintaining its secular nature. But to make explicit through instruction what was better off understood as an *implicit* relation was not only to undercut the operational value of this double stance: it was to lay open to native questioning the validity of the knowledge to be imparted. Native resistance to the truth of Christianity had always been a cause of immense frustration for missionaries, who often complained that they had to adopt a different, more demanding style of instruction in India. The Serampore missionary William Carey, for instance, dejectedly wrote that the rhetorical fervour of his lessons was often wasted on an audience that demanded proofs and demonstrations in its place. The government was more shrewd in assessing the source of the difficulty, and sensed that the natives resisted missionary claims not merely because they conflicted with perceptions derived from their own religions, but because the intention of conversion so overlay the content of instruction as to render its truth-value immaterial.

To disperse intention, and by extension authority in related fields of knowledge and inquiry, proposed itself as the best means of dissipating native resistance. As one government publication put it, 'If we lay it down as our rule to teach only what the natives are willing to make natural, viz., what they will freely learn, we shall be able by degrees to teach them all we know ourselves, without any risk of offending their prejudices'.[26] One of the great lessons taught by Gramsci, which this quotation amply corroborates, is that cultural domination operates by consent, indeed often preceding conquest by force. 'The supremacy of a social group manifests itself in two ways', he writes in the *Prison Notebooks*, 'as "domination" and as "intellectual and moral leadership" . . . It seems clear . . . that there can, and indeed must be hegemonic activity even before the rise of power, and that one should not count only on the material force which power gives in order to exercise an effective leadership'.[27] He argues that consent of the governed is secured primarily through the moral and intellectual suasion, a strategy clearly spelled out by the British themselves: 'The Natives must either be kept down by a sense of our power, or they must willingly submit from a conviction that we are more wise, more just, more humane, and more anxious to improve their condition than any other rulers they could have'.[28]

Implicit in this strategy is a recognition of the importance of self-representation, an activity crucial to what the natives 'would freely learn'. The answer to this last question was obvious to at least one member of the Council on Education: the natives' greatest desire, averred C. E. Trevelyan, was to raise themselves to the level of moral and intellectual refinement of their masters; their most driving ambition, to acquire the intellectual skills that confirmed their rulers as lords of the earth. Already, he declared, the natives had an idea that 'we have gained everything by our superior knowledge; that it is this superiority which has enabled us to conquer India, and to keep it; and they want to put themselves as much as they can upon an equality with us'.[29] If the assumption was correct that individuals willingly learned whatever they believed provided them with the means of advancement in the world, a logical method of overwhelming opposition was to demonstrate that the achieved material position of the Englishman was derived from the knowledge contained in English literary, philosophical, and scientific texts, a knowledge accessible to any who chose to seek it.

In effect, the strategy of locating authority in these texts all but effaced the sordid history of colonialist expropriation, material exploitation, and class and race oppression behind European world dominance. Making the Englishman known to the natives through the products of his mental labour served a valuable purpose in that it removed him from the plane of ongoing colonialist activity – of commercial operations, military expansion, administration of territories – and de-actualized and diffused his material presence in the process. In a crude reworking of the Cartesian axiom, production of thought defined the Englishman's true essence, overriding all other aspects of his identity – his personality, actions, behaviour. His material reality as a subjugator and alien ruler was dissolved in his mental output; the blurring of the man and his works effectively removed him from history. As the following statement suggests, the English literary text functioned as a surrogate Englishman in his highest and most perfect state: '[The Indians] daily converse with the best and wisest Englishmen through the medium of their works, and form ideas, perhaps higher ideas of our nation than if their intercourse with it were of a more personal kind'.[30] The split between the material and the discursive practices of colonialism is nowhere sharper than in the progressive rarefaction of the rapacious, exploitative, and ruthless actor of history into the reflective subject of literature.

How successful was the British strategy? [. . .] The fact that English literary study had its beginnings as a strategy of containment raises a host of questions about the interrelations of culture, state, and civil society and the modes of assertion of authority within that network of relations. Why, if the British were the unchallenged military power in India, was the exercise of direct force discarded as a means of maintaining social control? What accounts for the British readiness to turn to a disciplinary branch of knowledge to perform the task of administering the natives? What was the assurance that a disguised form of authority would be more successful in quelling a potential rebellion among the natives than a direct show of force? Why introduce English in the first place only to work at strategies to balance its secular tendencies with moral and religious ones?

These questions suggest a vulnerability in the British position that is most sharply felt when the history of British Rule is read in the light of the construction of an ideology. There is little doubt that a great deal of strategic manoeuvring went into the creation of a blueprint for social control in the guise of a humanistic programme of enlightenment. But merely to acknowledge this fact is not enough, for there is yet a further need to distinguish between strategy as unmediated assertion of authority and strategy as mediated response to situational imperatives. That is to say, it is important to decide whether British educational measures were elaborated from an uncontested position of superiority and strength, and as such are to be read as unalloyed expressions of ethnocentric sentiment, or whether that position itself was a fragile one which it was the role of educational decisions to fortify, given the challenge posed by historical contingency and confrontation.

[...] I have argued that the introduction of English literature represented an embattled response to historical and political pressures: to tensions between the Westminister Parliament and the East India Company, between Parliament and the missionaries, between the East India Company and the native elite classes. It is possible to study strategic effectiveness using only the techniques of literary, textual analysis, but it is equally possible that in the process the two kinds of strategies are reduced to a single category from which are excluded extratextual considerations, such as the exigencies of the political and historical situation, the variable power relationships between different groups, the specific composition, affiliation, and vested interests of the 'ruling class' over different periods of time. No doubt responsiveness both to historical change and to the subtleties of discursive practice at one and the same time requires unusual methodological skill and sophistication, and I am aware that this essay comes nowhere near achieving this goal. But I do hope that what will have emerged is a sense of the interpenetraion of different kinds of histories – social, cultural, political, literary.

Notes

1 Great Britain, *Parliamentary Debates*, 1813, **26**, p. 562.

2 Ninth Report of Select Committee on the Affairs of India, 17831; quoted in Eric Stokes, *The English Utilitarians and India* (Oxford, Clarendon Press, 1959), p. 2.

3 William Adam, *Reports on Vernacular Education in Bengal and Bihar*, Third Report (Calcutta, Calcutta University Press), p. 340.

4 Letter of Hastings to N. Smith; quoted in David Kopf, *British Orientalism and the Bengal Renaissance* (Berkeley and Los Angeles, University of California Press, 1969), p. 18.

5 Percival Spear, *Oxford History of Modern India 1740–1975* (Oxford, Oxford University Press, 1965), p. 89.

6 Stokes, p. 16.

7 Cf. 'To allure the natives of India to the study of European science and literature, we must, I think, engraft this study upon their own established methods of scientific and literary institutions, and particularly in all the public colleges or schools maintained or encouraged by government, good translations of the most useful European compositions on the subjects taught in them, may, I conceive, be introduced with the greatest advantage' (Paper by J. H. Harington, June 19, 1814, quoted in *Adam's Report on Vernacular Education in Bengal and Bihar*, p. 310.)

8 C.H. Philips, *The East India Company 1784–1834* (Manchester, Manchester University Press, 1940; rev. ed., 1961), p. 8.

9 Great Britain, *Parliamentary Debates*, 1813, **26**, p. 1027.

10 Great Britain, *Parliamentary Papers*, 1831–32, **9**, Appendix I, p. 486, Extract of Letter in the Public Department, from the Court of Directors to the Governor-General in Council, dated 6 September, 1813.

11 Thomas B. Macaulay, *Speeches*, ed. G. M. Young (London, Oxford University Press, 1935), p. 345.

12 *Atheneum* (1839), p. 108.

13 Great Britain, *Parliamentary Papers*, 1852–53, **32**, p. 266, Evidence of Horace Wilson.

14 Great Britain, *Parliamentary Papers*, 1852–53, **32**, p. 301, Evidence of the Rev. W. Keane.

15 Great Britain, *Parliamentary Papers*, 1852–53, **29**, p. 155, Evidence of Maj. F. Rowlandson.

16 Great Britain, *Parliamentary Papers*, 1832, **8**, p. 75, 'Observations on the State of Society'.

17 Quoted in M. G. Jones, *The Charity School Movement* (Cambridge, Cambridge University Press, 1938), p. 74.

18 Great Britain, *Parliamentary Papers*, 1852–53, **29**, p. 190, Minute of the Marquess of Tweeddale on Education, 4 July 1846.

19 *Madras Christian Instructor and Missionary Record*, **11**(4), (September 1844), p. 195.

20 All references are from *Parliamentary Papers*, 1852–53, **32**.

21 Great Britain, *Parliamentary Papers*, 1852–53, **32**, p. 185, Evidence of Charles Trevelyan.

22 Great Britain, *Parliamentary Papers*, 1852–53, **32**, p. 287, Evidence of Charles Cameron.

23 Ibid.

24 Northampton MS. William Carey to Andrew Fuller, 23 April, 1796; cited in M. A. Laird, *Missionaries and Education in Bengal 1793–1837* (Oxford, Clarendon Press, 1972), p. 56.

25 Great Britain, *Parliamentary Papers*, 1852–53, **32**, p. 412, Evidence of Alexander Duff.

26 Henry Sharp, ed., *Selections from Educational Records, Part I. 1781–1839* (Calcutta, Superintendent Government Printing, India, 1920).

27 Antonio Gramsci, *Selections from the Prison Notebooks of Antonio Gramsci*, ed. Quintin Hoare and Geoffrey Nowell Smith (London, Lawrence and Wishart, 1971), p. 57.

28 Minute of J. Farish dated 28 August 1838; Poll. Dept., Vol. 20/795, 1837–39 (Bombay Records); quoted in B. K. Boman-Behram, *Educational Controversies of India: the cultural conquest of India under British Imperialism* (Bombay, Taraporevala Sons and Co., 1942), p. 239.

29 Great Britain, *Parliamentary Papers*, 1852–53, **32**, p. 187, Evidence of Charles Trevelyan.

30 C. E. Trevelyan, *On the Education of the People of India* (London, Longman, Orme, Brown, Green, and Longmans, 1838), p. 176.

Source: Viswanathan, G. (1987) 'The beginnings of English literary study in British India', *Oxford Literary Review*, **9**, pp. 2–26.

7 BLACK BODIES, WHITE BODIES

TOWARD AN ICONOGRAPHY OF FEMALE SEXUALITY IN LATE NINETEENTH-CENTURY ART, MEDICINE AND LITERATURE

SANDER L. GILMAN

How do we organize our perceptions of the world? Recent discussions of this age-old question have centred around the function of visual conventions as the primary means by which we perceive and transmit our understanding of the world about us. Nowhere are these conventions more evident than in artistic representations, which consist more or less exclusively of icons. Rather than presenting the world, icons represent it. Even with a modest nod to supposedly mimetic portrayals it is apparent that, when individuals are shown within a work of art (no matter how broadly defined), the ideologically charged iconographic nature of the representation dominates. And it dominates in a very specific manner, for the representation of individuals implies the creation of some greater class or classes to which the individual is seen to belong. These classes in turn are characterized by the use of a model which synthesizes our perception of the uniformity of the groups into a convincingly homogeneous image. The resulting stereotypes may be overt, as in the case of caricatures, or covert, as in eighteenth-century portraiture. But they serve to focus the viewer's attention on the relationship between the portrayed individual and the general qualities ascribed to the class.

Specific individual realities are thus given mythic extension through association with the qualities of a class. These realities manifest as icons representing perceived attributes of the class into which the individual has been placed. The myths associated with the class, the myth of difference from the rest of humanity, is thus, to an extent, composed of fragments of the real world, perceived through the ideological bias of the observer. These myths are often so powerful, and the associations of their conventions so overpowering, that they are able to move from class to class without substantial alteration. In linking otherwise marginally or totally unrelated classes of individuals, the use of these conventions reveals perceptual patterns which themselves illuminate the inherent ideology at work.

While the discussion of the function of conventions has helped reveal the essential iconographic nature of all visual representation, it has mainly been limited to a specific sphere – aesthetics. And although the definition of the aesthetic has expanded greatly in the past decade to include everything from decoration to advertising, it continues to dominate discussions of visual conventions. Patterns of conventions are established within the world of art or between that world and parallel ones, such as the world of literature, but they go no further. We maintain a special sanctity about the aesthetic object which we deny to the conventions of representation in other areas.

This article is an attempt to plumb the conventions (and thus the ideologies) which exist at a specific historical moment in both the aesthetic and scientific spheres. I will assume the existence of a web of conventions within the world of the aesthetic – conventions which have elsewhere been admirably illustrated – but will depart from the norm by examining the synchronic existence of another series of conventions, those of medicine. I do not mean in any way to accord special status to medical conventions. Indeed, the world is full of overlapping and intertwined systems of conventions, of which the medical and the aesthetic are but two. Medicine offers an especially interesting source of conventions since we do tend to give medical conventions special 'scientific' status as opposed to the 'subjective' status of the aesthetic conventions. But medical icons are not more 'real' than 'aesthetic' ones. Like aesthetic icons, medical icons may (or may not) be rooted in some observed reality. Like them, they are iconographic in that they represent these realities in a manner determined by the historical position of the observers, their relationship to their own time, and to the history of the conventions which they employ. Medicine uses its categories to structure an image of the diversity of mankind; it is as much at the mercy of the needs of any age to comprehend this infinite diversity as any other system which organizes our perception of the world. The power of medicine, at least in the nineteenth century, lies in the rise of the status of science. The conventions of medicine infiltrate other seemingly closed iconographic systems precisely because of this status. In examining the conventions of medicine employed in other areas, we must not forget this power.

One excellent example of the conventions of human diversity captured in the iconography of the nineteenth century is the linkage of two seemingly unrelated female images – the icon of the Hottentot female and the icon of the prostitute. In the course of the nineteenth century, the female Hottentot comes to represent the black female *in nuce*, and the prostitute to represent the sexualized woman. Both of these categories represent the

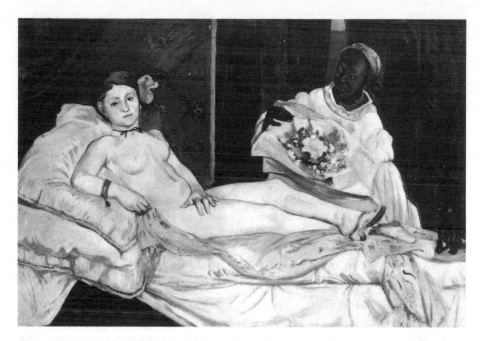

Figure 1 Edouard Manet, Olympia, *1863. Musée de l'Impressionisme, Paris (Réunion des musées nationaux).*

creation of classes which correspondingly represent very specific qualities. While the number of terms describing the various categories of the prostitute expanded substantially during the nineteenth century, all were used to label the sexualized woman. Likewise, while many groups of African blacks were known to Europeans in the nineteenth century, the Hottentot remained representative of the essence of the black, especially the black female. Both concepts fulfilled an iconographic function in the perception and the representation of the world. How these two concepts were associated provides a case study for the investigation of patterns of conventions, without any limitation on the 'value' of one pattern over another.

Let us begin with one of the classic works of nineteenth-century art, a work which records the idea of both the sexualized woman and the black woman. Edouard Manet's *Olympia*, painted in 1862–63 and first exhibited in the Salon of 1865, assumes a key position in documenting the merger of these two images (Figure 1). The conventional wisdom concerning Manet's painting states that the model, Victorine Meurend, is 'obviously naked rather than conventionally nude',[1] and that her pose is heavily indebted to classical models such as Titian's *Venus of Urbino* (1538), Francisco Goya's *Naked Maja* (1800), and Eugène Delacroix's *Odalisque* (1847), as well as other works by Manet's contemporaries, such as Gustave Courbet.[2] George Needham has shown quite convincingly that

Manet was also using a convention of early erotic photography in having the central figure directly confront the observer.[3] The black female attendant, based on a black model called Laura, has been seen as a reflex of both the classic black servant figure present in the visual arts of the eighteenth century as well as a representation of Baudelaire's *Vénus noire*.[4] Let us juxtapose the *Olympia*, with all its aesthetic and artistic analogies and parallels, to a work by Manet which Georges Bataille, among others, has seen as a modern 'genre scene' – the *Nana* of 1877 (Figure 2).[5] Unlike *Olympia*, *Nana* is modern, a creature of present-day Paris, according to a contemporary. But like *Olympia*, *Nana* was perceived as a sexualized female and is so represented. Yet in moving from a work with an evident aesthetic provenance, as understood by Manet's contemporaries, to one which was influenced by the former and yet was seen by its contemporaries as modern, certain major shifts in the iconography of the sexualized woman take place, not the least of which is the apparent disappearance of the black female.

The figure of the black servant in European art is ubiquitous. Richard Strauss knew this when he had Hugo von Hofmannsthal conclude their conscious evocation of the eighteenth century, *Der Rosenkavalier* (1911), with the mute return of the little black servant to reclaim the Marschallin's forgotten gloves.[6] But Hofmannsthal was also aware that one of the black servant's central functions in the visual arts of the eighteenth and nineteenth centuries was to sexualize the society in which he or she is found. The forgotten gloves, for instance, mark the end of the relationship between Octavian, the Knight of the Rose, and the Marschallin: the illicit nature of their sexual relationship, which opens the opera, is thereby linked to the appearance of the figure of the black servant, which closes the opera. When one turns to the narrative art of the eighteenth century – for example, to William Hogarth's two great cycles, *A Rake's Progress* (1733–34) and *A Harlot's Progress* (1731) – it is not very surprising that, as in the Strauss opera some two centuries later, the figures of the black servants mark the presence of illicit sexual activity. Furthermore, as in Hofmannsthal's libretto, they appear in the opposite sex to the central figure. In *A Harlot's Progress*, we see Moll Hackabout as the mistress of a Jewish merchant, the first stage of her decline as a sexualized female; also present is a young, black male servant (Figure 3). In the third stage of Tom Rakewell's collapse, we find him in a notorious brothel, the Rose Tavern in Covent Garden. The entire picture is full of references to illicit sexual activity, all portrayed negatively; present as well is the figure of a young female black servant.

The association of the black with concupiscence reaches back into the Middle Ages. The twelfth-century Jewish traveller Benjamin of Tudela wrote that

> at Seba on the river Pishon . . . is a people . . . who, like animals, eat of the herbs that grow on the banks of the Nile and in the fields.

Figure 2   Manet, Nana, *1877 (Elke Walford, Hamburger Kunsthalle).*

They go about naked and have not the intelligence of ordinary men. They cohabit with their sisters and anyone they can find . . . And these are the Black slaves, the sons of Ham.[7]

By the eighteenth century, the sexuality of the black, both male and female, becomes an icon for deviant sexuality in general; as we have seen, the black figure appears almost always paired with a white figure of the opposite sex. By the nineteenth century, as in the *Olympia,* or more

Figure 3   William Hogarth, A Harlot's Progress, *engraving, 1731 (Mary Evans Picture Library).*

crudely in one of a series of Viennese erotic prints entitled 'The Servant' (Figure 4), the central female figure is associated with a black female in such a way as to imply their sexual similarity. The association of figures of the same sex stresses the special status of female sexuality. In 'The Servant' the overt sexuality of the black child indicates the covert sexuality of the white woman. The relationship between the sexuality of the black woman and that of the sexualized white woman enters a new dimension when contemporary scientific discourse concerning the nature of black female sexuality is examined.

Buffon commented on the lascivious, ape-like sexual appetite of the black, introducing a commonplace of early travel literature into a 'scientific' context. He stated that this animal-like sexual appetite went so far as to lead black women to copulate with apes. The black female thus comes to serve as an icon for black sexuality in general. Buffon's view was based on a confusion of two applications of the great chain of being to the nature of the black. Such a scale was employed to indicate the innate difference between the races: in this view of mankind, the black occupied the antithetical position to the white on the scale of humanity. This poly-genetic view was applied to all aspects of mankind, including sexuality and beauty. The antithesis of European sexual mores and beauty is

Figure 4   Franz von Bayros, 'The Servant', ca. 1890.

embodied in the black, and the essential black, the lowest rung on the great chain of being, is the Hottentot. The physical appearance of the Hottentot is, indeed, the central nineteenth-century icon for sexual difference between the European and the black – a perceived difference in sexual physiology which puzzled even early monogenetic theoreticians such as Johann Friedrich Blumenbach.

Such labelling of the black female as more primitive, and therefore more sexually intensive, by writers like the Abbé Raynal would have been dismissed as unscientific by the radical empiricists of late eighteenth- and early nineteenth-century Europe. To meet their scientific standards, a paradigm was needed which would technically place both the sexuality and the beauty of the black in an antithetical position to that of the white. This paradigm would have to be rooted in some type of unique and observable physical difference; they found that difference in the distinction they drew between the pathological and the normal in the medical model. William Bynum has contended that nineteenth-century biology constantly needed to deal with the polygenetic argument. We see the validity of his contention demonstrated here, for the medical model assumes the polygenetic difference between the races.

It was in the work of J. J. Virey that this alteration of the mode of discourse – though not of the underlying ideology concerning the black female – took place. He was the author of the study of race standard in the early nineteenth century and also contributed a major essay (the only one on a specific racial group) to the widely cited *Dictionnaire des sciences médicales* (*Dictionary of medical sciences*) (1819).[8] In this essay, Virey summarized his (and his contemporaries') views on the sexual nature of black females in terms of acceptable medical discourse. According to him, their 'voluptuousness' is 'developed to a degree of lascivity unknown in our climate, for their sexual organs are much more developed than those of whites.' Elsewhere, Virey cites the Hottentot woman as the epitome of this sexual lasciviousness and stresses the relationship between her physiology and her physiognomy (her 'hideous form' and her 'horribly flattened nose'). His central proof is a dicussion of the unique structure of the Hottentot female's sexual parts, the description of which he takes from the anatomical studies published by his contemporary, Georges Cuvier.[9] According to Cuvier, the black female looks different. Her physiognomy, her skin colour, the form of her genitalia label her as inherently different. In the nineteenth century, the black female was widely perceived as possessing not only a 'primitive' sexual appetite but also the external signs of this temperament – 'primitive' genitalia. Eighteenth-century travellers to southern Africa, such as François Le Vaillant and John Barrow, had described the so-called Hottentot apron, a hypertrophy of the labia and nymphae caused by the manipulation of the genitalia and serving as a sign of beauty among certain tribes, including the Hottentots and Bushmen as well as tribes in Basutoland and Dahomey.[10]

The exhibition of 1810 of Saartjie Baartman, also called Sarah Bartmann or Saat-Jee and known as the 'Hottentot Venus', caused a public scandal in a London inflamed by the issue of the abolition of slavery, since she was exhibited 'to the public in a manner offensive to decency. She . . . does exhibit all the shape and frame of her body as if naked' (Figure 5). The state's objection was as much to her lewdness as to her status as an indentured black. In France her presentation was similar. Sarah Bartmann was not the only African to be so displayed: in 1829 a nude Hottentot woman, also called 'the Hottentot Venus', was the prize attraction at a ball given by the Duchess Du Barry in Paris. A contemporary print emphasized her physical difference from the observers portrayed. After more than five years of exhibition in Europe, Sarah Bartmann died in Paris in 1815 at the age of twenty-five. An autopsy was performed on her which was first written up by Henri de Blainville in 1816 and then, in its most famous version, by Cuvier in 1817.[11] Reprinted at least twice during the next decade, Cuvier's description reflected de Blainville's two

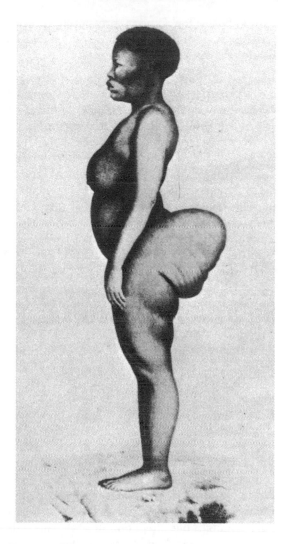

Figure 5   The Hottentot Venus (Georges Cuvier, 'Extraits d'observations faites sur le cadavre d'une femme connue à Paris et à Londres sous le nom de Vénus Hottentote', 1817).

intentions: the comparison of a female of the 'lowest' human species with the highest ape (the orangutan) and the description of the anomalies of the Hottentot's 'organ of generation'. It is important to note that Sarah Bartmann was exhibited not to show her genitalia but rather to present another anomaly which the European audience (and pathologists such as de Blainville and Cuvier) found riveting. This was the steatopygia, or protruding buttocks, the other physical characteristic of the Hottentot female which captured the eye of early European travellers. Thus the figure of Sarah Bartmann was reduced to her sexual parts. The audience which had paid to see her buttocks and had fantasized about the uniqueness of her genitalia when she was alive could, after her death and dissection, examine both, for Cuvier presented to 'the Academy the genital organs of this woman prepared in a way so as to allow one to see the nature of the labia.'[12]

Sarah Bartmann's sexual parts, her genitalia and her buttocks, served as the central image for the black female throughout the nineteenth century. And the model of de Blainville's and Cuvier's descriptions, which centre on the detailed presentation of the sexual parts of the black, dominates all medical description of the black during the nineteenth century. To an extent, this reflects the general nineteenth-century understanding of female sexuality as pathological: the female genitalia were of interest partly as examples of the various pathologies which could befall them but also because the female genitalia came to define the female for the nineteenth century. When a specimen was to be preserved for an anatomical museum, more often than not the specimen was seen as a pathological summary of the entire individual. Thus the skeleton of a giant or a dwarf represented 'giantism' or 'dwarfism'; the head of a criminal represented the act of execution which labelled him 'criminal'. Sarah Bartmann's genitalia and buttocks summarized her essence for the nineteenth-century observer, or, indeed, for the twentieth-century one, as they are still on display at the Musée de l'homme in Paris. Thus when one turns to the autopsies of Hottentot females in the nineteenth century, their description centres about the sexual parts. De Blainville (1816) and Cuvier (1817) set the tone, which is followed by A. W. Otto in 1824, Johannes Müller in 1834, William H. Flower and James Murie in 1867, and Luschka, Koch, and Görtz in 1869.[13] These presentations of Hottentot or Bushman women all focus on the presentation of the genitalia and buttocks. Flower, the editor of the *Journal of Anatomy and Physiology*, included his dissection study in the opening volume of that famed journal. His ideological intent was clear. He wished to provide data 'relating to the unity or plurality of mankind'. His description begins with a detailed presentation of the form and size of the buttocks and concludes with his portrayal of the 'remarkable development of the labia minoria, or nymphae, which is so general a characteristic of the Hottentot and Bushman race'. These were 'sufficiently well marked to distinguish these parts at once from those of any of the ordinary varieties of the human species'. The polygenetic argument is the ideological basis for all the dissections of these women. If their sexual parts could be shown to be inherently different, this would be a sufficient sign that the blacks were a separate (and, needless to say, lower) race, as different from the European as the proverbial orangutan. Similar arguments had been made about the nature of all blacks' (and not just Hottentots') genitalia, but almost always concerning the female. Edward Turnipseed of South Carolina argued in 1868 that the hymen in black women 'is not at the entrance to the vagina, as in the white woman, but from one-and-a-half to two inches from its entrance in the interior'. From this he concluded that 'this may be one of the anatomical marks of the non-unity of the races'.[14] His views were seconded in 1877 by C. H. Fort, who presented another six cases of this seeming anomaly.[15] In comparison, when one turns to the description of the autopsies of black males from approximately the same period, the absence of any discussion of the male genitalia whatsoever is striking. For example, William Turner, in his three dissections of male blacks in 1878, 1879, and 1896, makes no mention at all of the genitalia.[16] The uniqueness of the genitalia and buttocks of the black is thus associated primarily with the female and is taken to be a sign solely of an anomalous *female* sexuality.

By the mid-nineteenth century the image of the genitalia of the Hottentot had assumed a certain set of implications. The central view is that these anomalies are inherent, biological variations rather than adaptions. In Theodor Billroth's standard handbook of gynaecology, a detailed presentation of the 'Hottentot apron' is part of the discussion of errors in development of the female genitalia (*Entwicklungsfehler*). By 1877 it was a commonplace that the Hottentot's anomalous sexual form was similar to other errors in the development of the labia. The author of this article links this malformation with the overdevelopment of the clitoris, which he sees as leading to those 'excesses' which 'are called "lesbian love".' The concupiscence of the black is thus associated also with the sexuality of the lesbian.[17] In addition, the idea of a congenital error incorporates the disease model applied to the deformation of the labia in the Hottentot, for the model of degeneracy presumes some acquired pathology in one generation which is the direct cause of the stigmata of degeneracy in the next. Surely the best example for this is the concept of congenital syphilis as captured in the popular consciousness by Henrik Ibsen's drama of biological decay, *Ghosts*. Thus Billroth's 'congenital failure' is presupposed to have some direct and explicable etiology as well as a specific manifestation. While this text is silent as to the etiology, we can see the link established between the ill, the bestial, and the freak (pathology, biology, and medicine) in this view of the Hottentot's genitalia.

At this point, an aside might help explain both the association of the genitalia, a primary sexual characteristic, and the buttocks, a secondary sexual characteristic, in their role as the semantic signs of 'primitive' sexual appetite and activity. Havelock Ellis, in volume 4 of his *Studies in the Psychology of Sex* (1905), provided a detailed example of the great chain of being as applied to the perception of the sexualized Other. Ellis believed that there is an absolute scale of beauty which is totally objective and which ranges from the European to the black. Thus men of the lower races, according to Ellis, admire European women more than their own, and women of lower races attempt to whiten themselves with face powder. Ellis then proceeded to list the secondary sexual characteristics which comprise this ideal of beauty, rejecting the 'naked sexual organ(s)' as not 'aesthetically beautiful' since it is 'fundamentally necessary' that they 'retain their primitive characteristics'. Only people 'in a low state of culture' perceive the 'naked sexual organs as objects of attraction'.[18] The list of secondary sexual characteristics which Ellis then gives as the signs of a cultured (that is, not primitive) perception of the body – the vocabulary of aesthetically pleasing signs – begins with the buttocks. This is, of course, a nineteenth-century fascination with the buttocks as a displacement for the genitalia. Ellis gives it the quality of a higher regard for the beautiful. His discussions of the buttocks ranks the races by size of the female pelvis, a view which began with Willem Vrolik's claim in 1826 that a narrow pelvis is a sign of racial superiority and is echoed by R. Verneau's study in 1875 of the form of the pelvis among the various races.[19] Verneau uses the pelvis of Sarah Bartmann to argue the primitive nature of the Hottentot's anatomical structure. Ellis accepts this ranking, seeing the steatopygia as 'a simulation of the large pelvis of the higher races', having a compensatory function like face powder in emulating white skin. This view places the pelvis in an intermediary role as both a secondary as well as a primary sexual sign. Darwin himself, who held similar views as to the objective nature of human beauty, saw the pelvis as a 'primary [rather] than as a secondary . . . character' and the buttocks of the Hottentot as a somewhat comic sign of the primitive, grotesque nature of the black female.[20]

When the Victorians saw the female black, they saw her in terms of her buttocks and saw represented by the buttocks all the anomalies of her genitalia. In a mid-century erotic caricature of the Hottentot Venus, a white, male observer views her through a telescope, unable to see anything but her buttocks.[21] This fascination with the uniqueness of the sexual parts of the black focuses on the buttocks over and over again. In a British pornographic novel, published in 1899 but set in a mythic, antebellum Southern United States, the male author indulges his fantasy of flagellation on the buttocks of a number of white women. When he describes the one black, a runaway slave, being whipped, the power of the image of the Hottentot's buttocks captures him:

> She would have had a good figure, only that her bottom was out of all proportion. It was too big, but nevertheless it was fairly well shaped, with well-rounded cheeks meeting each other closely, her thighs were large, and she had a sturdy pair of legs, her skin was smooth and of a clear yellow tint.[22]

The presence of exaggerated buttocks points to the other, hidden sexual signs, both physical and temperamental, of the black female. This association is a powerful one. Indeed Freud, in *Three Essays on Sexuality* (1905), echoes the view that female genitalia are more primitive than those of the male, for female sexuality is more anal than that of the male.[23] Female sexuality is linked to the image of the buttocks, and the quintessential buttocks are those of the Hottentot.

We can see in Edwin Long's painting of 1882, *The Babylonian Marriage Market*, the centrality of this vocabulary in perceiving the sexualized woman (Figure 6). This painting was the most expensive work of contemporary art sold in nineteenth-century London. It also has a special

Figure 6   Edwin Long, The Babylonian Marriage Market, 1822 (Royal Holloway and Bedford New College).

place in documenting the perception of the sexualized female in terms of the great chain of aesthetic perception presented by Ellis. Long's painting is based on a specific text from Herodotus, who described the marriage auction in Babylon in which maidens were sold in order of comeliness. In the painting they are arranged in order of their attractiveness. Their physiognomies are clearly portrayed. Their features run from the most European and white (a fact emphasized by the light reflected from the mirror on to the figure at the far left) to the Negroid features (thick lips, broad nose, dark but not black skin) of the figure furthest to the observer's right. The latter figure fulfils all of Virey's categories for the appearance of the black. This is, however, the Victorian scale of sexualized women acceptable within marriage, portrayed from the most to the least attractive, according to contemporary British standards. The only black female present is the servant-slave shown on the auction block, positioned so as to present her buttocks to the viewer. While there are black males in the audience and thus among the bidders, the only black female is associated with sexualized white women as a signifier of their sexual availability. Her position is her sign and her presence in the painting is thus analogous to the figure of the black servant, Laura, in Manet's *Olympia*. Here, the linkage between two female figures, one black and one white, represents not the perversities of human sexuality in a corrupt society, such as the black servants signify in Hogarth; rather, it represents the internalization of this perversity in one specific aspect of human society, the sexualized female, in the perception of late nineteenth-century Europe.

In the nineteenth century, the prostitute is perceived as the essential sexualized female. She is perceived as the embodiment of sexuality and of all that is associated with sexuality – disease as well as passion. Within the large and detailed literature concerning prostitution written during the nineteenth century (most of which documents the need for legal controls and draws on the medical model as perceived by public health officials), the physiognomy and physiology of the prostitute are analysed in detail. We can begin with the most widely read early nineteenth-century work on prostitution, that of A. J. B. Parent-Duchatelet, who provides a documentation of the anthropology of the prostitute in his study of prostitution in Paris (1836).[24] Alain Corbin has shown how Parent-Duchatelet's use of the public health model reduces the prostitute to yet another source of pollution, similar to the sewers of Paris. Likewise in Parent-Duchatelet's discussion of the physiognomy of the prostitute, he believes himself to be providing a descriptive presentation of the appearance of the prostitute. He presents his readers with a statistical description of the physical types of the prostitutes, the nature of their voices, the colour of their hair and eyes, their physical anomalies, and their sexual profile in relation to childbearing and disease. Parent-Duchatelet's descriptions range from the detailed to the anecdotal. His discussion of the *embonpoint* of the prostitute begins his litany of external signs. Prostitutes have a 'peculiar plumpness' which is attributed to 'the great number of hot baths which the major part of these women take' – or perhaps to their lassitude, since they rise at ten or eleven in the morning, 'leading an animal life'. They are fat as prisoners are fat, from simple confinement. As an English commentator noted, 'the grossest and stoutest of these women are to be found amongst the lowest and most disgusting classes of prostitutes'.[25] These are the Hottentots on the scale of the sexualized female.

When Parent-Duchatelet considers the sexual parts of the prostitutes, he provides two sets of information which merge to become part of the myth of the physical anthropology of the prostitute. The prostitute's sexual parts are in no way directly affected by her profession. He contradicts the 'general opinion . . . that the genital parts in prostitutes must alter, and assume a particular disposition, as the inevitable consequence of their avocation' (P, p. 42). He cites one case of a women of fifty-one 'who had prostituted herself thirty-six years, but in whom, notwithstanding, the genital parts might have been mistaken for those of a virgin just arrived at puberty' (P, p. 43). Parent-Duchatelet thus rejects any Lamarckian adaptation as well as any indication that the prostitute is inherently marked as a prostitute. This, of course, follows from his view that prostitution is an illness of a society rather than of an individual or group of individuals. While he does not see the genitalia of the prostitute altering, he does observe that prostitutes were subject to specific pathologies of their genitalia. They are especially prone to tumours 'of the great labia . . . which commence with a little pus and tumefy at each menstrual period' (P, p. 49). He identifies the central pathology of the prostitute in the following manner: 'Nothing is more frequent in prostitutes than common abscesses in the thickness of the labia majora' (P, p. 50). Parent-Duchatelet's two views – first, that there is no adaption of the sexual organ and, secondly, that the sexual organ is especially prone to labial tumours and abscesses – merge in the image of the prostitute as developing, through illness, an altered appearance of the genitalia.

From Parent-Duchatelet's description of the physical appearance of the prostitute (a catalogue which reappears in most nineteenth-century studies of prostitutes, such as Josef Schrank's study of the prostitutes of Vienna), it is but a small step to the use of such catalogues of stigmata as a means of categorizing those women who have, as Freud states, 'an aptitude for prostitution' (SE, 7, 191).[26] The major work of nineteenth-century physical anthropology, public health, and pathology to undertake this was written by Pauline Tarnowsky. Tarnowsky, one of a number of Saint Petersburg female physicians in the late nineteenth century, wrote in the tradition of her eponymous colleague, V. M. Tarnowsky, the author of the standard work on Russian prostitution. His study appeared in both Russian and German and assumed a central role in the late nineteenth-century discussions of the nature of the prostitute.[27] She followed his more general study with a detailed investigation of the physiognomy of the prostitute.[28] Her categories remain those of Parent-Duchatelet. She describes the excessive weight of prostitutes, their hair and eye colour; she provides anthropometric measurements of skull size, a catalogue of their family background (as with Parent-Duchatelet, most are the children of alcoholics), and their level of fecundity (extremely low) as well as the signs of their degeneration. These signs deal with the abnormalities of the face: asymmetry of features, misshapen noses, overdevelopment of the parietal region of the skull, and the appearance of the so-called Darwin's ear. All of these signs are the signs of the lower end of the scale of beauty, the end dominated by the Hottentot. All of these signs point to the 'primitive' nature of the prostitute's physiognomy, for stigmata such as Darwin's ear (the simplification of the convolutes of the ear shell and the absence of a lobe) are a sign of the atavistic female.

In a later paper, Tarnowsky provided a scale of appearance of the prostitute, in an analysis of the 'physiognomy of the Russian prostitute'. At the upper end of the scale is the 'Russian Helen'. Here, classical aesthetics are introduced as the measure of the appearance of the sexualized female. A bit further on is one who is 'very handsome in spite of her hard expression'. Indeed, the first fifteen prostitutes on her scale 'might pass on the street for beauties'. But hidden even within these seeming beauties are the stigmata of criminal degeneration: black, thick hair; a strong jaw; a hard, spent glance. Some show the 'wild eyes and perturbed countenance along with facial asymmetry' of the insane.[29] Only the scientific observer can see the hidden faults, and thus identify the true prostitute, for prostitutes use superficial beauty as the bait for their clients. But when they age, their

> strong jaws and cheek-bones, and their masculine aspect . . . [once] hidden by adipose tissue, emerge, salient angles stand out, and the face grows virile, uglier than a man's; wrinkles deepen into the likeness of scars, and the countenance, once attractive, exhibits the full degenerate type which early grace had concealed.[30]

Change over time affects the physiognomy of the prostitute just as it does her genitalia, which become more and more diseased as she ages. For Tarnowsky, the appearance of the prostitute and her sexual identity are pre-established by heredity. What is most striking is that as the prostitute ages, she begins to appear more and more mannish. The link between the physical anomalies of the Hottentot and those of the lesbian appear in Billroth's *Handbuch der Frauenkrankheiten* (*Handbook of gynaecological diseases*); here, the link is between two further models of sexual deviancy, the prostitute and the lesbian. Both are seen as possessing the physical signs which set them apart from the normal.

The paper in which Tarnowsky undertook her documentation of the appearance of the prostitute is repeated word for word in the major late nineteenth-century study of prostitution. This study of the criminal woman, subtitled *The Prostitute and the Normal Woman*, written by Cesare Lombroso and his son-in-law, Guillaume Ferrero, was published in

1893.[31] Lombroso accepts Tarnowsky's entire manner of seeing the prostitute and articulates one further subtext of central importance in the perception of the sexualized woman in the nineteenth century. This subtext becomes apparent only by examining the plates in his study. Two of the plates deal with the image of the Hottentot female and illustrate the 'Hottentot apron' and the steatopygia. Lombroso accepts Parent-Duchatelet's image of the fat prostitute and sees her as similar to women living in asylums and to the Hottentot female. He regards the anomalies of the prostitute's labia as atavistic throwbacks to the Hottentot, if not the chimpanzee. Lombroso deems the prostitute to be an atavistic subclass of woman, and he applies the power of the polygenetic argument to the image of the Hottentot to support his views. Lombroso's text, in its offhanded use of the analogy between the Hottentot and the prostitute, simply articulates in images a view which had been present throughout the late nineteenth century. Adrien Charpy's essay of 1870, published in the most distinguished French journal of dermatology and syphilology, presented an analysis of the external form of the genitalia of 800 prostitutes examined at Lyons.[32] Charpy merged Parent-Duchatelet's two contradictory categories by describing all of the alterations as either pathological or adaptive. The initial category of anomalies is that of the labia; he begins by commenting on the elongation of the labia major in prostitutes, comparing this with the apron of the 'disgusting' Hottentots. The image comes as a natural one to Charpy, as it did to Lombroso two decades later. The prostitute is an atavistic form of humanity whose 'primitive' nature can be observed in the form of her genitalia. What Tarnowsky and Lombroso add to the equation is the parallel they draw between the seemingly beautiful physiognomy and this atavistic nature. Other signs were quickly found. Ellis saw, as one of the secondary sexual characteristics which determine the beautiful, the presence in a woman of a long second toe and a short fifth toe (see *SPS*, p. 164). The French physician L. Jullien presented clinical material concerning the anti-thetical case, the foot of the prostitute, which Lombroso in commenting on the paper immediately labelled as prehensile.[33] The ultimate of the throwbacks was, of course, the throwback to the level of the Hottentot or the Bushman – to the level of the lasciviousness of the prostitute. Ferrero, Lombroso's co-author, described prostitution as the rule in primitive societies and placed the Bushman at the nadir of the scale of primitive lasciviousness: adultery has no meaning for them, he asserted, nor does virginity; the poverty of their mental universe can be seen in the fact that they have but one word for 'girl, woman, or wife'.[34] The primitive is the black, and the qualities of blackness, or at least of the black female, are those of the prostitute. The work of a student of Lombroso's, Abele de Blasio, makes this grotesquely evident: he published a series of case studies on steatopygia in prostitutes in which he perceives the prostitute as being, quite literally, the Hottentot (Figure 7).[35]

The perception of the prostitute in the late nineteenth century thus merged with the perception of the black. Both categories are those of

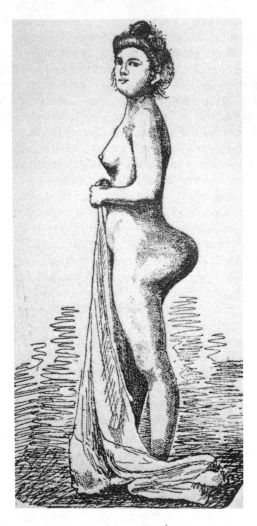

Figure 7   An Italian prostitute (Abele de Blasio, 'Steatopigia in prostitute', plate 1, 1905).

outsiders, but what does this amalgamation imply in terms of the perception of both groups? It is a commonplace that the primitive was associated with unbridled sexuality. This was either condemned, as in Thomas Jefferson's discussions of the nature of the black in Virginia, or praised, as in the fictional supplement written by Denis Diderot to Bougainville's voyages. It is exactly this type of uncontrolled sexuality, however, which is postulated by historians such as J. J. Bachofen as the sign of the 'swamp', the earliest stage of human history. Blacks, if both G. W. F. Hegel and Arthur Schopenhauer are to be believed, remained at this most primitive stage, and their presence in the contemporary world served as an indicator of how far mankind had come in establishing control over his world and himself. The loss of control was marked by a regression into this dark past – a degeneracy into the primitive expression of emotions in the form of either madness or unrestrained sexuality. Such a loss of control was, of course, viewed as pathological and thus fell into the domain of the medical model. For the medical model, especially as articulated in the public health reforms of the mid- and late nineteenth century, had as its central preoccupation the elimination of sexually transmitted disease through the institution of social controls; this was the project which motivated writers such as Parent-Duchatelet and Tarnowsky. The social controls which they wished to institute had existed in the nineteenth century but in quite a different context. The laws applying to the control of slaves (such as the 1685 French *code noir* and its American analogues) had placed great emphasis on the control of the slave as sexual object, both in terms of permitted and forbidden sexual contacts as well as by requiring documentation as to the legal status of the offspring of slaves. Sexual control was thus well known to the late eighteenth and early nineteenth century.

The linkage which the late nineteenth century established between this earlier model of control and the later model of sexual control advocated by the public health authorities came about through the association of two bits of medical mythology. The primary marker of the black is his or her skin colour. Medical tradition has a long history of perceiving this skin colour as the result of some pathology. The favourite theory, which reappears with some frequency in the early nineteenth century, is that the skin colour and attendant physiognomy of the black are the result of congenital leprosy.[36] It is not very surprising, therefore, to read in the late nineteenth century – after social conventions surrounding the abolition of slavery in Great Britain and France, as well as the trauma of the American Civil War, forbade the public association of at least skin colour with illness – that syphilis was not introduced into Europe by Christopher Columbus' sailors but rather that it was a form of leprosy which had long been present in Africa and had spread into Europe in the Middle Ages.[37] The association of the black, especially the black female, with the syphilophobia of the late nineteenth century was thus made manifest. Black females do not merely represent the sexualized female, they also represent the female as the source of corruption and disease. It is the black female as the emblem of illness who haunts the background of Manet's *Olympia*.

For Manet's *Olympia* stands exactly midway between the glorification and the condemnation of the sexualized female. She is the antithesis of the fat prostitute. Indeed, she was perceived as thin by her contemporaries, much in the style of the actual prostitutes of the 1860s. But Laura, the black servant, is presented as plump, which can be best seen in Manet's initial oil sketch of her done in 1862–63. Her presence in both the sketch and in the final painting emphasizes her face, for it is the physiognomy of the black which points to her own sexuality and to that of the white female presented to the viewer unclothed but with her genitalia demurely covered. The association is between these hidden genitalia and the signifier of the black. Both point to potential corruption of the male viewer by the female. This is made even more evident in that work which art historians have stressed as being heavily influenced by Manet's *Olympia*, his portrait *Nana*. Here the associations would have been quite clear to the contemporary viewer. First, the model for the painting was Henriette Hauser, called Citron, the mistress of the Prince of Orange. Secondly, Manet places in the background of the painting a Japanese crane, for which the French word (*grue*) was a slang term for prostitute. He thus labels the figure as a sexualized female. Unlike the classical pose of the *Olympia*, Nana is presented being admired by a well-dressed man-about-town (a *flâneur*). She is not naked but partially clothed. What Manet can further draw upon is the entire vocabulary of signs which, by the late nineteenth century, were associated with the sexualized female. Nana is fulsome rather than thin. Here Manet employs the stigmata of fatness to characterize the prostitute. This convention becomes part of the visualization of the sexualized female even while the reality of the idealized sexualized female is that of a thin female. Constantin Guys presents a fat, reclining prostitute in 1860, while Edgar Degas' *Madam's Birthday* (1879) presents an entire brothel of fat prostitutes. At the same time, Napoléon III's mistress, Marguerite Bellanger, set a vogue for slenderness. She was described as 'below average in size, slight, thin, almost skinny'.[38] This is certainly not Nana. Manet places her in a position *vis-à-vis* the viewer (but not the male observer in the painting) which emphasizes the line of her buttocks, the steatopygia of the prostitute. Also, Nana is placed in such a way that the viewer (but again not the *flâneur*) can observe her ear. It is, to no one's surprise, Darwin's ear, a sign of the atavistic female. Thus we know where the black servant is hidden in *Nana* – within Nana. Even Nana's seeming beauty is but a sign of the black hidden within. All her external stigmata point to the pathology within the sexualized female.

Manet's *Nana* thus provides a further reading of his *Olympia*, a reading which stresses Manet's debt to the pathological model of sexuality present during the late nineteenth century. The black hidden within *Olympia* bursts forth in Pablo Picasso's 1901 version of the painting: Olympia is presented as a sexualized black, with broad hips, revealed genitalia, gazing at the nude *flâneur* bearing her a gift of fruit, much as Laura bears a gift of flowers in Manet's original (Figure 8). But, unlike Manet, the artist is himself present in this work, as a sexualized observer of the sexualized female. Picasso owes part of his reading of the *Olympia* to the polar image of the primitive female as a sexual object, as found in the lower-class prostitutes painted by Vincent van Gogh or the Tahitian maidens à la Diderot painted by Paul Gauguin. Picasso saw the sexualized female as the visual analogue of the black. Indeed, in his most radical break with the impressionist tradition, *Les Demoiselles d'Avignon* (1907), he linked the inmates of the brothel with the black by using the theme of African masks to characterize their appearance. The figure of the male

Figure 8   Pablo Picasso, Olympia, *1901, New York (© DACS, 1991).*

represents the artist as victim. Picasso's parody points toward the importance of seeing Manet's *Nana* in the context of the medical discourse concerning the sexualized female which dominated the late nineteenth century.

The portrait of *Nana* is also embedded in a complex literary matrix which provides many of the signs needed to illustrate the function of the sexualized female as the sign of disease. The figure of Nana first appeared in Emile Zola's novel *L'Assommoir* (1877) in which she was presented as the offspring of the alcoholic couple who are the central figures of the novel. Here heredity assured the reader that she would eventually become a sexualized female – a prostitute – and, indeed, by the close of the novel she has run off with an older man, the owner of a button factory, and has begun her life as a sexualized female. Manet was captivated by the figure of Nana (as was the French reading public), and his portrait of her symbolically reflected her sexual encounters presented during the novel. Zola then decided to build the next novel in his Rougon-Macquart cycle about the figure of Nana as a sexualized female. Thus in Zola's *Nana* the reader is presented with Zola's reading of Manet's portrait of Nana. Indeed, Zola uses the portrait of the *flâneur* observing the half-dressed Nana as the centrepiece for a scene in the theatre in which Nana seduces the simple Count Muffat. Immediately before this meeting, Zola presents Nana's first success in the theatre (or, as the theatre director calls it, his brothel). She appears in a revue, unable to sing or dance, and becomes the butt of laughter until, in the second act of the revue, she appears unclothed on stage:

> Nana was in the nude: naked with a quiet audacity, certain of the omnipotence of her flesh. She was wrapped in a simple piece of gauze: her rounded shoulders, her Amazon's breasts of which the pink tips stood up rigidly like lances, her broad buttocks which rolled in a voluptuous swaying motion, and her fair, fat hips: her whole body was in evidence, and could be seen under the light tissue with its foamy whiteness.[39]

What Zola describes are the characteristics of the sexualized woman, the 'primitive' hidden beneath the surface: 'all of a sudden in the comely child the woman arose, disturbing, bringing the mad surge of her sex, inviting the unknown element of desire. Nana was still smiling: but it was the smile of a man-eater.' Nana's atavistic sexuality, the sexuality of the Amazon, is destructive. The sign of this is her fleshliness. And it is this sign which reappears when she is observed by Muffat in her dressing room, the scene which Zola found in Manet's painting:

> Then calmly, to reach her dressing-table, she walked in her drawers through that group of gentlemen, who made way for her. She had large buttocks, her drawers ballooned, and with breast well forward she bowed to them, giving her delicate smile. (N, p. 135)

Nana's childlike face is but a mask which conceals the hidden disease buried within, the corruption of sexuality. Thus Zola concludes the novel by revealing the horror beneath the mask: Nana dies of the pox. (Zola's pun works in French as well as in English and is needed because of the rapidity of decay demanded by the moral implication of Zola's portrait. It would not do to have Nana die slowly over thirty years of tertiary syphilis. Smallpox, with its play on 'the pox', works quickly and gives the same visual icon of decay.) Nana's death reveals her true nature:

> Nana remained alone, her face looking up in the light from the candle. It was a charnel-house scene, a mass of tissue-fluids and blood, a shovelful of putrid flesh thrown there on a cushion. The pustules had invaded the entire face with the pocks touching each other; and, dissolving and subsiding with the greyish look of mud, there seemed to be already an earthy mouldiness on the shapeless muscosity, in which the features were no longer discernible. An eye, the left one, had completely subsided in a soft mass of purulence; the other, half-open, was sinking like a collapsing hole. The nose was still suppurating. A whole reddish crust was peeling off one cheek and invaded the mouth, distorting it into a loathsome grimace. And on that horrible and grotesque mask, the hair, that beautiful head of hair still preserving its blaze of sunlight, flowed down in a golden

trickle. Venus was decomposing. It seems as though the virus she had absorbed from the gutters and from the tacitly permitted carrion of humanity, that baneful ferment with which she had poisoned a people, had now risen to her face and putrefied it. (*N*, pp. 464–65)

The decaying visage is a visible sign of the diseased genitalia through which the sexualized female corrupts an entire nation of warriors and leads them to the collapse of the French Army and the resultant German victory at Sedan. The image is an old one, it is *Frau Welt*, Madam World, who masks her corruption, the disease of being a woman, through her beauty. It reappears in the vignette on the title page of the French translation (1840) of the Renaissance poem *Syphilis* (Figure 9).[40] But it is yet more, for in death Nana begins to revert to the blackness of the earth, to assume the horrible grotesque countenance perceived as belonging to the world of the black, the world of the 'primitive', the world of disease. Nana is, like Olympia, in the words of Paul Valéry, 'pre-eminently unclean'.[41]

It is this uncleanliness, this disease, which forms the final link between two images of woman, the black and the prostitute. Just as the genitalia of the Hottentot were perceived as parallel to the diseased genitalia of the prostitute, so too the power of the idea of corruption links both images. Thus part of Nana's fall into corruption comes through her seduction by a lesbian, yet a further sign of her innate, physical degeneracy. She is corrupted and corrupts through sexuality. Miscegenation was a fear (and a word) from the late nineteenth-century vocabulary of sexuality. It was a fear not merely of interracial sexuality but of its results, the decline of the population. Interracial marriages were seen as exactly parallel to the barrenness of the prostitute: if they produced children at all, these children were weak and doomed. Thus Ellis, drawing on his view of the objective nature of the beauty of mankind, states that 'it is difficult to be sexually attracted to persons who are fundamentally unlike ourselves in racial constitution' (*SPS*, p. 176). He cites Abel Hermant to substantiate his views:

Differences of race are irreducible and between two beings who love each other they cannot fail to produce exceptional and instructive reactions. In the first superficial ebullition of love, indeed, nothing notable may be manifested, but in a fairly short time the two lovers, innately hostile, in striving to approach each other strike against an invisible partition which separates them. Their sensibilities are divergent; everything in each shocks the other; even their anatomical conformation, even the language of their gestures; all is foreign.[42]

It is thus the inherent fear of the difference in the anatomy of the Other which lies behind the synthesis of images. The Other's pathology is revealed in anatomy. It is the similarity between the black and the

Figure 9   Frontispiece. August Barthélemy, Syphilis, *1840.*

prostitute – as bearers of the stigmata of sexual difference and, thus, pathology – which captured the late nineteenth century. Zola sees in the sexual corruption of the male the source of political impotence and projects what is basically an internal fear, the fear of loss of power, on to the world.

The 'white *man's* burden' thus becomes his sexuality and its control, and it is this which is transferred into the need to control the sexuality of the Other, the Other as sexualized female. The colonial mentality which sees 'natives' as needing control is easily transferred to 'woman' – but woman as exemplified by the caste of the prostitute. This need for control was a projection of inner fears; thus, its articulation in visual images was in terms which described the polar opposite of the European male.

The roots of this image of the sexualized female are to be found in male observers, the progenitors of the vocabulary of images through which they believed themselves able to capture the essence of the Other. Thus when Freud, in his *Essay on Lay Analysis* (1926), discusses the ignorance of contemporary psychology concerning adult female sexuality, he refers to this lack of knowledge as the 'dark continent' of psychology (*SE*, **20** p. 212). In using this phrase in English, Freud ties the image of female sexuality to the image of the colonial black and to the perceived relationship between the female's ascribed sexuality and the Other's exoticism and pathology. It is Freud's intent to explore this hidden 'dark continent' and reveal the hidden truths about female sexuality, just as the anthropologist-explorers (such as Lombroso) were revealing the hidden truths about the nature of the black. Freud continues a discourse which relates the images of male discovery to the images of the female as object of discovery. The line from the secrets possessed by the 'Hottentot Venus' to twentieth-century psychoanalysis runs reasonably straight.

Notes

1 George Heard Hamilton *Manet and His Critics*, New Haven, Conn. (1954), p. 68.

2 For my discussion of Manet's works, I draw especially on Theodore Reff *Manet: 'Olympia'*, London (1976); and Werner Hofmann *Nana: Mythos und Wirklichkeit*, Cologne (1973); neither of these studies examines the medical analogies. See also Eunice Lipton 'Manet: a radicalized female imagery', *Artforum*, **13** (Mar. 1975), pp. 48–53.

3 See George Needham 'Manet, *Olympia*, and Pornographic Photography', in Thomas Ness and Linda Nochlin (eds) *Woman as Sex Object*, New York (1972) pp. 81–89.

4 See Philippe Rebeyrol 'Baudelaire et Manet', *Les Temps modernes*, **5** (Oct. 1949), pp. 707–25.

5 Georges Bataille *Manet* (trans. A. Wainhouse and James Emmons) New York (1956), p. 113. And see Hofmann, *Nana*.

6 See my *On Blackness without Blacks: Essays on the Image of the Black in Germany*, Boston (1982). On the image of the black, see Ladislas Bugner (ed.) *L'Image du noir dans l'art occidental* (3 vols), Paris (1976–); the fourth volume, not yet published, will cover the post-Renaissance period.

7 M. N. Adler (trans.) *The Itinerary of Benjamin of Tudela*, London (1907), p. 68.

8 See vol. 35, pp. 398–403 of J. J. Virey 'Nègre', *Dictionnaire des sciences médicales* (41 vols), Paris (1819).

9 See vol. 2, p. 151 of J. J. Virey *Histoire naturelle du genre humaine* (2 vols), Paris (1824).

10 See George M. Gould and Walter L. Pyle *Anomalies and Curiosities of Medicine*, Philadelphia (1901), p. 307; and Eugen Holländer *Aeskulap und Venus: Eine Kultur – und Sittengeschichte im Spiegel des Arztes*, Berlin (1928). Much material on the

SANDER L. GILMAN

indebtedness of the early pathologists to the reports of travellers to Africa can be found in the accounts of the autopsies that I will discuss in the text.

11 See Henri de Blainville 'Sur une femme de la race hottentote', *Bulletin des sciences par la société philomatique de Paris*, Paris (1816), pp. 183–90.

12 Georges Cuvier 'Extraits d'observations faites sur le cadavre d'une femme connue à Paris et à Londres sous le nom de Vénus Hottentote', *Mémoires du Museum d'histoire naturelle*, 3 (1817), pp. 259–74; repeated with plates in Geoffrey Saint-Hilaire and Frédéric Cuvier *Histoire naturelle des mammifères avec des figures originales* (2 vols), Paris (1824), vol. 1, pp. 1–23. The substance of the autopsy is given in Flourens *Journal complémentaire du dictionnaire des sciences médicales*, 4 (1819), pp. 145–49; and in Jules Cloquet *Manuel d'anatomie de l'homme descriptive du corps humaine*, Paris (1825), pl. 278. Cuvier's presentation of the 'Hottentot Venus' forms the major signifier for the image of the Hottentot as sexual primitive in the nineteenth century.

13 See Adolf Wilhelm Otto *Seltene Beobachtungen zur Anatomie, Physiologie, und Pathologie gehörig*, Breslau (1816), p. 135; Johannes Müller 'Ueber die äusseren Geschlechtstheile der Buschmänninnen', *Archiv für Anatomie, Physiologie, und wissenschaftliche Medizin* (1834), pp. 319–45; W. H. Flower and James Murie 'Account of the dissection of a bushwoman', *Journal of Anatomy and Physiology*, 1 (1867), pp. 189–208; and Hubert von Luschka, A. Koch and E. Görtz 'Die äusseren Geschlechtsheile eines Buschweibes', *Monatsschrift für Geburstkunde*, 32 (1868), pp. 343–50. The popularity of these accounts can be seen by their republication in extract for a lay audience. These extracts also stress the sexual anomalies described. See *Anthropological Review*, 5 (July 1867), pp. 319–24, and *Anthropological Review*, 8 (Jan. 1870), pp. 89–318.

14 Edward Turnipseed 'Some facts in regard to the anatomical differences between the negro and white races', *American Journal of Obstetrics*, 10 (1871), 32, 33.

15 See Fort, C. H. 'Some corroborative facts in regard to the anatomical difference between the negro and white races', *American Journal of Obstetrics*, 10 (1877), pp. 258–59. Paul Broca was influenced by similar American material (which he cites from the *New York City Medical Record*, 15 Sept. 1868) concerning the position of the hymen; see his untitled note in the *Bulletins de la société d'anthropologie de Paris*, 4 (1869), pp. 443–44. Broca, like Cuvier before him, supported a polygenetic view of the human races.

16 See William Turner 'Notes on the dissection of a negro', *Journal of Anatomy and Physiology*, 13 (1878), pp. 382–86; 'Notes on the dissection of a second negro', *Journal of Anatomy and Physiology*, 14 (1879), pp. 244–48; and 'Notes on the dissection of a third negro', *Journal of Anatomy and Physiology*, 31 (1896), pp. 624–26.

17 H. Hildebrand 'Die Krankheiten der äusseren weiblichen Genitalien' in Theodor Billroth (ed.) *Handbuch der Frauenkrankheiten* (3 vols), Stuttgart (1885–86), vol. 3, pp. 11–12. See also Thomas Power Lowry (ed.) *The Classic Clitoris: Historic Contributions to Scientific Sexuality*, Chicago (1978).

18 Havelock Ellis *Studies in the Psychology of Sex*, vol. 4, *Sexual Selection in Man*, Philadelphia (1920), p. 158; all further references to this work in the text are abbreviated *SPS*.

19 See Willem Vrolik *Considérations sur la diversité du bassin des différentes races humaines*, Amsterdam (1826); and Verneau, *Le bassin dans les sexes et dans les races*, Paris (1875), pp. 126–29.

20 Charles Darwin *The Descent of Man and Selection in Relation to Sex*, Princeton, N.J. (1881), 2:317, and see 2:345–46.

21 See John Grand-Carteret *Die Erotik in der französischen Karikatur* (trans. Cary von Karwarth and Adolf Neumann), Vienna (1909), p. 195.

22 [Hugues Rebell?] *The Memories of Dolly Morton: The Story of a Woman's Part in the Struggle to Free the Slaves: An Account of the Whippings, Rapes, and Violences That*

Preceded the Civil War in America with Curious Anthropological Observations on the Radical Diversities in the Conformation of the Female Bottom and the Way Different Women Endure Chastisement, Paris (1899), p. 207.

23 See vol. 7, pp. 186–87, esp. n. 1, of Sigmund Freud *The Standard Edition of the Complete Psychological Works of Sigmund Freud*, ed. and trans. James Strachey (24 vols), London (1953–74); all further references to this work in the text are abbreviated *SE* with volume and page numbers included.

24 See vol. 1, pp. 193–244 of A. J. B. Parent-Duchatelet *De la prostitution dans la ville de Paris* (2 vols), Paris (1836).

25 Parent-Duchatelet, A. J. B. *On Prostitution in the City of Paris*, London (1840), p. 38; all further references to this work in the text are abbreviated *P*. It is exactly the passages on the physiognomy and appearance of the prostitute which this anonymous translator presents to his English audience as the essence of Parent-Duchatelet's work.

26 See my 'Freud and the prostitute: male stereotypes of female sexuality in *fin de siècle* Vienna', *Journal of the American Academy of Psychoanalysis*, **9** (1981), pp. 337–60.

27 See V. M. Tarnowsky *Prostitutsija i abolitsioniszm*, Petersburg (1888); and *Prostitution und Abolitionismus*, Hamburg (1890).

28 See Pauline Tarnowsky *Etude anthropométrique sur les prostituées et les voleuses*, Paris (1889).

29 Tarnowsky 'Fisiomie di prostitute russe', *Archivio di psichiatria, scienze penali e antropologia criminale*, **14** (1893), pp. 141–42; my translation.

30 *Ibid.*, p. 141; my translation.

31 See Cesare Lombroso and Guillaume Ferrero *La donna deliquente: La prostituta e la donna normale*, Turin (1893); esp. pp. 349–50, 361–62, and 38.

32 See Adrien Charpy 'Des organes génitaux externes chez les prostituées', *Annales des dermatologie*, **3** (1870–71), pp. 271–79.

33 See L. Jullien 'Contribution à l'étude de la morphologie des prostituées', in *Quatrieme Congrès international d'anthropologie criminelle, 1896*, Geneva (1897), pp. 348–49.

34 See Ferrero (1892) 'L'atavisme de la prostitution', *Revue scientifique*, pp. 136–41.

35 See A. de Blasio 'Steatopigia in prostitute', *Archivio di psichiatria*, **26** (1905), pp. 257–64.

36 See Winthrop D. Jordan *White over Black: American Attitudes toward the Negro, 1550–1812*, New York (1977), pp. 3–43.

37 See Iwan Bloch *Der Ursprung der Syphilis; Eine medizinische und kulturgeschichtliche Untersuchung* (2 vols), Jena (1901–11).

38 Reff, *Manet: 'Olympia'*, pp. 58 and 118. (See Note 2.)

39 Emile Zola *Nana*, trans. Charles Duff, London (1953), p. 27; all further references to this work in the text are abbreviated *N*.

40 See August Barthélemy (trans.) *Syphilis: Poème en deux chants*, Paris (1840). This is a translation of a section of Fracastorius' Latin poem on the nature and origin of syphilis. The French edition was in print well past mid-century.

41 Paul Valéry, quoted in Bataille, *Manet*, p. 65. (See Note 5.)

42 Abel Hermant, quoted in Ellis, *Studies in the Psychology of Sex*, **4**, p. 176, n. 1. (See Note 18.)

Source: Gates, H. L. Jr. (ed.) (1987) *Race, Writing, and Difference*, Chicago, University of Chicago Press.

8 RACISM, REPRESENTATION, PSYCHOANALYSIS

CLAIRE PAJACZKOWSKA AND LOLA YOUNG

What might a psychoanalytic perspective contribute to an understanding of racism? Far from explaining it away as an individual pathology, the psychoanalytic emphasis on the complex and often painful transactions between the psychic and social can reveal how deeply racism permeates not only the institutions of a post-colonial society like Britain, but also the ways in which we experience ourselves and others. Nowhere is this more evident than in Frantz Fanon's pioneering studies of the emotional dynamics of negrophobia and its effects on the Black subject. In that spirit, this article examines the way in which our ordinary identities are mediated through symbolic categories that are themselves profoundly racialized. We look in particular at the complex systems of representation embodied in two popular texts, the British film *Mona Lisa* and Toni Morrison's Pulitzer Prize-winning novel *Beloved*. We have selected these because of the contrast they offer. One is a film that uses destructive stereotypes, the other a novel that traces and counteracts the damage caused by such stereotypes. We are thus responding to Fanon's call for a psychoanalysis of racism that both deconstructs negrophobia and contributes to the affirmation and celebration of autonomous Black culture.

There is a long history which unites psychoanalysis and antiracist struggle. It has been suggested that psychoanalysis was forged from the cumulative wit of hundreds of generations of Jewish survival of persecution and diaspora, and that the systematic understanding of the psyche was initially the need to understand the oppressor, to anticipate the next blow, in order to deflect it and continue with self realization. The insights of psychoanalysis have, to some extent, become part of twentieth-century common sense, but it remains to be fully integrated into this generation of antiracist struggle.

We begin by introducing some key psychoanalytic concepts that are valuable in analysing texts and the ways in which they interact with cultural forms to produce a subjective sense of self, or identity, for the spectator or reader. We suggest what light these concepts might cast on one of the most important, but least examined, features of racism: that is, ordinary white identity. We then offer our analyses of *Mona Lisa* and *Beloved*.

As it is part of our argument that a psychoanalytic perspective makes it possible to draw on intuition, experience and memory in a critical account of racism, we should perhaps acknowledge our own investment in this project. This article has developed from joint teaching over a number of years, particularly teaching a course 'Representing Other Cultures', as part of an undergraduate course in Cultural History. The section on *Mona Lisa* is written by Claire Pajaczkowska that on *Beloved* by Lola Young. The latter especially draws on the way the book interacts with the reader's own intuition, experience and memory in an attempt to acknowledge the usually implicit personal investment in theoretical work.

Psychoanalytic concepts

The starting point of our analysis is that the capacity for racism is based on innate human characteristics, but that this capacity is not necessarily activated by society in a destructive way. Although racism exists as a subjective structure it also exists as an objective reality, produced by the history of imperialism, colonialism and exploitation. How, then, do subjective structures influence objective reality, and, conversely, how do external structures become part of our inner reality? How does history interact with memory to produce our sense of personal, familial, group, institutional, national and international identity? Because culture is an intermediate space, in which we find the subjective and objective realities of memory and history represented in the form of narratives and dramas, it is both fascinating and instructive to analyse. In order to link narrative scenarios to their symbolic and historic meanings we have drawn especially on a number of psychoanalytic concepts.

Trauma

The first concept is that of trauma; originally derived from the Greek word meaning 'wound' or 'injury' but defined analytically as 'an event in the subject's life defined by its intensity, by the subject's inability to respond adequately to it, and by the upheaval and long-lasting effects that it brings about in psychical organisation' (Laplanche and Pontalis, 1988, p. 465). This psychoanalytic account of trauma shows that unless experiences can be symbolized in a way that is both subjectively and objectively true, the human subject is deprived of its fundamental link with others. The human subject loses the community of communication, and deprivation of this link creates a loss comparable in scale to the emotional loss of an infant separated from its mother. The sense of identity of a Black person trying to recover her history and culture within the combination of White narcissism and denial that passes for 'history' in most post-colonial societies, is one that will necessarily contain the 'trauma' of an intense life event for which the culture provides no symbolic equivalents and to which the subject is therefore unable to respond adequately. What is a history without representation? What is the identity of a person for whom reading and writing were illegal, the family illegal as was the case under slavery? Is not such deprivation in fact a theft? The trauma of slavery is evident in the realization that although its reality must be represented, in order to become real, the reality of its dehumanization of Black people is one for which there are no adequate words.

Trauma is a concept which depends, for its meaning, on several other concepts central to the psychoanalytic explanation of life, and before turning to the more detailed textual analysis of the film and the novel four of these will be introduced.

The unconscious

The concept most fundamental to psychoanalysis is that of the unconscious mind. The existence of an unconscious mind is a hypothesis proposed by Freud in the late nineteenth century to account for patterns which he saw emerging across symptoms, dreams, fantasies and memories, common to both 'pathological' and 'normal' behaviour. He understood the unconscious mind to be a highly structured form of subjective reality, analogous in logic to the emotional world of infants and children, which continues to be active in adult life. In textual analysis the existence of the unconscious is discovered in the patterns underlying texts' narrative, imagery, vocabulary, characters and symbols. In ideology the unconscious mind is evident in the meanings and values attributed to human differences and is especially evident in the meanings racism attributes to physical and visual difference.

Identification

Identification is a process which may be conscious or unconscious, comprising the processes of introjection, projection and judgement, and through which people are able to find the links of identity and difference amongst themselves. The emotional process of identification has physiological precursors in the development of infants. Thus the introjection of meanings, symbols, images or concepts of another person is based on what was once a physical process of 'taking in' food, warmth, love. Projection of oneself onto other people or concepts is also based on their physical expulsions and rejections. Both introjection and projection are central parts of healthy identity, are innate characteristics of the human subject, but both can be misused for the purposes of defence. In racism these processes are used to maintain violently exploitative structures of identity. Film and literature employ the viewer/reader's identification, providing characters and situations which are introjected and become part of the reader's imaginative world. Similarly, the reader projects onto the text, either its characters or its scenario, aspects of his or her own experience, fantasy or memory which brings the texts 'to life' or endows them with meaning.

Denial

Another concept linked to the unconscious and identification is that of denial or disavowal. The mechanism of projection, when employed as a defense, can serve to protect the subject from knowledge of its own ambivalence. In order to deny knowledge of its own ruthlessness and aggression the subject has to maintain the fiction that 'foreigners are dirty' or that 'black men are violent'. Often sexuality is combined with aggression, and also experienced as 'dirty', in which case thoughts will be doubly denied or disavowed and will become projected onto whichever screen or scapegoat is socially condoned. Denial is a powerful emotional defence against acknowledging painful, distressing or troubling know-ledge. It is also the widespread reaction of most White people when asked to consider the reality of racism. This is an attitude described by the American writer James Baldwin as the 'sin of ignorance', or simply not wanting to know. What most people do not want to know about is their own capacity for aggression, whether this is expressed in the form of violence or indifference, and the knowledge thus remains unconscious, so that much racism, for example, is enacted in the guise of virtue. The emotional state produced by denial is one of blankness, and the role of blankness in sustaining White identity as normal and as 'undefined' will be discussed in greater detail below.

The Oedipus complex

Named after the protagonist of the Greek tragic myth, the Oedipus complex refers to the persistence of infantile reality within the adult unconscious. The small child becomes passionately attached, desirous and possessive of the parent of the opposite sex and ambivalently attached to the parent of the same sex. The desire and aggression cannot be satisfied, the small child cannot 'win', and the impossibility of the triangular structure results in the child's realization of his own helplessness, the difference between the generations and some degree of self consciousness. In adults this predicament exists only as an aspect of unconscious mental life, or in a symbolic form in narratives or drama. Psychoanalysts and structuralist literary critics note the similarity between narrative structure and oedipal structure; some have suggested that these are equivalent with the textual form reflecting an external, cultural version of the subjective, oedipal form. We have noted how racist ideology weaves fantasies of sexuality and power and how these find expression in dramas, narratives and imagery.

Whiteness as an absent centre

The analytic concepts described above make it possible to articulate the absent centre of White identity. The identity of White culture is 'absent' in a number of senses, both political and subjective. Within European history descriptions of Whiteness are absent due to denial of imperialism, and this leaves a blank in the place of knowledge of the destructive effects of wielding power. An identity based on power never has to develop consciousness of itself as responsible, it has no sense of its limits except as these are perceived in opposition to others. The blankness of the identity of empire covers an ambivalence which is often unconscious, and which, consequently, can most readily be perceived in the representations it creates of the colonial 'other'; representations which are projections of the 'split off' parts of the self. If we take three aspects of 'ordinary' identity in our culture, those of being White, being middle class and being male, we find processes which maintain this identity as a cultural norm, an absence, a negativity, with the power to define itself only in terms of what it designates its opposites. If Whiteness is assumed, in European culture, to be an identity without boundaries, without definition, without question, what will happen when this identity becomes defined in terms of its historical determinants and in terms of its subjective limits? If White identity is dependent on comparisons between itself and its others, it thereby lacks integrity; and much of White identity is contradictory, fragmented, disintegrated, projecting itself onto series of imaginary dramas, narratives, scenarios. The White and middle class male ego, shored up in its power to define what is real, for itself, will tend to characterize any threatening, negative, unreasonable attributes as Black, working class or feminine elements or characteristics. Why is White identity so resistant to self awareness and what is its missing content? Catherine Hall's (1989 and 1991) historical research on British, White, male, middle class identity in the second half of the nineteenth century is especially useful here. Her detailed study of the British Colonial presence in Australia and Jamaica shows how the brutal, often sadistic, politics of colonial administrators were based on the ideology of middle class masculinity of the time. According to that ideology men were supposed, above all else, to be independent. It was a highly idealized and fictional version of independence, held to be a personal virtue and moral goal throughout these men's education, that led to the ruthless control, exploitation and punishment of all perceived occurrences of dependence, especially the imaginary dependence of others. The characteristics of dependence were typically attributed, by colonial administrators, to the indigenous peoples. The literature and imagery of that time are replete with examples of fantasies of indolence and greed; of natives waiting passively to be fed, without effort, by bountiful nature, fantasies of uncontrolled sexuality and fecundity. All of these fantasies bore no relation to the actual predicament of the indigenous peoples, but formed what can now be recognized as the disowned, 'split off' or disavowed aspects of the 'independent' man's self identity. The colonists' inability to differentiate between their projection and their real predicament resulted from the blankness at the centre of White identity and concealed the extremely sadistic means habitually employed to suppress and control rebellion.

Different historical accounts of the causes of imperialism, slavery and racism accord different kinds of determinacy to ideological processes. There are many reasons why the middle classes of mid-nineteenth century Britain might want to deny their dependency. As a class they were economically dependent on the surplus value produced by waged labour, a dependency that was systematically misrepresented to assuage their guilt. Also the middle class often emulated their idea of aristocracy, along with having an ambivalent envy of the parasitic wealth of this class. Men may well have envied the social and economic parasitism of middle class femininity, despite the Victorians' idealization of 'home' life. These factors are historically specific, but since this ideology of the overvaluation of independence seems still to be current in contemporary definitions of masculinity it is useful to explore the significance of its subjective components.

In the place of negativity, the blankness or absence of self reflection, let's put the concept of narcissism or excessive self regard to the exclusion of external reality. Narcissism can often be used as a defence against feelings of helplessness, the traumatic loss of self regard. Joan Riviere, a psychoanalyst writing in 1937, maintained that any blow to adult narcissism is emotionally evocative of earliest traumas of life such as the loss of infantile omnipotence, traumas that are forgotten or repressed into the unconscious. 'Psychoanalysis can trace this anxiety of dependence back through countless situations to the very early one experienced by us all in babyhood . . . A baby at the breast is actually completely dependent on someone else, but has no fear of this.' When the immature ego experiences frustration of the immediate satisfaction of its needs it reacts with overwhelming anger, loss and threatened destruction. 'It is our first experience of something like death, a recognition of the non-existence of something, of an overwhelming loss, both in ourselves and in others as it seems' (Riviere, 1937, p. 8). The infantile response to separation indicates the intensity and power of the sensations and emotions at stake in the adult unconscious. Because the infantile experience is repressed it will exist as an unconscious memory of threat, and it is the intensity of the pressure exerted by this memory that lies beneath the blankness identified as the absent centre of White identity. Overlaid onto the primary narcissistic wound are the other threats of loss of identity, control, status, power, belonging, safety, decorum; ego losses which threaten traditional identities of gender, class, ethnicity and nation. We have described the process of projection as one of the psychic mechanisms fundamental to racism, and can now further note that unless the primary experience of dependence is recognized as a subjective reality, as part of the self, the anxiety and threat it represents for the ego will continue to be projected outwards onto other people, classes, genders, races, nations in a way that will tend to be destructive.

It has been suggested (Glasser, 1985, p. 409) that men tend to project their sexuality onto the idea of women, that is, that men tend to experience their sexuality as something external to themselves. This is possibly because mental mechanisms are to some extent based on bodily processes, and the external male sexual organs, with their involuntary and hence alarming changes, symbolize sexual response as occurring 'outside' the self and its control. Western culture has further exacerbated this mental capacity by evolving representations which tend to depict women as sexual objects thereby disabling men from integrating their own sexuality, and facilitating their location of sexuality in the image or idea of woman.

As we have noted, representations of anger and aggression tend to be projected onto Black people. The fear of loss of individuality is projected onto the idea of the 'masses', so that the working class becomes a mirror reflecting disowned envy and discontent. These projections leave White, middle class, male identity as one of safety, power, control, independence and contentment, perhaps smug or self-righteous. Yet this is an illusory identity because it is actually highly dependent on its others to shore up its sense of security, to reflect back the disowned parts of itself as inferior, contemptible, dependent, frightened or threatening, perhaps excremental. The illusory identity needs narratives constantly to reaffirm its fictitious centrality. This is what is meant by the 'androcentrism' and 'ethnocentrism' of cultural forms where emotional and intellectual distortions are created in order to shore up the narcissistic illusion of the centrality of White, masculine, middle class identity.

Mona Lisa

An audience at the cinema is also projecting aspects of itself onto characters and predicaments in the narrative of the film. This is part of the process of identification described above; and as Laura Mulvey has analysed (Mulvey, 1975), the audience is in a state of heightened narcissism where both desire and sadism are displaced, leaving an emptiness in the viewing subject with a consequent craving for the action and passion represented in the narrative. The film *Mona Lisa* is a vehicle for the split off aspects of a White and middle class identity. Its title refers

Figure 1   Splitting: George (Bob Hoskins) and Simone (Cathy Tyson) in Mona Lisa *(UK, directed by Neil Jordan, 1986) (© 1986 HandMade Films (1985) Partnership).*

to the popular concept of culture, Leonardo's masterpiece, the painting that people feel they ought to admire or revere whether it has any meaning for them or not. The title also refers to a popular song, the soundtrack of the film, which laments the enigmatic appeal of the idea of woman for man. The film's narrative revolves around the enigma of a young Black woman, Simone, who is chauffeured to her assignments as a call girl by an ineffectual working class criminal, George. In the film it is the enigma of Simone's sexuality that is investigated, controlled, possessed and finally destroyed. George needs to discover whatever it is that she does behind closed doors. Mystery was unbearable for the man and was transformed, through narrative, into mastery.

In *Mona Lisa* the illusion that a sadistic masculinity is ultimately benevolent is maintained through a series of displacements of guilt. George is caricatured as the affable criminal, as a passive victim, never responsible for the violence which surrounds him, and which is always associated with the visual presence of Black people within the camera frame and composition. Following his release from prison after a seven year sentence, George is mystified by his wife's angry response to his naive return home, and his violent outburst at her is portrayed as purely reactive. Even George's criminality seems to have consisted mainly of his ineffectuality, his gullibility for getting the blame for somebody else's actions. Although the narrative revolves around his journey through an urban underworld of prostitution, illicit sex, drug dependence and destitution, even George's motivating curiosity is not his own; he is 'given' the job of being Simone's driver, and given orders to find out what it is that she does with her clients. He is given another mission to find a lost girl, a lost innocence, and descends into a dark labyrinth of nighttime London. To every possible interrogation he can safely reply that he was only following orders, although the audience must temper their identification with George with a certain amount of contempt for his sheer ineffectuality, symbolized by the small stature of the actor playing George. Even his imagination is not his own: having made himself a tourist in his own unconscious he finds what he didn't know he was looking for, a panoramic view of infantile sexualities. All forms of perversion are represented and are associated with drug dependency, then the combination of uncontrolled or deviant sexuality with pathological dependency becomes signified by Simone's Blackness. Simone's colour becomes a metaphor for all that is 'bad' within George, and because she represents a split-off part of him she is also represented as being hopelessly involved in a symbiotic relationship, a caricature of lesbianism. The stereotype of the prostitute enables George to displace his incestuous wishes, his own schoolgirl daughter is a stranger to him after his years in prison, she is an adolescent and her strangeness and sexuality are a threat to his paternal integrity. In order to maintain his daughter as an object of pure affection George's imagination regresses to the nineteenth century morality that deemed prostitution 'a necessary institution, drawing away the distasteful but inevitable waste products of male lustfulness', and he splits the daytime world of his blonde daughter from the nighttime world of Simone's prostitution. The stereotype of the prostitute represents danger by condensing a double dependency – men's dependency on 'illicit' sex, and women's dependency on men's money, so that prostitutes are doubly despised. Simone's colour adds a third meaning to this icon, and gives further narrative 'justification' for her punishment. The anxiety generated by sadistic debasement without guilt becomes represented in the film's visual style, with its dimly lit street scenes, sordid interiors, the oversaturated colours of the nightclubs, the trendiness of high street fashion, the decaying remains of Brighton pier, all of which represent a mood of melancholia in masquerade.

Eventually the narrative reaches its climax and the tantalizing underworld of desire and fear destroys itself in an orgiastic frenzy of voyeurism, a chase with guns, violence, and an oedipal parricide. Simone 'disappears' from reality, last seen framed in the rear view mirror of George's car. Was she a figment of his imagination? An image he conjured up from memory and fantasy while driving his car, a masturbation fantasy? A part of his identity? George never has to resolve this problem because the film simply annihilates the underworld, returns us to an autumnal park scene with

Figure 2   Projection: 'Simone represents the "bad" mother who could not be possessed or controlled by the son, whose sexuality is a threatening enigma to him, who seems to be betraying him . . .' Mona Lisa, (© 1986 HanddMade Films (1985) Partnership).

naturalistic lighting where George has been reunited with his daughter and his pal, and restored to his rightful place in the world as a car mechanic. The concluding triangle erases the existence of the Black people central to the narrative, and offers a 'post-feminist' world which has destroyed any need for the role of wife and mother.

The film represents a dramatic enactment of the kinds of fantasies an oedipal boy uses to attack all forms of maturity and integrity, but especially the idea of woman. Simone represents the 'bad' mother who could not be possessed or controlled by the son, whose sexuality is a threatening enigma to him, who seems to have betrayed him and is therefore blackened by being equated with the son's sexualized hatred. The narrative represents an oedipal journey in which action results from the desire to avenge seven years' imprisonment for an unspecified crime for which the victim feels himself to have been wrongly accused. The action consists of an investigation into the sexuality of a woman and detection of what it is that men and women do behind closed doors. The desire to know conclusively and the desire to retrieve a lost child lead to a spectacular drama choreographing all forms of perverse, infantile sexuality, and climaxing in a parricidal murder. This sequence parallels Freud's description of human psychosexual development. Infantile sexuality leads to the Oedipus complex, an impossible desire to possess the mother, a burning curiosity about the secrets of the parents' reproductive power, the desire to see everything and to know everything. The impossibility of this predicament reactivates other losses, such as the loss of infantile omnipotence and the loss of the breast described above by Joan Riviere, giving rise to anger and immense frustration. Repression of both incestuous and parricidal wishes take place and with this a recognition of the father as authority (represented in the film by the court case), the capacity for conscience, guilt and concern, the superego. This is followed by seven years or so of latency (the prison years) and the onset of adolescent sexuality which reactivates the unconscious oedipal predicament (the drama between Simone and George). Unconscious guilt is experienced as a vague feeling of discomfort, threat, anxiety or danger, reflected in the film's visual style and in its investigative narrative.

The film is destructive and regressive in its use of stereotype because it represents dependency as intolerable, as excremental, and because it projects this onto working class, Black and feminine realities. It sensationalizes despair as spectacle and represents sensuality as desperate without acknowledging the sensuality of audience voyeurism. It addresses the audience as a rather smug middle class, with a sense of moral superiority of having culture whilst the proletarians have only pornography, detective stories and high street shopping, of having careers or unalienated work whilst others have only semi-criminal ways of earning a living, and of having family life or love whereas the others have only sadistic and debased sexualities. Despite the film's self consciously anti-naturalistic style, and the many references to other fiction genres, the pastiche of *film noir* and the detective thriller, the narrative and the visual style work to reinforce contemporary ideologies of white, middle class masculinity which are deeply destructive in undermining the recognition of responsibility, and which deny the need to work together for social change based on interdependence and respect.

Memory, history and Beloved

This account is a meditation on Toni Morrison's *Beloved* which uses the text to ask questions about history, to think about some teaching issues, and to try to ascertain what benefits might be gained through an acknowledgement of a relationship between our theoretical work and personal circumstances. Both the form and the terms in which *Beloved* is expressed and the emphasis given to remembering and speaking the unspeakable past as a means of understanding and progressing forward from the often overwhelming present, evoke certain psychoanalytic concepts such as the notion of the 'talking cure'.

Beloved is set in the period after the American Civil War (1861–1865) known as the Reconstruction. The action starts in Cincinnati and returns through flashbacks to events which occurred at the ironically named 'Sweet Home' plantation in Mississippi. After an absence of 18 years one of the ex-'Sweet Home' boys, Paul D, intervenes in the female household which is comprised of Sethe and her youngest daughter Denver, and the ghost of Sethe's eldest daughter, named Beloved. The narrative is concerned with the reasons why Beloved's life was tragically cut short, and tells of how she returns as a young adult, her ghost having been ejected forcibly from 124 (Bluestone Road) by Paul D.

By assembling the fragments of their individual and collective memories, Sethe, Paul D – who becomes Sethe's lover – Baby Suggs, Beloved's grandmother, and Denver, Beloved's younger sister, come to understand and to articulate the events and emotions experienced in the past. It is these past conditions which inform the way they experience the present and suggest possibilities for working at the future.

Morrison writes of Sethe's main preoccupation as being that of 're-memory'. The act of 're-memory' entails the piecing together of fragments of memory, myth and facts to form a coherent account of experiences previously denied in one way or another. These 're-memories' are temporally fluid, merging past with present and are a conscious act of reclamation.

> Some things you forget. Other things you never do . . . If a house
> burns down, it's gone, but the place – the picture of it stays, and not
> just in my re-memory, but out there in the world. What I remember
> is a picture floating out there outside my head. I mean, even if I
> don't think it, even if I die, the picture of what I did, or knew or saw
> is still out there. Right in the place where it happened. (Morrison,
> 1987, p. 36)

The first time I read *Beloved*, I was in the USA, south of the Mason-Dixon line in Virginia. The geographical and emotional position I occupied contributed another dimension to my reading and comprehension. I could 'see' my forebears labouring in the cotton fields, singing their scathing attacks on their slave-owners. I thought of those of us who – like Sethe – are unable to identify our mothers, have experienced fractured childhoods or have been unwillingly separated from our parents for various reasons. I felt I could begin to understand the meaning and significance of 're-memory' and its bearing on our world-views. The heritage of the struggle for freedom and human rights, and to reclaim the past is fundamental to the evolution of Black cultures not only in the USA but throughout the African diaspora.

I'd bought the book months before I read it. In fact, I had actively avoided reading it because at that moment in my personal history, having just experienced a devastating loss which echoed other episodes of dispossession and distress, I didn't feel I would be capable of dealing with what I thought would be yet more emotional devastation, centred around loss and deprivation. When I did come to read the book, it was not just the actual narrative or my identification with Sethe and her daughters Denver and Beloved which I found so demanding, it was also having to recognize my complicity in erasing sections of my memory in order to survive. It is precisely that strategy which Sethe uses, that of recognizing that the 'future was a matter of keeping the past at bay' (p. 42). Personal and collective survival is based on the repression of the memory of past events which resurface, sometimes through madness. It seems self-evident that we cannot engage with the future before we have disentangled the past. Deprivation, humiliation, the 'middle passage',[1] slavery; all such experiences are unspeakable and the text acknowledges that but it also suggests ways in which these events may be articulated.

A sense of being located historically and socially is fundamental to a sense of belonging and participating in the creative processes of a particular culture. If cultural belonging-ness resides in those discourses which call upon collective memory, then with a lack of access to the elements of that memory, along with a sense of dislocation comes a feeling of loss of cultural cohesion.

Slavery radically destabilized Africa and resulted in the undermining and fragmentation of cultural self identity both for those who underwent the process of dispersal and disruption and for their descendants. Black people are frequently in the position of having to piece together distorted fragments of the past and of past selves in order to re-create a self-determined picture of individual and collective cultural identities. Reclamation of the past through 'remembering' is considered to be virtually a moral obligation by some African-Americans since the official histories have failed to document and acknowledge the meanings of the experiences of their ancestors.

It is clear from statements that she has made and from the wealth of detail in the book that Morrison has been most thorough in her research and built this text on several verifiable incidents from female slave and abolitionist accounts of the period. This is notable because those slave narratives – the literary predecessors of *Beloved* – which are most accessible, have been frequently written by men telling of the ordeals undergone in attempting to escape captivity. These ordeals often involved severe tests of mental resourcefulness and extreme physical duress.

Such narratives, in addition to continuing the struggle for emancipation, served as a literary mechanism to attempt to reclaim Black masculinity by demonstrating the qualities such as courage, determination, rationality and so on, admired in and by White men: the attributes that White manhood could not attribute to Blacks. The effect of this predominance of Black men's writings has been to regard the male version of slavery as a representative model of slave existence and resistance, and there is an acute lack of historical accounts of Black women as autonomous and determining participants during the periods of slavery, emancipation and reconstruction.

So with Black women's experiences not foregrounded in narratives of slavery written by Black men and also denied a place in 'White' accounts of history, how are Black women to relate to history? By drawing attention to the circumstances under which Sethe makes her escape, Toni Morrison gives women's experience of slavery a voice and, most importantly, a language through Sethe. Sethe is an active historical agent as opposed to a passive victim or an absence. In making these comments, the intention is not to disparage those remarkable acts of heroism and courage that Black men carried out against extremely oppressive odds. The issue being raised is that there is another facet to the incompleteness of documentation about this period.

Sethe's – and Denver's and Beloved's – re-telling of their narratives is an affirmation of their 'selves' in opposition to a world designed to obliterate all traces of self-determined being. Sethe is pregnant with her fourth child when she is subjected to a humiliating ordeal by Schoolteacher's sons just before she makes her escape as they suck milk from her breasts. Surviving a beating from Schoolteacher – the new owner of 'Sweet Home' – Sethe almost dies during her escape as she gives birth to Denver, named after the 'whitegirl' who assisted in the delivery in a rickety boat.

There is a conscious evocation and a reaffirmation of the power and heritage of African folk memory through the use of the supernatural and the uncanny, and the merging of fantasy, myth and history to form 'magical realism'. The use of the supernatural as a normal part of everyday life alongside the historical accounts of slavery is a departure from the literary tradition of much early writing although the naturalizing of the supernatural is part of an African-American oral heritage and has its beginnings in various African cultural traditions.

The grandmother Baby Suggs belongs to a distinctive tradition within African-American writing: a wise and protective grandparent. Baby Suggs' benign presence is that of a protector and a provider with magical intuition, whose strategy for survival deflects the brutality she has had to endure without a sense of self pity or victimization. Baby Suggs testifies to the pain and deprivations endured by the community by observing 'Not a house in the country ain't packed to its rafters with some dead Negro's grief' (p. 5). She is important because against the odds, she survives and defies, and provides familial continuity through her knowledge and exposition of the past.

Beloved herself is a spiritual manifestation of history; she is the embodiment of the sixty million and more dead and enslaved Africans, returned to reclaim her space and haunt us throughout the narrative with her enigmatic existence. Nobody is left untouched by her return but, like the past she represents she can function as an oppressive force, stimulating pain, shame and paralysing guilt, or she can function as a liberator from the shackles of past trauma and sustained humiliation and serve to inspire positive and productive action for personal – and perhaps societal – transformation. However, as Amy Denver the 'whitegirl' says, 'anything dead coming back to life hurts' (p. 35) and there is no denying the pain involved in the act of revelation.

The need for an articulation of the processes of self-discovery and re-memory is part of the continuing search of African-American literature of the twentieth century. The quest is for a personal and collective identity based on self-esteem which can survive in a racist society, for the expression of a specific 'Black consciousness' and for a way of expressing oral and cultural traditions in a language which escapes the entrapment of dominant discourses. Whereas enslaved ancestors '. . . sang it out and beat it up, garbling the words so they could not be understood; tricking the words so their syllables yielded up other meanings' (p. 108), contemporary Black authors, having identified the oppressor's language for what it is – the imagination of the dominant culture embodied in words – use, control and expand the vocabulary to create something that speaks to the experiences of Black communities. In doing so they combat White people's lack of perception of Blacks as individuated beings. An example of this, demonstrated in *Beloved* and common practice during slavery, is the way in which the men who are enslaved on the 'Sweet Home' plantation under the relatively 'benign' regime of the Garners are stripped of individual identities and each named 'Paul' followed by an initial.

For the sake of the (separate) survival of both Blacks and Whites, White Americans have had to undergo a process of re-construction which refers not only to the economic, social and cultural sphere but also to the realm of the psyche. Whites have had to re-construct the reality of their past taking into account the distortions, self-deception and denials that constitute many European versions of 'history'. In order to maintain the self-deception and claim validity for certain interpretations of historical events, distortions in the accounts of the past and disavowal of the implications of their forebears' involvement in slavery have typified literary, dramatic and cinematic renderings of the period, certainly in American popular culture.

The invisible White presence is at once clearly defined and less than significant in *Beloved*. The most important feature of 'race' dealt with is not the relationship of Black slaves to their White owners: it is the relationships within the community and how the community deals with the problems laid at their doorsteps. Individual Whites are in one sense peripheral. Whites frequently attempt to make Blacks invisible in cultural production by ignoring or subordinating presence through crass stereotyping. This is reflected in the limited range of characterizations offered through cultural products and is self-evident on studying particular texts. White American reconstruction writers in particular portrayed a constant stream of brutal rapists, tragic 'mulattos' and sexually promiscuous Blacks, and it is against this backdrop that African-American writers work.

The process of projection as described in the introduction to this article is recognized in *Beloved* and is described as White people getting rid of their negative feelings about themselves by discharging their anger with themselves onto Blacks. According to Laplanche and Pontalis, 'Projection emerges . . . as the primal means of defence against those endogenous excitations whose intensity makes them too unpleasurable: the subject projects these outside so as to be able to flee from them (e.g., phobic avoidance) and protect himself from them . . . the subject now finds himself obliged to believe completely in something that is henceforth subject to the laws of external reality.' (Laplanche and Pontalis, 1988, p. 352).

As previously indicated, however, the act of disavowal affects and – in part at least – determines 'external reality' since facets of that reality are denied. Through an analysis of the recurring stereotypes mentioned above, it is possible to identify a cycle whereby (White) anxiety and guilt is apparently resolved through projection and denial and disavowal of the reality of a traumatizing realization. The emotional flow is from anxiety to denial to projection: then to distortion upon which enactment is based and from there, there is further denial. This cycle is important politically because the enactment phase involves the mechanics of individual, institutional and state racisms.

As the institution of slavery necessitated sustained inhumanity towards fellow human beings – requiring the ruthless and violent subordination of Blacks – slaves had to be viewed as non-humans, as property, so that it was then acceptable to ill-treat them. As James Baldwin has pointed out, White people's own inhumanity was projected onto Blacks and this mis-recognition of what constituted brutality was enacted through master–slave relations, determined by slave-holders. However, such acts are not without cost to the oppressor. Since Blacks were – and still are – a living

reminder of the horrors perpetrated in the name of economic development, civilization or whatever, many White were horrified and disgusted
by Blacks. Of course this set of ideas regarding Blacks' status as human
beings is wholly inconsistent with notions of reason, the logic of
'Enlightenment' and so on, and that is why the representations in White
cultural products are distorted to fit the scheme: the distortion has then to
be defended through repetition and elaboration (Baldwin, 1988, p. 3).
Since guilt underpins White anxiety about Blacks, many Whites know
and fear that their status in society – in the world – is partially due to
their capacity to brutalize people for their own advantage. Even non-
racist Whites benefit from the fact of their Whiteness at the expense of
Blacks. So our disproportionately low presence in historical representations and mainstream culture should not be surprising: it is a part of the
enactment phase of the cycle referred to previously.

Frantz Fanon asserted that 'race' and sex need to be considered in
conjunction with each other since many of the anxieties that Whites have
about Blacks are of a sexual nature. The lascivious, sexually debased
Black is the distorted representation which allowed the continued sexual
abuse of female slaves and the lynching and castration of male slaves.
Bred like animals, subjected to abuse and forbidden to marry and to form
stable, long-term relationships, the attempts to control Black fertility and
sexuality were the reflection of Whites' attempts to regulate their own
sexuality according to the socio-sexual morality of the time. The idealization of White female sexual purity and the valorization of 'masculine'
characteristics such as courage, autonomous action and independence fed
into the repression of sexuality in favour of a celebration of 'masculinity'
and 'femininity'. A classic example of the alleged threat posed by Black
male hypersexuality to White American femininity can be found in D. W.
Griffith's film *The Birth of a Nation* (1915). A more contemporary British
example appears in *Mona Lisa*, in the character of Anderson (Clarke
Peters). The brute male negro unable to control his excessive sexual
energy is characterized as a pimp who preys on White schoolgirls, plying
them with drugs and beating them up when they inevitably fail to satisfy
him.

Morrison pin-points White male sexual anxiety in relation to Black men
through an ambivalent exchange which we are told Garner (the first
owner of the 'Sweet Home' plantation) is fond of initiating:

'Y'all got boys,' he told them. 'Young boys, old boys, picky boys,
stroppin boys. Now at Sweet Home, my niggers is men every one of
em. Bought em thataway, raised em thataway. Men every one.'
  'Beg to differ, Garner. Ain't no nigger men.'
  'Not if you scared, they ain't.' Garner's smile was wide. 'But if you
a man yourself, you'll want your niggers to be men too.'
  'I wouldn't have no nigger men round my wife.'
It was the reaction Garner loved and waited for. 'Neither would I,'

Figure 3   D. W. Griffith's Birth of a Nation *(1915) is an epic account of the defeated South in the aftermath of the American Civil War. It presents a story of unscrupulous Northerners unleashing blacks on a defenceless population. In one episode Gus, a black soldier, rapes a white girl. In response, her brother ('the Little Colonel') creates the Ku Klux Klan to avenge her and recreate the South. As played by the blacked-up white actor Walter Long, Gus embodies evil and bestiality (BFI Stills, Posters and Designs).*

he said. 'Neither would I,' and there was always a pause before the neighbor, or stranger, or peddler, or brother-in-law or who ever it was got the meaning. Then a fierce argument, sometimes a fight, and Garner came home bruised and pleased, having demonstrated one more time what a real Kentuckian was: one tough enough and smart enough to make and call his niggers men. (p. 11)

Slavery represented the perfect mechanism through which personal space was tamed, controlled and drained of emotional investment and meaning. Human beings were converted into commodities and sold to the highest bidder. In the slave economy, the body was stripped of individuality and robbed of all possessions. Individual identities and names were taken and mothers and fathers, daughters and sons were separated. Even mothers' breasts are robbed of their milk. These dehumanizing experiences resulted in psychic trauma in the course of which language and voice were literally and figuratively destroyed, and the ability to communicate severely impaired. The slave economy necessitated the control of fertility through selective breeding, prevented mothers from 'owning' their children and destabilized sexual relationships.

Under this regime, whatever Sethe produced was taken from her and ultimately used against her. Sethe made the ink which the Schoolteacher used to write pseudo-scientific anthropological studies, seeking to establish the linking characteristics between animals and Africans. Sethe was forcibly separated from her two sons and Beloved, so that they could escape to relative freedom. This takes place before Beloved was named and before Sethe had the chance to empty her breasts of milk. The separation and connection of motherhood was intensified through slavery. Through the unfolding of Sethe's narrative, Morrison convincingly demonstrates why Sethe can say by way of explanation of her killing her eldest daughter 'that what she had done was right because it came from true love'. Rather than see Beloved live through that which, '. . . Baby Suggs died of, what Ella knew, what Stamp saw and what made Paul D tremble. That anybody white could take your whole self for anything that came to mind. Not just work, kill, or maim you but dirty you. Dirty you so bad, you couldn't like yourself anymore. Dirty you so bad you forgot who you were and couldn't think it up' (p. 251).

Beloved, though, is not judgemental: neither Sethe's infanticide nor White people's behaviour are condemned. In the introduction to *The Mother Daughter Plot: Narrative, Psychoanalysis, Feminism*, Marianne Hirsch says, 'The novel contains more than judgement: it contains the stories that precede and follow judgement, the stories that form and surround the relationship of mother and daughter during slavery and in post-abolition times' (Hirsch, 1989, p. 7).

A fabrication woven from fear, anxiety, fantasy and myth formed the backcloth for the initial encounter between Europeans and Africans. This was not conducive to the production of an open, equitable relationship. However, despite the denials, distortions and disruptions which characterized our dispersal, in the same way that Sethe constructs herself from the fragments of memory and re-memory that become available to her, so may peoples of a diaspora manage to achieve authority over the recreation of the self after the many attempts to destroy it. The identification within the text of the necessity to rebuild the past from fragments and the idea of 'rememory' has particular resonance in the context of a desire on the part of many people to see the past through a sentimentalized haze. Although much of what she writes generally advocates a rootedness in the past and a reference to origins and traditions, Morrison's work is not based on a nostalgia for the past. The issue is one of how useful to any of us is a history which denies its more disturbing aspects.

Implications for teaching

I would now like to pose some questions related to teaching which uses *Beloved* as a focus and to indicate some of the difficulties raised by working on this text in a British context. In particular, the way in which slavery has been dealt with in the teaching of British history is characterized by a lack of emphasis on Britain's involvement in the slave trade and the absence of information about how Africans resisted slavery and struggled to abolish it both in this country and in the Caribbean. In terms of how slavery is approached in literature, in films and on television, again we are identifying an absence rather than a negative presence. If it is dealt with at all in cultural products, the standard manner of describing the actuality of slavery is to re-present the condition of enslavement in the ways in which it is conventionally expressed through the educational system.

In this country at any rate, Africa's loss and the enslavement of the sixty million to whom *Beloved* is dedicated has been enshrined in a mythology which seeks to purify the actions of the pro-slavery plantocracy and, to some extent, justify the prolonged brutality. Some of the unimaginably terrible conditions during the 'middle passage' of the triangular slave trade are illustrated in various school texts and isolated vicious incidents are described. However, this does not invalidate my main contention. The semiotician Roland Barthes describes a process of 'inoculation' whereby a limited number of inhumane actions are admitted by the perpetrators: this 'immunizes the contents of the collective imagination by means of a small inoculation of acknowledged evil; one thus protects it against the risk of a generalized subversion' (Barthes, 1973, p. 42).

One of the results of this selective approach to this period of history has been that generations of children, Black and White, have been led to believe in a series of misrepresentative narratives masquerading as objective historical fact. These narratives indict the actions of *other* nations and invoke Britain as being the country that fought *against* slavery, *against* the barbarity of Europeans and Americans, rather than being prime instigators, responsible for more than half of the international trade in human beings during the period between 1791 and 1806 (Fryer, 1984).

If this collective historical amnesia and national disavowal typifies British accounts of slavery, how are we to relate to Morrison's belief that modern history begins with slavery? A way of avoiding the crucial issues about guilt and responsibility, and the acts of denial implicit in that question, is to answer that Morrison's consciousness is determined by, and culturally and historically specific to, the African-American situation. It is clear that whatever the temporal and cultural specificity of Morrison's *Beloved*, her narrative also corresponds to current national and international features of 'race'. As anyone who is aware of events in continental Europe realizes, there are a number of potentially depressing features on the current 'race relations' landscape.[2] Another issue is that with many White academics there is a sense of a lack of knowledge of, or engagement with, what might be termed Black experience. Given this reluctance, one question might be: is there a correlation between how much Whites know of Black people's experiences and how much they can become involved with what the text has to offer? A related issue is whether or not White people might read the text differently from Black readers.

If there are small numbers of Black students in a group, those students can become the uncomfortable focus of the course-work in which the class is immersed. In fact, they may – and I have experienced this myself both as lecturer and student in predominantly White gatherings – come to embody the text for White people in the group. There is a moment in which skin colour becomes both an accusation and a judgement. It can also be a mystification; a way of saying 'you can't know it in the same way that I live it'. Through an approach which encourages students to identify for themselves the resonances of *Beloved* with their own histories and present lives, it is possible to have fruitful intra-cultural dialogue and hopefully an inter-cultural one as well.

The point of raising these issues in terms of Black readers and White readers is not to homogenize or to deny intra-group differences but to suggest broad areas for further examination. I am not suggesting that there are definitive answers to these questions and I would like to point out that the questions are problematic in themselves. The reluctance of many White academics to actively support and encourage what amounts to a less ethnocentric, more diverse approach to developing curricula, has been likened to the reluctance of the early venture capitalists to travel inland from the Guinea coast. They are not yet ready it seems – for a number of reasons – to venture into the interior of the 'dark continent'. Perhaps a crucial question would be: is it possible for White academics to venture into the interior without colonizing it?

Notes

1 The 'middle passage' refers to the transfer of slaves from Africa to the Caribbean across the Atlantic Ocean. This is probably one of the least documented aspects of the slave-trade

but what is clear is that the conditions on board the ships involved in the trade were appalling. The death rate of slaves in transit over a period of a 100 years (between 1680 and 1780), averaged one in eight. Slaves were herded together, kept in spaces not big enough for them to sit up, systematically flogged, virtually starved and thrown overboard if weak or sickly.

2 For instance, in Britain there is the apparent demise of antiracist movements, the slow process of systemic change in institutions, the lack of significant progress in educational achievement and so on. In France, there are politicians who are elected on openly racist platforms. In Germany, officially there is no such thing as 'racism', only 'hostility towards foreigners'. I am not pointing out these events in order to spread a paralysis of the will through despair but to indicate the relevance of *Beloved* for us all.

References

Baldwin, J. (1988) 'A talk to teachers' in Simonson, R. and Walker, S. (eds) *The Graywolf Annual Five Multicultural Literacy*, Minnesota, Graywolf Press.

Barthes, R. (1973) *Mythologies*, London, Paladin.

Ellison, R. (1972) *Invisible Man*, New York, Plume.

Fryer, P. (1984) *Staying Power: The History of Black People in Britain*, London, Pluto Press.

Glasser, M. (1985) 'The weak spot: observations on male sexuality' *International Journal of Psychoanalysis*, **66**.

Hall, C. (1989) 'The economy of intellectual prestige: Thomas Carlyle, John Stuart Mill and the case of Governor Eyre', *Cultural Critique*, **12** (Spring).

Hall, C. (1991) 'Missing stories: gender and ethnicity in England in the 1830s and '40s' in Grossberg, L., Nelson, C. and Treitler, P. (eds) *Cultural Studies Now and in the Future*, London, Routledge.

Hirsch, M. (1989) *The Mother Daughter Plot: Narrative, Psychoanalysis, Feminism*, Indianapolis, Indiana University Press.

Laplanche, J. and Pontalis, J. B. (1988) *The Language of Psychoanalysis*, London, Karnac.

Morrison, T. *Beloved* (1987) New York, Plume.

Mulvey, L. (1975) 'Visual pleasure and narrative cinema', *Screen*, **16**(3).

Mulvey, L. (1989) 'Visual pleasure and narrative cinema' in *Visual and Other Pleasures*, London, Macmillan.

Riviere, J. and Klein, M. (1937) *Love, Hate and Reparation*, London, Hogarth.

9 THE FACT OF BLACKNESS

FRANTZ FANON

'Dirty nigger!' Or simply, 'Look, a Negro!'

I came into the world imbued with the will to find a meaning in things, my spirit filled with the desire to attain to the source of the world, and then I found that I was an object in the midst of other objects.

Sealed into that crushing objecthood, I turned beseechingly to others. Their attention was a liberation, running over my body suddenly abraded into non-being, endowing me once more with the agility that I had thought lost, and by taking me out of the world, restoring me to it. But just as I reached the other side, I stumbled, and the movements, the attitudes, the glances of the others fixed me there, in the sense in which a chemical solution is fixed by a dye. I was indignant; I demanded an explanation. Nothing happened. I burst apart. Now the fragments have been put together again by another self.

As long as the black man is among his own, he will have no occasion, except in minor internal conflicts, to experience his being through others. There is of course the moment of 'being for others', of which Hegel speaks, but every ontology is made unattainable in a colonized and civilized society. It would seem that this fact has not been given sufficient attention by those who have discussed the question. In the *Weltanschauung* of a colonized people there is an impurity, a flaw that outlaws any ontological explanation. Someone may object that this is the case with every individual, but such an objection merely conceals a basic problem. Ontology – once it is finally admitted as leaving existence by the wayside – does not permit us to understand the being of the black man. For not only must the black man be black; he must be black in relation to the white man. Some critics will take it on themselves to remind us that this proposition has a converse. I say that this is false. The black man has no ontological resistance in the eyes of the white man. Overnight the Negro has been given two frames of reference within which he has had to place himself. His metaphysics, or, less pretentiously, his customs and the sources on which they were based, were wiped out because they were in conflict with a civilization that he did not know and that imposed itself on him.

The black man among his own in the twentieth century does not know at what moment his inferiority comes into being through the other. Of course I have talked about the black problem with friends, or, more rarely, with American Negroes. Together we protested, we asserted the equality of all men in the world. In the Antilles there was also that little gulf that exists among the almost-white, the mulatto, and the nigger. But I was satisfied with an intellectual understanding of these differences. It was not really dramatic. And-then . . .

And then the occasion arose when I had to meet the white man's eyes. An unfamiliar weight burdened me. The real world challenged my claims. In the white world the man of colour encounters difficulties in the development of his bodily schema. Consciousness of the body is solely a negating activity. It is a third-person consciousness. The body is surrounded by an atmosphere of certain uncertainty. I know that if I want to smoke, I shall have to reach out my right arm and take the pack of cigarettes lying at the other end of the table. The matches, however, are in the drawer on the left, and I shall have to lean back slightly. And all these movements are made not out of habit but out of implicit knowledge. A slow composition of my *self* as a body in the middle of the spatial and temporal world – such seems to be the schema. It does not impose itself on me; it is, rather, a definitive structuring of the self and of the world – definitive because it creates a real dialectic between my body and the world.

For several years certain laboratories have been trying to produce a serum for 'denegrification'; with all the earnestness in the world, laboratories have sterilized their test tubes, checked their scales, and embarked on researches that might make it possible for the miserable Negro to whiten himself and thus to throw off the burden of that corporeal malediction. Below the corporeal schema I had sketched a historico-social schema. The elements that I used had been provided for me not by 'residual sensations and perceptions primarily on a tactile, vestibular, kinesthetic, and visual character',[1] but by the other, the white man, who had woven me out of a thousand details, anecdotes, stories. I thought that what I had in hand was to construct a physiological self, to balance space, to localize sensations, and here I was called on for more.

'Look, a Negro!' It was an external stimulus that flicked over me as I passed by. I made a tight smile.

'Look, a Negro!' It was true. It amused me.

'Look, a Negro!' The circle was drawing a bit tighter. I made no secret of my amusement.

'Mama, see the Negro! I'm frightened!' Frightened! Frightened! Now they were beginning to be afraid of me. I made up my mind to laugh myself to tears, but laughter had become impossible.

I could no longer laugh, because I already knew that there were legends, stories, history, and above all *historicity*, which I had learned about from Jaspers. Then, assailed at various points, the corporeal schema crumbled, its place taken by a racial epidermal schema. In the train it was no longer a question of being aware of my body in the third person but in a triple person. In the train I was given not one but two, three places. I had already stopped being amused. It was not that I was finding febrile coordinates in the world. I existed triply: I occupied space. I moved towards the other . . . and the evanescent other, hostile but not opaque, transparent, not there, disappeared. Nausea . . .

I was responsible at the same time for my body, for my race, for my ancestors. I subjected myself to an objective examination, I discovered my blackness, my ethnic characteristics; and I was battered down by tom-toms, cannibalism, intellectual deficiency, fetishism, racial defects, slave-ships, and above all else, above all: 'Sho' good eatin'.'

On that day, completely dislocated, unable to be abroad with the other, the white man, who unmercifully imprisoned me, I took myself far off from my own presence, far indeed, and made myself an object. What else could it be for me but an amputation, an excision, a haemorrhage that spattered my whole body with black blood? But I did not want this revision, this thematization. All I wanted was to be a man among other men. I wanted to come lithe and young into a world that was ours and to help to build it together.

But I rejected all immunization of the emotions. I wanted to be a man, nothing but a man. Some identified me with ancestors of mine who had been enslaved or lynched: I decided to accept this. It was on the universal level of the intellect that I understood this inner kinship – I was the grandson of slaves in exactly the same way in which President Lebrun was the grandson of tax-paying, hard-working peasants. In the main, the panic soon vanished.

In America, Negroes are segregated. In South America, Negroes are whipped in the streets, and Negro strikers are cut down by machine-guns. In West Africa, the Negro is an animal. And there beside me, my neighbour in the university, who was born in Algeria, told me: 'As long as the Arab is treated like a man, no solution is possible.'

'Understand, my dear boy, colour prejudice is something I find utterly foreign . . . But of course, come in, sir, there is no colour prejudice among us . . . Quite, the Negro is a man like ourselves . . . It is not because he is black that he is less intelligent than we are . . . I had a Senegalese buddy in the army who was really clever . . .'

Where am I to be classified? Or, if you prefer, tucked away?

'A Martinican, a native of "our" old colonies.'

Where shall I hide?

'Look at the nigger! . . . Mama, a Negro! . . . Hell, he's getting mad . . . Take no notice, sir, he does not know that you are as civilized as we . . .'

My body was given back to me sprawled out, distorted, recoloured, clad in mourning in that white winter day. The Negro is an animal, the Negro is bad, the Negro is mean, the Negro is ugly; look, a nigger, it's cold, the nigger is shivering, the nigger is shivering because he is cold, the little boy is trembling because he is afraid of the nigger, the nigger is shivering with cold, that cold that goes through your bones, the handsome little boy is trembling because he thinks that the nigger is quivering with rage, the little white boy throws himself into his mother's arms: Mama, the nigger's going to eat me up.

All round me the white man, above the sky tears at its navel, the earth rasps under my feet, and there is a white song, a white song. All this whiteness that burns me . . .

I sit down at the fire and I become aware of my uniform. I had not seen it. It is indeed ugly. I stop there, for who can tell me what beauty is?

Where shall I find shelter from now on? I felt an easily identifiable flood mounting out of the countless facets of my being. I was about to be angry. The fire was long since out, and once more the nigger was trembling.

'Look how handsome that Negro is! . . .'

'Kiss the handsome Negro's ass, madame!'

Shame flooded her face. At last I was set free from my rumination. At the same time I accomplished two things: I identified my enemies and I made a scene. A grand slam. Now one would be able to laugh.

The field of battle having been marked out, I entered the lists.

What! While I was forgetting, forgiving, and wanting only to love, my message was flung back in my face like a slap. The white world, the only honourable one, barred me from all participation. A man was expected to behave like man. I was expected to behave like a black man – or at least like a nigger. I shouted a greeting to the world and the world slashed away my joy. I was told to stay within bounds, to go back where I belonged.

They would see, then! I had warned them, anyway. Slavery? It was no longer even mentioned, that unpleasant memory. My supposed inferiority? A hoax that it was better to laugh at. I forgot it all, but only on condition that the world not protect itself against me any longer. I had incisors to test. I was sure they were strong. And besides . . .

What! When it was I who had every reason to hate, to despise, I was rejected? When I should have been begged, implored, I was denied the slightest recognition? I resolved, since it was impossible for me to get away from an *inborn complex*, to assert myself as a BLACK MAN. Since the other hesitated to recognize me, there remained only one solution: to make myself known.

In *Anti-Semite and Jew* (p. 95), Sartre says: 'They [the Jews] have allowed themselves to be poisoned by the stereotype that others have of them, and they live in fear that their acts will correspond to this stereo-type ... We may say that their conduct is perpetually overdetermined from the inside.'

All the same, the Jew can be unknown in his Jewishness. He is not wholly what he is. One hopes, one waits. His actions, his behaviour are the final determinant. He is a white man, and, apart from some rather debatable characteristics, he can sometimes go unnoticed. He belongs to the race of those who since the beginning of time have never known cannibalism. What an idea, to eat one's father! Simple enough, one has only not to be a nigger. Granted, the Jews are harassed – what am I thinking of? They are hunted down, exterminated, cremated. But these are little family quarrels. The Jew is disliked from the moment he is tracked down. But in my case everything takes on a *new* guise. I am given no chance. I am overdetermined from without. I am the slave not of the 'idea' that others have of me but of my own appearance.

I move slowly in the world, accustomed now to seek no longer for upheaval. I progress by crawling. And already I am being dissected under white eyes, the only real eyes. I am *fixed*. Having readjusted their microtomes, they objectively cut away slices of my reality. I am laid bare. I feel, I see in those white faces that it is not a new man who has come in, but a new kind of man, a new genus. Why, it's a Negro!

I slip into corners, and my long antennae pick up the catchphrases strewn over the surface of things – nigger underwear smells of nigger – nigger teeth are white – nigger feet are big – the nigger's barrel chest – I slip into corners, I remain silent, I strive for anonymity, for invisibility. Look, I will accept the lot, as long as no one notices me!

'Oh, I want you to meet my black friend ... Aimé Césaire, a black man and a university graduate ... Marian Anderson, the finest of Negro singers ... Dr Cobb, who invented white blood, is a Negro ... Here, say hello to my friend from Martinique (be careful, he's extremely sensitive) ...'

Shame. Shame and self-contempt. Nausea. When people like me, they tell me it is in spite of my colour. When they dislike me, they point out that it is not because of my colour. Either way, I am locked into the infernal circle.

I turn away from these inspectors of the Ark before the Flood and I attach myself to my brothers, Negroes like myself. To my horror, they too reject me. They are almost white. And besides they are about to marry white women. They will have children faintly tinged with brown. Who knows, perhaps little by little ...

I had been dreaming.

'I want you to understand, sir, I am one of the best friends the Negro has in Lyons.'

The evidence was there, unalterable. My blackness was there, dark and unarguable. And it tormented me, pursued me, disturbed me, angered me.

Negroes are savages, brutes, illiterates. But in my own case I knew that these statements were false. There was a myth of the Negro that had to be destroyed at all costs. The time had long since passed when a Negro priest was an occasion for wonder. We had physicians, professors, statesmen. Yes, but something out of the ordinary still clung to such cases. 'We have a Senegalese history teacher. He is quite bright . . . Our doctor is coloured. He is very gentle.'

It was always the Negro teacher, the Negro doctor; brittle as I was becoming, I shivered at the slightest pretext. I knew, for instance, that if the physician made a mistake it would be the end of him, and of all those who came after him. What could one expect, after all, from a Negro physician? As long as everything went well, he was praised to the skies, but look out, no nonsense, under any conditions! The black physician can never be sure how close he is to disgrace. I tell you, I was walled in: No exception was made for my refined manners, or my knowledge of literature, or my understanding of the quantum theory.

I requested, I demanded explanations. Gently, in the tone that one uses with a child, they introduced me to the existence of a certain view that was held by certain people, but, I was always told, 'We must hope that it will very soon disappear.' What was it? Colour prejudice.

> It [colour prejudice] is nothing more than the unreasoning hatred of one race for another, the contempt of the stronger and richer peoples for those whom they consider inferior to themselves, and the bitter resentment of those who are kept in subjection and are so frequently insulted. As colour is the most obvious outward manifestation of race it has been made the criterion by which men are judged, irrespective of their social or educational attainments. The light-skinned races have come to despise all those of a darker colour, and the dark-skinned peoples will no longer accept without protest the inferior position to which they have been relegated.[2]

I had read it rightly. It was hate; I was hated, despised, detested, not by the neighbour across the street or my cousin on my mother's side, but by an entire race. I was up against something unreasoned. The psycho-analysts say that nothing is more traumatizing for the young child than his encounters with what is rational. I would personally say that for a man whose only weapon is reason there is nothing more neurotic than contact with unreason.

I felt knife blades open within me. I resolved to defend myself. As a good tactician, I intended to rationalize the world and to show the white man that he was mistaken.

In the Jew, Jean-Paul Sartre says, there is a sort of impassioned imperialism of reason: for he wishes not only to convince others that he is right; his goal is to persuade them that there is an absolute and unconditioned value to rationalism. He feels himself to be a missionary of the universal; against the universality of the Catholic religion, from which he is excluded, he asserts the 'catholicity' of the rational, an instrument by which to attain to the truth and establish a spiritual bond among men.[3]

And, the author adds, though there may be Jews who have made intuition the basic category of their philosophy, their intuition

has no resemblance to the Pascalian subtlety of spirit, and it is this latter – based on a thousand imperceptible perceptions – which to the Jew seems his worst enemy. As for Bergson, his philosophy offers the curious appearance of an anti-intellectualist doctrine constructed entirely by the most rational and most critical of intelligences. It is through argument that he establishes the existence of pure duration, of philosophic intuition; and that very intuition which discovers duration or life, is itself universal, since anyone may practise it, and it leads towards the universal, since its objects can be named and conceived.[4]

With enthusiasm I set to cataloguing and probing my surroundings. As times changed, one had seen the Catholic religion at first justify and then condemn slavery and prejudices. But by referring everything to the idea of the dignity of man, one had ripped prejudices to shreds. After much reluctance, the scientists had conceded that the Negro was a human being; *in vivo* and *in vitro* the Negro had been proved analogous to the white man: the same morphology, the same histology. Reason was confident of victory on every level. I put all the parts back together. But I had to change my tune.

That victory played cat and mouse; it made a fool of me. As the other put it, when I was present, it was not; when it was there, I was no longer. In the abstract there was agreement: the Negro is a human being. That is to say, amended the less firmly convinced, that like us he has his heart on the left side. But on certain points the white man remained intractable. Under no conditions did he wish any intimacy between the races, for it is a truism that 'crossings between widely different races can lower the physical and mental level . . . Until we have a more definite knowledge of the effect of race-crossings we shall certainly do best to avoid crossings between widely different races.'[5]

For my own part, I would certainly know how to react. And in one sense, if I were asked for a definition of myself, I would say that I am one who waits; I investigate my surroundings, I interpret everything in terms of what I discover, I become sensitive.

In the first chapter of the history that the others have compiled for me, the foundation of cannibalism has been made eminently plain in order that I may not lose sight of it. My chromosomes were supposed to have a few thicker or thinner genes representing cannibalism. In addition to the *sex-linked*, the scholars had now discovered the *racial-linked*.* What a shameful science!

But I understand this 'psychological mechanism'. For it is a matter of common knowledge that the mechanism is only psychological. Two centuries ago I was lost to humanity, I was a slave for ever. And then came men who said that it all had gone on far too long. My tenaciousness did the rest; I was saved from the civilizing deluge. I have gone forward.

Too late. Everything is anticipated, thought out, demonstrated, made the most of. My trembling hands take hold of nothing; the vein has been mined out. Too late! But once again I want to understand.

Since the time when someone first mourned the fact that he had arrived too late and everything had been said, a nostalgia for the past has seemed to persist. Is this that lost original paradise of which Otto Rank speaks? How many such men, apparently rooted to the womb of the world, have devoted their lives to studying the Delphic oracles or exhausted themselves in attempts to plot the wanderings of Ulysses! The pan-spiritualists seek to prove the existence of a soul in animals by using this argument: a dog lies down on the grave of his master and starves to death there. We had to wait for Janet to demonstrate that the aforesaid dog, in contrast to man, simply lacked the capacity to liquidate the past. We speak of the glory of Greece, Artaud says; but, he adds, if modern man can no longer understand the *Choephoroi* of Aeschylus, it is Aeschylus who is to blame. It is tradition to which the anti-Semites turn in order to ground the validity of their 'point of view'. It is tradition, it is that long historical past, it is that blood relation between Pascal and Descartes, that is invoked when the Jew is told, 'There is no possibility of your finding a place in society'. Not long ago, one of those good Frenchmen said in a train where I was sitting: 'Just let the real French virtues keep going and the race is safe. Now more than ever, national union must be made a reality. Let's have an end of internal strife! Let's face up to the foreigners (here he turned towards my corner) no matter who they are.'

It must be said in his defence that he stank of cheap wine; if he had been capable of it, he would have told me that my emancipated-slave blood could not possibly be stirred by the name of Villon or Taine.

An outrage!

The Jew and I: since I was not satisfied to be racialized, by a lucky turn of fate I was humanized. I joined the Jew, my brother in misery.

An outrage!

* In English in the original. (Translator's note.)

At first thought it may seem strange that the anti-Semite's outlook should be related to that of the Negrophobe. It was my philosophy professor, a native of the Antilles, who recalled the fact to me one day: 'Whenever you hear anyone abuse the Jews, pay attention, because he is talking about you.' And I found that he was universally right – by which I meant that I was answerable in my body and in my heart for what was done to my brother. Later I realized that he meant, quite simply, an anti-Semite is inevitably anti-Negro.

You come too late, much too late. There will always be a world – a white world – between you and us . . . The other's total inability to liquidate the past once and for all. In the face of this affective ankylosis of the white man, it is understandable that I could have made up my mind to utter my Negro cry. Little by little, putting out pseudopodia here and there, I secreted a race. And that race staggered under the burden of a basic element. What was it? *Rhythm!* Listen to our singer, Léopold Senghor:

> It is the thing that is most perceptible and least material. It is the archetype of the vital element. It is the first condition and the hallmark of Art, as breath is of life: breath, which accelerates or slows, which becomes even or agitated according to the tension in the individual, the degree and the nature of his emotion. This is rhythm in its primordial purity, this is rhythm in the masterpieces of Negro art, especially sculpture. It is composed of a theme – sculptural form – which is set in opposition to a sister theme, as inhalation is to exhalation, and that is repeated. It is not the kind of symmetry that gives rise to monotony; rhythm is alive, it is free . . . This is how rhythm affects what is least intellectual in us, tyrannically, to make us penetrate to the spirituality of the object; and that character of abandon which is ours is itself rhythmic.[6]

Had I read that right? I read it again with redoubled attention. From the opposite end of the white world a magical Negro culture was hailing me. Negro sculpture! I began to flush with pride. Was this our salvation?

I had rationalized the world and the world had rejected me on the basis of colour prejudice. Since no agreement was possible on the level of reason, I threw myself back towards unreason. It was up to the white man to be more irrational than I. Out of the necessities of my struggle I had chosen the method of regression, but the fact remained that it was an unfamiliar weapon; here I am at home; I am made of the irrational; I wade in the irrational. Up to the neck in the irrational. And now how my voice vibrates!

> Those who invented neither gunpowder nor the compass
> Those who never learned to conquer steam or electricity
> Those who never explored the seas or the skies
> But they know the farthest corners of the land of anguish
> Those who never knew any journey save that of abduction

Those who learned to kneel in docility
Those who were domesticated and Christianized
Those who were injected with bastardy . . .

Yes, all those are my brothers – a 'bitter brotherhood' imprisons all of us alike. Having stated the minor thesis, I went overboard after something else.

. . . But those without whom the earth would not be the earth
Tumescence all the more fruitful
than
the empty land
still more the land
Storehouse to guard and ripen all
on earth that is most earth
My blackness is no stone, its deafness
hurled against the clamour of the day
My blackness is no drop of lifeless water
on the dead eye of the world
My blackness is neither a tower nor a cathedral
It thrusts into the red flesh of the sun
It thrusts into the burning flesh of the sky
It hollows through the dense dismay of its own pillar of patience.[7]

Eyah! the tom-tom chatters out the cosmic message. Only the Negro has the capacity to convey it, to decipher its meaning, its import. Astride the world, my strong heels spurring into the flanks of the world, I stare into the shoulders of the world as the celebrant stares at the midpoint between the eyes of the sacrificial victim.

But they abandon themselves, possessed, to the essence of all things, knowing nothing of externals but possessed by the movement of all things

uncaring to subdue but playing the play of the world
truly the eldest sons of the world
open to all the breaths of the world
meeting-place of all the winds of the world
undrained bed of all the waters of the world
spark of the sacred fire of the world
flesh of the flesh of the world,
    throbbing with the very movement of the world![8]

Blood! Blood! . . . Birth! Ecstasy of becoming! Three-quarters engulfed in the confusions of the day, I feel myself redden with blood. The arteries of all the world, convulsed, torn away, uprooted, have turned towards me and fed me.

'Blood! Blood! All our blood stirred by the male heart of the sun.'[9]

Sacrifice was a middle point between the creation and myself – now I went back no longer to sources but to The Source. Nevertheless, one had to distrust rhythm, earth-mother love, this mystic, carnal marriage of the group and the cosmos.

In *La vie sexuelle en Afrique noire*, a work rich in perceptions, De Pédrals implies that always in Africa, no matter what field is studied, it will have a certain magico-social structure. He adds:

> All these are the elements that one finds again on a still greater scale in the domain of secret societies. To the extent, moreover, to which persons of either sex, subjected to circumcision during adolescence, are bound under penalty of death not to reveal to the uninitiated what they have experienced, and to the extent to which initiation into a secret society always excites to acts of *sacred love*, there is good ground to conclude by viewing both male and female circumcision and the rites that they embellish as constitutive of minor secret societies.[10]

I walk on white nails. Sheets of water threaten my soul on fire. Face to face with these rites, I am doubly alert. Black magic! Orgies, witches' sabbaths, heathen ceremonies, amulets. Coitus is an occasion to call on the gods of the clan. It is a sacred act, pure, absolute, bringing invisible forces into action. What is one to think of all these manifestations, all these initiations, all these acts? From every direction I am assaulted by the obscenity of dances and of words. Almost at my ear there is a song:

> First our hearts burned hot
> Now they are cold
> All we think of now is Love
> When we return to the village
> When we see the great phallus
> Ah how then we will make Love
> For our parts will be dry and clean.[11]

The soil, which only a moment ago was still a tamed steed, begins to revel. Are these virgins, these nymphomaniacs? Black Magic, primitive mentality, animism, animal eroticism, it all floods over me. All of it is typical of peoples that have not kept pace with the evolution of the human race. Or, if one prefers, this is humanity at its lowest. Having reached this point, I was long reluctant to commit myself. Aggression was in the stars. I had to choose. What do I mean? I had no choice . . .

Yes, we are – we Negroes – backward, simple, free in our behaviour. That is because for us the body is not something opposed to what you call the mind. We are in the world. And long live the couple, Man and Earth! Besides, our men of letters helped me to convince you; your white civilization overlooks subtle riches and sensitivity. Listen:

Emotive sensitivity. *Emotion is completely Negro as reason is Greek.*
[Author's italics.] Water rippled by every breeze? Unsheltered soul
blown by every wind, whose fruit often drops before it is ripe? Yes,
in one way, the Negro today is richer *in gifts than in works.*
[Author's italics.] But the tree thrusts its roots into the earth. The
river runs deep, carrying precious seeds. And, the Afro-American
poet, Langston Hughes, says:

> I have known rivers
> ancient dark rivers
> my soul has grown deep
> like the deep rivers.

The very nature of the Negro's emotion, of his sensitivity,
furthermore, explains his attitude towards the object perceived with
such basic intensity. It is an abandon that becomes need, an active
state of communion, indeed of identification, however negligible the
action – I almost said the personality – of the object. A rhythmic
attitude: The adjective should be kept in mind.[12]

So here we have the Negro rehabilitated, 'standing before the bar', ruling
the world with his intuition, the Negro recognized, set on his feet again,
sought after, taken up, and he is a Negro – no, he is not a Negro but the
Negro, exciting the fecund antennae of the world, placed in the
foreground of the world, raining his poetic power on the world, 'open to all
the breaths of the world'. I embrace the world! I am the world! The white
man has never understood this magic substitution. The white man wants
the world; he wants it for himself alone. He finds himself predestined
master of this world. He enslaves it. An acquisitive relation is established
between the world and him. But there exist other values that fit only my
forms. Like a magician, I robbed the white man of 'a certain world', for
ever after lost to him and his. When that happened, the white man must
have been rocked backward by a force that he could not identify, so little
used as he is to such reactions. Somewhere beyond the objective world of
farms and banana trees and rubber trees, I had subtly brought the real
world into being. The essence of the world was my fortune. Between the
world and me a relation of coexistence was established. I had discovered
the primeval One. My 'speaking hands' tore at the hysterical throat of the
world. The white man had the anguished feeling that I was escaping from
him and that I was taking something with me. He went through my
pockets. He thrust probes into the least circumvolution of my brain.
Everywhere he found only the obvious. So it was obvious that I had a
secret. I was interrogated; turning away with an air of mystery, I
murmured:

> Tokowaly, uncle, do you remember the nights gone by
> When my head weighed heavy on the back of your patience or
> Holding my hand your hand led me by shadows and signs

The fields are flowers of glowworms, stars hang on the bushes, on
    the trees
Silence is everywhere
Only the scents of the jungle hum, swarms of reddish bees that
    overwhelm the cricket's shrill sounds,
And covered tom-tom, breathing in the distance of the night.
You, Tokowaly, you listen to what cannot be heard, and you explain
    to me what the ancestors are saying in the liquid calm of the
    constellations,
The bull, the scorpion, the leopard, the elephant, and the fish we
    know,
And the white pomp of the Spirits in the heavenly shell that has no
    end,
But now comes the radiance of the goddess Moon and the veils of the
    shadows fall.
Night of Africa, my black night, mystical and bright, black and
    shining.[13]

I made myself the poet of the world. The white man had found a poetry in which there was nothing poetic. The soul of the white man was corrupted, and, as I was told by a friend who was a teacher in the United States, 'The presence of the Negroes beside the whites is in a way an insurance policy on humanness. When the whites feel that they have become too mechanized, they turn to the men of colour and ask them for a little human sustenance.' At last I had been recognized, I was no longer a zero.

I had soon to change my tune. Only momentarily at a loss, the white man explained to me that, genetically, I represented a stage of development: 'Your properties have been exhausted by us. We have had earth mystics such as you will never approach. Study our history and you will see how far this fusion has gone.' Then I had the feeling that I was repeating a cycle. My originality had been torn out of me. I wept a long time, and then I began to live again. But I was haunted by a galaxy of erosive stereotypes: the Negro's *sui generis* odour . . . the Negro's *sui generis* good nature . . . the Negro's *sui generis* gullibility . . .

I had tried to flee myself through my kind, but the whites had thrown themselves on me and hamstrung me. I tested the limits of my essence; beyond all doubt there was not much of it left. It was here that I made my most remarkable discovery. Properly speaking, this discovery was a rediscovery.

I rummaged frenetically through all the antiquity of the black man. What I found there took away my breath. In his book *L'abolition de l'esclavage* Schoelcher presented us with compelling arguments. Since then, Frobenius, Westermann, Delafosse – all of them white – had joined the chorus: Ségou, Djenné, cities of more than a hundred thousand people; accounts of learned blacks (doctors of theology who went to Mecca to interpret the Koran). All of that, exhumed from the past, spread with its insides out, made it possible for me to find a valid historical place. The white man was wrong, I was not a primitive, not even a half-man, I belonged to a race that had already been working in gold and silver two thousand years ago. And too there was something else, something else that the white man could not understand. Listen:

What sort of men were these, then, who had been torn away from their families, their countries, their religions, with a savagery unparalleled in history?

Gentle men, polite, considerate, unquestionably superior to those who tortured them – that collection of adventurers who slashed and violated and spat on Africa to make the stripping of her the easier.

The men they took away knew how to build houses, govern empires, erect cities, cultivate fields, mine for metals, weave cotton, forge steel.

Their religion had its own beauty, based on mystical connections with the founder of the city. Their customs were pleasing, built on unity, kindness, respect for age.

No coercion, only mutual assistance, the joy of living, a free acceptance of discipline.

Order – Earnestness – Poetry and Freedom.

From the untroubled private citizen to the almost fabulous leader there was an unbroken chain of understanding and trust. No science? Indeed yes; but also, to protect them from fear, they possessed great myths in which the most subtle observation and the most daring imagination were balanced and blended. No art? They had their magnificent sculpture, in which human feeling erupted so unrestrained yet always followed the obsessive laws of rhythm in its organization of the major elements of a material called upon to capture, in order to redistribute, the most secret forces of the universe . . .[14]

Monuments in the very heart of Africa? Schools? Hospitals? Not a single good burgher of the twentieth century, no Durand, no Smith, no Brown even suspects that such things existed in African before the Europeans came . . .

But Schoelcher reminds us of their presence, discovered by Caillé, Mollien, the Cander brothers. And, though he nowhere reminds us that when the Portuguese landed on the banks of the Congo in 1498, they found a rich and flourishing state there and that the courtiers of Ambas were dressed in robes of silk and brocade, at least he knows that Africa had brought itself up to a juridical concept of the state, and he is aware, living in the very flood of imperialism, that European civilization, after all, is only one more civilization among many – and not the most merciful.[15]

I put the white man back into his place; growing bolder, I jostled him and told him point-blank, 'Get used to me, I am not getting used to anyone'. I shouted my laughter to the stars. The white man, I could see, was resentful. His reaction time lagged interminably . . . I had won. I was jubilant.

'Lay aside your history, your investigations of the past, and try to feel yourself into our rhythm. In a society such as ours, industrialized to the highest degree, dominated by scientism, there is no longer room for your sensitivity. One must be tough if one is to be allowed to live. What matters now is no longer playing the game of the world but subjugating it with integers and atoms. Oh, certainly, I will be told, now and then when we are worn out by our lives in big buildings, we will turn to you as we do to our children – to the innocent, the ingenuous, the spontaneous. We will turn to you as to the childhood of the world. You are so real in your life – so funny, that is. Let us run away for a little while from our ritualized, polite civilization and let us relax, bend to those heads, those adorably expressive faces. In a way, you reconcile us with ourselves.'

Thus my unreason was countered with reason, my reason with 'real reason'. Every hand was a losing hand for me. I analysed my heredity. I made a complete audit of my ailment. I wanted to be typically Negro – it was no longer possible. I wanted to be white – that was a joke. And, when I tried, on the level of ideas and intellectual activity, to reclaim my negritude, it was snatched away from me. Proof was presented that my effort was only a term in the dialectic:

> But there is something more important: The Negro, as we have said, creates an anti-racist racism for himself. In no sense does he wish to rule the world: he seeks the abolition of all ethnic privileges, wherever they come from; he asserts his solidarity with the oppressed of all colours. At once the subjective, existential, ethnic idea of *negritude* 'passes,' as Hegel puts it, into the objective, positive, exact idea of *proletariat*. 'For Césaire,' Senghor says, 'the white man is the symbol of capital as the Negro is that of labour . . . Beyond the black-skinned men of his race it is the battle of the world proletariat that is his song.'
>
> That is easy to say, but less easy to think out. And undoubtedly it is no coincidence that the most ardent poets of negritude are at the same time militant Marxists.
>
> But that does not prevent the idea of race from mingling with that of class: The first is concrete and particular, the second is universal and abstract; the one stems from what Jaspers calls understanding and the other from intellection; the first is the result of a psychobiological syncretism and the second is a methodical construction based on experience. In fact, negritude appears as the minor term of a dialectical progression: The theoretical and practical assertion of the supremacy of the white man is its thesis; the

position of negritude as an antithetical value is the moment of negativity. But this negative moment is insufficient by itself, and the Negroes who employ it know this very well; they know that it is intended to prepare the synthesis or realization of the human in a society without races. Thus negritude is the root of its own destruction, it is a transition and not a conclusion, a means and not an ultimate end.[16]

When I read that page, I felt that I had been robbed of my last chance. I said to my friends, 'The generation of the younger black poets has just suffered a blow that can never be forgiven'. Help had been sought from a friend of the coloured peoples, and that friend had found no better response than to point out the relativity of what they were doing. For once, that born Hegelian had forgotten that consciousness has to lose itself in the night of the absolute, the only condition to attain to consciousness of self. In opposition to rationalism, he summoned up the negative side, but he forgot that this negativity draws its worth from an almost substantive absoluteness. A consciousness committed to experience is ignorant, has to be ignorant, of the essences and the determinations of its being.

Orphée Noir is a date in the intellectualization of the *experience* of being black. And Sartre's mistake was not only to seek the source of the source but in a certain sense to block that source:

Will the source of Poetry be dried up? Or will the great black flood, in spite of everything, colour the sea into which it pours itself? It does not matter: Every age has its own poetry; in every age the circumstances of history choose a nation, a race, a class to take up the torch by creating situations that can be expressed or transcended only through Poetry; sometimes the poetic impulse coincides with the revolutionary impulse, and sometimes they take different courses. Today let us hail the turn of history that will make it possible for the black man to utter 'the great Negro cry with a force that will shake the pillars of the world' (Césaire).[17]

And so it is not I who make a meaning for myself, but it is the meaning that was already there, pre-existing, waiting for me. It is not out of my bad nigger's misery, my bad nigger's teeth, my bad nigger's hunger that I will shape a torch with which to burn down the world, but it is the torch that was already there, waiting for that turn of history.

In terms of consciousness, the black consciousness is held out as an absolute density, as filled with itself, a stage preceding any invasion, any abolition of the ego by desire. Jean-Paul Sartre, in this work, has destroyed black zeal. In opposition to historical becoming, there had always been the unforeseeable. I needed to lose myself completely in negritude. One day, perhaps, in the depths of that unhappy romanticism . . .

In any case I *needed* not to know. This struggle, this new decline had to take on an aspect of completeness. Nothing is more unwelcome than the commonplace: 'You'll change, my boy; I was like that too when I was young . . . you'll see, it will all pass.'

The dialectic that brings necessity into the foundation of my freedom drives me out of myself. It shatters my unreflected position. Still in terms of consciousness, black consciousness is immanent in its own eyes. I am not a potentiality of something, I am wholly what I am. I do not have to look for the universal. No probability has any place inside me. My Negro consciousness does not hold itself out as a lack. It *is*. It is its own follower.

But, I will be told, your statements show a misreading of the processes of history. Listen then:

> Africa I have kept your memory Africa
> you are inside me
> Like the splinter in the wound
> like a guardian fetish in the centre of the village
> make me the stone in your sling
> make my mouth the lips of your wound
> make my knees the broken pillars of your abasement
> AND YET
> I want to be of your race alone
> workers peasants of all lands . . .
> . . . white worker in Detroit black peon in Alabama
> uncountable nation in capitalist slavery
> destiny ranges us shoulder to shoulder
> repudiating the ancient maledictions of blood taboos
> we roll away the ruins of our solitudes
> If the flood is a frontier
> we will strip the gully of its endless
> covering flow
> If the Sierra is a frontier
> we will smash the jaws of the volcanoes
> upholding the Cordilleras
> and the plain will be the parade ground of the dawn
> where we regroup our forces sundered
> by the deceits of our masters
> As the contradiction among the features
> creates the harmony of the face
> we proclaim the oneness of the suffering
> and the revolt
> of all the peoples on all the face of the earth
>   and we mix the mortar of the age of brotherhood
>   out of the dust of idols.[18]

Exactly, we will reply, Negro experience is not a whole, for there is not merely *one* Negro, there are *Negroes*. What a difference, for instance, in this other poem:

> The white man killed my father
> Because my father was proud
> The white man raped my mother
> Because my mother was beautiful
> The white man wore out my brother in the
>   hot sun of the roads
> Because my brother was strong
> Then the white man came to me
> His hands red with blood
> Spat his contempt into my black face
> Out of his tyrant's voice:
> 'Hey boy, a basin, a towel, water.'[19]

Or this other one:

> My brother with teeth that glisten at the compliments of hypocrites
> My brother with gold-rimmed spectacles
> Over eyes that turn blue at the sound of the Master's voice
> My poor brother in dinner jacket with its silk lapels
> Clucking and whispering and strutting through the drawing rooms
>   of Condescension
> How pathetic you are
> The sun of your native country is nothing more now than a shadow
> On your composed civilized face
> And your grandmother's hut
> Brings blushes into cheeks made white by years of abasement and
>   *Mea culpa*
> But when regurgitating the flood of lofty empty words
> Like the load that presses on your shoulders
> You walk again on the rough red earth of Africa
> These words of anguish will state the rhythm of your uneasy gait
> I feel so alone, so alone here![20]

From time to time one would like to stop. To state reality is a wearing task. But, when one has taken it into one's head to try to express existence, one runs the risk of finding only the non-existent. What is certain is that, at the very moment when I was trying to grasp my own being, Sartre, who remained The Other, gave me a name and thus shattered my last illusion. While I was saying to him:

> 'My negritude is neither a tower nor a cathedral,
> it thrusts into the red flesh of the sun,
> it thrusts into the burning flesh of the sky,
> it hollows through the dense dismay of its own pillar
> of patience . . .'

while I was shouting that, in the paroxysm of my being and my fury, he was reminding me that my blackness was only a minor term. In all truth, in all truth I tell you, my shoulders slipped out of the framework of the world, my feet could no longer feel the touch of the ground. Without a Negro past, without a Negro future, it was impossible for me to live my Negrohood. Not yet white, no longer wholly black, I was damned. Jean-Paul Sartre had forgotten that the Negro suffers in his body quite differently from the white man.* Between the white man and me the connexion was irrevocably one of transcendence.†

But the constancy of my love had been forgotten. I defined myself as an absolute intensity of beginning. So I took up my negritude, and with tears in my eyes I put its machinery together again. What had been broken to pieces was rebuilt, reconstructed by the intuitive lianas of my hands.

My cry grew more violent: I am a Negro, I am a Negro, I am a Negro . . .

And there was my poor brother – living out his neurosis to the extreme and finding himself paralysed:

The Negro:	I can't, ma'am.
Lizzie:	Why not?
The Negro:	I can't shoot white folks.
Lizzie:	Really! That would bother them, wouldn't it?
The Negro:	They're white folks, ma'am.
Lizzie:	So what? Maybe they got a right to bleed you like a pig just because they're white?
The Negro:	But they're white folks.

A feeling of inferiority? No, a feeling of non-existence. Sin is Negro as virtue is white. All those white men in a group, guns in their hands, cannot be wrong. I am guilty. I do not know of what, but I know that I am no good.

The Negro:	That's how it goes, ma'am. That's how it always goes with white folks.
Lizzie:	You too? You feel guilty?
The Negro:	Yes, ma'am.[21]

It is Bigger Thomas – he is afraid, he is terribly afraid. He is afraid, but of what is he afraid? Of himself. No one knows yet who he is, but he knows that fear will fill the world when the world finds out. And when the world

* Though Sartre's speculations on the existence of The Other may be correct (to the extent, we must remember, to which *Being and Nothingness* describes an alienated consciousness), their application to a black consciousness proves fallacious. That is because the white man is not only The Other but also the master, whether real or imaginary.
† In the sense in which the word is used by Jean Wahl in *Existence humaine et transcendance* (Neuchâtel, La Baconnière, 1944).

knows, the world always expects something of the Negro. He is afraid lest the world know, he is afraid of the fear that the world would feel if the world knew. Like that old woman on her knees who begged me to tie her to her bed:

'I just know, Doctor: Any minute that thing will take hold of me.'

'What thing?'

'The wanting to kill myself. Tie me down, I'm afraid.'

In the end, Bigger Thomas acts. To put an end to his tension, he acts, he responds to the world's anticipation.[22]

So it is with the character in *If He Hollers Let Him Go*[23] – who does precisely what he did not want to do. That big blonde who was always in his way, weak, sensual, offered, open, fearing (desiring) rape, became his mistress in the end.

The Negro is a toy in the white man's hands; so, in order to shatter the hellish cycle, he explodes. I cannot go to a film without seeing myself. I wait for me. In the interval, just before the film starts, I wait for me. The people in the theatre are watching me, examining me, waiting for me. A Negro groom is going to appear. My heart makes my head swim.

The crippled veteran of the Pacific war says to my brother, 'Resign yourself to your colour the way I got used to my stump; we're both victims'.[24]

Nevertheless with all my strength I refuse to accept that amputation. I feel in myself a soul as immense as the world, truly a soul as deep as the deepest of rivers, my chest has the power to expand without limit. I am a master and I am advised to adopt the humility of the cripple. Yesterday, awakening to the world, I saw the sky turn upon itself utterly and wholly. I wanted to rise, but the disembowelled silence fell back upon me, its wings paralysed. Without responsibility, straddling Nothingness and Infinity, I began to weep.

Notes

1 Jean L'hermitte, *L'Image de notre corps*, Paris, Nouvelle Revue critique, 1939, p. 17.

2 Sir Alan Burns, *Colour Prejudice*, London, Allen and Unwin, 1948, p. 16.

3 Jean-Paul Sartre, *Anti-Semite and Jew*, New York, Grove Press, 1960, pp. 112–13.

4 Ibid., p. 115.

5 Jon Alfred Mjoen, 'Harmonic and disharmonic race-crossings', The Second International Congress of Eugenics (1921), *Eugenics in Race and State*, vol. II, p. 60, quoted in Sir Alan Burns, op. cit., p. 120.

6 'Ce que l'homme noir apporte', in Claude Nordey, *L'Homme de couleur*, Paris, Plon, 1939, pp. 309–10.

7 Aimé Césaire, *Cahier d'un retour au pays natal*, Paris, Présence Africaine, 1956, pp. 77–8.

8 Ibid., p. 78.

9 Ibid., p. 79.

10 De Pédrals, *La vie sexuelle en Afrique noire*, Paris, Payot, p. 83.

11 A. M. Vergiat, *Les rites secrets des primitifs de l'Oubangui*, Paris, Payot, 1951, p. 113.

12 Léopold Senghor, 'Ce que l'homme noir apporte', in Nordey, op. cit., p. 205.

13 Léopold Senghor, *Chants d'ombre*, Paris, Editions du Seuil, 1945.

14 Aimé Césaire, Introduction to Victor Schoelcher, *Esclavage et colonisation*, Paris, Presses Universitaires de France, 1948, p. 7.

15 Ibid., p. 8.

16 Jean-Paul Sartre, *Orphée Noir*, preface to *Anthologie de la nouvelle poésie nègre et malgache*, Paris, Presses Universitaires de France, 1948, pp. xl ff.

17 Ibid., p. xliv.

18 Jacques Roumain, 'Bois-d'Ebène', Prelude, in *Anthologie de la nouvelle poésie nègre et malgache*, p. 113.

19 David Diop, 'Le temps du martyre', in ibid., p. 174.

20 David Diop, 'Le Renégat'.

21 Jean-Paul Sartre, *The Respectful Prostitute*, in *Three Plays*, New York, Knopf, 1949, pp. 189, 191. Originally, *La Putain respectueuse*, Paris, Gallimard, 1947. See also *Home of the Brave*, a film by Mark Robson.

22 Richard Wright, *Native Son*, New York, Harper, 1940.

23 By Chester Himes, Garden City, Doubleday, 1945.

24 *Home of the Brave*.

Source: Fanon, F. (1970) 'The fact of blackness' from *Black Skins, White Masks*, Chapter 5, London, Paladin (first published in French, 1952 and in English, Grafton Books, 1968).

PART 3

COMMUNITY AND DIASPORA

10 COLONIALISM AND HUMANISM

ROBERT YOUNG

'Come, then, comrades, the European game has finally ended,' wrote Frantz Fanon. 'It is a question of the Third World starting a new history.'[1] But how to write a new history when, as Aimé Césaire observed, the only history is white?[2] The critique of the structures of colonialism might seem a marginal activity in relation to the mainstream political issues of literary and cultural theory, catering only for minorities or for those with a specialist interest in colonial history. But although it is concerned with the geographical peripheries of metropolitan European culture, its long-term strategy is to effect a radical restructuring of European thought and, particularly, historiography.

This has not been a matter of setting up the critique of colonialism in opposition to European culture but rather of demonstrating the extent to which they are already deeply implicated within each other. European thought since the Renaissance would be as unthinkable without the impact of colonialism as the history of the world since the Renaissance would be inconceivable without the effects of Europeanization. So it is not an issue of removing colonial thinking from European thought, of purging it, like today's dream of 'stamping out' racism. It is rather a question of repositioning European systems of knowledge so as to demonstrate the long history of their operation as the effect of their colonial other, a reversal encapsulated in Fanon's observation: 'Europe is literally the creation of the Third World' (p. 81). We should not assume either that the anti-colonialism has been confined to our own age: sympathy for the oppressed other, and pressure for decolonization, is as old as European colonialism itself.[3] What has been new in the years since the Second World War during which, for the most part, the decolonization of the European empires has taken place, has been the accompanying attempt to decolonize European thought and the forms of its history as well. It thus marks that fundamental shift and cultural crisis currently charac- terized as postmodernism.

This project could be said to have been initiated in 1961 by Fanon's *The Wretched of the Earth*. The book is both a revolutionary manifesto of decolonization and the founding analysis of the effects of colonialism upon colonized peoples and their cultures. Throughout, the Third World is put forward as a radical alternative to the contemporary order of world power and its two rival ideologies of capitalism and socialism. Despite the influence of Sartre, Fanon has little time for the central contention of the

Critique of Dialectical Reason, published only the year before, that men as self-conscious agents create the totality of history. He quickly points to what this means when put in the colonial context:

> The settler makes history and is conscious of making it. And because he constantly refers to the history of his mother country, he clearly indicates that he himself is the extension of that mother country. Thus the history which he writes is not the history of the country which he plunders but the history of his own nation in regard to all that she skims off, all that she violates and starves (p. 40).

If men make history, here Fanon shows how the men and women who are the objects of that history are condemned to immobility and silence. It is to these men and women that his own book is addressed. His criticism of Europe does not stop at the violent history of colonial appropriation. For the effect of colonialism, he suggests, is to dehumanize the native; a process which, paradoxically, finds its justification in the values of Western humanism. This humanism Fanon consistently attacks and ridicules. So, for example, in the Conclusion, he urges his readers:

> Leave this Europe where they are never done talking of Man, yet murder men everywhere they find them, at the corner of every one of their own streets, in all the corners of the globe. For centuries they have stifled almost the whole of humanity in the name of a so-called spiritual experience . . .
> That same Europe where they were never done talking of Man, and where they never stopped proclaiming that they were only anxious for the welfare of Man: today we know with what sufferings humanity has paid for every one of their triumphs of the mind (p. 251).

As might have been expected, it was this aspect of Fanon's critique which particularly affected Sartre. In the *Critique of Dialectical Reason* Sartre rejects the humanist notion that there is an ahistorical essence of man, although the book is still founded on an attempt to put a very European 'Man' at the centre of history. Doubtless Fanon's intervention can be added to the list of reasons why Sartre's project foundered.

'Decolonization', Fanon comments, 'which sets out to change the order of the world is, obviously, a programme of complete disorder' (p. 27), and no more so than in the disorder it sets up in the values attached to European humanism. Sartre's remarkable Preface to *The Wretched of the Earth*, which, by contrast, is specifically addressed to the European reader, marks the opening move by a European in the critique of European culture from the perspective of its involvement in colonialism. Sartre does not try to come to terms with contemporary history by lamenting the decline of the West, nor does he merely acknowledge the violence of the history of European domination. The significance of Sartre's essay stems from the fact that he acknowledges that, although he himself had spent the past few years trying to correct Marxism's economism to a humanism, humanism itself, often validated among the highest values of European civilization, was deeply complicit with the violent negativity of colonialism, and played a crucial part in its ideology. The formation of the ideas of human nature, humanity and the universal qualities of the human mind as the common good of an ethical civilization occurred at the same time as those particularly violent centuries in the history of the world now known as the era of Western colonialism. The effect of this was to dehumanize the various subject-peoples: in Sartre's words, 'to wipe out their traditions, to substitute our language for theirs and to destroy their culture without giving them ours' (p. 1).

Now, however, that disorder is being reversed. 'For we in Europe too are being decolonized', Sartre announces:

> that is to say that the settler which is in every one of us is being savagely rooted out. Let us look at ourselves, if we can bear to, and see what is becoming of us. First, we must face that unexpected revelation, the striptease of our humanism. There you can see it, quite naked, and it's not a pretty sight. It was nothing but an ideology of lies, a perfect justification for pillage; its honeyed words, its affectation of sensibility were only alibis for our aggression (p. 21).

It was the recognition of this use of the human as a highly politicized category which led to the sustained critique of 'Man' by a broad range of post-war thinkers in the movement known as 'anti-humanism'. Few politico-intellectual projects have generated as much controversy, hostility, and, ironically but perhaps symptomatically, intolerance. What is striking is that few of those defending humanism ever ask where anti-humanism came from. The standard definition states that it is derived from the critique of Marxist humanism initiated by Lévi-Strauss and Althusser against Sartre and others such as Garaudy in the French Communist Party. But this account hardly tells us more than that the critique of Marxist humanism came from the anti-humanists. Taking Althusser's strategic homogenization of all humanisms into one on trust, it altogether neglects the Marxist-humanist attempt, by Lukács, Sartre, and others, to found a 'new humanism' which would substitute, for the Enlightenment's conception of man's unchanging nature, a new 'historical humanism' that would see 'man as a product of himself and of his own activity in history'.[4] But that very historical activity formed the basis for the critiques of both kinds of humanism by non-European writers such as Césaire and Fanon. This version of anti-humanism starts with the realization of humanism's involvement in the history of colonialism, which shows that the two are not so easily separable. For from the colonial perspective, humanism began as a form of legitimation produced as a self-justification by the colonizers for their own people, but later, as what Abdul JanMohammed has distinguished as the 'dominant' phase of colonialism shifted to the 'hegemonic' phase of neocolonialism, humanism was utilized as a form of ideological control of the colonized peoples.[5] This in turn set the structures of neocolonialism in place ready for decolonization. Fanon describes it as follows:

> The colonialist bourgeoisie, in its narcissistic dialogue, expounded by the members of its universities, had in fact deeply implanted in the minds of the colonized intellectual that the essential qualities remain eternal in spite of all the blunders men may make: the essential qualities of the West, of course (p. 36).

So those universal essential features which define the human mask over the assimilation of the human itself with European values; an identification perhaps clearest in the Marxist definition of history which states that if history is the product of human actions, then it only can be said to begin properly when 'primitive' societies give way to (European) civilization. To criticize humanism in this context therefore does not mean that you do not like human beings and have no ethics – the gist of certain attacks on 'anti-humanism' – but rather the reverse. It questions the use of the human as an explanatory category that purports to provide a rational understanding of 'man' – an assumed universal predicated on the exclusion and marginalization of his Others, such as 'woman' or 'the native'.

A good example of such a questioning can be found in Roland Barthes' short essay, 'The Great Family of Man'.[6] Barthes is discussing the well-known photographic exhibition which is organized around the fiction of the universality of fundamental human experiences. Barthes points to the way that 'The Family of Man' projects the myth of a global human community in two stages: first, there is an emphasis on difference – a multiplicity of exotic varieties of everyday activities of work, play, birth, death, etc. are compiled; but such diversity is only introduced so that it can be taken away again in the name of an underlying unity which implies that at some level all such experiences are identical, despite their wide cultural and historical differences, that underneath there is one human nature and therefore a common human essence. Barthes argues that such humanism, so reassuring at the sentimental level, functions simply to override differences 'which we shall here quite simply call "injustices"':

> Any classic humanism postulates that in scratching the history of men a little, the relativity of their institutions or the superficial diversity of their skins (but why not ask the parents of Emmet Till, the young Negro assassinated by the Whites what *they* think of *The Great Family of Man*?), one very quickly reaches the solid rock of a universal human nature (p. 101).

No one, of course, denies that there are universal facts, such as birth or death. But take away their historical and cultural context, and anything which is said about them can only be tautological. As Chandra Talpade Mohanty observes, 'that women mother in a variety of societies is not as significant as the *value* attached to mothering in these societies'.[7] Similarly, Barthes argues that the suggestion that work is as natural as birth or death negates its historicity, its different conditions, modes, and ends – specificities which matter to such an extent,

> that it will never be fair to confuse in a purely gestural identity the colonial and the Western worker (let us also ask the North African workers of the Goutte d'Or district in Paris what they think of *The Great Family of Man*) (p. 102).

As his examples show, Barthes consistently places the claimed universal values of humanism in the ironic perspective of the facts of Western colonialism and racism. This is reinforced by what is perhaps the best known analysis of *Mythologies*, the *Paris-Match* cover of a young black soldier in French uniform saluting the tricolour. Barthes demonstrates how this photograph has a meaning, namely the reinforcement of a colonial ideology, the family of the French Empire: 'that all her sons, without any colour discrimination, faithfully serve under her flag, and that there is no better answer to the detractors of an alleged colonialism than the zeal shown by this Negro in serving his so-called oppressors' (p. 116).[8]

As Barthes' analyses indicate, the French critique of humanism was conducted from the first as a part of a political critique of colonialism. Colonial discourse analysis, therefore, shows why 'anti-humanism' was not merely a philosophical project. The anti-humanists charged that the category of the human, however exalted in its conception, was too often invoked only in order to put the male before the female, or to classify other 'races' as subhuman, and therefore not subject to the ethical prescriptions applicable to 'humanity' at large. As Sartre put it: 'Humanism is the counterpart of racism: it is a practice of exclusion'.[9] This contradiction, according to Fanon, was resolved in the following way:

> Western bourgeois racial prejudice as regards the nigger and the Arab is a racism of contempt; it is a racism which minimises what it hates. Bourgeois ideology, however, which is the proclamation of an essential equality between men, manages to appear logical in its own eyes by inviting the sub-men to become human, and to take as their prototype Western humanity as incarnated in the Western bourgeoisie (p. 131).

A classic example of this kind of double logic would be John Stuart Mill's basing his argument for liberty on the prior division of the world into cultures of civilization and barbarism; or, at the level of aesthetics, the anthropologizing of Kant's notion of the universal claim in questions of taste into the basis for the claims by European critics that the perceptions and experiences represented by European writers achieve the status of universal human truths, without any knowledge as to whether this could possibly be so or not.[10] How universal would the Shakespearian 'human' values of the English have been to the people, say, of the city of Benin as they watched the sacking of their city in commemoration of Queen Victoria's 1897 Jubilee? Fanon gives us an answer:

> The violence with which the supremacy of white values is affirmed and the aggressiveness which has permeated the victory of these values over the ways of life and of thought of the native mean that, in revenge, the native laughs in mockery when Western values are mentioned in front of him (p. 33).

Every time a literary critic claims a universal ethical, moral, or emotional instance in a piece of English literature, he or she colludes in the violence of the colonial legacy in which the European value or truth is defined as the universal one.

The structuralist critique of humanism was produced in the context of the general refusal to acknowledge that such violence is intrinsic to Western culture and not simply accidental to it. Structuralism's so-called 'decentring of the subject' was in many respects itself an ethical activity, derived from a suspicion that the ontological category of 'the human' and 'human nature' had been inextricably associated with the violence of Western history. If the human is itself revealed as a conflictual concept it can no longer be presented as an undisturbed ethical end. As is well known, the preoccupation with the 'problem of the subject' was concerned to articulate the ways in which human subjects are not unitary essences but products of a conflictual psychic and political economy. One way of addressing this difficulty was to redefine the self through the model of the different grammatical positions which it is obliged to take up in language, which disallow the centrality and unity of the 'I' assumed by humanism. It is precisely this inscription of alterity within the self that can allow for a new relation to ethics: the self has to come to terms with the fact that it is also a second and a third person. The Foucauldian redefinition of the self according to its position within language, for example, showed how once engaged in any kind of linguistic activity it is displaced, decentred, and variously positioned as a subject according to different systems, institutions, forms of classification and hierarchies of power. As Gayatri Spivak puts it, 'structuralists question humanism by exposing its hero – the sovereign subject as author, the subject of authority, legitimacy, and power', a critique which extends to the connection between the production of the humanist subject and the general process of colonialism by which Europe consolidated itself politically as sovereign subject of the world.[11] With the West's gradual loss of suzerainty, the First World is now having to come to terms with the fact that it is no longer always positioned in the first person with regard to the Second or Third Worlds. As Sartre put it, 'Europe is springing leaks everywhere. What then has happened? It is simply that in the past we made history and now it is being made of us' (p. 23).

A particularly symptomatic example of this strategic blindness and refusal to come to terms with the violence intrinsic to Western culture is the way in which Fascism and the Holocaust are often presented as if they were a unique aberration, a dark perversion of Western rationalism or a particular effect of German culture. Here the differences between the French and the Frankfurt school, which has remained curiously oblivious to the whole problem of colonialism, becomes most apparent. It took a Césaire or a Fanon to point out that Fascism was simply colonialism brought home to Europe.[12] Sartre spells out the implications of this argument:

> Liberty, equality, fraternity, love, honour, patriotism and what have
> you. All this did not prevent us from making anti-racial speeches
> about dirty niggers, dirty Jews and dirty Arabs. High-minded people,
> liberal or just soft-hearted, protest that they were shocked by such
> inconsistency; but they were either mistaken or dishonest, for with
> us there is nothing more consistent than a racist humanism since
> the European has only been able to become a man through creating
> slaves and monsters (p. 22).

Sartre, however, is in many ways more sanguine than the more fervent anti-humanists who were unwilling to recognize humanism as a conflictual concept, divided against itself. He demonstrates why a straightforward anti-humanism was always problematic in so far as it never recognized that the contradictory structure of humanism made difficulties for the assumption that it could simply be opposed. For humanism is itself already anti-humanist. That is the problem. It necessarily produces the non-human in setting up its problematic boundaries. But at the same time, it can also produce positive effects. As even Althusser recognized, humanism found genuinely revolutionary echoes in Third-World struggles.[13] The question then becomes whether we should – and whether we can – differentiate between a humanism which harks back critically, or uncritically, to the mainstream of Enlightenment culture and Fanon's new 'new humanism' which attempts to reformulate it as a non-conflictual concept no longer defined against a sub-human other. For to some extent Europe itself fulfils this function in Fanon. [...] The contradictions of humanism continue to perplex anti-colonialist thought.

What is clear is that such challenges as Fanon's to the limits of Western ethnocentricity have had the effect of decentring and displacing the norms of Western knowledge: questioning, for example, the assumptions of Western historicist history as an ordered whole with a single meaning, or of Western nationalist discourse which, as Homi Bhabha puts it, 'normalizes its own history of expansion and exploitation by inscribing the history of the other in a fixed hierarchy of civil progress'.[14] In addition to the rewriting of the history of non-European histories and culture, analysis of colonialism therefore shifts the perspectives of European history and culture so as to interrogate the fundamental structures and assumptions of Western knowledge. The legacy of colonialism is as much a problem for the West as it is for the scarred lands in the world beyond.

Notes

1 Frantz Fanon, *The Wretched of the Earth* (trans. Constance Farrington), Harmonds-worth, Penguin (1967), pp. 251–4. Further references will be cited in the text.

2 Aimé Césaire, *Discourse on Colonialism* (trans. Joan Pinkham), New York, Monthly Review Press (1972), p. 54.

3 As is evident from Marcel Merle's extremely useful anthology, *L'Anticolonialisme européen, de Las Casas à Marx*, Paris, Colin (1969); see also Peter Hulme, *Colonial Encounters: Europe and the Native Caribbean, 1492–1797*, London, Methuen (1986); and Tzvetan Todorov, *Nous et les autres: La Réflexion française sur la diversité humaine*, Paris, Seuil (1989).

4 Georg Lukács, *The Historical Novel* (trans. Hannah and Stanley Mitchell), London, Merlin Press (1962), pp. 28–9. For contemporary discussions of humanism, see also Sartre's Conclusion to *Being and Nothingness* (trans. Hazel E. Barnes), New York, Philosophical Library (1958); *Existentialism and Humanism* (trans. Philip Mairet), London, Methuen (1948); Maurice Merleau-Ponty *Humanism and Terror* (trans. J. O'Neill), Evanston, Northwestern University Press (1964); Heidegger 'Letter on Humanism', in Krell, D. F. (ed.) *Basic Writings*, London, Routledge and Kegan Paul (1978), pp. 193–242; and Louis Althusser 'Marxism and Humanism', in *For Marx* (trans. Ben Brewster), London, New Left Books (1969), pp. 219–47; and 'Reply to John Lewis' in *Essays in Self-Criticism* (trans. Grahame Lock), London, New Left Books (1976), pp. 33–99. A detailed account of some of the recent arguments about the complexities of the problems involved in humanism can be found in Kate Soper's *Humanism and Anti-Humanism*, London, Hutchinson (1986).

5 Abdul R. JanMohammed, 'The Economy of Manichean Allegory: The Function of Racial Difference in Colonialist Literature' *Critical Inquiry* 12(1) (1985), pp. 61–2.

6 Roland Barthes, 'The Great Family of Man' in *Mythologies* (trans. Annette Lavers), London, Jonathan Cape (1972), pp. 100–2. Further references will be cited in the text.

7 Chandra Talpade Mohanty 'Under Western Eyes: Feminist Scholarship and Colonial Discourses' *Boundary* 2 (12:3/13:1) (1984), p. 340.

8 Compare Paul Gilroy's analysis of the 1983 Conservative Election poster, 'Labour Says He's Black, Tories say He's British' in *There Ain't No Black in the Union Jack: The Cultural Politics of Race and Nation*, London, Hutchinson (1987), pp. 57–9.

9 Jean-Paul Sartre *Critique of Dialectical Reason: I. Theory of Practical Ensembles* (trans. Alan Sheridan-Smith), London, New Left Books (1976), p. 752.

10 Mill 'On Liberty' in Robson, J. M. (ed.) *Collected Works of John Stuart Mill*, London, Routledge and Kegan Paul (1963–), vol. 18, p. 224, 'Considerations on Representative Government'; 19, pp. 562–77 'Of the government of dependencies by a free state'; and 'Thoughts on Parliamentary Reform', vol. 19, p. 324. For detailed analysis of Mill's views in relation to India, see Eric Stokes *The English Utilitarians and India*, Oxford, Clarendon

Press (1959); Kant, *The Critique of Judgement* (trans. James Creed Meredith), Oxford, Clarendon Press (1952).

11 Spivak, *In Other Worlds*, p. 202. It should be obvious from the present discussion that I disagree with Spivak's argument that imperialism constitutes a 'symptomatic blank in contemporary Western anti-humanism'.

12 Aimé Césaire, *Discourse on Colonialism*, pp. 14–15; Fanon, *The Wretched of the Earth*, pp. 71, 80; cf. also Paul Virilio, *Speed and Politics* (trans. Mark Polizzotti), New York, Semiotext(e) (1986), 106ff.

13 Louis Althusser and Etienne Balibar, *Reading Capital* (trans. Ben Brewster), London, New Left Books (1970), p. 141.

14 Homi Bhabha 'Sly Civility', *October* **34** (1985), p. 74. With respect to this Western time, contrast the essays in the special issue of *Diogenes* **42** (1963) 'Man and the Concept of History in the Orient'.

Source: Young, R. (1990) *White Mythologies: Writing History and the West*, London, Routledge.

11 NEW ETHNICITIES

STUART HALL

I have centred my remarks on an attempt to identify and characterize a significant shift that has been going on (and is still going on) in black cultural politics. This shift is not definitive, in the sense that there are two clearly discernible phases – one in the past which is now over and the new one which is beginning – which we can neatly counterpose to one another. Rather, they are two phases of the same movement, which constantly overlap and interweave. Both are framed by the same historical conjuncture and both are rooted in the politics of antiracism and the postwar black experience in Britain. Nevertheless I think we can identify two different 'moments' and that the difference between them is significant.

It is difficult to characterize these precisely, but I would say that the first moment was grounded in a particular political and cultural analysis. Politically, this is the moment when the term 'black' was coined as a way of referencing the common experience of racism and marginalization in Britain and came to provide the organizing category of a new politics of resistance, amongst groups and communities with, in fact, very different histories, traditions and ethnic identities. In this moment, politically speaking, 'The Black experience', as a singular and unifying framework based on the building up of identity across ethnic and cultural difference between the different communities, became 'hegemonic' over other ethnic/racial identities – though the latter did not, of course, disappear. Culturally, this analysis formulated itself in terms of a critique of the way blacks were positioned as the unspoken and invisible 'other' of predominantly white aesthetic and cultural discourses.

This analysis was predicated on the marginalization of the black experience in British culture; not fortuitously occurring at the margins, but placed, positioned at the margins, as the consequence of a set of quite specific political and cultural practices which regulated, governed and 'normalized' the representational and discursive spaces of English society. These formed the conditions of existence of a cultural politics designed to challenge, resist and, where possible, to transform the dominant regimes of representation – first in music and style, later in literary, visual and cinematic forms. In these spaces blacks have typically been the objects, but rarely the subjects, of the practices of representation. The struggle to come into representation was predicated on a critique of the degree of fetishization, objectification and negative figuration which are so much a feature of the representation of the black subject. There was a concern not simply with the absence or marginality of the black experience but with its simplification and its stereotypical character.

The cultural politics and strategies which developed around this critique had many facets, but its two principal objects were: first the question of access to the rights to representation by black artists and black cultural workers themselves. Secondly, the *contestation* of the marginality, the stereotypical quality and the fetishized nature of images of blacks, by the counter-position of a 'positive' black imagery. These strategies were principally addressed to changing what I would call the 'relations of representation'.

I have a distinct sense that in the recent period we are entering a new phase. But we need to be absolutely clear what we mean by a 'new' phase because, as soon as you talk of a new phase, people instantly imagine that what is entailed is the *substitution* of one kind of politics for another. I am quite distinctly *not* talking about a shift in those terms. Politics does not necessarily proceed by way of a set of oppositions and reversals of this kind, though some groups and individuals are anxious to 'stage' the question in this way. The original critique of the predominant relations of race and representation and the politics which developed around it have not and cannot possibly disappear while the conditions which gave rise to it – cultural racism in its Dewsbury form – not only persists but positively flourishes under Thatcherism.[1] There is no sense in which a new phase in black cultural politics could replace the earlier one. Nevertheless it is true that as the struggle moves forward and assumes new forms, it does to some degree *displace*, reorganize and reposition the different cultural strategies in relation to one another. If this can be conceived in terms of the 'burden of representation', I would put the point in this form: that black artists and cultural workers now have to struggle, not on one, but on two fronts. The problem is, how to characterize this shift – if indeed, we agree that such a shift has taken or is taking place – and if the language of binary oppositions and substitutions will no longer suffice. The characterization that I would offer is tentative, proposed in the context of this conference mainly to try and clarify some of the issues involved, rather than to pre-empt them.

The shift is best thought of in terms of a change from a struggle over the relations of representation to a politics of representation itself. It would be useful to separate out such a 'politics of representation' into its different elements. We all now use the word representation, but, as we know, it is an extremely slippery customer. It can be used, on the one hand, simply as another way of talking about how one images a reality that exists 'outside' the means by which things are represented: a conception grounded in a mimetic theory of representation. On the other hand the term can also stand for a very radical displacement of that unproblematic notion of the concept of representation. My own view is that events, relations, structures do have conditions of existence and real effects, outside the sphere of the discursive; but that only within the discursive, and subject to its specific conditions, limits and modalities, do they have or can they be constructed within meaning. Thus, while not wanting to expand the territorial claims of the discursive infinitely, how things are represented and the 'machineries' and regimes of representation in a culture do play a *constitutive*, and not merely a reflexive, after-the-event, role. This gives questions of culture and ideology, and the scenarios of representation – subjectivity, identity, politics – a formative, not merely an expressive, place in the constitution of social and political life. I think it is the move towards this second sense of representation which is taking place and which is transforming the politics of representation in black culture.

This is a complex issue. First, it is the effect of a theoretical encounter between black cultural politics and the discourses of a Eurocentric, largely white, critical cultural theory which in recent years has focused so much analysis on the politics of representation. This is always an extremely difficult, if not dangerous, encounter. (I think particularly of black people encountering the discourses of poststructuralism, postmodernism, psychoanalysis and feminism.) Secondly, it marks what I can only call 'the end of innocence', or the end of the innocent notion of the essential black subject. Here again, the end of the essential black subject is something which people are increasingly debating, but they may not have fully reckoned with its political consequences. What is at issue here is the recognition of the extraordinary diversity of subjective positions, social experiences and cultural identities which compose the category 'black'; that is, the recognition that 'black' is essentially a politically and culturally *constructed* category, which cannot be grounded in a set of fixed transcultural or transcendental racial categories and which therefore has no guarantees in Nature. What this brings into play is the recognition of the immense diversity and differentiation of the historical and cultural experiences of black subjects. This inevitably entails a weakening or fading of the notion that 'race' or some composite notion of race around the term black will either guarantee the effectivity of any cultural practice or determine in any final sense its aesthetic value.

We should put this as plainly as possible. Films are not necessarily good because black people make them. They are not necessarily 'right-on' by virtue of the fact that they deal with the black experience. Once you enter the politics of the end of the essential black subject you are plunged headlong into the maelstrom of a continuously contingent, unguaranteed, political argument and debate: a critical politics, a politics of criticism. You can no longer conduct black politics through the strategy of a simple set of reversals, putting in the place of the bad old essential white subject, the new essentially good black subject. Now, that formulation may seem to threaten the collapse of an entire political world. Alternatively, it may be greeted with extraordinary relief at the passing away of what at one time seemed to be a necessary fiction. Namely, either that all black people are good or indeed that all black people are *the same*. After all, it is one of the predicates of racism that 'you can't tell the difference because they all look the same'. This does not make it any easier to conceive of how a politics can be constructed which works with and through difference, which is able to build those forms of solidarity and identification which make common struggle and resistance possible but without suppressing the real heterogeneity of interests and identities, and which can effectively draw the political boundary lines without which political contestation is impossible, without fixing those boundaries for eternity. It entails the movement in black politics, from what Gramsci called the 'war of manoeuvre' to the 'war of position' – the struggle around positionalities. But the difficulty of conceptualizing such a politics (and the temptation to slip into a sort of endlessly sliding discursive liberal-pluralism) does not absolve us of the task of developing such a politics.

The end of the essential black subject also entails a recognition that the central issues of race always appear historically in articulation, in a formation, with other categories and divisions and are constantly crossed and recrossed by the categories of class, of gender and ethnicity. (I make a distinction here between race and ethnicity to which I shall return.) To me, films like *Territories*, *Passion of Remembrance*, *My Beautiful Laundrette* and *Sammy and Rosie Get Laid*, for example, make it perfectly clear that this shift has been engaged; and that the question of the black subject cannot be represented without reference to the dimensions of class, gender, sexuality and ethnicity.

Difference and contestation

A further consequence of this politics of representation is the slow recognition of the deep ambivalence of identification and desire. We think about identification usually as a simple process, structured around fixed 'selves' which we either are or are not. The play of identity and difference which constructs racism is powered not only by the positioning of blacks as the inferior species but also, and at the same time, by an inexpressible envy and desire; and this is something the recognition of which fundamentally *displaces* many of our hitherto stable political categories, since it implies a process of identification and otherness which is more complex than we had hitherto imagined.

Racism, of course, operates by constructing impassable symbolic boundaries between racially constituted categories, and its typically binary system of representation constantly marks and attempts to fix and naturalize the difference between belongingness and otherness. Along this frontier there arises what Gayatri Spivak calls the 'epistemic violence' of the discourses of the Other – of imperialism, the colonized, orientalism, the exotic, the primitive, the anthropological and the folkloric.[2] Consequently the discourse of antiracism had often been founded on a strategy of reversal and inversion, turning the 'Manichean aesthetic' of colonial discourse up-side down. However, as Fanon constantly reminded us the epistemic violence is both outside and inside, and operates by a process of splitting on both sides of the division – in here as well as out here. That is why it is a question, not only of 'black-skin, white-skin' but of *'Black-skin, white masks'* – the internalization of the self-as-other. Just as masculinity always constructs femininity as double – simultaneously Madonna and Whore – so racism constructs the black subject: noble savage and violent avenger. And in the doubling, fear and desire double for one another and play across the structures of otherness, complicating its politics.

Recently I've read several articles about the photographic texts of Robert Mapplethorpe – especially his inscription of the nude, black male – all written by black critics or cultural practitioners.[3] These essays properly begin by identifying in Mapplethorpe's work the tropes of fetishization, the fragmentation of the black image and its objectification, as the forms of their appropriation within the white, gay gaze. But, as I read, I know that something else is going on as well in both the production and the reading of those texts. The continuous circling around Mapplethorpe's work is not exhausted by being able to place him as the white fetishistic gay photographer; and this is because it is also marked by the surreptitious return of desire – that deep ambivalence of identification which makes the categories in which we have previously thought and argued about black cultural politics and the black cultural text extremely problematic. This brings to the surface the unwelcome fact that a great deal of black politics, constructed, addressed and developed directly in relation to questions of race and ethnicity, has been predicated on the assumption that the categories of gender and sexuality would stay the same and remain fixed and secured. What the new politics of represent-ation does is to put that into question, crossing the questions of racism irrevocably with questions of sexuality. That is what is so disturbing, finally, to many of our settled political habits about *Passion of Remembrance*. This double fracturing entails a different kind of politics because, as we know, black radical politics has frequently been stabilized around particular conceptions of black masculinity, which are only now being put into question by black women and black gay men. At certain points, black politics has also been underpinned by a deep absence or more typically an evasive silence with reference to class.

Another element inscribed in the new politics of representation has to do with the question of ethnicity. I am familiar with all the dangers of 'ethnicity' as a concept and have written myself about the fact that ethnicity, in the form of a culturally constructed sense of Englishness and a particularly closed, exclusive and regressive form of English national identity, is one of the core characteristics of British racism today.[4] I am also well aware that the politics of antiracism has often constructed itself in terms of a contestation of 'multi-ethnicity' or 'multi-culturalism'. On the other hand, as the politics of representation around the black subject shifts, I think we will begin to see a renewed contestation over the meaning of the term 'ethnicity' itself.

If the black subject and black experience are not stabilized by Nature or by some other essential guarantee, then it must be the case that they are constructed historically, culturally, politically – and the concept which refers to this is 'ethnicity'. The term ethnicity acknowledges the place of history, language and culture in the construction of subjectivity and identity, as well as the fact that all discourse is placed, positioned, situated, and all knowledge is contextual. Representation is possible only because enunciation is always produced within codes which have a history, a position within the discursive formations of a particular space and time. The displacement of the 'centred' discourses of the West entails putting in question its universalist character and its transcendental claims to speak for everyone, while being itself everywhere and nowhere. The fact that this grounding of ethnicity in difference was deployed, in the discourse of racism, as a means of disavowing the realities of racism and repression does not mean that we can permit the term to be permanently colonized. That appropriation will have to be contested, the term disarticulated from its position in the discourse of 'multiculturalism' and transcoded, just as we previously had to recuperate the term 'black', from its place in a system of negative equivalences. The new politics of representation therefore also sets in motion an ideological contestation around the term, 'ethnicity'. But in order to pursue that movement further, we will have to retheorize the concept of *difference*.

It seems to me that, in the various practices and discourses of black cultural production, we are beginning to see constructions of just such a new conception of ethnicity: a new cultural politics which engages rather than suppresses *difference* and which depends, in part, on the cultural construction of new ethnic identities. Difference, like representation, is also a slippery, and therefore, contested concept. There is the 'difference' which makes a radical and unbridgeable separation: and there is a 'difference' which is positional, conditional and conjunctural, closer to Derrida's notion of *différance*, though if we are concerned to maintain a politics it cannot be defined exclusively in terms of an infinite sliding of the signifier. We still have a great deal of work to do to *decouple* ethnicity, as it functions in the dominant discourse, from its equivalence with nationalism, imperialism, racism and the state, which are the points of attachment around which a distinctive British or, more accurately, English ethnicity have been constructed. Nevertheless, I think such a project is not only possible but necessary. Indeed, this decoupling of ethnicity from the violence of the state is implicit in some of the new forms of cultural practice that are going on in films like *Passion* and *Handsworth Songs*. We are beginning to think about how to represent a non-coercive and a more diverse conception of ethnicity, to set against the embattled, hegemonic conception of 'Englishness' which, under Thatcherism, stabilizes so much of the dominant political and cultural discourses, and which, because it is hegemonic, does not represent itself as an ethnicity at all.

This marks a real shift in the point of contestation, since it is no longer only between antiracism and multiculturalism but inside the notion of ethnicity itself. What is involved is the splitting of the notion of ethnicity between, on the one hand the dominant notion which connects it to nation and 'race' and on the other hand what I think is the beginning of a positive conception of the ethnicity of the margins, of the periphery. That is to say, a recognition that we all speak from a particular place, out of a particular history, out of a particular experience, a particular culture, without being contained by that position as 'ethnic artists' or film-makers. We are all, in that sense, *ethnically* located and our ethnic identities are crucial to our subjective sense of who we are. But this is also a recognition that this is not an ethnicity which is doomed to survive, as Englishness was, only by marginalizing, dispossessing, displacing and forgetting other ethnicities. This precisely is the politics of ethnicity predicated on difference and diversity.

The final point which I think is entailed in this new politics of representation has to do with an awareness of the black experience as a *diaspora* experience, and the consequences which this carries for the process of unsettling, recombination, hybridization and 'cut-and-mix' – in short, the process of cultural *diaspora-ization* (to coin an ugly term) which it implies. In the case of the young black British films and film-makers under discussion, the diaspora experience is certainly profoundly fed and nourished by, for example, the emergence of Third World cinema; by the African experience; the connection with Afro-Caribbean experience; and the deep inheritance of complex systems of representation and aesthetic traditions from Asian and African culture. But, in spite of these rich cultural 'roots', the new cultural politics is operating on new and quite distinct ground – specifically, contestation over what it means to be 'British'. The relation of this cultural politics to the past; to its different 'roots' is profound, but complex. It cannot be simple or unmediated. It is (as a film like *Dreaming Rivers* reminds us) complexly mediated and transformed by memory, fantasy and desire. Or, as even an explicitly political film like *Handsworth Songs* clearly suggests, the relation is inter-textual – mediated, through a variety of other 'texts'. There can, therefore, be no simple 'return' or 'recovery' of the ancestral past which is not re-experienced through the categories of the present: no base for creative enunciation in a simple reproduction of traditional forms which are not transformed by the technologies and the identities of the present. This is something that was signalled as early as a film like *Blacks Britannica* and as recently as Paul Gilroy's important book, *There Ain't No Black in the Union Jack*.[5] Fifteen years ago we didn't care, or at least I didn't care, whether there was any black in the Union Jack. Now not only do we care, we must. [. . .]

Notes

This article is based on a talk delivered to the conference *Black Film, British Cinema*, Institute of Contemporary Arts, London, February 1988.

1 The Yorkshire town of Dewsbury became the focus of national attention when white parents withdrew their children from a local school with predominantly Asian pupils, on the grounds that 'English' culture was no longer taught on the curriculum. The contestation of multicultural education from the right also underpinned the controversies around Bradford headmaster Ray Honeyford. See, Paul Gordon, 'The New Right, race and education': *Race and Class*, **24**(3), Winter 1987.

2 Gayatri C. Spivak, *In Other Worlds: essays in cultural politics*, London, Methuen, 1987.

3 Kobena Mercer, 'Imaging the black man's sex' in Patricia Holland *et al.* (eds) *Photography/Politics: Two*. Comedia/Methuen, 1987 and various articles in *Ten.8*, **22**, 1986, an issue on 'Black experiences' edited by David A. Bailey.

4 Stuart Hall, 'Racism and reaction' in *Five Views on Multi-Racial Britain*, London, Commission for Racial Equality, 1978.

5 Paul Gilroy, *There Ain't No Black in the Union Jack: the cultural politics of race and nation*, London, Hutchinson, 1987.

12 BRITISH ASIAN MUSLIMS AND THE RUSHDIE AFFAIR

TARIQ MODOOD

In 1989 'Rushdie' became a racial taunt in Britain. Prison warders were reported as reading passages from *The Satanic Verses* (hereafter *SV*) to a Muslim prisoner, and racial tension and racist attacks in Muslim/Asian areas increased. While some Muslims saw 'the Rushdie affair' in terms of the Crusades, liberal intellectuals, while deploring the growing racism, saw it as a call to arms on behalf of the Enlightenment. Whatever the cause – racism, liberalism or passionate bibliophilia – no minority in the context of British race relations has been as friendless as Muslims in spring 1989 (not helped of course by their failure to disassociate themselves from the Ayatollah's *fatwa*).[1] Yet Muslims did not crumble in the face of this widespread and at times hysterical opposition. They unashamedly remained indignant, regardless of the reputation of infamy that their anger gave rise to.[2] Where, one has to ask, did that anger and defiance come from?

Muslims in a European society

There are now probably over a million Muslims (i.e. people born and brought up as Muslims) in Britain and this figure is bound to grow if for no other reason than that Muslims are much younger than the rest of the population and have large families.[3] About two-thirds are of South Asian origin: over 400,000 from Pakistan, perhaps 120,000 from Bangladesh and up to 100,000 each from India and East Africa. The remainder are from the Middle East (120,000 Arabs, 75,000 Turks and Cypriots, 50,000 Iranians) and a small number from black Africa. While it would be foolish to suppose that all these form a single religio-political group it ought not to be overlooked that they form part of a larger European presence. The number of Muslims in both France (primarily N. African Arabs) and West Germany (mainly Turks) is more than double that in the UK and the total in the European Community is over six million.[4] The anti-*SV* street demonstrations were largely confined to the UK and achieved their intensity by the passion of a South Asian Islam missing in other countries, but it would be false to suppose that the conditions for Muslim action are singular to Britain. The depth of French Arabophobia, where cultural-racism has a greater intensity than colour-racism, and the current celebration of German ethnicity suggest the very opposite – indeed, the row in France about the right of Muslim girls to wear headscarves in state schools has been dubbed 'the French Rushdie affair'. Our own Rushdie affair should therefore not be seen as a pathology or as a once-and-for-all matter but as the first of what will probably be a series of major political battles to determine the shape of the rights of Muslims in European society – and, indeed, as part of the international struggle between a hegemonic West and rebellious Muslims reviving from a slumber with dreams of past glories.[5]

I shall confine my attention to UK South Asian Muslims, and particularly the Pakistanis settled in fairly large-sized communities in towns and cities such as Bradford and Birmingham. It may be an exaggeration – though not a wholly wild one – to suppose that they represent the leading edge of a six-million force in Europe but it is undeniable that it is they who are the force behind the *SV* demonstrations both nationally and internationally, that they are the most charged with Islamic fervour and that they are the group that British society is currently being forced to adjust to or defeat.

Throughout the 1980s, of the nine non-white groups identified in the Labour Force Survey, Pakistanis and Bangladeshis have suffered the highest rates of unemployment, have the lowest number of educational qualifications and the highest profile in manual work; and this is true in each respect not just for women but also men, and not just for the middle-aged (the first generation) but also the young. They have had the most adverse impact from immigration laws and rules, they have the worst housing and suffer from the highest levels of attacks on person and property. Of all groups, Pakistanis are least found in London and the South-East for they came mainly to work in the run-down mills and factories of the North and Midlands and have in consequence suffered most from the 'shake-out' of the early 1980s and benefited least from the recent growth. If a racial underclass exists in Britain, here it is. The first step in understanding the anti-*SV* militancy is to recognize that we are talking about a semi-industrialized, newly urbanized working class community that is only one generation away from rural peasantry. For despite the explanations offered by the pundits – political manipulation, fundamentalism or even unqualified racism – it is an incontrovertible fact that the demonstrations and the book-burnings were above all spontaneous working-class anger and hurt pride. How can it be that the most socially deprived and racially harassed group should bear all this and explode in anger on an issue of religious honour? Socio-economic categories, like sociologically reductive conceptions of race and racism, barely begin to help us understand the phenomenon. To do that it is necessary to make at least a brief incursion into ethnic history, for the explanation lies in a deep-rooted conservatism and a religious devotionalism that cannot be picked up by an ahistorical sociology or a purely materialistic history.

Besieged conservatism

The Muslim world has created many historical empires and its relation to the West has not always been that of an inferior; on the contrary, continental Europeans can remember a time when they trembled before the conquering might of Islam, and Muslims can remember when Europe was synonymous with backwardness and they were the leaders in civilization and technology, one of the legacies of which was the renaissance of Western Europe. It has, like any civilization, faced major epochal challenges. In the early medieval period it was a theological intellectualism. It was defeated by the establishment of a dogmatic unifying Islam which proved disastrous for philosophical, critical and, ultimately, religious thinking, the price of which is paid to this day. In the early modern period the problem came to be conceived by many as one of eclecticism. It was felt by many, such as Shah Waliullah of Delhi (1703–64), that the spread of Muslim power and the mass conversions had brought into Islam a wide range of beliefs, superstitions, religious practices and social customs of the new Muslims and of conquered peoples such as the Hindus, such that Islam was no longer the simple, rational, anti-idolatrous, egalitarian faith that had made history. In this sense of impurity and decline are the origins of the major modern reform movements: fundamentalism and modernism. Each insisted on the need to break with historically received orthodoxy and to return to a fresh study of the Quran and the Prophet as exemplar either in order to re-enact it and shut out all other influences (fundamentalism) or in order to distil its universal message from its historical manifestation so as to apply it to new historical circumstances (modernism).

It is worth noting, if only to puncture the arrogance of European progressivism, that Islam enlightenment in the form of Shah Waliullah's historical contextualism preceded its European counterpart. These reform movements were, however, born at a time of political weakness: Muslim power in India was being thretened by the rising religious and political militancy of the Hindu Marathas and the Sikhs (itself partly a reaction to Islamic re-assertiveness) and within the next 100 years virtually the whole Muslim world was to come under European hegemony and, in the case of India, colonial rule.

From that point onwards Muslim thought, whether reformist or conservative, was mixed up with a response to the West. Modernist reform came to mean acceptance of existing political realities and adoption of a Western framework of ideas. The response of the more orthodox as well as the uneducated, on the other hand, was a retreat into a dogmatic citadel in order to hold on to something uncorrupted by the West in the context of comprehensive political subordination. For the first time in history the Muslim world found itself totally unable in the realm of ideas to defend itself against the aggressor, let alone to impress the aggressor with any form of living, as opposed to historical, brilliance. In the last two centuries Islam, in so far as it was capable of putting up any show at all, seems to have lost all the intellectual and ideological battles. Yet it has survived. Its survival and resilience lay in the fact that its masses were not easily overawed by the new civilization. It survived in the stubborn conservatism of the religious establishment and the ordinary people, above all the peasantry, who retained, indeed nourished, a collective memory of Islamic hegemony. They hung on to their Islam by a blind adherence to custom, tradition and religion.[6] The price of this defiant conservatism which allowed little space for critical thought has been little, slow and hesitant renewal of internal traditions, and only a superficial encounter with Western ideas, for the latter have not been seen as a resource but a threat. Forms of behaviour, of course, outlive their usefulness (nationalism in Western Europe is a good example) but it does not mean that they automatically disappear (Ulster is a good example). People nurtured over generations in a besieged conservatism cannot easily give it up (my father can remember when preachers in Delhi denounced electricity as unIslamic; he therefore is disturbed but not surprised when he hears sermons against television – the medium, not the message – in Brent).[7] They are unlikely to give it up where they perceive Western secular hegemony to be undefeated and certainly not when it is audaciously contemptuous and stridently intolerant of their core values. They will not be tempted into lusher pastures when they experience, on the one hand, racist rejection and violence, and on the other hand pressures to change fast and into a culture that they deem to be decadent and a mortal enemy to Islam and decency.

Continuity and change

Before we look further into the religious–political make-up of the British Asian Muslim, especially Pakistani, community, it would be useful to bear in mind some other indicators of whether distinctively Asian attitudes are or are not being reproduced in Britain. For the kind of defensive traditionalism I am postulating is obviously not confined to religion in any narrow sense; if Asian Muslim attitudes are undergoing change on a wide front then religion will not be immune, and, conversely, if those attitudes are showing relatively small shifts between generations this too will have implications for the whole of community relations. I do not have the space to review it here but there is now considerable and growing evidence that on a whole range of issues to do with sex, gender roles, arranged marriage, mixed marriages, female dress, family authority and honour, extended family and preservation of cultural identity, second generation attitudes are closer to those of their parents and hence to their peers in the sub-continent than to their British peers.[8] Sex is absolutely central. In a secular, hedonistic society sex is usually seen as a paradigm of pleasure and of self-chosen relationships, some of which may turn out to be serious. Asian and especially Asian Muslim views are typically pre-modern. While Asian culture has a strong strain of romantic fantasy (most notably evidenced in films) the primary use of sex is to sustain one's, and ultimately the groom's, family. One's happiness is typically not postulated as independent of one's family's well-being. The average Pakistani in Britain, for instance, feels a strong sense of not only belonging to an extended family but also to a *birādari* (kinship group) of which a branch is in Britain but the centre of which is in Pakistan.[9] Even where this feeling is relatively weak amongst the young, that may be because they are young rather than because they are simply outgrowing it: as they get married and slowly become involved in the financial affairs and decision-making of the *birādari* they may come to have a more palpable sense of belonging.

I do not want to exaggerate the continuity (for there is genuine change and adaptation) nor to encourage a static conception of culture (that would be false and a disservice to good community relations) nor to deny that there are a significant number of exceptions (middle-class London is full of them). The evidence, however, not only supports my general thesis but intimates a further interesting development. It is perhaps a cliché, post-Rushdie, to say that the 1960s liberal assumptions about immigration and 'melting-pot' seem facile compared with the perceptiveness of Enoch Powell on, say, native English chauvinism and Asian community formation[10] (these can of course be separated from his prescription of massive repatriation or prophecy of racial war). What to date has been less noticed is how inappropriate the American three-generation model of immigrants (derived from white experience in a country that was not as a whole hostile to their presence) is to Asian experience in Britain. That model postulates that the immigrants slave and self-sacrifice to see their children succeed in the new country; the second generation assimilate and conform to succeed; the grandchildren, assured of acceptance and advancement, have a romantic yearning for their ancestral roots. British racism, however, extorts such a high price for the success of the second stage that Asian teenagers – in Bradford, Brick Lane and Southall – are beginning to say 'so far it is we who have had to make all the changes, now it is the turn of the British to change to accept the fact of our existence'.[11] This new ethnic assertiveness is likely to be more than a teenage fashion for it arises from genuine social conditions and a sense of threat to identity and will challenge the stereotype that Asians are passive and accepting.

Deobandis, Barelvis and Fundamentalists

One cannot discuss British Muslim political perspectives without discussing 'fundamentalism'. It is the word on every lip and journalistic pen and it is what editors want to know about when they commission articles. I have three comments to make on fundamentalism. First, I shall offer a definition; secondly, I shall contend that fundamentalism is virtually non-existent among Asian Muslims and played an insignificant part in the demonstrations and book-burnings; and, finally, that there is a real likelihood that fundamentalism will now become attractive to a portion of Muslim youth.

The term 'fundamentalism' originally arose to describe the literalist attitude of certain American Protestant sects to the Bible. As such, it cannot be directly transposed on to Muslims for the vast majority of Muslims, including those in Britain, are Sunnis who, incidentally, owe no allegiance whatsoever to Shiite Ayatollahs, and who, unlike the Shia, take all passages in the Quran literally rather than metaphorically. I understand fundamentalism in Sunni Islam to consist of the following beliefs:

(i) to recapture the essence of one's faith one needs to return to the source, namely the Quran and prophet Muhammad as the perfect model of a Muslim in personal life and public affairs and to reject all other historical accretions and contemporary norms as un-Islamic;

(ii) this source is not just a moral vision or a body of ethical principles but a comprehensive and indivisible way of life and the sole legitimate basis for positive law in all its details, all social institutions and all aspects of personal life and with appropriate leadership and effort can be implemented in any time or place for it is of universal authority, eternally valid and yet capable of a single correct interpretation;

(iii) no modern society, including most if not all the Muslim states, is or is endeavouring to be Islamic and Muslims in all societies, especially where they are a majority, are under an obligation to work to create an Islamic state.

A Sunni fundamentalist, then, believes that Islam is a totally systematic, self-sufficient set of ideas that owes nothing to history and can be enacted in a single uniform way of life which is the life that God meant for humankind and which it is the duty of all Muslims to approximate to as much as possible and in as many spheres of life as the distribution of political power between Muslims and non-Muslims allows (though Muslims have a further duty to improve this distribution in favour of 'true' Muslims as circumstances allow).

My Sunni (in the British context, let's say Muslim) fundamentalist is undoubtedly an ideal type and the definition is offered as such and not as a set of necessary and sufficient conditions.[12] Nevertheless, I believe that my definition is far superior to the popular usage when the term usually means no more than 'militant Muslim'. [. . .] I doubt if there are more than a few thousand fundamentalists in Britain and most of them are likely to be in London rather than Bradford, in offices rather than factories. Asian fundamentalists are urban, educated and middle-class: British Asian Muslims have rural peasant origins and are only now coming to a point where they can produce individuals for whom the ideological rigour of fundamentalism and studied rejection of Western ideas is attractive and possible. If then the angry book-burners are not fundamentalists what are they?

The majority of Pakistanis in this country are Barelvis; the majority of the remainder are Deobandis. Both these sects have their origins in the reformist movement set in motion by Shah Waliullah but came into existence in post-1857 British India. They were concerned with ways of maintaining Islam as a living social force in a non-Muslim polity and ruling culture. The Deobandis, taking their name from a school founded in Deoband, near Delhi, came to focus primarily on education and on keeping alive in the seminaries Muslim medieval theological and juristic doctrines. They saw politics as an unequal struggle and tried to be as independent as possible of the British state. Their anti-Britishness took the form of withdrawal and non-cooperation rather than of active confrontation but they took great care to shut out not only British and Hindu influences but also Shia. Through active proselytization they built up a mass following as well as an international reputation in Islamic learning and more recently a world-wide organization called Tablīgh-i-Jamaat. It is represented in Britain with a national headquarters in Dewsbury, W. Yorkshire, and has an active presence in Birmingham. The Deobandis currently show all signs of remaining true to their traditions that a good Muslim should seek in-depth knowledge of the doctrines of Islam, create a self-sufficient community and strengthen the faith of or convert lost souls. The Deobandis have no notion of an Islamic state and studiously avoid a clash with the powers that be.

The Barelvis are more numerous nationally, form the core of Bradford's Muslim working class and are part of the traditions of Sufi mysticism and Indian folk-religions. Deriving their name from Ahmed Riza Khan of Bareilly (1856–1921) theirs is an Islam of personalities; the Prophet Muhammad, for instance, is imbued with a metaphysical significance and devotional reverence that goes well beyond what some would regard as orthodox and has been called 'the mythification of Muhammad'.[13] Their religious heroes are not confined to the Prophet and the early Arab Muslims but include a galaxy of minor and major saints who, contrary to more reformist Islam, can intercede with God on behalf of petitioners. Additionally they hold dear many customs and superstitions that have no justification in the Quran but have been acquired from other sources, usually from the rich soil of India, and are no doubt a reminder of the religion of their forefathers before conversion to Islam during the period of Muslim rule. Their easy-going Islam (in matters of doctrine and worship; they are even more puritanical on matters of sex than other Muslim sects) is also reflected in attitudes to politics.

While, unlike the Deobandis, they are not apolitical they, unlike the fundamentalists, have no political grand plan; under the Raj they co-operated with and were favoured by British rule, were not at the forefront in the Independence movement and it has been said that 'flexibility is a feature of their behaviour'.[14] Their religious passion is usually aroused when their doctrines and forms of worship are denounced by Deobandis and fundamentalists as un-Islamic historical accretions. This intense sectarianism has led to and continues to lead to serious violence in Pakistan and there are not many towns in England which have mosques and have not witnessed such a clash.

The leading fundamentalist movement in South Asia, the Jamaat-i-Islami, was founded in 1941 by Sayyid Abul Ala Mawdudi (1903–1979), one of the leading and most influential Muslim thinkers of this century. My earlier definition of fundamentalism sums up this philosophical outlook. In Pakistan, Jamaat is both a religious movement and an overt political party with a highly authoritarian Leninist cadre structure. While it has never made any electoral headway it has come to be a force in the universities and the education system, in the officer ranks of the army and civil police. Mawdudi's ethical vision and intellectually systematic representation of Islam were attractive to the idealistic educated young when in contrast the Westernized ruling and commercial class, while paying lip-service to Islam, not only seemed to offer no alternative ethical vision of society, but seemed to lack standards of public service and personal morality. It has been said of the first decade of Pakistan's history that 'the liberals are strong (i.e. are in power), but liberalism is weak'.[15] The remarks fit not just the country as a whole but the liberals themselves: not only did they fail to impress their outlook upon the country but their personal convictions were too weak even to guide their own behaviour.

With this background of religious backwardness at the bottom and secular hypocrisy and selfishness at the top Mawdudi, with a Platonic contempt for democracy, tried to create an authentic Islamic intelligentsia to rival the existing Westernized one. Jamaat became the leading ideological force among the non-Westernized urban middle and lower-middle classes of Pakistan with influence and support in many other Muslim countries, above all in the Egyptian Muslim Brotherhood and the Saudi Arabian establishment from whom it has received generous funding. Originally composed of idealists with high standards of personal integrity, its agitprop tactics played a key role in thrusting Islamic issues into the centre of Pakistani politics, but came to involve it increasingly in social disorder and the toppling of governments. As a result, on the one hand the leadership of the Jamaat in the 1970s and 1980s passed into non-ideological hands and it became extremely thuggish with university branches becoming gun-toting fascist paramilitary organizations. On the other hand, under Zia, the leadership became part of the circle of government and Jamaat enjoyed considerable government patronage and moved from religious radicalism to become an arch-conservative religious legitimizer of a military dictatorship.[16] The Jamaat is represented in Britain by the Islamic Foundation in Leicester and the UK Islamic Mission. It is very small in number compared with the Deobandis or Barelvis and has negligible working class community links, but with Saudi money and support it is better nationally and internationally organized than the other two. Its two organizations are avowedly propagandistic and represent as far as I can tell the old-style idealism, but within the constraints of Saudi political and international interests.

Pragmatism and religious politics

South Asian Muslims, especially Pakistanis, in Britain are then represented by three tendencies: Deobandi apolitical conservative revivalists, Barelvi devotionalists with a pro-British Raj history and a small network of Saudi-backed middle-class fundamentalists.[17] How is it then that they can be portrayed as a radical assault upon British values, a threat to the state and an enemy to good race relations? Informed opinion seems to be that Muslims put the dogmas of Islam above a value for the norms of political conduct and debate as developed in a civil society; that Muslims insist on mixing up religion and politics. There is, however, far more error than truth in this as once again a quick glance at Pakistan will show. The Pakistani electorate is as thoroughly pragmatic and non-ideological as it is possible to be. Pakistanis think it unthinkable that politics should challenge what after all is the grounding of their society, Islam; but they do not expect politics to be deduced from religious propositions or read out of texts. They see Islam as the core of their cultural heritage and a source of national identity rather than as a rule-book to be put into practice. They expect a harmony at some abstract level between Islam and politics (as we all expect a harmony between ethics and politics) but have no ideological formula for how to bring this about and they certainly have never desired the state to be led by religionists. Hence the consistently poor showing of the Jamaat and other religious parties in every election and the absence of popular support for Zia's Islamicization. The ambivalent and pragmatic understanding of the relations between religion and politics that I am pointing to is well illustrated by the fact that though Z. A. Bhutto found it necessary to call his political programme *Islamic Socialism* he in fact won the 1970 election on a socialist platform despite 113 *fatwas* against socialism (so much for the power of *fatwas* in politics; and these, unlike in the Rushdie case, were decrees of their own spiritual leaders not a Shiite Ayatollah). The

Barelvis, I might add, no less than the Deobandis steadfastly take the view that spiritual mentors (*pirs*) have no right to pronounce on political matters.

This pragmatic approach is very evident in the participation of Asian Muslims in British politics as has been acutely observed by John Rex. Rex recognized the different sectarian strands among Muslims in Birmingham (its 80,000 Muslims are the single largest settlement in Britain), but argues that while all are deeply antipathetic to British sexual habits and modes of family life and anxious about such influences upon their children from British schools; believe that Islam is a higher form of morality than that practised by most of the natives; and are indifferent to ideological socialism and capitalism; they nevertheless are all deeply accommodationist when it comes to politics. The pragmatic approach in politics could not be better evidenced than by the fact that despite having a social ethic that is close to that of the moral right, they overwhelmingly support the Labour Party as the best vehicle to defend their material interests. Rex concludes with the prediction that though the issue of schooling could become a difficult political issue, in general 'Muslim society in Britain will be characterized by a political quietism qualified by a drive to sustain and promote a distinctive type of marriage and family life.'[18]

Based on the evidence of the mid-1980s, a time in any case when Asian Muslims were overshadowed by black activism and the emergence of Indian economic success, this was a somewhat complacent but not an unreasonable conclusion.[19] Judging by the conventional understanding of the Rushdie affair one would suppose that the fault in Rex's analysis was that he failed to make allowance for fundamentalism. In fact the anger against *SV* had nothing to do with fundamentalism – or indeed Khomeni. Virtually every practising Muslim was offended by passages from the book and shocked that it was written by a Muslim of whom till then the Asian community were proud. Rushdie has argued that the *mullahs* whipped up the ordinary Muslims for their own political motives.[20] The truth is that all the religious zealots had to do was simply quote from *SV* for anger, shame and hurt to be felt. It is important to be clear that *SV* was not objected to as an intellectual critique of their faith (libraries are full of those); for the average Muslim the vulgar language, the explicit sexual imagery, the attribution of lustful motives – without any evidence – to the holy Prophet, in short the reduction of their religion to a selfish sexual appetite[21] was no more a contribution to literary discourse than pissing upon the Bible is a theological argument. While it was a member of staff of the Islamic Foundation in Leicester that first alerted the Muslim world to the book, and while in Britain quiet representations to the publishers and the government were made by the middle-class Asian and Arab Muslims of London, it was not until the Bradford Barelvis picked up the issue that the public registered something was up. The passion and intensity of the street demonstrations was a product of Barelvi devotionalism, which normally even other Muslims think is excessive in the exalted status it confers on Muhammad. It was the cultists not the Calvinists, that were the driving force of the protest – and more by their example than by any national organization. While just about the whole of Britain was denouncing the fundamentalists, in fact the Sunni fundamentalists, either of their own will or because of Saudi pique at Iran, were among the first to begin to tone things down. As for the Shia fundamentalists, their small number and lack of organic links with the wider Muslim community here makes them incapable of taking the lead.

What perhaps cannot be denied and is worth noting is that by his intervention the Ayatollah rose in Asian estimation. Not because the majority wished Rushdie killed, let alone wanted to kill him. It was because he was considered to have stood up for Islamic dignity and sensibilities against the West and in contrast to Arab silence. Initially, Asian Muslims had looked to Saudi Arabia as the spiritual leader of Sunni Islam to speak out. They were baffled by the silence and dismayed when they recalled the trouble that that government had gone to to prevent the showing of *Death of a Princess* on British television: were the Guardians of the Holy places more concerned with the honour of the royal family than of Muhammad?[22] The group, however, that Asian Muslims felt most let down by was the London secular Asian intelligentsia (a minority only of whom are of course Muslim). Not only did they not even attempt to act as an intermediary and prevent a polarization – the least that they could have done – but some of their leading lights joined the public vilification of Muslims. Collective declarations were issued deploring the actions of 'fundamentalists' and groups were set up with titles such as 'Women Against Fundamentalism' thus reinforcing the dismissive tactic that all assertive or angry Muslims were just extreme fundamentalists. By using the media's language they reinforced a racist stereotype of Muslims as fundamentalists, which, if excusable in those who have no first-hand knowledge of Muslims, in Asians and Muslims was shocking. It reveals the frightening power of media caricatures over knowledge gained by direct acquaintance. Of course the shock of the *fatwa* led to confusion and mistakes on all sides, and an understandable fear for the life of Salman Rushdie emotionally clouded many a judgement. Nevertheless, the ease with which the popular stereotypes of Muslims found a home in the minds of the Asian intelligentsia reveals a profound division which may well have long-term consequences which Britain may come to regret. In any case, the creation of an Anglicized middle/intellectual class which does not understand and/or feel responsible for its own ethnic working class is, I believe, the single most worrying trend in the Muslim and other Asian communities.

I argued earlier that the opportunity for fundamentalism in Pakistan arose from the inadequacies of an intelligentsia that had cut itself off from its roots and that the initial fundamentalist project was to create an alternative intelligentsia that was rooted in Islam rather than in Western culture. My expectation is that this too, in so far as it is possible in a Western society, will be the focus of Muslim fundamentalist activity here. Reports from all over the country suggest that Asian Muslim youth are deserting the bars and clubs and returning to the mosques and religious classes.[23] By the summer of 1989 it was the youths who were marching in the streets and looking for action though their initial reaction had been cooler than their fathers'. With the education and social experience that Britain has given them, and will give those who are currently at school, they may well find the faith of their parents too simple in its devotionalism and too accommodating in its political outlook. As Francis Robinson has incisively argued, we should

> expect support from the Jamaat in Britain to be proportionately rather greater than in Pakistan. First because here all Muslims are confronted directly by the challenges of Western civilization, and to these the Jamaat offers the most complete and systematic answer. And second because Muslims in Britain are favourably placed socio-logically. Religious fundamentalism seems to flourish amongst those who are in a state of transition from one society to another . . .[24]

The Rushdie affair was the hour of the simple devotionalist: we may yet have the hour of the educated fundamentalist. Nature abhors a vacuum and the desertion of the secular intelligentsia has created one. No longer can they be looked to as role-models let alone for moral leadership; their example, instead, is being used by the traditionalists as further evidence of how 'Westoxification' corrupts. My personal view, however, is that fundamentalism, at least as a political force, say, as an Islamic party,[25] will remain as an ideological fringe and will continue to suffer from its dependency upon the ultra-conservative, indeed, feudal Saudi Arabian establishment. One of the many unfortunate consequences of *SV* may, however, be that the not unreasonable assumption that a couple of generations of experience in the West would lead Muslims, in line with the Jews, to develop a liberal modernist interpretation of their faith can no longer, to put it at its mildest, be taken for granted.[26] Our philosophies of race relations will, however, I believe, be radically recast in the 1990s and Islamic reassertion and communalism will be one of the primary reasons. It is important that Muslims be in this debate. I would therefore like to devote my final section to considering critically some aspects of the concept of racial equality and minority status and their relationship to the Muslim experience.

Racial equality and minority rights

'Fight racism, not Rushdie': stickers bearing this slogan were worn by many who wanted to be on the same side as the Muslims.[27] It was well meant but betrayed a poverty of understanding. It is a strange idea that when somebody is shot in the leg one says 'Never mind, the pain in the elbow is surely worse.' The root problem is that contemporary antiracism defines people in terms of their colour; Muslims – suffering all the problems that antiracists identify – hardly ever think of themselves in terms of their colour. And so, in terms of their own being, Muslims feel most acutely those problems that the antiracists are blind to; and respond weakly to those challenges that the antiracists want to meet with most force. And there is no way out of this impasse if we remain wedded to a concept of racism that sees only colour discrimination as a cause and material deprivation as a result. We need concepts of race and racism that can critique socio-cultural environments which devalue people because of their physical differences but also because of their membership of a cultural minority and, critically, where the two overlap and create a double disadvantage.[28] Such concepts should help us to understand that any oppressed group feels its oppression most according to those dimensions of its being which *it* (not the oppressor) values the most; moreover, it will resist its oppression from those dimensions of its being from which it derives its greatest collective psychological strength. For this and further reasons I shall come to below, Muslims cannot easily, confidently or systematically assume the moral high ground on the issue of colour racism; their sense of being and their surest convictions about their devaluation by others comes from their historical community of faith and their critique of 'the West'. Authentic 'anti-racism' for Muslims therefore will inevitably have a religious dimension and take a form in which it is integrated to the rest of Muslim concerns. Antiracism begins (i.e. ought to begin) by accepting oppressed groups on their own terms (knowing full well that these will change and evolve) not by imposing a spurious identity and asking them to fight in the name of that.[29] The new strength among Muslim youth in, for example, not tolerating racial harassment, owes no less to Islamic re-assertion than to metropolitan antiracism: people don't turn and run when something they care about is under attack. The racist taunt 'Rushdie!' rouses more self-defence than 'black bastard!'

Muslims need to be part of the re-thinking I speak of and at the same time must admit that they have something not only to teach but to learn from the antiracist, for Muslim thinking too is inadequate to the current situation.[30] The Quranic teaching is that people are to be valued in terms of virtue not colour or race. Muslims insist that there is no divinely favoured race and that the Quran is God's message to the whole of mankind. They take pride in the fact that Islam is a genuine multi-ethnic religion (Christianity is the only other) and point to the fact that one of the first converts to Islam was Bilal, a black slave (Arab trade in black slaves having pre-dated the same by Europeans) and that in Muslim history there have been several black rulers and generals in racially mixed societies. This then is the standard Muslim view on racial equality. Like all 'colour-blind' approaches it has two weaknesses.

First, it is too weak to prevent racial and ethnic prejudice. While it was strong enough, unlike its Christian and secular Western counterparts, to prevent the development of official and popular ideologies of racism, it is not the case that Islam has banished racism. Arab racism is such that most Pakistanis would prefer to work in Britain than in Saudi Arabia for a higher income; racist humiliations from shop-keepers, taxi-drivers, catering staff and so on have become a regular feature of the pilgrimage to Mecca for the diverse ethnic groups of Islam. Asians have no fewer racial stereotypes about white and blacks than these groups have about Asians or about each other.[31]

The second weakness flows from the first. A 'colour-blind' approach is unable to sanction any programme of positive action to tackle the problem once it is acknowledged to exist. The 1976 Race Relations Act has provisions for, say, employers to identify under-representation of racial minorities in the workforce and to target within certain limits those groups for recruitment. It is not obvious that strictly Muslim thinking can consistently support this. Some very recent Muslim position statements seem to express a reluctance for, what is essential to positive action, heightening racial categories. Indeed, one goes as far as to say that 'we believe that it is very unhelpful to look at human relations in Britain on the basis of race', while another asserts 'there is only one race, the human race'.[32] This is, as I have said, because Muslims (and indeed most other minority communities) do not see themselves in terms of colour and do not want a public identity that emphasizes colour. The way out is a concept of race that not only allows minorities a purchase upon their mode of being but, equally importantly, also upon how white British society defines them – that is to say upon their mode of oppression. While radical anti-racists are, as it were, religion-blind and culture-blind, it would be foolish for a non-white group not to recognize the existence of colour racism and how it, as well as culture racism, affects them and their life-chances. For that would rob them of effective strategies as well as alliances with other non-white groups to oppose the various dimensions of racism and its effects.[33] To develop such thinking one cannot – *pace* fundamentalism – rely solely on Quranic concepts.

I believe that we are slowly learning that our concepts of racial equality need to be tuned not just to guaranteeing that individuals of different hues are treated alike but also to the fact that Britain now encompasses communities with different norms, cultures and religions. Hence racial equality cannot always mean that our public institutions and the law itself must treat everybody as if they were the same – for that will usually mean treating everybody by the norms and convenience of the majority. Local authorities have been discovering this, especially with regards to schools, usually in the glare of adverse publicity, and English common law has quietly and sensibly gone a long way down this road.[34] Yet here, too, our thinking is far from clear. Some Muslims believe that they have the answer. What is urged is some variation of the *millat* system, a form of religious-based communal pluralism which reached its most developed form in the Ottoman Empire whereby ethnic minorities ran their own communal affairs with a minimum of state interference. The British in India allowed the development of a Muslim family law with its own separate courts and much the same proposal was put to John Patten, the Home Office Minister with responsibility for community relations, by a Muslim delegation in the summer of 1989. The idea, hardly surprisingly, was rejected out of hand and I do not wish to argue for it. Nevertheless, I do think Britain can usefully consider aspects of Muslim historical experience for I do not think equality is possible without some degree of pluralism.

Once again dialogue, learning from a variety of traditions, is the way forward, for Muslim views of pluralism are not as they stand adequate either. They fail to confer equality of citizenship in some crucial respects. Islam insists on a fundamental equality between all Muslims; it insists on the rights of non-Muslims in a Muslim state to lead their lives according to their own norms and customs; it insists on the right of minorities to enjoy the full protection of the state; it does not, however, even as an ideal, allow them to be senior members of the major branches of the state nor propagate an ideology which challenges that of the state, i.e. Islam.[35] Under Jamaat's influence, Zia's Islamicization went even further and created separate electorates so non-Muslims could not influence the election of Muslim legislators. Historically, Muslim minorities have accordingly sought a tolerance-cum-pluralism not formal equality; the UK offers its Muslims a formal equality but is not yet willing to acknowledge in its institutional and legal arrangements the existence of a Muslim community which, for instance, can be deeply hurt and provoked to violence by forms of literature that the majority of citizens have become used to tolerating. The question of the interrelationship between equality and pluralism lies I believe at the heart of future British race relations and it is one on which Muslim thought will and ought to focus.

For however appalled we might be by 'the hang 'em and flog 'em' interpreters of the Quranic verses, that should not obscure for any of us, Muslims and non-Muslims, that 'the Rushdie affair' is not about the life of Salman Rushdie nor freedom of expression, let alone Islamic fundamentalism or book-burning or Iranian interference in British affairs. The issue is of the rights of non-European religious and cultural minorities in the context of a secular hegemony. Is the Enlightenment big enough to legitimize the existence of pre-Enlightenment religious enthusiasm or can it only exist by suffocating all who fail to be overawed by its intellectual brilliance and vision of Man?

Notes

1 Tariq Modood, 'Religious anger and minority rights', *Political Quarterly*, July 1989, pp. 280–284.

2 Shabbir Akhtar, *Be Careful with Muhammad!* London, 1989. Akhtar's book is the only full-scale (what he calls) fundamentalist presentation of the Muslim case and worth reading for that reason. I argue later in the article, however, that Muslim anger does not owe anything to (what I call) fundamentalism.

3 All available figures are estimates. I have relied on the Labour Force Survey data of 1985–87 for the larger groups, (which is very similar to *Social Trends*, 1989) and on 'Strategy and Plan (1987–1992)' of UK Islamic Missions for the smaller groupings.

4 Muhammad Anwar, 'Employment patterns of Muslims in Western Europe', *Journal* (Institute of Muslim Minority Affairs), 1 (1984). This, rather than libertarianism, is the reason why France and West Germany forced Sir Geoffrey Howe to toughen his stand against Khomeini's *fatwa*.

5 M. Ali Kettani, *The Muslim Minorities*, Leicester, The Islamic Foundation, 1979, p. 12 writes 'al-Andalusia is very much alive in the heart of every Muslim' and even someone as sophisticated as Rana Kabbani believes that 'the loss of Spain is not just a dusty entry in Arab history books but almost a contemporary event, prefiguring more recent catastrophes and in particular the loss of Palestine'. *Letter to Christendom*, London, Virago, 1989, pp. 2–3.

6 More than one commentator has seen parallels with East European Jewry: E. Mortimer, *Faith and Power: The Politics of Islam*, London, Faber, 1982, p. 403; M. Ruthven, *Islam in the World*, London, Penguin, 1984, p. 326.

7 A Government of Pakistan survey recently found the vast majority of those with a reputation for religious learning to be barely literate. Hamza Alavi, 'Pakistan and Islam: ethnicity and ideology' in Fred Halliday and Hamza Alavi (eds), *State and Ideology in the Middle East and Pakistan*, London, Macmillan, 1987, pp. 80–81. Most *imams* employed to lead prayers in British mosques are from this pool although attempts are under way to produce British trained personnel.

8 See, for example, M. Anwar, *Young Muslims in a Multi-Cultural Society*, Leicester, Islamic Foundation, reprinted 1986; John Rex and Sasha Josephides, 'Asian and Greek Cypriot associations and identity' in J. Rex, D. Joly and C. Wilpert (eds) *Immigrant Associations in Europe*, Aldershot, Gower, 1987; Alison Shaw, *A Pakistani Community in Britain*, Oxford, 1988; 'Race survey shock', *Daily Express*, 30 August 1989.

9 Shaw, *op. cit.*, is excellent in her account of the workings of the *birādari* system in Oxford.

10 One particular phrase of Powell is lodged in my brain. It goes something like: 'When an Englishman looks into the face of Asia he sees whom he will have to contest for his land.' What is remarkable is that it was said at an early moment in the process of Asian immigration when commentators of all political complexions assumed that social conflict would take a white–black form.

11 See, for example, Yasmin Alibhai, 'Home truths', *Observer* (Colour Supplement), 19 November 1989, pp. 46–49.

12 My archetype is Abul Ala Mawdudi. See, for example his *The Islamic Way of Life*, ed. Kurshid Ahmad and Khurram Murad, and *Human Rights in Islam*, both published by The Islamic Foundation, Leicester, 1986 and 1976 respectively.

13 Fazlur Rahman, *Islam and Modernity*, University of Chicago Press, 1982, p. 41.

14 Francis Robinson, *Varieties of South Asian Islam*, Centre for Research in Ethnic Relations, 1988, p. 10. This is the single most helpful guide on Asian Muslim groups in Britain. See also Jorgen S. Nielsen, *Muslim Immigration and Settlement in Britain*, Centre for the Study of Islam and Christian–Muslim Relations, 1984, Research Paper 21.

15 Wilfred Cantwell Smith, *Islam in Modern History*, Princeton, Princeton University Press, 1957, p. 236.

16 Leonard Binder, 'Islam, ethnicity and the state in Pakistan: an overview' in Ali Banuazizi and Myron Weiner, *The State, Religion and Ethnic Politics, Afghanistan, Iran and Pakistan*, Syracuse, 1986, p. 262.

17 There is also Ahl-e-Hadith, an older brand of fundamentalism which publishes *The Straight Path* and which due to the charismatic leadership of the late Maulana Mypurey has been quite influential in Birmingham, and one or two other groups too small to mention, see Robinson, *op. cit.*

18 John Rex, 'The urban sociology of religion and Islam in Birmingham' in Thomas Gerholm and Yngve Georg Lithman (eds) *The New Islamic Presence in Western Europe*, Mansell, 1988, p. 217.

19 On the latter see 'Britain's browns', *Economist*, 28 October 1989, pp. 25–28 – one of the few really good pieces of journalism on the Asian community.

20 'Choice between light and dark', *Observer*, 22 January 1989.

21 This is well brought out in Bhikhu Parekh 'Between holy text and moral void', *New Statesman and Society*, 24 March 1989, pp. 29–33 – the first article in the British media that showed any understanding of the Muslim anger.

22 Hence placards such as 'Shame on Arab Leaders' and 'Ayatollah, You Will Never Walk Alone' have been evident at demonstrations (David Caute, 'The Holy War', *New Statesman and Society*, 2 June 1989). See Akhtar, *op. cit.*, pp. 80–88 for a discussion of the response of the Arabs: his claim, however, that the Saudis were able to get the New Zealand government to ban *SV* (p. 93) is comprehensively denied by the High Commission in London.

23 For example, Fazlun Khalid, 'When fools rushed in', *Impact International*, 8 September 1989.

24 Robinson, *op. cit.*, p. 20.

25 Led by white converts and with hardly any community consultation an Islamic Party of Great Britain was set up in September 1989.

26 For examples of Islamic modernism, see note 13. See also W. Montgomery Watt, *Islamic Fundamentalism and Modernity*, London, 1988, for some critical advice to Muslims.

27 Consider: 'Had Rushdie been white, the left would almost certainly have condemned (*SV*) as patronizing prejudice against an already oppressed racial minority', Akhtar, *op. cit.*, p. 110. It is because most Muslims believe this that they now consider (if they did not previously do so) the left's interest in racial minorities is only as a political pawn. I remember reading that there was the same feeling in Brixton when after the riots the left began arriving.

28 See my 'Colour, class and culture: the three Cs of race', *Equal Opportunities Review*, March 1990. See Dervla Murphy, *Tales from Two Cities*, London, 1987, for an excellent account of how racism is far more potent when it focuses on not just colour but also culture.

29 For how the antiracist concept of Black harms Asians, see my '"Black", racial equality and Asian identity', *New Community*, Spring, 1988.

30 For an example of Muslim thinking on race, see M. Aman Hobohm, 'Islam and the racial problem' in Altaf Gauhar (ed.) *The Challenge of Islam*, London, Islamic Council of Europe, 1978, pp. 268–283.

31 Akhtar's rhetorical defence of Muslim prejudices about the West is, 'as we learn in the race relations industry, prejudice without power can safely be ignored', *op. cit.*, p. 52. Perhaps in future the 'industry' will want to be more careful about such hostages to fortune.

32 UK Action Committee on Islamic Affairs, *The British Muslim Response to Mr. Patten*, 1989, p. 11; Akhtar, *op. cit.*, p. 7.

33 Interestingly, Rex reports that Muslim leaders in Birmingham 'suggested that if the West Indians had any equivalent of the mosques they would be more likely to gain employment and less likely to riot. There was indeed some interest in converting West Indians and a small number have in fact become Muslims', *op. cit.*, p. 215.

34 Sebastian Poulter, 'Cultural pluralism and its limits – a legal perspective', CRE–Runnymede Trust Conference on Pluralism, October 1989; and his *English Law and Ethnic Minority Customs*, London, 1986.

35 See, for example, the account of the minimum principles of an ideal Islamic state agreed to by a 1949 conference of all major sects in Pakistan, Allahbuklish K. Brohi, 'Mawlana Abul Ala Mawdudi: the man, the scholar, the reformer' in K. Ahmad and Z. I. Ansari, *Islamic Perspectives*, The Islamic Foundation, Leicester, 1979, pp. 296–299.

Source: Modood, T. (1990) 'British Asian Muslims and the Rushdie affair', *Political Quarterly*, **61**(2), pp. 143–60.

13 FUNDAMENTALISM, MULTICULTURALISM AND WOMEN IN BRITAIN

NIRA YUVAL-DAVIS

When you read books on fundamentalism, it becomes clear how central the issue of women is to fundamentalist movements. This may be made explicit – 'Muslim fundamentalists have obsessive concern with the role of women' – or it may be implicit in the discussion of, for example, abortion – 'Opposition to abortion has become the unifying cause of the New Right, Protestant Fundamentalists and Right-to-Life Catholics' (Hyman, 1985, p. 23; Reichley, 1985, p. 320). Many authors observe that this concern is relatively new, dating from the rise of the second wave of feminism in the late 1960s and early 1970s. In this article, I offer an explanation of why women, their role, and above all their control, have become central to the fundamentalist agenda in this way. I also examine this phenomenon as it has manifested itself in contemporary Britain. My argument is that the conforming of women to the strict confines of womanhood defined by fundamentalist religious codes is a precondition for the maintenance and reproduction of their symbolic order. Furthermore, this control of women is often the link between religious fundamentalism, secular political and ideological movements, and states. Unpacking constructions of woman-hood by these movements throws into question some of the common-sense (including academic common-sense) attributions of ethnic and gender difference applied by antiracist as well as by racist discourses. I shall, therefore, also look at the connection between the constructions of cultural difference and the fundamentalist control of women.

'Fundamentalism', especially as it had been used in the media around the Rushdie affair, has become so confused with the abusive labelling of Muslims and their racialization as the collective 'barbaric Other', that some authors have suggested dispensing with the term altogether (Modood, this volume; Rex, 1990). Despite that, and while struggling against anti-Muslim racism, I still consider it important to identify and analyse fundamentalism as a specific (although heterogeneous) social phenomenon which cross-cuts religions and cultures, with particular implications in relation to women. In Britain, it has been the Rushdie affair and mass demonstrations in protest not only against the book *The Satanic Verses* and its author but also against the ways the state privileges Christianity, which have put the issue of fundamentalism at the heart of the political debate. But different fundamentalist movements – Christian, Jewish, Sikh and Hindu as well as Muslim – have been growing in Britain during the past few years, partly as a result of international developments and partly as a result of the situation in Britain itself.

Fundamentalism

The Concise Oxford Dictionary defines fundamentalism as: 'Strict maintenance of traditional orthodox religious beliefs, such as the inerrancy of Scripture and literal acceptance of the creeds as fundamentals of Protestant Christianity'. Indeed, the first religious groupings to be called fundamentalist were American Protestant churches, which in 1919 established the World Christian Fundamentalist Association – based on a series of Bible conferences which took place between 1865 and 1910 (Chalfant *et al.*, 1981). Given this origin, it has been argued that the term fundamentalism should be applied only to Protestant Christians, although even in this case some authors suggest that 'Because of its prejudical character . . . it is not a useful title for Evangelicals today' (Packer, 1958, p. 169). Some Muslim leaders have insisted that they are not fundamentalists, just devout Muslims. Others, like Rowe (1990), would apply the label to Muslims, but argue that one cannot put Christian and Muslim fundamentalists in the same category because of the different nature of the two religions.

Without underestimating the specific historical and cultural constructions of different religions, however, I would argue two things. First, heterogeneity exists not only among religions but also within them. We need to be sceptical of essentialist notions and look at the historical conditions which construct specific fundamentalist movements, beyond looking at what is common to them all. Not only is Islam different in different Muslim states: the role and meaning of fundamentalist Islam for second-generation Pakistanis who have grown up as a racial minority in the north of England, for example, are very different from its role for Iranians who have come to London as refugees. And there would be very important differences between black and white evangelical Christianity, between Orthodox Judaism inside and outside Israel, or even between Anglicanism in England and Scotland. Second, beyond all these differences there are two interconnected features common to all fundamentalist religious movements. They claim their version of religion to be the only true one and feel threatened by pluralist systems of thought, and so justify the use of political means to impose it on all members of their religion. Fundamentalist militancy therefore has to be differentiated from liberation theologies which, while deeply religious and political, co-operate with, rather than subjugate, non-religious political struggles for freedom.

The original fundamentalist movement arose in the USA as a response to the 'Social Gospel' which liberalized religion and had strong progressive elements. Fundamentalist movements all over the world are basically political movements with religious articulations, which seek in various ways and in varied circumstances to harness modern state and media powers to the service of their gospel. This gospel is presented as the only valid form of the religion. It may rely heavily on sacred texts, but it can also be more experiential and linked to charismatic leadership. Politically, fundamentalism aligns itself with different political trends in different countries and manifests itself in different forms. It can appear as an orthodoxy – a maintenance of traditional values – or as a revivalist radical phenomenon, dismissing impure and corrupt forms of religion in a 'return' to original sources. Jewish fundamentalism in Israel, for example, has appeared as both right-wing Zionism, for which the establishment of the Israeli state has been a positive religious act, and as non-Zionist, if not anti-Zionist, which sees in the Israeli state a convenient source for gaining economic and political powers. In Islam, fundamentalism has appeared as a return to the Koranic text (fundamentalism of the madrasa) and as a return to the religious law, the Sharia (fundamentalism of the 'ulama') (Roy, 1985, p. 122). In the USA, there is a distinction between 'fundamentalists' in the original sense of those who call to go back to the biblical text, and those 'born-again' Christians who rely much more on emotional religious experiences. Reichley (1985) defines fundamentalism as an 'extreme form of evangelicalism'. Another important difference among fundamentalist movements is between movements of dominant majorities within states which look for universal domination in society and fundamentalist movements among minorities who aim to use state and media powers and resources to promote and impose their gospel primarily within their specific constituencies which are usually defined in ethnic terms. (Identifying heterogeneous forms of fundamentalist movements in this way does not invalidate the proposition that fundamentalism is a specific social phenomenon. All major social movements, including national, socialist and feminist movements, have been similarly heterogeneous.)

The rise of fundamentalism is linked to the crisis of modernity (Bauman, 1991), to a general sense of despair and disorientation, in which there is no clear societal moral order. This has moved people from all over the world to go back to religion as a source of solace, stability, and identity. In the West the most influential fundamentalist movement has been the evangelical movement which is at the heart of the Moral Majority in the USA. In the Third World, and among Third World minorities in the West, the rise of fundamentalism is intimately linked with the failure of nationalist and socialist movements to bring about successful liberation from oppression, exploitation and poverty. Religion has also been utilized by militants as an 'indigenous' ideology with which to mobilize the 'masses' and to confront racism, imperialism and superpower interventions. Since the Iranian revolution, this development has affected not only

Muslims in other countries, but also Jews, Sikhs, Hindus and other religions in which fundamentalist movements have grown. As Amrita Chhachhi (1990) argues, however, religious fundamentalist movements sponsored by Third World states, such as those in Southern Asia, have grown not in opposition, but as a way of accommodating the penetration of capitalist relations into the labour market. In addition, of course, specific local conditons have also contributed to the rise of these movements.

The British case

The Rushdie affair has produced in Britain a preoccupation with fundamentalist issues which has been deeply confusing, creating divisions both within the Left and the Right. During the mass demonstration by Muslims in London in June 1989, for example, there was a counter-demonstration by the newly formed Women Against Fundamentalism. They wanted to register their voice in opposition to the fundamentalist leadership and to its demands concerning Rushdie and the extension of the blasphemy law, but especially to challenge its position on the role of women. The Anti-Fascist League took part in the main demonstration, emphasizing the Muslims' right to resist racism and struggling against those fascists who opposed the demonstration on racist and nationalist grounds. Another fascist organization supported the demonstration, seeing it as the Muslim expression of their inherently different and separate cultural-national essence. However, both factions of fascists as well as the Muslim fundamentalists were opposed to the Women Against Fundamentalism. Equally unusual, if not unholy, alliances and splits have been reported, for example, around the *Sacred Cows* pamphlet, published in 1989, in which the feminist novelist Fay Weldon argued for a return to explicitly assimilationist policies in the nation's schools.

The position of Women Against Fundamentalism is related to the different political ideologies with which fundamentalist movements have aligned themselves. For many years, one of the unchallenged 'truths' of the Left has been that anti-imperialism is inherently progressive. Khomeini's Iranian revolution was supported, at least initially, by large sections of the Left because it was clearly anti-western and anti-imperialist. By extension, any attempt to criticize and challenge the authority of fundamentalist leaders has been interpreted as racist. They have been taught by multiculturalist and antiracist strategists to hold as sacred the 'autonomy' of minority 'communities' and to view them as internally homogeneous. Similarly, those who uphold the fashionable 'identity politics', in which the organizing principle is around legitimizing people's differences and uniqueness in the public as well as in the private spheres, could not challenge what has been claimed by fundamentalist leaders to be the essence of their 'cultural difference'. At the same time, some of the New Right in Britain, although deeply racist, have presented the cohesive, tightly controlled, industrious model of 'the Asian family' as highly conducive to the type of moral system they want to strengthen in the society. In this way, there has been collusion between Christian and Muslim fundamentalism.

Paradoxically, fundamentalism in Britain has been encouraged by different political forces *both* to homogenize and unite the British collectivity in religious and cultural terms, *and* to heterogenize and atomize it. This was possible, first, because of the particular relationship between religion and the state in Britain, and, secondly, because of the relationship between fundamentalism and multicultural policies.

Religion and state

There has never been full separation between religion and the state in Britain. This is all too often ignored in the analysis both by the Left and by sociologists of religion. The hidden or explicit assumption has been that in modern states, nationalism has replaced religion, which has either disappeared in the secularized society, or at least withdrawn into the private arena. So the enquiry into religion in Britain has predominantly focused on attitudes, beliefs and membership of religious organizations.

According to *Social Trends* (1989), less than twenty per cent of the population are members of religious organizations, and only fifteen per cent are members of Trinitarian churches, such as the established and Catholic churches. Seventy-five per cent of the population have a religious affiliation, however, the majority being to the established churches. In a survey carried out by the Independent Television Authority in 1970, eight out of every ten Britons felt the Christian identity of Britain to be very important or important to them. This is the context in which the notion of Englishness expressed by Enoch Powell in his 'rivers of blood' speech in 1968 has to be understood. Powell called for the repatriation of black immigrants in Britain before bloody confrontations take place between them and the English, as there is no way that these inherently different immigrants could ever assimilate with the English. Research on the contents of the mail Powell received after his speech showed that the primary reason given by correspondents for supporting him was their fear for 'the English way of life'. Christianity, apparently, is one of the most important factors in this perceived 'way of life'. This can also be seen in the remarks of David Jenkins, now the Bishop of Durham, who wrote about *The British, their Identity and their Religion* in 1975: 'The more I considered what it means in specific terms to be distinctively English, Scottish or Welsh, the more important became the place of religious inheritance in the process of definition' (p. vii).

The Christianity of Britain is not just a question of religious affiliation, however, nor even just of British nationalist ideology. It is anchored in law, and extends beyond the symbolism of the Queen being the titular head of the churches of England and of Scotland. The church hierarchy participates in the legislative process. The two archbishops and twenty-four bishops are members of the House of Lords: they are 'the Lords Spiritual'. It is the duty of the Prime Minister to appoint the archbishop, and that decision will be influenced by his or her religious affiliation and attitudes. Even though it is seldom invoked, the blasphemy law exists to protect the Church of England from attacks that would not be illegal if directed against other religions. Perhaps most significantly for the future, under the 1988 Education Reform Act all state schools are required to have a daily act of Christian worship.

In such ways, the legal status of Christianity as the ideological cement of the national culture is affirmed. This in turn confers a degree of legitimacy on church leaders when they express opinions on such social and political issues as poverty and homelessness. Although these may cause some discomfort to the government, this construction assumes a correspondence between national and religious identity which marginal-ized non-established churches, and especially non-Christians, as only partial members of the British national collectivity. They are defined to a lesser or greater extent as outsiders.

Fundamentalism and multiculturalism

While membershp of the established churches fell by fourteen per cent between 1987 and 1990, membership of minority churches such as spiritualists and Jehovah's Witnesses rose by twenty-six per cent. Non-Christian religions, especially Islam and Sikhism, almost doubled their membership. Religious affiliation has thus come, in different ways, to signify collective identity among ethnic minorities in Britain. This phenomenon can be attributed in part to global developments and to the rise of religious fundamentalist movements in the countries of origin of non-Christians living in Britain. Hindu fundamentalists, for example, have raised funds to send blessed bricks to build a temple in India. The phenomenon is, however, also a result of the multiculturalist policies prevalent in the British educational system and in other parts of its race relations industry. Although these policies aimed to legitimize hetero-geneity in British national culture, they have in fact created a space for separatist and fundamentalist movements which seek to impose uniform-ity and homogeneity on all their adherents.

There have been many attempts to deal with the related problems of racism and the absorption by the mainstream society of minorities drawn from the old empire who settled in Britain after the war. The policy of multiculturalism, despite some misgivings by both the Left and the Right, has been widely adopted as a more tolerant way forward towards integration than full assimilation into a 'British way of life'. It has been accepted as a tool of social policy and in education where it was first articulated. Its premises were clearly articulated in 1977 by the Inner London Education Authority.

> The Authority serves a city where the presence of people of diverse cultures with different patterns of belief, behaviour and language is of great importance . . . Recognizing this, we have reaffirmed our determination to sustain a policy which will ensure that, within a society which is cohesive though not uniform, cultures are respected, differences recognized and individual identities are ensured.
> (ILEA, 1977)

Fundamentalist leaderships have been the main beneficiaries of the adoption of multiculturalist norms. Although sometimes portrayed as 'medievalists who have rejected British values', their demands upon the British state have been articulated within this framework. It has provided their chief ideological weapon. They have argued for the extension of the blasphemy law to Islam and for separate schools in the name of equal rights. Within the terms of the multiculturalist consensus, which sees racism not as a form of institutionalized inequality but as a matter of different mutually exclusive ways of life which must be preserved, their arguments are unanswerable. Minority communities are defined by their culture, which has increasingly been constructed as a matter of religious identity (Anthias and Yuval-Davis, 1992).

So, for example, children in 'multicultural' schools are taught about various religious holidays as one way of acquainting them with other cultures, and community relations boards and local councils have been financing mosques and temples (but usually not churches – even if black churches) as a major part of their 'race relations' work. The racialization of religion, especially Islam, reached a new peak after the Rushdie affair. Groups previously known by national or regional origin – Pakistani, Mirpuri, Bengali, and Punjabi, for example – are now all seen as part of a single Muslim community. This categorization of minority communities in primarily religion terms assumes them to be internally unified, homogeneous entities with no class or gender differences or conflicts. Women's demands for freedom and equality are seen as being outside 'cultural traditions' (often themselves only half understood), and therefore not legitimate. The most conservative versions are often considered to be the most 'authentic'. Appeals to culture and tradition have been used to attack women's autonomous organizing.

Women and fundamentalism

Women affect and are affected by ethnic and national processes in several major ways (see Yuval-Davis and Anthias, 1989). Some of these are central to the project of fundamentalism, which attempts to impose its own unitary religious definition on the collectivity and its symbolic order. The 'proper' behaviour of women is used to signify the difference between those who belong to the collectivity and those who do not. Women are also seen as the 'cultural carriers' of the collectivity who transmit it to the future generation, and the 'proper' control of women in terms of marriage and divorce ensures that children who are born to those women are not only biologically but also symbolically within the boundaries of the collectivity. The control of women and the 'patriarchal family' are thus central to fundamentalism. Often they are seen as the panacea for all social ills.

> A widespread evangelical conviction is that stability in the home is the key to the resolution of other social problems. Once wanderers came 'home' and the poor acquired the sense of responsibility found in strong Christian familiality, poverty could cease.
> (Marsdan, 1980, p. 37)

Women's desertion of their proper social role might therefore mean a social disaster: 'Woman has such a degree of biological disability and such huge family responsibilities as to preclude her leaving purdah in a well ordered society' (Pundah Mandrudi, quoted in Hyman, 1985, p. 24).

The link between fundamentalism and women's oppression has been recognized by women in many countries where they have established organizations to fight against fundamentalism. In Britain, Women Against Fundamentalism was established in London in spring 1989. Although the immediate impulse was the public debate around the Rushdie affair, the organization encompasses a broad range of women's groups and individuals from different ethnic and religious backgrounds (Christian, Muslim, Hindu, Jewish, etc.). It is campaigning against fundamentalism in all religions, although it does not define itself as anti-religious. Its members see the exclusive focus of the media on Muslim fundamentalism as part of the racism of British society. The preoccupations of Women Against Fundamentalism coalesce around three central areas of struggle: separate religious schools, especially for girls; women's refuges; and women's reproductive rights.

Separate schools

Separate religious schools are one of the major demands of fundamentalist leaders: most of the pressure is for single-sex schools, especially for girls. In Britain it has never been compulsory for schooling to be conducted through state education. Private schools have educated the elite, and voluntary-aided schools have been the semi-private system in which religious schools (mostly Church of England and Catholic) have been partially financed by the state. One of the key demands of Muslim fundamentalists has been to establish such voluntary-aided schools for their communities. Until now most of them have been rejected by Her Majesty's Inspectorate because their standards have been too low.

Single-sex schooling for girls has been considered by some feminists to enhance their academic achievement. Without boys in the classroom, they argue, girls are less affected by traditional sexual divisions of academic interests and less intimidated by the boys. This feminist thinking, however, assumes a structure and curriculum similar to those of a mixed school. This is not the case where religious schools are concerned. Most of the private Muslim schools which have been established in Britain, with the exception of a couple of seminaries, are for girls only. Their purpose is clearly to bring up girls to be dutiful wives and mothers. They teach creation theories in science (like Christian fundamentalists) and offer inadequate facilities for achieving academic qualifications. Although most Asian parents would probably prefer single-sex education, they would not want to send their daughters to such schools. Even fewer would risk their sons' futures. Few parents would publicly oppose a religious demand, however. By making separate education for girls a central plank of the national campaign, Muslim fundamentalists have shown a keen aware-ness of the fears of their constituency. Their discourse ties the control of girls to the dangers in growing up in a secular society in the 'morally degenerate' West. A few years ago in Manchester there was a successful community campaign, in which Asian feminists were involved, to stop a state school from being converted into a Muslim school. In the more intimidating atmosphere following the Rushdie affair and the greater cohesion behind Muslim demands, such a campaign might now be more difficult to organize.

Though Muslim fundamentalists are the most vocal, they are by no means the only groups demanding separate schools. Ultra-orthodox Jews, Seventh-Day Adventists, Sikh and Hindu groups have all done the same. These demands are likely to be fuelled by the increasingly inadequate funding of many schools and the often severe shortage of teachers. In the East End of London, for instance, where Britain's biggest Bangladeshi community is settled, thousands of their children were without school places in 1989 and 1990. At the same time, local voluntary-aided Catholic schools had vacancies, but these were not available to them. A better state education and an end to discrimination and racial harassment in schools are the answers to these problems. This is the goal towards which a broad-based alliance, in which some members of Women Against Fundamentalism are also involved, is fighting.

In the late 1980s and early 1990s, the Labour Party embraced fundamentalist demands for separate schools in the name of equal rights. Its education spokesperson, Jack Straw, who has a large Muslim constituency, has suggested that people opposing these demands are racist. Labour MPs have also argued that one should not oppose those demands for state aid of separate schools because these children are from the working classes and without state aid their private schools would be too poorly resourced. Only those willing to challenge the multicultural consensus have opposed this view. Unfortunately, some, like Fay Weldon, have done so by calling for a return to integrationist policies which adhere to a set of 'British values' assumed to be embraced by the nation. Women Against Fundamentalism has opposed both views, arguing instead that the British state needs to be secularized and that there should be an end to state support for all religious schools.

Women's refuges

Women's refuges were initially established by the feminist movement to provide women with a separate space away from their husbands' violent attempts to control them. In the early 1980s, autonomous black women's groups took up the issue of domestic violence and began to argue for funding for refuges from local councils. They had to fight on several fronts. They were bitterly opposed by conservative community leaders who denied that domestic violence existed, or insisted that it was a problem to be solved by traditional mechanisms within the community. Some white feminists also felt that separate refuges were incompatible with the central idea of the women's movement – the notion of 'sisterhood'. Black women, mostly from the antiracist movement, argued that there was a need for Asian, and sometimes Afro-Caribbean, women to have separate spaces to live with people who understood the pressures they felt, including dealing with racism. But the essential aim of all refuges was the same – to provide an alternative space outside the family for women who had suffered from domestic violence.

Anxious to be seen to be implementing equal opportunity policies, some councils – mostly Labour-led – did fund these refuges, even though they provoked community backlash. Now the problem of domestic violence is so widely recognized that a claim to provide advice or other services to deal with it is a significant factor in gaining funding for a variety of community organizations. This has lead to a sharp turnabout. Community leaders who had earlier opposed the provision of refuges are now applying for funding themselves. But they are using their services for the purpose of reintegrating women into the family. The notion of 'cultural difference' has turned the idea of a refuge on its head. New refuges are being funded solely on the basis of religious allegiance. This is part of a more general process in which the conservative patriarchy that used to lead community organizations is beginning, in some cases, to be replaced by young militant fundamentalists who venture into areas like refuges, from which the 'old guard' shied away. In other areas councils have tried to impose religious leaders onto the management committees of refuges as a form of 'community control'. Feminist women, by definition, were deemed 'outsiders' to 'the community' even if they worked in areas where they grew up.

Reproductive rights

In the USA, the issue of abortion has united the New Right, Protestant fundamentalists and Catholics in common cause (Reichley, 1985, p. 320). Ron Paul, a gynaecologist and a congressman, typifies their rhetoric in his comments on abortion and liberty.

> The acceptance of abortion, the growth of bureaucratic government, double-digit interest rates and the loss of freedom are all interrelated. They are all a result of a lack of understanding and concern for natural rights bestowed on us by our Creator.
> (Paul, 1983, p. 9)

In Britain, the picture is more complicated. In 1990, for example, an act of parliament on embryo research was passed and radical new restrictions on the availability of abortion were rejected. Although united on the question of good family life as a basis for social stability, many representatives of the New Right have distanced themselves from the irrationality of the radical pro-life lobby. Similarly, the Anglican Church, which in 1980 supported the Catholic bishops' opposition to abortion, has put women's health before a foetus's right and has not become part of the 'pro-life' lobby.

Although less dominant than its American counterpart, the pro-life movement in Britain is powerful and is closely linked to religious fundamentalism. (Abortion clinics have been picketed by anti-abortionists inspired and coached by Rescue, an organization that is part of the evangelical Moral Majority in the US, for instance.) The abortion issue, as well as the wider issue of women's reproductive rights, has always been at the heart of the feminist agenda, as well as that of the 'pro-life' movement. In Britain there has also been a long tradition of Irish feminists supporting women from Ireland – both south and north – who have had to go to mainland Britain to have an abortion as a result of the political power of the Catholic Church. Women Against Fundamentalism have demonstrated in front of the Irish embassy in London in support of feminists appealing to the European Court of Human Rights to overturn a decision by the Irish Supreme Court that advising and directing women to abortion facilities outside Ireland is unconstitutional.

Fundamentalism and women's empowerment

Britain is still far from being a fundamentalist country. Its Moral Majority is smaller and less overtly political than in the USA; its black and non-Christian fundamentalists are still part of oppressed racialized minorities.

Nevertheless, the close ties between the state and Christianity, on the one hand, and the collapse of antiracism into a multiculturalism which equates culture with religion, on the other hand, provide a fertile ground in which the influence of fundamentalist militants can grow. This has direct implications for the possibility of women's empowerment.

Traditional gender relations have been subjected to many challenges in the past few decades, both in the West and in the Third World. The state often becomes a focal point for struggles to retain control of women within changing social and economic circumstances. As Amrita Chhachhi convincingly shows in the context of South Asia, fundamentalist religious movements can be sponsored by the state as part of this struggle. She describes how the incorporation of women into the labour market often encourages, rather than weakens, patriarchal control over them, although the form of such control might change. Often, when the threat to patriarchal social control arises, the state steps in as a third actor, 'providing a coincidence of capitalist and patriarchal interests' (1990, p. 5), and partriarchal control shifts from individual men to the state. In the West, equal opportunities legislation and the legalization of abortion were prompted by the changing role of women in the labour market as well as by the increasing influence of the feminist movement. It is within such contexts that we also have to observe the struggles for and against fundamentalism.

One of the interesting questions to look at is why some women have been attracted to fundamentalist movements as a source of empowerment (Afshar, 1989). It is clear that in certain circumstances, being part of a fundamentalist organization provides girls (and it is mostly unmarried girls or at least those as yet without children) with a place where they can find refuge from the pressures of both sexism and racism. Moreover, the authority of such affiliation might legitimize defiance against parents, peer group and school and thus provide a kind of empowerment that other forms of rebellion could not. This empowerment, however, is within the strict control of the male leaderships of fundamentalist movements and subjected to a narrow definition of 'a woman's place'. Chhachhi compares it to the type of attraction which fascist movements have had for women despite the clearly subordinate roles in which these placed them. The basic question is not, therefore, whether the women in fundamentalist movements feel empowered or not. It is more important to ask, what are the parameters of this empowerment? What limitations does it impose on women and what kinds of women does it disempower (e.g. gay women, older single, childless women)? And what are the overall implications, including for women, of the religious ideologies and movements within which this sense of empowerment has been achieved?

Issues of racism and sexism are interwoven in intricate ways. This is no reason always to prioritize one struggle in favour of the other, however. The task ahead is to find effective ways to confront the contradictions and conflicts within minority communities as well as oppression and racism in the state and society at large. To find ways to resolve the tension between autonomy and tolerance, diversity and equality. To have the right to dissent and oppose both racism and fundamentalism. And sexism.

Acknowledgement

This paper could not have been written without the work and discussions I have carried on with Women Against Fundamentalism in general and Gita Sahgal (my co-editor on *Refusing Holy Orders: women and fundamentalism in Britain*, Virago Press, 1992) in particular. This paper is a further development of a paper I wrote with her for *Marxism Today*, 'Refusing Holy Orders', March 1990. In its present form the paper was presented at the International Sociological Association conference, Madrid 1990, and is included in a special issue on Gender, Ethnicity and Race of the *Revue Internationale de Sociologie*, 1991, edited by S. Allen, F. Anthias and myself.

References

Afshar, Haleh (1989) 'Three generations of women in Bradford', paper presented at the Conference of Socialist Economists conference.

Anthias, Floya and Yuval-Davis, Nira (1992) *Racialized Boundaries: ethnic, gender, colour and class divisions and the anti-racist struggle*, London, Routledge.

Bauman, Zygmunt (1991) *Modernity and Ambivalence*, Cambridge, Polity Press.

Chalfant, Paul H., Beckley, Robert E. and Palmer, C. Eddie (1981) *Religion in Contemporary Society*, Palo Alto, CA, Mayfield Publications.

Chhachhi, Amrita (1990) 'The state, religious fundamentalism and women', unpublished paper.

Hyman, Anthony (1985) *Muslim Fundamentalism*, The Institute for the Study of Culture, 174.

Inner London Education Authority (1977) *Multi-ethnic Education*, London, ILEA publication.

Jenkins, David (1975) *The British, their Identity and their Religion*, London, SCS Press.

Johnson, Stephen D. and Tamney, Joseph B. (eds) (1986) *The Political Role of Religion in the USA*, Boulder, CO, Westview Press Inc.

Marsdan, George M. (1980) *Fundamentalism and American Culture*, Oxford, Oxford University Press.

Modood, Tariq (1990) 'British Asian Muslims and the Rushdie affair', *Political Quarterly*, 61(2). Reprinted in this volume.

Packer, J. I. (1958) *'Fundamentalism' and the Word of God*, London, Inter-Varsity Fellowship.

Paul, Ron (1983) *Abortion and Liberty*, Texas, The Foundation for Rational Economics and Education.

Reichley, James A. (1985) *Religion in American Political Life*, Washington DC, The Brookings Institute.

Rex, John (1990) paper on Muslims in Birmingham presented at a conference on *New Debates in Black Politics*, Warwick University, May.

Rowe, Arthur (1990) comments written on G. Sahgal and Yuval-Davis' paper 'Refusing Holy Orders' in *Marxism Today*, March 1990, unpublished.

Roy, Oliver (1985) 'Fundamentalism, traditionalism and Islam', *TELOS*, 65, Fall.

Sahgal, Gita and Yuval-Davis, Nira (1990) 'Refusing Holy Orders', *Marxism Today*, March.

Social Trends (1989) HMSO.

Weldon, Fay (1989) *Sacred Cows*, London, Chatto and Windus.

Yuval-Davis, Nira and Anthias, Floya (1989) *Woman–Nation–State*, London, Macmillan.

LIST OF CONTRIBUTORS

Avtar Brah teaches at Birkbeck College, University of London. She was previously lecturer in education at the Open University and has held research posts at the Universities of Leicester and Bristol. She has published widely on gender, 'race' and ethnicity, and on education and employment issues. Her latest publication is *Working Choices: South Asian young Muslim women and the labour market* (Department of Employment, 1992).

Philip Cohen is senior research fellow at the Polytechnic of East London, where he directs the New Ethnicities Initiative. Before that he directed a research and curriculum development project on tackling cultures of racism in schools at the London Institute of Education. He contributed to *Multiracist Britain* (Macmillan, 1988).

Frantz Fanon was born in Martinique in 1921. He practised as a psychiatrist in Algeria, where he was extremely critical of the colonial war being conducted by the French. His first book, *Black Skins, White Masks*, was published in 1948. Later works such as *A Dying Colonialism* and *The Wretched of the Earth* became manifestos for Third World liberation struggles. He died in 1961.

Sander L. Gilman is the Goldwin Smith Professor of Humane Studies at Cornell University and professor of the history of psychiatry at Cornell Medical College. He is an intellectual and literary historian and the author or editor of over twenty-seven books, including the basic study of the visual stereotyping of the mentally ill, *Seeing the Insane* (John Wiley, 1982). His most recent book is *Sexuality: an illustrated history* (John Wiley, 1989).

Paul Gilroy teaches in the Sociology Department at Goldsmiths' College, University of London. He is author of *There Ain't No Black in the Union Jack* (Hutchinson, 1987).

Stuart Hall is professor of sociology at the Open University. He was previously director of the Centre for Cultural Studies at the University of Birmingham. His major publications include *Policing the Crisis: mugging, the state and law and order* (Macmillan Press, 1978), *Resistance through Rituals: youth subcultures in post-war Britain* (ed. with Tony Jefferson) (Hutchinson, 1976), and *Hard Road to Renewal: Thatcherism and the crisis of the left* (Verso, 1990).

Caroline Knowles is senior lecturer in sociology at the Polytechnic of East London. She has also taught at universities in Nigeria and Canada. She is author of *Race, Discourse and Labourism* (Routledge, 1992).

Sharmila Mercer works as a human resources consultant in Queensland, Australia. She was previously Women's Adviser to Islington Borough Council.

Tariq Modood is currently a visiting research fellow at Nuffield College, Oxford. He taught political theory at a number of British universities and worked for five years in racial equality policy, including a period as Principal Employment Officer at the Commission for Racial Equality in London. He is presently writing a book on the changing nature of the concept of 'race' in contemporary Britain.

Claire Pajaczkowska is senior lecturer in contemporary cultural studies at Middlesex Polytechnic. She is a member of the editorial advisory board of the journal *Free Associations*.

Ali Rattansi is lecturer in sociology at City University, London. He was previously lecturer in the School of Education at the Open University and chair of the course *'Race', Education and Society*. He is author of *Marx and the Division of Labour* (Macmillan, 1982) and co-editor (with R. Boyne) of *Postmodernism and Society* (Macmillan, 1990) and (with D. Reeder) of *Radicalism and Education* (Lawrence and Wishart, 1992).

Gauri Viswanathan is assistant professor in the Department of English and Comparative Literature at Columbia University, New York.

Lola Young is lecturer in film/media studies at the Polytechnic of West London. She has written several articles on the subject of 'race', gender and cultural politics.

Robert Young is fellow in English at Wadham College, Oxford, and joint editor of the *Oxford Literary Review*. He is author of *White Mythologies: writing history and the West* (Routledge, 1990).

Nira Yuval-Davis is reader in ethnic and gender studies at Thames Polytechnic, London, and a member of Women Against Fundamentalism. She is co-editor with F. Anthias of *Woman–Nation–State* (Macmillan, 1989) and with H. Bresheeth of *The Gulf War and the New World Order* (Zed Books, 1991). Her most recent books are with F. Anthias, *Racialized Boundaries: ethnic, gender, colour and class divisions and the anti-racist struggle* (Routledge, 1992) and with G. Sahgal, *Refusing Holy Orders: women and fundamentalism in Britain* (Virago, 1992).

INDEX

Phizacklea, A., 31, 32–3
Picasso, Pablo, 190–1
pluralism, 273–4
 see also cultural pluralism
police
 attitude to race, 85, 87, 89–90, 91–2
 and racial violence, 64–5, 74–5
political activity by black communities,
 134
political constituency, 121–2, 140
political struggles, 122
politics
 and fundamentalism, 280
 and Islam, 268–9
 and racism, 51–3, 55
positive action, 273
positive images, 34
Powell, Enoch, 53, 264, 275, 282
power, 3, 57
 identity based on, 202
 racism as, 75, 83, 139
prejudice, 3, 25–9, 38, 57, 75, 80–1
projection, 200, 201, 204, 213
propaganda, 34
prostitute, icon of, 172–3, 184–7, 193
psychoanalysis, 96
 feminism and, 142
 racism and, 198–218

Quran, 272

race, culture and, 1, 3, 50, 53–4, 55, 57, 80
Race Relations Act 1976, 273
racial abuse
 in schools, 21
 suppression of, 96–7
racial discourses, 27, 36–7, 67–70, 86–94
racial envy, 90
racial equality, and minority rights, 271–4
racial oppression, 72, 109
racial underclass, 261
racialization of place, 92
racialization of time, 92
racism, 2, 3–4, 5, 36–8, 63, 255
 and antiracists, 29–35, 52–6, 60–1
 change in, 32
 differences in, 138
 different responses to, 133
 discussion about, 68–70
 and education, 13, 14–15, 17, 20–4, 28
 and ethnicity, 57–8, 257–8
 explanations of, 74–86
 and gender and class, 137–8
 histories of, 133
 and humanism, 247
 institutional, 35, 74–5, 76, 79
 Islam and, 272–3

models of, 69
and nationalism, 53–4, 56
origins, 80–1, 84
in politics, 51–3
psychoanalysis and, 198–218
and rationality, 3, 30, 33, 42n, 81, 82
and sexism, 110–12, 138
struggles against, 112–13
by teachers, 21–2, 28
theories of, 70–4
and the women's movement, 114–16
racism awareness training (RAT), 96–7
radical feminism, 132
radical holism, 77, 78, 79
Ramazanoglu, C., 115, 138
Rampton, Anthony, 12, 16
rational choice, 82, 83
rationalism, and reduction of prejudice, 33,
 42n
Rattansi, Ali, 6
reductionism, 31, 63, 77–8, 126
Reeves, F., 14
Reichley, J. A., 280
relative autonomy rule, 95–6
religion, 161–2
 and fundamentalism, 279–81
 literature and, 163–5
 and native education in India, 158–62
 as source of identity, 280, 283–4
 and the state, 282–4
religious schools, 285–7
representation, politics of, 253–4, 255, 256,
 257
representations, 34, 171, 172, 252–3, 257
 see also images
reproduction, 107–8, 288
resistance, 73–4
 to antiracism, 32, 33
 black feminism and, 112–14
Rex, John, 19, 269
Riviere, Joan, 203
Robinson, Francis, 271
Rushdie, Salman, 260, 269, 270, 278

Sammy and Rosie Get Laid (film), 40, 255
sanctions against racial abuse, 96, 97
Sankofa, 34
Sartre, Jean-Paul, 235, 237, 238
 on humanism, 244–5, 247, 249
 on Jews, 223–4, 226
Sarup, Madan, 31
Satanic Verses, The (Salman Rushdie), 2,
 49
 demonstrations against, 261, 269, 278,
 281
Scarman, Lord, 13, 17
Schoelcher, Victor, 223, 224